James A. Michener

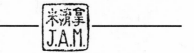

A Bibliography

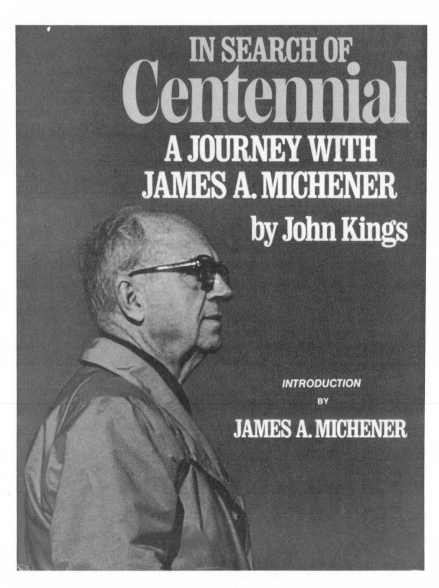

IN SEARCH OF
Centennial
A JOURNEY WITH JAMES A. MICHENER
by John Kings

INTRODUCTION
BY
JAMES A. MICHENER

In Search of Centennial. C.028.

James A. Michener

A Bibliography

David A. Groseclose

Foreword by
James A. Michener

State House Press
Austin Texas
1996

Library of Congress Cataloging-in-Publication Data

Groseclose, David A., 1942-
James A. Michener : a bibliography / David A. Groseclose :
foreword by James A. Michener
p. cm.
Includes bibliographical references and index.
ISBN 1-880510-23-5 (hc : alk. paper).
ISBN 1-880510-24-3 (ltd. ed. : alk. paper)
1. Michener, James A. (James Albert), 1907-
—Bibliography. I. Title.

Z8572.4.G76 1995
[PS3525.I19]
016.813'54—dc20   95-13090

Printed in the United States of America

FIRST EDITION

STATE HOUSE PRESS
P.O. Box 15247
Austin, Texas 78761

dedicated to my wife Karen Anne

Japanese Prints. A.015.

ACKNOWLEDGMENTS

Many thanks to those who helped and encouraged.
Tom Bost, Bookseller specializing in James A. Michener, Colorado Springs, Colorado

David Adickes, Houston, Texas
Patricia and Allen Ahearn, Quill & Brush, Rockville, Maryland
Tom Allee, Greenwood Village, Colorado
Patricia Andrews, Researcher, Washington, D.C.
Arizona State University Library
Barbara Bass, Special Collections & Archives Asst., Kent State University, Kent, Ohio
The Bent Cover, June and Jay Patton, Phoenix, Arizona
Alice L. Birney, Manuscript Division, Library of Congress
A. Richard Boera, Lyndonville, Vermont
Book Gallery, Mike Riley, Tanya Fahey, Phoenix, Arizona
Bruce Cheeseman, Archivist, King Ranch, Kingsville, Texas
Don Conover, President, Taurine Bibliophiles of America, Newtown, Pennsylvania
Fleur Cowles, London, England
Pam Cressman, Librarian, Central Bucks High School West, Doylestown, Pennsylvania
A. Grove Day, Honolulu, Hawaii, (before his death in 1994)
John "Al" de Vere, Al's Family Bookstore, Phoenix, Arizona
Susan Drury, Author's League Fund, New York, New York
Wendell Eckholm, Tucson, Arizona
Mark Frazier, Washington, D. C.
Edward Fuller, McCabe Library Special Collections, Swarthmore College, Swarthmore, Pa.
John Fulton, Sevilla, Spain
Charles Gersch, New York, New York
Georgann Giovagnoli, Swarthmore College Alumni Office, Swarthmore, Pennsylvania
Lawrence Grobel, Los Angeles, California
Ben, John, and Susan Groseclose
Zirel Handler, Anti-Defamation League of B'nai B'rith, New York, New York
Bill Hirsch, Phoenix, Arizona
Norma Johnson, A B C Bookstore, Phoenix, Arizona
Paul Johnson, Evergreen, Colorado
Melanie M. Jones, Doylestown, Pennsylvania
Kevin Keane, Minneapolis, Minnesota
John Kings, Austin, Texas
Bobbie Jean Klepper, Permian Historical Society Archivist, University of Texas, Odessa
Sherry Latshaw, Development Secretary, The Hill School, Pottstown, Pennsylvania
Dexter Mapel, The Book Island, Tempe, Arizona
Charles W. Melvin, M.D., Florence, Alabama
Barbara Monrad, Evergreen, Colorado
Ingrid "Twink" Monrad, Tucson, Arizona
Steve Montgomery, Phoenix, Arizona
Richard Murian, Alcuin Books, Phoenix, Arizona
Erik Nelson, Executive Director, Emlen House Prod., Fort Washington, Pennsylvania

(ACKNOWLEDGMENTS CONTINUED)

Paradise Valley Community College, Shelley Witten, Librarian, Paradise Valley, Arizona

Doris E. Phelps, Austin, Texas

Phoenix Public Library Inter-Library Loan Department: Thelma H. Wacker, former Supv. and Sonia Enriquez, Sheila Miller, Maritza Jerry, Rose Martin

LaRue W. Piercy, Greeter and Historian, Mokuaikaua Church, Kailua, Kona, Hawaii

Bonita Porter, Bonita Porter - Books, Litchfield Park, Arizona

Patrick Price, Ballantine Books, New York, New York

Mary Anne Ramirez, Books, Inc., Phoenix, Arizona

James W. Roberts, The Oriental Bookshelf, St. Petersburg, Florida

Elaine Rosenthal, New York, New York

Polly Chandler Alexander Schatz, Arlington, Virginia

Olga Seham, Associate Editor, Random House, New York, New York

State House Press, Debbie Brothers, Tom Munnerlyn, Erik Mason

Henry Toledano, Books etc., Rare Books, San Francisco, California

University of Alaska, Gretchen Lake, Archivist, Rasmuson Library, Fairbanks

Louis A. Heib, University of Arizona Library Special Collections, Tucson, Arizona

University of Hawaii at Manoa, Eleanor Au, Head, Special Collections & Nancy J. Morris, Ph.D., Head, Archives & Manuscripts

University of Northern Colorado, Betty Mooso & Mary L. Linscome, University Libraries, Archives, Greeley, Colorado

University of West Florida, Allen Josephs, Pensacola, Florida

Robert Vavra, El Cajon, California

Willow Creek Books, Nancy and Don Colberg, Englewood, Colorado

Table of Contents

Tales of the South Pacific. A.003.

Foreword

When I saw the prodigious amount of work David Groseclose had done in compiling this record I thought it regrettable that neither he nor any other commentator had referred to my two earliest appearances in print. Although they were dramatic and worthy of comment, neither gave any evidence that I would spend my life within the printed word. They were, frankly, disasters.

When I was nine or ten I joined a gang of kids my own age for a midsummer swim in Pine Run, a trivial streamlet near our town. While in the water I noticed that Sam Horner, a boy bigger than I and stronger, was in apparent difficulty, so I swam out to help him regain safety on the shore. Someone noticed this as an act of heroism and reported it to our local newspaper, which ran a headline: Local Lad a Hero. Saves His Companion.

For one day I basked in this boyhood glory, but on the third day I ran into Sam Horner, the boy whose life I had ostensibly saved. Without any preamble or explanation he started punching me about the face and head and when I staggered back, totally bewildered, he growled as he stood over me: 'Saved my life? You nearly drowned me. Got in my way as I was making it to shore.'

Sam and I were friends no longer and I was left to ruminate, at that early age, on the vagaries of the printed word, a mystery which still perplexes me.

The second incident was an even greater disaster, one whose consequences would remain with me throughout my life. My family lived at the north end of town in an area that had always been called Germany because of those sturdy immigrants who had concentrated there in the preceding century. Five houses down from ours a benevolent old German shoemaker plied his trade, was kind to his neighbors, and tolerant of the children who stopped by his little shop to watch him at work. He was an admirable citizen and my best friend among the town adults.

Foreword

But in 1918, when I was eleven and caught up in the patriotic fervor of World War One, I remembered that on our shoemaker's wall rested a framed chromolithograph in full color depicting Kaiser Wilhelm in military uniform. Bursting with civic pride, I alone marched down to the shop and without saying a word to my dear friend, ripped down his portrait of the Kaiser, took it out in the street before his shop and, to the applause of adult watchers, burned the hateful visage, a fact which was duly recorded in the press with a heading something like Local Lad Heroically Smashes Image of the Kaiser. Now I was a certified patriot with no outraged Sam Horner to punch me out again.

But the incident did not end there, for as I ripped the portrait from the wall and carried it triumphantly out of the shop, I chanced to see the old man staring at me in disbelief. His pain at seeing one of his young friends behaving in this cruel manner did not bring tears to his eyes, but it did transfix him, and his confused glare followed me out the door.

Throughout the rest of my life I would never forget that incredulous stare. His eyes followed me, haunted me, and returned time and again as I stood on the threshold of doing some inane act. I learned what self-induced misery was. I knew what a wrong act was. I had tasted the bitter fruit that an overweening chauvinism can produce, and I dedicated myself to a life which would in the future avoid such nonsense.

If the works which are listed here carry any central message, it is that brotherhood is one of the world's positive assets and that attention to the sensibilities of others, whether individuals or nations, is a way to avoid terrible error. The accusatory eyes of the old shoemaker have monitored my public behavior, and I have never again marched into the unprotected home of an old man, or old nation, and torn down cherished symbols in order to gain a momentary taste of so-called heroism. There have been few heroes in what I have written but a great deal of humanity.

—JAMES A. MICHENER
Texas Center for Writers
Austin, Texas
July, 1994

Introduction

I wish I could tell you about the South Pacific. The way it actually was.
The endless ocean. The infinite specks of coral we called islands.

Thus began the literary odyssey of James A. Michener in **Tales of the South Pacific**. From the South Pacific Michener has ventured into, and transported his readers to, every corner of the world and beyond.

Although his novel-writing career began in 1946, he had amassed many works previously. He was the Editor-in-Chief of his Doylestown High School Newspaper, *The Torch*. He authored numerous works of poetry, essays, drama, and sports articles for both his high school and college publications. After graduation from college, he wrote sports articles for a local newspaper. While pursuing post-graduate programs and teaching, he published articles on education, sociology and teaching. He joined Macmillan Publishing Company as an Associate Editor in the school textbook division in 1940. World War II interrupted his editing job at Macmillan and took him to the South Pacific as an enlisted member of the United States Navy where he attempted to write an account of the tedium, loneliness, frustrations, and ennui of the war.

Since that time, Michener has written twenty-three major works of fiction. He has also written significant works of non-fiction including five on the subject of Japanese art and others on international relations, travel, American government, sports, writing, and his autobiography.

The topics of his writings have varied as much as the geographical characteristics of the world he has covered. His writing has spanned almost seventy years and continues still, so this bibliographical study has not been a trivial task. There are not many Americans who do not know his name.

Over the past six years, I have collected and compiled bibliographic material from libraries and librarians at Swarthmore, the University of Northern Colorado, the Library of Congress, Arizona State University, and the Phoenix and Denver public libraries. Extensive information was collected through the OCLC (On-line College Library Consortium) and from NewsBank, periodical indexes, copies of college theses, collectors' and bookstore owners' personal knowledge, publishers' records, critics' reviews, watching movies and documentaries, listening to tapes, and visiting with others who suffer from 'Micheneritis.' I have enjoyed many hours reading, cataloging, searching, collecting, learning, researching, and verifying information. Along with a substantial number of readers, I have learned much from Michener's writing: art, history, politics, race relations, war, sports, music, and even geology, paleontology, and archeology. It is impossible to read Michener's writings and not feel and appreciate his attitudes of compassion and understanding expressed in his recurring themes of brotherhood and tolerance of the differences of the cultural, religious, and ethnic groups that populate the world we live in.

The scope and depth of Michener's writings is reflected in the extension of his materials to theater, movies, television, and other media. Both **Tales of the South Pacific** and **Sayonara** have been adapted to the musical theater. Nine feature films have been produced based upon his writings. These include **Return to Paradise** (1953), **The Bridges at Toko-ri** (1954), **Men of the Fighting Lady** (1954), **Sayonara** (1957), **Until They Sail** (1957), **South Pacific** (1958), **Hawaii** (1966), **The Hawaiians** (1970), and **Caravans** (1978). Three major TV miniseries have been produced: **Centennial** (1978), **Space** (1985), and **Texas** (1994).

Michener has also narrated and appeared in a series of over twenty PBS documentaries. In addition, **Adventures in Paradise**, a weekly sixty minute series based on stories by Michener, was broadcast from 1959 to 1962.

During the course of his writing career, Michener has donated his working papers, manuscripts, and materials to many libraries and repositories. Very early in his writing career, under a program initiated by the Library of Congress, he began to deposit his papers and business records there. In an article dated October 16, 1983, in the *Los Angeles Herald Examiner*, he states,

> *But several years ago, Congress did a dastardly thing: They said that the papers of a writer were of no value whatsoever! (Congressional legislation attempting to plug tax loopholes made it illegal for writers and public figures to donate their papers to libraries and then take a tax write-off for the appraised value.) So I got angry and said to hell with the Library of Congress. To say that the manuscript of 'Hamlet' is*

only worth the paper it is written on is ridiculous. Of course, the
congressmen exempted themselves from this law. So the memos
and speeches of some son-of-a-bitch politician, who is one step
ahead of the sheriff, are worth $100,000. Yet the manuscript of
'Death of a Salesman' is worth $3. That is so repulsive to me. I
decided to have no part of them or their library. I stopped giving
my papers there and now send them to a variety of universities. I
haven't decided yet where I will put 'Poland'.

Since that time, Michener has donated his various drafts, research materials, original manuscripts, and other items related to his writing to the following institutions:

Swarthmore College possesses the materials related to **The Covenant**. In addition, Swarthmore seeks to acquire all copies of Michener's printed works. In 1981, the library published a "Register" of Michener's papers and works. The information has been updated in electronic form, but has never been republished by Swarthmore.

The University of Northern Colorado has a large exhibit, housed in the James A. Michener Library, showing the steps of production of **Centennial,** along with the various related materials.

The Talbot County Free Library of Easton, Maryland, has **Chesapeake.**

The University of Texas has **Texas, Space** and **Poland**.

University of Alaska, Fairbanks Archives, has **Alaska.**

The University of Miami, Miami, Florida, has **Journey, Caribbean, Six Days in Havana, The World is My Home, Writer's Handbook, Mexico,** and **Creatures of the Kingdom.**

A special section of original correspondence between Michener and A. Grove Day, along with the first manuscript of **Rascals in Paradise,** is contained in the Special Collections Division of the Thomas Hale Hamilton Library, University of Hawaii at Manoa, Honolulu, Hawaii. These were a gift from A. Grove Day in 1966.

In pursuit of a lifelong interest in art, the Micheners amassed valuable collections that they donated to public institutions and universities. The Honolulu Academy of Arts houses the James A. Michener Collection consisting of approximately 6,000 works of Ukiyo-e prints. The University of Texas is the repository of the James A.

Introduction

Michener Collection which contains American artists' works created in Michener's lifetime. Approximately 300 pieces comprise the Michener Collection which he and Mari Michener have contributed to the University of Texas at Austin since 1970.

It has been a disappointment to have to omit from this bibliography the endless foreign editions of Michener's works. Mr. Michener is particularly proud, for example, that The **Bridge at Andau** went into fifty-three foreign editions, primarily because the state department felt that it was an admirable revelation of the communist system. Because of the enormity of the task of acquiring, inspecting, and compiling the translation of the bibliographical information for each of the numerous editions in order to compile a complete and accurate listing, it was impossible to attempt such a listing of the hundreds of foreign editions at this time. To give a flavor of the enormity of the task, a sample record of only two of Mr. Michener's books reveals that **Hawaii** has been translated into thirteen different languages and **Texas** has been translated into ten languages.

The compilation of the foreign titles, the correction of inevitable errors, the addition of never-ending elusive materials, and the introduction of new materials will be addressed in a subsequent edition. As this bibliography goes to press, the list continues.

In **The World Is My Home,** Michener acknowledges appreciation for friends who want to name fine libraries in his honor and is proud that he helped transform an old jail in Doylestown into a center for the arts. Yet he is more pleased that three great universities have created training programs for young writers that he either started or assisted in starting. He concludes: *But mostly, I would want to be remembered by that row of solid books that rest on library shelves throughout the world.*

This bibliography is a testament to the fulfillment of that wish.

—DAVID GROSECLOSE
Phoenix, Arizona
1995

A CHRONOLOGY

OF THE PUBLISHED WRITINGS, COLLECTIONS, SETS, AND WORKS EDITED BY

JAMES A. MICHENER

"I was born with a passionate desire to communicate, to organize experience, to tell tales that dramatize the adventures which listeners might have had. I have been that ancient man who sat by the campfire at night and regaled the hunters with imaginative accounts of their prowess that morning in tracking down their prey. The job of an apple tree is to bear apples. The job of a storyteller is to tell stories, and I have concentrated on that obligation."

—James A. Michener
"The Old Apple Tree"
THE EAGLE AND THE RAVEN
Austin, Texas: State House Press, 1990

A Chronology

James A. Michener

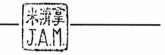

A Bibliography

*"Writer, scholar, diplomat, Buck's County Squire, connoisseur of art
and music, patron, man of reason and concern, thinker and doer, sport's
enthusiast, but above all gentleman, . . .
This is James A. Michener."*

–Helen M. Strauss
A TALENT FOR LUCK
New York: Random House, 1979

Selected Writings of James A. Michener. A.012.

A.
Works Authored
or Edited
by James A. Michener

"Michener is known for his long novels, often spanning hundreds, even thousands of years, and telling the stories of multiple generations of people. His descriptions and the story lines are both informative and entertaining, but he is often criticized for creating characters who lack the heroic stature to make them memorable literary personalities. As I see it, the reason is that the real hero of Michener stories is the historical sweep of events and ideas, not individuals. His fictional characters are more like real people, with a combination of defects and attributes which blurs their image as villains or heroes. They are not soap opera stereotypes strutting about in a melodrama. Rather, they are supporting actors on life's stage, and the remarkable thing is that despite their ordinariness, the things they do have consequences which become a part of history."

—Don Conover
La Busca, December, 1993

THE STORY OF JAPANESE PRINTS

THE
Floating
World

An account of the life and death of an art, of the men
who made it and of the lusty age in which they flourished.
65 illustrations, including 40 in full color.

BY JAMES A · MICHENER

The Floating World. A.009.

A.I
Descriptive
Bibliography
of First Editions

The descriptive bibliography is organized chronologically to provide relevant information in identifying the first editions and first published sets and collections of James A. Michener. The information regarding the title pages, the copyright pages, the bindings, and the dustjackets is a quasi-facsimile of the transcription. The printed lines are separated by a slash. Script and italics have been used where they appear on the originals. Calligraphy and special descriptions are noted in brackets.

Color descriptions of the bindings and dustjackets are based upon Munsell color charts and descriptions according to the ISCC-NBS Method of Designating Colors and Color Names Dictionary.

Subsequent printings of each work are listed in Section A.II.

THE FUTURE OF THE SOCIAL STUDIES

Proposals for an Experimental Social-Studies Curriculum

JAMES A. MICHENER

Editor

Harold Rugg
600 West End Ave.

THE NATIONAL COUNCIL FOR THE
SOCIAL STUDIES

1939

The Future of the Social Studies. A.001.

Section A.I - Descriptive Bibliography of First Editions

A.001 THE FUTURE OF THE SOCIAL STUDIES.
("The Problem of the Social Studies") [1939]

Title Page: THE FUTURE OF THE / SOCIAL STUDIES / Proposals for an Experimental / Social Studies Curriculum / James A. Michener / *Editor* / THE NATIONAL COUNCIL FOR THE SOCIAL STUDIES / 13 Lawrence Hall, Kirkland Street / Cambridge, Massachusetts

Copyright: COPYRIGHT 1939 / BY / NATIONAL COUNCIL FOR THE SOCIAL STUDIES / GEORGE BANTA PUBLISHING COMPANY / MENASHA, WISCONSIN, U.S.A.

Contents: [i] title; [ii] copyright; [iii-iv] foreword; [v] contents; [vi] blank; [1] 2-5 The Problem of the Social Studies, James A. Michener; 6-178 text of fifteen additional essays by miscellaneous authors.

Collation: [i-vi] [1] 2-178; 8" x 11"

Binding: Light greenish blue (172) wraps, with five staples at the centerfold. Front: [moderate blue (182) print] THE FUTURE OF THE / SOCIAL STUDIES / Proposals for an Experimental / Social-Studies Curriculum / JAMES A. MICHENER / *Editor* / THE NATIONAL COUNCIL FOR THE / SOCIAL STUDIES / 1939. Back: YEARBOOKS OF THE NATIONAL COUNCIL / FOR THE SOCIAL STUDIES / [descriptions of the first through tenth yearbooks] / THE SECRETARY 13 LAWRENCE HALL, HARVARD UNIVERSITY / CAMBRIDGE, MASSACHUSETTS.

Dust Jacket: None.

Price: Distributed free to the members of the National Council for the Social Studies.

Notes: Twenty social studies teachers were requested to submit their opinions of 'the specific content, the types of content, or types of experience' to include in an ideal curriculum for the elementary and secondary schools. This book is a compilation of the answers received. Michener was the Editor of the compilation and also served on the Committee on Publications which solicited the opinions. He wrote the first essay titled "The Problem of the Social Studies."

Section A.I - Descriptive Bibliography of First Editions

A.002 THE UNIT IN THE SOCIAL STUDIES [1940]

Title Page: [rule] / HARVARD WORKSHOP SERIES: NO. 1 / [rule] / THE UNIT IN / THE SOCIAL STUDIES / BY / JAMES A. MICHENER / Colorado State College of Education / AND / HAROLD M. LONG / Glens Falls High School, Glens Falls, New York / WITH AN INTRODUCTION BY / HOWARD E. WILSON / Harvard University / [rule] / Published by the Graduate School of Education / Harvard University, Cambridge, Massachusetts / PRICE, 75 CENTS / [rule]

Copyright: COPYRIGHT 1940 / BY THE COMMITTEE ON PUBLICATIONS / HARVARD GRADUATE SCHOOL OF EDUCATION / REPRINTED BY LEW A. CUMMINGS COMPANY / CAMBRIDGE, MASS.

Contents: [i] title; [ii] copyright; iii-iv FOREWORD; v TABLE OF CONTENTS; [vi] blank; 1-91 text; 92-103 SELECTED BIBLIOGRAPHY; 104-108 BIBLIOGRAPHY OF SELECTED SAMPLE UNITS.

Collation: [i-ii] iii-v [vi] 1-108; 5 7/8" x 9"

Binding: Bright red paper wraps. Front: HARVARD WORKSHOP SERIES: No. 1 / THE UNIT IN / THE SOCIAL STUDIES / JAMES A. MICHENER AND HAROLD M. LONG / [within ruled rectangle] [illustration of 3 students seated at study desks in library] / GRADUATE SCHOOL OF EDUCATION / HARVARD UNIVERSITY - CAMBRIDGE, MASSACHUSETTS. Spine: ? Back: Blank.

Dust Jacket: None

Price: $.75

Notes: Written with Harold M. Long. This publication resulted from a summer workshop in Social Studies at the Harvard Graduate School of Education. It attempts to arrange social studies materials in units for teaching purposes. The first paper discusses the meaning of the term *unit*. The next four papers are sample units for use of teachers and pupils. [Not seen by bibliographer. Information courtesy of Tom Bost.]

Section A.I - Descriptive Bibliography of First Editions

A.003 TALES OF THE SOUTH PACIFIC [1947]

Title Page: [triple rule framed border] TALES OF / *The South Pacific* / BY / JAMES A. MICHENER / NEW YORK / THE MACMILLAN COMPANY / 1947

Copyright: Copyright, 1946, 1947, by / THE CURTIS PUBLISHING COMPANY / Copyright, 1947, by / JAMES A. MICHENER / [rule] / All rights reserved --- no part of this book may be / reproduced in any form without permission in writ- / ing from the publisher, except by a reviewer who / wishes to quote brief passages in connection with a / review written for inclusion in magazine or newspaper. / [rule] / *First Printing* / PRINTED IN THE UNITED STATES OF AMERICA / BY VAIL - BALLOU PRESS, INC., BINGHAMTON, N. Y.

Contents: [i] half title; [ii] publisher's device and places of publication; [iii] title; [iv] copyright; v Contents; [vi] blank; [vii] second half title; [viii] blank; 1-326 text; [327-328] blank.

Collation: [i-iv] v [vi-viii] 1-326 [327-328]; 5 1/2" x 8 3/8"

Binding: Brownish orange (54) cloth. Front: Blank. Spine: [all strong blue (178) print] [three horizontal rules] [vertical] MICHENER *Tales of the South Pacific* MACMILLAN. [three horizontal rules]. Back: Blank.

Dust Jacket: [Illustration of destroyer cruising the coastline of a mountainous South Sea island, in multiple hues of green, blue and purple, covers front and spine.] Front: [black print] TALES OF THE / South Pacific / [white print] James A. Michener / [vertical at right edge, very illegible, but appears to be] J.O.H. Cosgrave II [the illustrator ?]. Spine: [vertical] [black print] TALES OF THE / South Pacific [moderate yellowish pink (39) print] MICHENER Macmillan. Back: [top left] [photograph of the author in military shirt.] [to right of photo] JAMES A. / MICHENER / [biographical sketch of the author]. Front flap: [machine clipped at top and bottom] [vertical at top right] $3.00 / [blurb]. Back flap: [continuation of blurb]. (Two variants of the front flap have been noted. One is machine clipped on the top and bottom and has the $3.00 price at the top, vertical at the right edge. The second is unclipped and has the $3.00 price horizontal at the bottom. Both are believed to be first edition dust jackets).

Price: $3.00

Notes: A collection of tales of the exploits of men at war in the Pacific in World War II displaying the emotions, frustrations, tedium, and anxiety of waiting for the conflict which ultimately must come. This was Michener's first published novel and won the Pulitzer Prize in 1948. Macmillan intended to release this book in 1946, but the sale of some stories to the *Saturday Evening Post* delayed publication by Macmillan until 1947. The original title page dated 1946 was replaced with a tipped-in title page dated 1947. There is one known copy with the original 1946 title page located at the University of Pennsylvania. It does not have a dust jacket and the front cover has an outline illustration of a destroyer cruising a mountainous coastline. The two *Post* articles preceding book publication were "The Remittance Man," December 14, 1946, and "Best Man in de Navy," January 18, 1947.

7

Section A.I - Descriptive Bibliography of First Editions

A.004 THE FIRES OF SPRING [1949]

Title Page: JAMES A. MICHENER / THE / FIRES / OF / SPRING / [a scene of rolling hills incorporates a two story Random House publisher's device into the illustration] / RANDOM HOUSE / NEW YORK

Copyright: FIRST PRINTING / *Copyright, 1949, by James A. Michener / All rights reserved under International and Pan-American Copyright / Conventions. Published in New York by Random House, Inc., and simultaneously in Toronto, Canada, by Random House of Canada, / Limited. / Manufactured in the United States of America / Designed by Marshall Lee*

Contents: [i] half title; [ii] By / James A. Michener [previous works]; [iii] title; [iv] copyright; [v] dedication; [vi] blank; [vii] CONTENTS; [viii] blank; [1] [chapter heading] THE POORHOUSE; [2] blank; 3-495 text; [496] blank.

Collation: [i-viii] [1-2] 3-495 [496]; 5 3/8" x 8 3/16"

Binding: Grayish blue (186) cloth. Front: James A. Michener signature stamped in gold. Spine: [within top half dark green (146) panel, in gold print] JAMES A. / MICHENER / THE / FIRES / OF / SPRING / RANDOM / HOUSE / [narrow gray stripe] [decorative device on lower narrow dark green panel]. Back: Blank.

Dust Jacket: White and black. Front: [printed in a spectrum of hues progressing from deep purple to purple to red purple to red to yellow red to green yellow to green to deep green] THE / FIRES OF / SPRING / A NOVEL BY / JAMES A. / MICHENER / [vertical from bottom to top, along right edge, black print] author of TALES OF THE SOUTH PACIFIC • PULITZER PRIZE WINNER 1947. Spine: [black with panels of light purplish pink (249), light yellow (86), light yellow green (119), and very light green (143)] [white print] THE [within light purplish pink panel] FIRES OF / [within light yellow panel] SPRING / [white print] A NOVEL BY / [within light yellow green panel] JAMES A. / [within very light green panel] MICHENER / [white publisher's device] / [white print] RANDOM HOUSE. Back: [full page photograph of the author] [bottom right, below photograph] Blackstone Studios, Inc. / JAMES A. MICHENER. Front flap: [top right] $3.50 / [blurb]. Back flap: [continuation of blurb] Jacket design by Sam Sugar / RANDOM HOUSE / *Publishers of* The American College Dictionary.

Price: $3.50

Notes: Michener's second major work of fiction, **The Fires of Spring** follows the childhood and growth to adulthood of a fictional David Harper. His experiences in a poorhouse, his adventures in cross-country hitch-hiking, his job experience as a shortchange artist in a carnival show, his awkward encounters with infatuation and young love, and educational development all bear striking resemblance to Michener's own life. Michener originally planned to title this *"The Homeward Journey."*

8

Section A.I - Descriptive Bibliography of First Editions

A.005 RETURN TO PARADISE [1951]

Title Page: RETURN TO / *Paradise* / by / JAMES A. MICHENER / [publisher's device] / RANDOM HOUSE • NEW YORK

Copyright: Copyright, 1951, by James A. Michener / Copyright 1951, by / The Curtis Publishing Company / All rights reserved under International and / Pan-American Copyright Conventions. / Published in New York by Random House, Inc., / and simultaneously in Toronto, Canada, by / Random House of Canada, Limited. / Manufactured in the United States of America / FIRST PRINTING

Contents: [i] half title; [ii] By / James A. Michener [previous works]; [iii] title; [iv] copyright; [v] dedication; [vi] blank; [vii] CONTENTS; [viii] blank; [1] second half title; [2] blank; 3-437 text; [438-440] blank.

Collation: [i-viii] [1] [2] 3-437 [438-440]; 5 1/2" x 8 3/16"

Binding: Grayish yellow-green (122) cloth. Front: [dark green (146) publisher's device on bottom left]. Spine: [contains horizontal dark green decorative floral designs alternating from top to bottom with horizontal gold rules crossing the spine] [within a dark green horizontal panel at top in gold print] James A. Michener [within a wide dark green panel at mid-spine in gold print] Return / to / Paradise / [within a dark green horizontal panel at the bottom in gold print] Random House. Back: Blank. Green top stain.

Dust Jacket: Varying hues of brown and yellow. Repeating silhouette illustration of island native standing in outrigger canoe at sunset continues to spine and back. Front: [white print] By the author of TALES OF THE SOUTH PACIFIC / return / to / paradise / JAMES A. MICHENER. Spine: [white print] JAMES A. / MICHENER / return / to / paradise / [publisher's device] / RANDOM HOUSE. Back: [same as front]. Front flap: [top right] $3.50 / A Book-of-the-Month-Club Selection / [rule] / [blurb] / Jacket design by Arthur Williams / from a color photo by Charles Allmon / RANDOM HOUSE, INC. / [other imprints]. Back flap: [photograph of the author] / JAMES A. MICHENER / Author of / TALES OF THE SOUTH PACIFIC / (Pulitzer Prize-winner, 1947) / • / THE FIRES OF SPRING / • / SOUTH PACIFIC / A musical play by / Richard Rodgers and / Oscar Hammerstein, 2nd / Book by / Oscar Hammerstein, 2nd and Joshua Logan / Adapted from James A. Michener's / *Tales of the South Pacific.*

Price: $3.50

Notes: A series of informative essays involving island locales in the South Pacific, each essay followed by a fictional story related to the theme and locale of the essay. Chapters from the book were published as magazine articles prior to book publication. The following articles appeared in *Holiday*: "The Atoll," May, 1950, (introductory paragraphs were added and the article was titled "Circles in the Sea"); "Fiji," June, 1950; "Mynah Birds," July, 1950, (titled "Myna Birds"); "Guadalcanal," August, 1950; "Australia," November, 1950; "New Guinea," December 1950; "New Zealand," January, 1951; "Polynesia," March, 1951. And, in *Today's Woman*: "The Jungle," February, 1951. At least some copies marked "FIRST PRINTING" were distributed by Book-of-the-Month Club and are indistinguishable from the Random House first edition, except for the small BOMC green dot at the bottom right of the back cover, and the differences in the dust jacket. The BOMC dust jacket has no price on the top right corner of the front flap or rule on the front flap and states "BOOK-OF-THE-MONTH CLUB SELECTION," instead of "A Book-of-the-Month-Club Selection." The BOMC back flap states "BOOK-OF-THE-MONTH' above the photograph of the author and "PRINTED IN U.S.A." and the number "053" at bottom.

Section A.I - Descriptive Bibliography of First Editions

A.006 THE VOICE OF ASIA [1951]

Title Page: *THE / VOICE / OF / ASIA* / BY JAMES A. MICHENER / RANDOM HOUSE • NEW YORK / [publisher's device]

Copyright: FIRST PRINTING / *Copyright, 1951, by James A. Michener / All rights reserved under International and Pan-American Copy- / right Conventions. Published in New York by Random House, / Inc., and simultaneously in Toronto, Canada, by Random House / of Canada, Limited. / Manufactured in the United States of America*

Contents: [i] half title; [ii] By / James A. Michener [previous works]; [iii] title; [iv] copyright; [v] dedication; [vi] blank; vii-xi CONTENTS; [xii] blank; [1] second half title; [2] blank; 3-338 text; [339-340] blank.

Collation: [i-vi] vii-xi [xii] [1-2] 3-338 [339-340]; 5 3/8" x 8 1/4"

Binding: Grayish yellow (90) cloth. Front: Blank. Spine: [bonsai style decorative devices in gold on top and bottom quarters of spine] [within the dark blue (183) panel covering mid-half of spine, in gold print] [horizontal letters in two vertical columns] *THE VOICE / OF ASIA* / [horizontal at bottom of panel] JAMES A. / MICHENER / RANDOM / HOUSE. Back: Blank. End maps [Asia and the South Pacific]. Blue top stain.

Dust Jacket: Moderate red (15), grayish purplish blue (204), grayish yellow (90). Front: [thick blue rule at top edge] [white print on red top two-thirds] The / VOICE / of ASIA / [oriental illustration of Japanese harbor, village, and trees] / [on blue bottom-third] [white print] JAMES A. MICHENER / [grayish yellow print] Author of *Tales of the South Pacific & Return to Paradise* / [white print] At first-hand an acknowledged authority examines & evalu- / ates in human terms the changed outlook of the Asiatic / world toward the West. Spine: [continuation of blue rule from front] [on red top two-thirds] [at mid-spine in grayish yellow print] The / VOICE / of ASIA / [continuation of illustration from front] / [on blue bottom-third in grayish yellow print] JAMES A. / MICHENER / [moderate red publisher's device] / [grayish yellow print] Random / House. Back: [off-white] [squiggly grayish yellow rule] / [blue print] What the Critics Said about / James A. Michener's *Return to Paradise* / (A BOOK-OF-THE-MONTH CLUB SELECTION) / [squiggly grayish yellow rule] / [blurbs]. Front flap: [top right] $3.50 / [comments by the author regarding the importance of Asia to Americans] / [at bottom] A RANDOM HOUSE BOOK / Jacket design by Leo Manso. Back flap: [blue print] Books by / James A. Michener / • [list of previous works].

Price: $3.50

Notes: First hand observations of the people of Asia, its religious problems, economic questions and social revolutions. Michener says "I have tried to share with you what the people of Asia told me." This book is based upon a series of fifteen newspaper articles appearing in the *New York Herald Tribune* between May 2, 1951, and May 18, 1951. The Literary Guild edition is distinguishable from the Random House first edition by dark blue (183) binding with a moderate red (15) panel on the spine. It also has a moderate red top stain. The Literary Guild dust jacket omits the price at the top right corner of the front flap. It omits "A RANDOM HOUSE BOOK" below JAMES A. MICHENER, and states "BOOK CLUB EDITION," at the bottom right of the front flap. The back flap is blank except for "PRINTED IN U.S.A." at the bottom. The back states "Great Writers on Reading" with quotes by Montaigne, Gibbon, Whitman, Thoreau, and Trollope.

Section A.I - Descriptive Bibliography of First Editions

A.007 THE BRIDGES AT TOKO-RI [1953]

Title Page: THE / BRIDGES / AT / TOKO-RI / JAMES A. MICHENER / [publisher's device] / RANDOM HOUSE

Copyright: Copyright, 1953, by James A. Michener / All rights reserved under International and Pan-American / Copyright Conventions. Published in New York by Random / House, Inc., and simultaneously in Toronto, Canada, / by Random House of Canada, Limited. / Library of Congress Catalog Card Number: 52-7129 / Manufactured in the United States of America

Contents: [i] half title; [ii] blank; [iii] title; [iv] copyright; [v] dedication; [vi] blank; [1] [chapter heading] SEA; [2] blank; 3-146 [147] text; [148] blank; [149-150] ABOUT THE AUTHOR; [151-152] blank.

Collation: [i-vi] [1-2] 3-146 [147-152]; 5 1/4" x 8"

Binding: Moderate blue (182) cloth and dark blue (183) cloth. The top three-fifths of the front, back, and spine is moderate blue, and the bottom two-fifths is dark blue with a horizontal gold rule crossing the cover and spine at the bottom of the moderate blue cloth. Front: Blank. Spine: [vertical silver print] MICHENER [horizontal gold print] THE / BRIDGES / AT / TOKO-RI / [silver publisher's device] / [vertical silver print] RANDOM HOUSE. Back: Blank. (four variants have been noted with no determination of priority: white endpapers with no top-stain; white end papers with blue top-stain; blue endpapers with no top-stain; blue endpapers with blue top-stain).

Dust Jacket: Multi-colored, but predominantly dark blue. [illustration of jets bombing the bridges at Toko-ri covers the front and spine] Front: [brilliant greenish blue (168) print] A STORY OF INDIVIDUAL HEROISM / [strong yellow (84) print] The Bridges / at Toko-ri / [brilliant greenish blue (168) print] A NOVEL BY / [white print] JAMES A. MICHENER / [strong yellow print] author of TALES OF THE SOUTH PACIFIC and RETURN TO PARADISE. Spine: [white print] James A. / Michener / [strong yellow print] The / Bridges / at / Toko-ri / [at bottom] [white publisher's device] / [strong yellow print] Random / House. Back: [photograph of author with biographical sketch]. Front flap: [top right] $2.50 / "Where did we get such men?" / [blurb] / RANDOM HOUSE, INC. / [other imprints] / Jacket design by H. Lawrence Hoffman. Back flap: [continuation of biographical sketch from back].

Price: $2.50

Notes: A portrayal of American involvement in curbing communism in Asia. The exploits of aircraft carriers and pilots in the Korean War, it was published in its entirety in *Life* magazine on July 6, 1953, prior to book publication. There is no statement of "First Printing" on the copyright page of the first edition. This is an exception to the standard practice at Random House of identifying first editions on the copyright page. See "A Collector's Guide to Publishers," *Firsts: Collecting Modern First Editions,* 4:4 (1994/04) 42-43. Subsequent printings are so stated on the copyright page.

A.008 SAYONARA [1954]

Title Page: [double title page] [on verso] [horizontal letters in vertical column at left edge] RANDOM HOUSE NEW YORK [publisher's device] [on recto] [illustration of birds in flight] [angled] SAYONARA / James A. Michener

Copyright: First Printing / Copyright, 1953, 1954, by James A. Michener / All rights reserved under International and / Pan-American Copyright Conventions. / Published in New York by Random House, Inc., / and simultaneously in Toronto, Canada, by / Random House of Canada, Limited. / Library of Congress Catalog Number: 54-5953 / Manufactured in the United States of America / by H. Wolff, New York / Design: Marshall Lee

Contents: [i] half title; [ii] blank; [iii] By James A. Michener [previous works]; [iv-v] double title; [vi] copyright; [vii] dedication; [viii] blank; [1] second half title; [2] blank; 3-243 text; [244] blank; [245] ABOUT THE AUTHOR; [246-248] blank.

Collation: [i-viii] [1-2] 3-243 [244-248]; 5 1/4" x 8"

Binding: Black cloth binding with front and back covers covered with a wide vertical band of light brown (57) paper, leaving a strip along the spine and edges uncovered. [at top, angled slightly, silver print] SAYONARA [at bottom right, stamped in strong red (12) print] [publisher's device]. Spine: [angled upward, from left to right, silver print] SAYONARA / [horizontal dark pink (6) print] JAMES A. / MICHENER [horizontal stong red print in vertical column at lower right edge of spine] RANDOM HOUSE. Back: Blank. Light brown top stain.

Dust Jacket: Front and spine are multi-hued light brown (57) simulated grasscloth. Front: [white print] A New Novel by [strong yellow (84) print] James A. Michener [white print] author of / TALES OF THE SOUTH PACIFIC and RETURN TO PARADISE / [strong red outlined in black] [Japanese character] / [white print] Sayonara / [strong yellow print] A JAPANESE-AMERICAN / LOVE STORY / [strong red outlined in black] Japanese character / [lower right in strong yellow print] Hoffman. Spine: [strong yellow print] James A. / Michener / [vertical white print] Sayonara / [strong red print publisher's device, shaded in black] [horizontal] [strong yellow print] RANDOM / HOUSE. Back: [blurb by Pearl Buck and a photograph and biographical sketch of the author]. Front flap: [top right] $3.50 / [blurb] / [bottom right] 1/54 [bottom] Jacket designed by H. Lawrence Hoffman. Back flap: [top right] [for *The Bridges at Toko-ri*] $2.50 / [blurb about *The Bridges at Toko-ri*] / RANDOM HOUSE, INC. / [publisher's address and other imprints] / Printed in U.S.A.

Price: $3.50

Notes: A World War II Japanese-American love story first published under the title "Sayonara Means Goodbye," *McCalls*, October, November, and December, 1953. The BOMC edition has gray and black binding with a gray dot in the bottom right of the back. The BOMC dust jacket is almost identical to the first edition dust jacket, but lacks the price of **Sayonara** ($3.50) on the top right front flap and the price of **The Bridges at Toko-ri** ($2.50) on the top right back flap.

Section A.I - Descriptive Bibliography of First Editions

A.009 THE FLOATING WORLD [1954]

Title Page: *The Floating / World /* [illustration of Japanese woman in kimono] / Random House, New York / [oriental version of publisher's device]

Copyright: FIRST PRINTING / Copyright, 1954, by James A. Michener. / All rights reserved under / International and Pan-American / Copyright Conventions. / Published in New York by / Random House, Inc., / and simultaneously / in Toronto, Canada, / by Random House of Canada, Limited. / Library of Congress Catalog Card Number: / 54-7812 / Manufactured in the / United States of America / Grateful acknowledgment is made for the following: Quotation from the Faubion Bowers' / Japanese Theater by permission of Hermitage House, New York; from Henry P. Bowie's / On the Laws of Japanese Painting reprinted through permission of Dover Publications, / Inc., New York ($4.50); from Arthur Davison Ficke's Chats on Japanese Prints by / permission of Ernest Benn Limited, London; from Frederick William Gooken's / Katsukawa Shunsho by permission of The Art Institute of Chicago; from Judson D. / Metzgar's Adventures in Japanese Prints (Dawson's Book Shop, Los Angeles) by per- / mission of the author; from Hans Alexander Mueller's How I Make Woodcuts and / Wood Engravings by permission of the author and American Artists Group, New / York; from A. L. Sadler's The Maker of Modern Japan by permission of George Allen / & Unwin, Ltd., London; from Waldmar von Seidlitz' A History of Japanese Color / Prints by permission of William Heinemann, Ltd., London.

Contents: [i] half title; [ii] James A. Michener [previous works]; [iii] title; [iv] copyright; v-viii An Explanation; ix-x Contents; xi-xii Illustrations; [1] second half title; [2] blank; 3-257 text; 258-357 The Prints; 358-359; Prices; 360 Chronological Chart; 361-378 Biographies; 379-390 Bibliography; 391-403 Index and Glossary; [404] ABOUT THE AUTHOR. Black top stain.

Collation: [i-iv] v-xii [1-2] 3-403 [404]; 6 1/8" x 9 3/16"

Binding: Black cloth. Front: [the right side is covered with a simulated moire pattern of irregular very pale blue (184) and bluish gray (191) wavy pattern on white] [left side is black cloth containing a Japanese style bluish gray publisher's device]. Spine: [gold stamped oriental style print] Michener / The / Floating / World / [horizontal gray letters, in a vertical column at right edge] RANDOM HOUSE. Back: Blank.

Dust Jacket: Light brown (57). Front: THE STORY OF JAPANESE PRINTS / [at right side] reproduction of Plate No. 34 from the book] / [at left of print] [pale yellow (89) calligraphy] THE / Floating / World / [small black calligraphy] An account of the life and death of an art, of the men / who made it and of the lusty age in which they flourished. / 65 illustrations, including 40 in full color. / [pale yellow] BY JAMES A • MICHENER. Spine: [pale yellow] THE [pale yellow calligraphy] Floating / World / [reproduction of cover print] / [pale yellow calligraphy] JAMES A. / MICHENER / [publisher's device] / RANDOM / HOUSE. Back: Large reproduction of Plate No. 25 from the book. Front flap: [top right] $8.75 / [blurb] / [bottom right] 12/54. Back flap: [biographical sketch of the author] / [previous works] / RANDOM HOUSE, INC. / [publisher's address and imprints] / Printed in USA.

Price: $8.75

Notes: An account of the origins and demise of an art form covering the period 1660 to 1860. Michener lists four goals in writing this book: 1. To provide an account of the birth and death of an art. 2. To identify the need for society to continue to foster original thought and expression. 3. To illustrate the detriment created by government regulating art and its quenching of innovation and originality. 4. To promote awareness and development of our own unequaled national collection of Japanese art.

Section A.I - Descriptive Bibliography of First Editions

A.010 THE BRIDGE AT ANDAU [1957]

Title Page: THE / BRIDGE / AT / ANDAU / James A. Michener / RANDOM HOUSE NEW YORK / [publisher's device]

Copyright: FIRST PRINTING / © Copyright, 1957, by James A. Michener / All rights reserved under International and Pan-American Copyright / Conventions. Published in New York by Random House, Inc., and / simultaneously in Toronto, Canada, by Random House of Canada, Limited. / Library of Congress Catalog Card Number: / 57-8158 / Manufactured in the United States of America / by H. Wolff, New York

Contents: [i] half title; [ii] BY James A. Michener [previous works]; [iii] title; [iv] copyright; [v] dedication; [vi] blank; [vii] CONTENTS; [viii] blank; [ix] x-xi foreword; [xii] blank; [1] second half title; [2] blank; [3] 4-270 text; [271] Editor's note; [272] blank; [273] ABOUT THE AUTHOR; [274-276] blank.

Collation: [i-ix] x-xi [xii] [1-3] 4-270 [271-276]; 5 1/4" x 8"

Binding: Grayish yellow (90) cloth. Front: Blank. Spine: [vivid red (11) print] THE / BRIDGE / AT / ANDAU / [black print between two large black panels covering most of the spine] / James A. / Michener / [at bottom of lower black panel] [grayish yellow print] [silhouette of publisher's device] / RANDOM HOUSE. Back: Blank. Deep pink (3) top stain.

Dust Jacket: White. Front: [black print] [to the left] JAMES A. / [to the right] MICHENER / [to the left] [grayish brown (61) print] The heroic story of the revolt / by the Hungarian people / that made crystal clear / to the world the / true face of communism / [illustration of Hungarian freedom fighter holding machine gun] [partially superimposed on illustration in vivid red (11) print] THE / BRIDGE / AT ANDAU. Spine: [vivid red print] THE / BRIDGE / AT / ANDAU / [black print] JAMES A. / MICHENER / [grayish brown silhouette of publisher's device] [black print] RANDOM / HOUSE. Back: [full page biographical sketch of the author]. Front flap: [top right] $3.50 / [blurb] / [bottom right] 3/57. Back flap: [continuation of blurb from front flap] / Jacket design by Daniel Schwartz / RANDOM HOUSE, INC. / [publisher's address and other imprints] / Printed in U.S.A.

Price: $3.50

Notes: Michener's firsthand account of the story of Hungarian refugees' fleeing Hungary following the 1956 revolt against communism. Excerpts were published in *Reader's Digest* in March and May, 1957, for which he received the Overseas Press Club Award for best foreign affairs article. Book club jackets can be distinguished by the absence of the price at the top, and "3/57" at the bottom right of the front flap. The Christian Herald's Family Bookshelf Selection is so stated at the bottom of its front flap. The Book-of-the-Month Club selection is believed to state "Special De Luxe Edition" in the top right corner of the front flap.

Section A.I - Descriptive Bibliography of First Editions

A.011 RASCALS IN PARADISE. Written with A. Grove Day [1957]

Title Page: RASCALS / IN / PARADISE / BY *James A. Michener* / AND *A. Grove Day* / RANDOM HOUSE [publisher's device] NEW YORK

Copyright: FIRST PRINTING / © Copyright, 1957, by James A. Michener and A. Grove Day / All rights reserved under International and Pan-American Copyright / Conventions. Published in New York by Random House, Inc., and simul- / taneously in Toronto, Canada, by Random House of Canada, Limited. / Library of Congress Catalog Card Number: 57-5364 / Designed by Philip Grushkin / Manufactured in the United States of America

Contents: [i] half title; [ii] Books by James A. Michener [previous works] Books by A. Grove Day [previous works]; [iii] title; [iv] copyright; [v] dedication; [vi] blank; [vii] CONTENTS; [viii] blank; [1] second half title; [2] blank; 3-354 text; 355-360 Selected Bibliography; 361-374 Index; [375] blank; [376] ABOUT THE AUTHORS.

Collation: [i-viii] [1-2] 3-374 [375-376]; 6" x 8 15/16"

Binding: Grayish yellow (90) cloth. Front: [centered, stamped in gold] [tropical version publisher's device]. Spine: [gold rule] [gold print within black panel] RASCALS / IN / PARADISE / [gold rule] [gold print within second black panel] *James A. Michener* / AND / *A. Grove Day* / [gold rule] [gold print within third black panel] [tropical version of publisher's device] / RANDOM HOUSE / [gold rule]. Back: Blank. End paper maps of South Pacific Ocean. Grayish purple (228) top stain.

Dust Jacket: [photograph of South Sea Islands and shores, in multiple tones of blue, covers front, spine, and front flap]. Front: [brilliant yellow (83) print] Rascals in / Paradise / [white calligraphy] True Tales of High Adventure in the South Pacific / [brilliant yellow print] BY James A. Michener / AND A. Grove Day. Spine: [brilliant yellow print] Rascals / in / Paradise / [white print] Michener / AND / Day / [white] [publisher's device] / RANDOM / HOUSE. Back: [half-page photograph of the authors, by Captain William J. Lederer] / Biographical sketch of the authors. Front flap: [top right] $4.75 / [within a pale yellow (89) panel] [blurb] / [bottom right of panel] 6/57. Back flap: [continuation of blurb from front flap] / Jacket design by Hollis Holland / from a color photo by Charles Allman / [publisher's device] / RANDOM HOUSE, INC. / [publisher's address and other imprints] / Printed in U.S.A.

Price: $4.75

Notes: The chronicles of ten historical figures who sought paradise and riches in the South Pacific, from the 16th century to the present.

Section A.I - Descriptive Bibliography of First Editions

A.012 SELECTED WRITINGS OF JAMES A. MICHENER:
With a Special Foreword by the Author [1957]

Title Page: SELECTED / WRITINGS / OF / JAMES A. / MICHENER / [decorative device] / With a special Foreword by the Author / [publisher's device] / THE MODERN / LIBRARY / NEW YORK

Copyright: FIRST MODERN LIBRARY EDITION, 1957 / © Copyright, 1957, by Random House, Inc. / Copyright, 1947, 1951, 1953, by James A. Michener / Copyright, 1950, 1951, by The Curtis Publishing Company / All rights reserved under International / and Pan American Copyright conventions / Library of Congress Catalog Card Number: 57-6493 / [publisher's] Random House IS THE PUBLISHER OF The Modern Library / BENNETT CERF • DONALD S. KLOPFER / MANUFACTURED IN THE UNITED STATES OF AMERICA BY H. WOLFF

Contents: [i] half-title; [ii] blank; [iii] title; [iv] copyright; [v] dedication; [vi] blank; vii-xi foreword; [xii] blank; [xiii] contents; [xiv] blank; [1] from / Tales / of the / South / Pacific; [2] blank; 3-425 text; [426] blank; [427-434] catalog.

Collation: [i-vi] vii-xi [xii] [1-2] 3-425 [426-434]; 4 5/8" x 7"

Binding: Moderate red (15) cloth. Front: [within a black panel framed by double gold rule] [gold print] SELECTED / WRITINGS / OF / JAMES A. / MICHENER / [within the double ruled frame stamped in gold] [publisher's device]. Spine: [stamped in gold] [publisher's device] / [within black panel framed by gold rule in gold print] Selected / Writings / of / James A. / Michener / • / MODERN / LIBRARY. Back: blank. Black top stain.

Dust Jacket: Black front and spine and white back. Front: [white print] Selected Writings of James A. / [wood-grained gold print] MICHENER / [circular facsimile of ship's porthole framing illustration of island native in an outrigger canoe] / [white print] Including stories and articles from TALES OF THE SOUTH PACIFIC, / RETURN TO PARADISE, and THE VOICE OF ASIA, as well as a complete / novel, THE BRIDGES AT TOKO-RI. With a special Foreword by the Author. / A MODERN LIBRARY BOOK. Spine: [white print] Selected / Writings / of / James A. / MICHENER / [at bottom] [black publisher's device silhouette on pale gold circle] / 296. Back: [advertisement and cutout mail-in order coupon for other Modern Library titles]. Front flap: [top right] $1.65 / a copy / No. 296 / blurb. Back flap: [short list of other Modern Library publications]. Reverse side of jacket: [top] WHICH OF THESE 379 OUTSTANDING BOOKS DO YOU WANT TO READ? / [complete list of then current titles published by Modern Library].

Price: $1.65

Notes: A collection of novels, stories, and essays which serves as an informative, compassionate guide to understanding the transition of Asia from the past to the future. The first edition dust jacket, reverse side, should state "WHICH OF THESE 379 OUTSTANDING BOOKS DO YOU WANT TO READ?" Later jackets will not have the 379. (Some authorities have indicated that the number on the 1st edition dust jacket could be 377 or 378, but these numbers are probably incorrect resulting from minor errors in Modern Library publication records for the years in question. Information courtesy of Henry Toledano, at Books, etc., San Francisco, CA.)

Section A.I - Descriptive Bibliography of First Editions

A.013 THE HOKUSAI SKETCHBOOKS: Selections from the Manga [1958]

Title Page: [double title page] [on verso] [illustration of Japanese man leaning on cane] / Self-portrait of Hokusai / as an old man. / From a brush-drawing. / [on recto] [between heavy framed rules] JAMES A. MICHENER / THE / HOKUSAI / SKETCH- / BOOKS / SELECTIONS FROM THE MANGA / [across the bottom of both verso and recto, beneath the framed rule] Rutland • Vermont • • Tokyo Japan • • • • • • CHARLES • E • TUTTLE • COMPANY

Copyright: Published by the / Charles E. Tuttle Company / of Rutland, Vermont & Tokyo, Japan / with editorial offices at / 15 Edogawa-cho, Bunkyo-ku, Tokyo / Copyright in Japan, 1958 / by James A. Michener / All rights reserved / throughout the world / Library of Congress / Catalog Card No. 58-9983 / First edition, 1958 / Book design & typography by M. Weatherbee / Layout of decorations by M. Kuwata / Text set & printed by Toppan Printing Co., Tokyo / Plates engraved & printed by Kyodo Printing Co., Tokyo / Binding by Okamoto Bindery, Tokyo / Manufactured in Japan

Contents: [1] [Japanese characters in double ruled frame at top right]; [2-3] double title; [4] copyright; [5] dedication; [6] blank; [7] CONTENTS; [8] blank; [9] ESSAY; 10-272 text; 273 ODDMENTS; 274-275 Caption Runovers; 276-277 Breakdown of Plates; 278-279 Acknowledgments; 280-286 Index.

Collation: [1-9] 10-286; 6 3/8" x 10 1/8"

Binding: Blackish blue (100) cloth with top fifth covered with moderate yellowish pink (29) cloth. Front: [at top right, within white vertical panel framed by black rule] [six vertical Japanese characters]. Spine: [gold print] [within moderate yellowish pink top fifth] THE / HOKUSAI / SKETCH- / BOOKS / [in gold print on blackish blue cloth] MICHENER / TUTTLE.

Dust Jacket: Top three-fourths, grayish yellow (90), bottom one-fourth, light olive gray (112). Front: [top right] [vivid red vertical panel with concave corners framed with black rule, containing Japanese characters and decorative device] [at center is illustration of hunched over Japanese printmaker with Japanese youth standing on his back holding paintbrush which has just painted the title] [black print] THE / HOKUSAI / SKETCH- / BOOKS / [below paintbrush] SELECTIONS FROM / THE [vivid red print] MANGA [within light olive gray area are numerous illustrations of Japanese block print figures] [at bottom] [black print] BY / [vivid red print] JAMES A. MICHENER. Spine: [black print] MICHENER / [within vivid red vertical panel with concave corners framed with black rule in vertical black print] THE HOKUSAI SKETCHBOOKS / [at bottom in black print] TUTTLE. Back: "Books to Span the East and West" [blurbs on eight publications] / Charles E. Tuttle Company : Publishers. Front flap: [top right] In Far East. $? / In the U.S. $10.00 / [blurb] [bottom right] Jacket design by M. Kuwata, Incorporating / title-page decoration of Manga Vol. XI. Back flap: [continuation of blurb]. Decorative cardboard shipping case.

Price: In the U.S. $10.00

Notes: A survey of a series of Japanese woodblock-printed volumes titled "Hokusai Manga" or "Hokusai's Sketches from Life" published between 1814 and 1878 in Japan.

Section A.I - Descriptive Bibliography of First Editions

A.014 HAWAII [1959]

Title Page: Hawaii / James A. Michener / [publisher's device] / RANDOM HOUSE [decorative device] / NEW YORK

Copyright: FIRST PRINTING / © Copyright, 1959, by James A. Michener / All rights reserved under International and Pan-American Copyright / Conventions. Published in New York by Random House, Inc., and / simultaneously in Toronto, Canada, by Random House of Canada, Limited. / Library of Congress Catalog Card Number: 59-10815 / Manufactured in the United States of America by H. Wolff, New York

Contents: [i] half title; [ii] BY JAMES A. MICHENER [previous works]; [iii] title; [iv] copyright; [v] Dedication; [vi] blank; [vii] author's explanatory note; [viii] blank; [ix] Contents; [x] blank; [1] [chapter heading] From the Boundless Deep; [2] blank; [3] 4-937 text; [938] blank; [939-947] GENEALOGICAL CHARTS; [948] blank; [949] ABOUT THE AUTHOR; [950] blank.

Collation: [i-x] [1-3] 4-937 [938-950]; 5 3/4" x 8 7/16"

Binding: White cloth. Front: Blank. Spine: [vertical multi-colored print with each letter of the title colored separately as follows: strong purplish red (255), strong orange (50), brilliant greenish blue (168), light purple (222), brilliant blue (177), light purplish pink (249)] Hawaii / [vertical at right edge in black print] *James A. Michener* / [vertical at left edge, black print] RANDOM HOUSE / [publisher's device]. Back: Blank. Front end map: "The Coming of the Peoples." Back end map: "The Islands." Pale blue (185) top stain.

Dust Jacket: White. Front: [multi-colored print with each letter of the title colored separately as follows: moderate purple (223), moderate olive green (125), strong yellow (84), strong yellow green (117), deep purplish pink (248), moderate purplish red (258)] Hawaii / [black print] *a novel by* / JAMES A. MICHENER / [moderate purplish red print] *a Random House Book* / [multi-colored illustration of Hawaii coast and mountains]. Spine: [each letter of title colored separately, as on front cover] Hawaii / [black print] James A. / Michener / [black publisher's device] [moderate purplish red print] RANDOM HOUSE. Back: [full page photograph of the author]. Front flap: [top right] $6.95 / [blurb] / Jacket design by S. K. A. Associates / [bottom right] 11/59. Back flap: [biographical sketch of the author] / *A Book-of-the-Month Club selection* / RANDOM HOUSE, INC. / [publisher's address] / Printed in U.S.A. / [bottom right, vertical at edge] W. Suschitzky.

Price: $6.95.

Notes: A poetic depiction of the geological processes which created the islands, followed by a fictional account of the cross-cultural peopling of Hawaii. Book-of-the-Month Club distributed copies marked "First Printing" which are only distinguishable by the small indented BOMC square at the bottom right of the back cover, and lack of top stain. The BOMC dust jacket is identical to the first edition dust jacket except the price ($6.95) is missing from the top right of the front flap.

Section A.I - Descriptive Bibliography of First Editions

A.015 JAPANESE PRINTS: From the Early Masters to the Modern [1959]

Title Page: JAPANESE PRINTS / FROM THE / EARLY MASTERS / TO THE / MODERN / by James A. Michener / with Notes on the Prints by / RICHARD LANE / with the cooperation of / THE HONOLULU ACADEMY OF ARTS / CHARLES E. TUTTLE COMPANY: PUBLISHERS / RUTLAND, VERMONT & TOKYO, JAPAN

Copyright: Published by the / Charles E. Tuttle Company of / Rutland, Vermont & Tokyo, Japan / with editorial offices at / 15 Edogawa-cho, Bunkyo-ku, Tokyo / Copyright in Japan, 1959 / by James A. Michener / All rights reserved / Library of Congress Catalog / Card No. 59-10410 / First printing, 1959 / Book design and typography by Kaoru Ogimi / Color plates by the Kyodo Printing Co., Tokyo / Gravure plates by the Inshokan Printing Co., Tokyo / Letter Press by the Kenkyusha Printing Co., Tokyo / MANUFACTURED IN JAPAN

Contents: [1] half title; [2] tipped in color Japanese print; [3] title; [4] copyright; 5 TABLE OF CONTENTS; 6-8 LIST OF ARTISTS AND PRINTS; [9] second half title; [10] [illustration of kneeling Japanese woman in kimono]; 11-24 INTRODUCTION; 25-250 text and prints; 251-282 NOTES ON THE PRINTS; 283-284 BIBLIOGRAPHY; 285-287 INDEX; [288] blank.

Collation: [1-4] 5-8 [9-10] 11-287 [288]; 8 15/16" x 12 1/16"

Binding: Light olive (106) cloth. Front: [grayish red (19) embossed raw silk insert of woodblock print by Choki (Plate 173 in the book)]. Spine: [black print at top] MICHENER / [vertical gold print] JAPANESE PRINTS / [black print at bottom] TUTTLE. Back: Blank.

Dust Jacket: Front, back, and spine contain a multi-colored illustration of Plate 173 by Choki titled "The Courtesan Tsukasa-dayu" against a silver background. Front: [lower right quarter in black calligraphy] Japanese Prints / [moderate orange (53) print] FROM THE / EARLY MASTERS / TO THE / MODERN / [black calligraphy] James A. Michener. Spine: [yellowish white (92) calligraphy] MICHENER / Japa- / nese / Prints / [black print] TUTTLE. Front flap: [at angle, across top right] In / Far East / Y4,500 or $12.50 / [broken rule] / In the U.S. $15.00 / [blurb] / Jacket design by M. Kuwata, using a section / of a woodblock print by Choki (see Plate 173). Back flap: [woodblock print of author] / HIRATSUKA UN'ICHI: "Portrait of James A. Michener" / Woodblock print, monochrome, 1957. 19.8 x 25cm. / [biographical sketch of the author]. Decorative cardboard shipping case.

Price: In Far East ¥4,500 or $12.50; In the U.S. $15.00

Notes: Michener communicates his understanding, love, and enthusiasm for Japanese prints in this collection of 257 plates, including 55 in full color. The final section of the book contains notes by Richard Lane.

Section A.I - Descriptive Bibliography of First Editions

A.016 REPORT OF THE COUNTY CHAIRMAN [1961]

Title Page: *James A. Michener* / REPORT / of the / COUNTY / CHAIRMAN / [x in box] / publisher's device] / *Random House : New York*

Copyright: *FIRST PRINTING / © Copyright, 1961, by James A. Michener / All rights reserved under International and Pan-American Copyright / Conventions. Published in New York by Random House, Inc., and / simultaneously in Toronto, Canada, by Random House of Canada, Limited. / Library of Congress Catalog Card Number: 61-10872 / Manufactured in the United States of America / by H. Wolff, New York*

Contents: [i] half title; [ii] BOOKS BY JAMES A. MICHENER [previous works]; [iii] title; [iv] copyright; [v] dedication; [vi] blank; [vii] Contents; [viii] blank; [1] second half title; [2] blank; [3] 4-310 text; [311] ABOUT THE AUTHOR; [312] blank.

Collation: [i-viii] [1-3] 4-310 [311-312]; 5 3/8" x 8"

Binding: Moderate greenish blue (173) cloth. Front: [black handwritten signature] *James A. Michener* / [gold print] COUNTY CHAIRMAN / [two blind stamped boxes containing X's, one at left and one at right side]. Spine: [all gold print] [within a black panel, ruled in gold at top and bottom] REPORT / of the / COUNTY / CHAIRMAN / [blue outline of box containing blue X] / *James A.* / *Michener* / [below black panel] [publisher's device] / RANDOM / HOUSE. Back: Blank. Deep pink (3) top stain.

Dust Jacket: White. Front: [double vertical moderate red (15) rules at left edge] [typewriter print] [black print] Report of the / County / Chairman / by / [moderate red print print] JAMES A. / MICHENER / [black small print] Since it seems likely that the 1960 Presidential Elec- / tion will long remain a matter of speculation for his- / torians, I think it might be of interest to have a fac- / tual record of the reflections of a citizen who found / himself involved in the campaign at the precinct level. / The comments that follow are as honest as I can make / them and they provide a chart of the alternate hopes / and fears with which I followed the course of John F. / Kennedy to the Presidency. Spine: [black star] / [black print] Report / of the / County / Chairman / [moderate red print] JAMES A. / MICHENER / [black publisher's device] / [moderate red print] Random / House.   Back: [full page photograph of Johnny Walsh, Jim Michener, and Sam Thompson. Front flap: [top right] $3.95 / [blurb] / [bottom] Jacket design by Paul Bacon [bottom right] 3/61. Back flap: [continuation of blurb from front flap] / [biographical sketch of the author] / RANDOM HOUSE, INC. / [publisher's address and other imprints] / Printed in U.S.A. [vertical at lower right edge] Maddox, Doylestown, Pa.

Price: $3.95

Notes: A journal of Michener's efforts in the election process as county chairman of John Kennedy's 1960 Presidential campaign.

Section A.I - Descriptive Bibliography of First Editions

A.017 THE MODERN JAPANESE PRINT: An Appreciation [1962]

Title Page: JAMES A. MICHENER / THE MODERN JAPANESE PRINT / AN APPRECIATION / *with ten original prints by* / HIRATSUKA UN'ICHI • MAEKAWA SEMPAN / MORI YOSHITOSHI • WATANABE SADAO • KINOSHITA TOMIO / SHIMA TAMAMI • AZECHI UMETARO • IWAMI REIKA / YOSHIDA MASAJI • MAKI HAKU / [Red Japanese woodblock character] / *Rutland, Vermont* / CHARLES E. TUTTLE COMPANY / *Tokyo, Japan*

Copyright: European Representatives / Continent: BOXERBOOKS, INC., Zurich / British Isles: PRENTICE-HALL INTERNATIONAL, INC., London / Published by Charles E. Tuttle Co., of Rutland, Vermont & Tokyo, Japan / with editorial offices at / 15 Edogawa-cho, Bunkyo-ku, Japan / Copyright in Japan, 1962, by James A. Michener / Library of Congress Catalog Card No. 62-17555 / PRINTED IN JAPAN

Colophon: This book has been designed and produced by / Meredith Weatherby with the collaboration of Masakazu Kuwata, Takeshi / Yamazaki and Satoru Iwamoto at the Tokyo offices of the Charles E. Tuttle / Company, Inc. The text was set by hand in Perpetua type and / printed by Kenkiusha, Limited, Tokyo and the specially reinforced binding / was done at the Okamoto Bindery, Tokyo. The text paper is handmade / Kyokushi, sometimes called Japanese vellum, with a high content of fibers / from the mitsumata and cotton plants, made and watermarked expressly for / this edition by Nakajo Sampei at Iamoto, Imadate Town, Imadate County, / Fukui Prefecture. The blocks for the prints have been destroyed and the type / distributed after producing the limited edition of 510 copies, 475 of which are / for sale. This copy is no.___.

Laid in Message: On a label laid in on the limitation page "To the Ten Signatures of distinguished Print Artists in / this book I am privileged to add my own as a token of faith in the enduring / value of their work. / James A. Michener [signature] / Bucks County, Pennsylvania / Summer, 1962"

Contents: [1] half title; [2] blank; [3] title; [4] copyright; 5 TABLE OF CONTENTS; [6] blank; 7-12 INTRODUCTION; [13] 14-52 text and tipped in prints [the prints are each individually signed by the artist, and are mounted on gray matting, unpaginated, and inserted as an extra page between the regular paginations]; 53-54 IN CONCLUSION; 55 COLOPHON; [56] blank.

Collation: [1-4] 5 [6] 7-12 [13] 14-55 [56]; 15 5/8" x 20 7/8"

Binding: Back, spine, and left one-third of the front are grayish red (19) cloth. The middle-third of the front is grayish yellowish pink (32) cloth. The right-third of the front is moderate red (15) cloth. All gold print. Front: [top left, embossed gold woodblock illustration on grayish red and grayish yellowish pink sections] [bottom right, on grayish yellowish pink and moderate red sections] THE MODERN / JAPANESE / PRINT. Spine: [vertical] MICHENER - THE MODERN JAPANESE PRINT - TUTTLE. Back: Blank.

Dust Jacket: None. Japanese cedar wood slipcase. The slipcase has the same woodblock design that appears on the title page burned into the wood. The slipcase is in turn enclosed in a stout protector of corrugated paper, with special reinforced corners.

Price: [$150.00]

A.017 THE MODERN JAPANESE PRINT: An Appreciation [1962] (continued)

Notes: From a review of 275 prints submitted by 120 artists, ten contemporary Japanese artists were selected in a competition judged by a panel of U.S. and Japanese art experts as best representing the "richness and power of the modern Japanese print." This limited edition has not been seen by the bibliographer. Information about the limited edition was provided by Charles W. Melvin, M.D. The first popular edition was issued in 1968, and is described as follows.

First Popular Edition

Contents: The contents of this popular edition are substantially the same as the limited edition except the half-title page lists Michener's previous works and a publisher's foreword is added at page 7, extending the length of the book by two pages.

Binding: Yellowish gray (93) cloth. Front: [Vivid red (11) print] JAMES A. MICHENER / [black print] THE MODERN / JAPANESE PRINT / [stamped vivid red woodblock illustration]. Spine: [vertical black print] MICHENER THE MODERN JAPANESE PRINT TUTTLE. Back: Blank.

Dust jacket: Pale yellow green (121). Front: [large illustration from the book (page 35) titled BIRDS by Shima Tamami] / [above illustration in black print] JAMES A. MICHENER / THE MODERN / JAPANESE PRINT / [below illustration] AN APPRECIATION. Spine: [vertical] [black print] MICHENER THE MODERN JAPANESE PRINT / [white print] AN APPRECIATION [black print] TUTTLE. Back: [blurb by Alan Priest, *New York Herald Tribune*] / CHARLES E. TUTTLE COMPANY: PUBLISHERS / Rutland, Vermont & Tokyo, Japan. Front flap: [top right] $5.00 / [blurb] [bottom right] In / Japan / ¥ 1260 / or $3.50. Back flap: [biographical sketch of the author] / Printed in Japan.

Section A.I - Descriptive Bibliography of First Editions

A.018 CARAVANS [1963]

Title Page: [double title page] [across both verso and recto is a line silhouette of sand dunes] [on verso] [publishers device] / RANDOM HOUSE NEW YORK / [on recto] *Caravans* / a novel by / James A. / MICHENER

Copyright: Quotation on pages 52-53 from the 11th Edition Encyclopedia Britan- / nica, published in 1910. Reprinted by permission. / FIRST PRINTING / © *Copyright, 1963*, by Random House, Inc. / All rights reserved under / International and Pan-American Copyright / Conventions. Published in New York by Random House, Inc., and / simultaneously in Toronto, Canada, by Random House of Canada, Limited. / *Library of Congress Catalog Card Number: 63-16152* / MANUFACTURED IN THE UNITED STATES OF AMERICA

Contents: [i] half title; [ii] blank; [iii] BOOKS BY JAMES A. MICHENER [previous works]; [iv-v] double title; [vi] copyright; [vii] dedication; [viii] blank; [1] second half title; [2] blank; [3] 4-336 text; [337]339-341 Note to the Reader; [342-344] blank.

Collation: [i-viii] [1-3] 4-336 [337] 338-341 [342-344]; 5 5/8" x 8 3/8"

Binding: Black cloth. Front: [the left three-fourths of the cover is blind stamped with vertical irregular wavy lines] [at right, gold print] JAMES A. / MICHENER. Spine: [continuation of vertical wavy lines from front, in strong red orange (35)] [horizontal gold print] Caravans [vertical gold print] JAMES A. / MICHENER / [publisher's device] RANDOM HOUSE. Back: Blank.

Dust Jacket: Brownish orange (54) at top one-quarter fading into moderate brown (58) at bottom three-quarters. Front: [at top] [illustration of camel caravan crossing desert] / [vivid yellow (82) print] Caravans / [strong orange (50) calligraphy] a novel by / [white print] JAMES A. / MICHENER / [vivid yellow print] A Random House Book. Spine: [at top, a continuation of the illustration from the front] / [white print] Caravans / [vivid yellow print] JAMES A. / MICHENER / [strong orange print] [publisher's device] / RANDOM HOUSE. Back: [full page photograph of the author] / PHOTO: *Baldanza, Kabul, Afghanistan* / JAMES A. MICHENER. Front flap: [top right] $5.95 / C. / R.H. / [blurb] / JACKET DESIGN BY BARRY MARTIN / *A Book-of-the-Month selection* / [bottom right] 8/63. Back flap: [list of author's previous works] / RANDOM HOUSE, INC. / [publisher's address] / Printed in the U.S.A. End maps "AFGHANISTAN." Moderate red (15) top stain.

Price: $5.95

Notes: A travelogue of post-war Afghanistan, containing a fictional narrative of a disillusioned American coed who marries an Afghan engineer and then escapes to a wandering caravan. BOMC dust jacket front flap states at the top right "BOOK-OF-THE-MONTH CLUB * SELECTION" and omits the $5.95 / C. / R. H. The bottom of the front flap states "*Trademark of Book-of-the-Month Club, Inc. / Reg. U.S. Pat. Off. and in Canada" and omits "A Book-of-the-Month Club selection 8/63". The back flap states "BOOK-OF-THE-MONTH" at top and has an "*055" at bottom right.

Section A.I - Descriptive Bibliography of First Editions

A.019 THE SOURCE [1965]

Title Page: The / SOURCE / rule / *a novel by* / JAMES A. / MICHENER / [publisher's device] / *Random House New York*

Copyright: FIRST PRINTING / © *Copyright, 1965, by Random House, Inc.* / All rights reserved under International and Pan-American Copyright / Conventions. Published in New York by Random House, Inc., and / simultaneously in Toronto, Canada, by Random House of Canada / Limited. / Manufactured in the United States of America / *by H. Wolff, New York* / DESIGNED BY TERE LOPRETE / MAPS AND DIAGRAMS BY JEAN-PAUL TREMBLAY / *Library of Congress catalog card number: 65-11255*

Contents: [i-ii] blank; [iii] half title; [iv] BOOKS BY JAMES A. MICHENER [previous works]; [v] title; [vi] copyright; [vii-viii] acknowledgments; [ix] Contents; [x] blank; [xi] author's explanatory note; [xii] blank; [1-2] THE TELL, illustration and explanation; 3-909 text; [910] blank; [911] note; [912-915] end paper maps; [916] blank.

Collation: [i-xii] [1-2] 3-909 [910-916]; 5 5/8" x 8 3/8"

Binding: Light bluish green (163) cloth. Front: [irregular strong blue (178) horizontal lines representing geological strata] [centered between the top 3 and bottom 3 strata, printed in gold, is a horizontal figure of the goddess ASTARTE]. Spine: [horizontal gold print] *The* / SOURCE / [lines continued from front] *James A.* / *Michener* / [lines continued from front] [gold print] [publisher's device] / RANDOM HOUSE. Back: Blank. Front end map: THE LOCALE. Back end map: THE GALILEE / 1964 C.E. Moderate orange (53) top stain.

Dust Jacket: Black. Front: [white print] THE / SOURCE [white rule] [strong orange (50) print] James A. / Michener / [within oval outline, strong orange, brilliant greenish blue (168), and grayish red (19) illustration of moon over Tell] / [brilliant greenish blue print] A RANDOM HOUSE NOVEL. Spine: [thick strong orange rule] / [white print] THE / SOURCE / [brilliant greenish blue rule] / [strong orange print] James A. / Michener / [white rule] [brilliant greenish blue] [publisher's device] / [RANDOM / HOUSE / [thick rule]. Back: [photograph of the author, at the ruins of Tell Beth-shan, overlooking the Jordan valley] / PHOTO: Captain Lawrence F. Danz, U.S.N. / [description of photo and quotation from 1 SAMUEL 31:9-10]. Front flap: [top right] $7.95 / [blurb] / [bottom right] 5/65. Back flap: [continuation of blurb from front flap] / RANDOM HOUSE, INC. / [publisher's address and other imprints] / PRINTED IN U.S.A. / JACKET DESIGN BY GUY FLEMING.

Price: $7.95

Notes: An archeological excavation of a fictional site in Israel revealing, at different levels, the 12,000 year history of the region's people and societies. BOMC dust jacket front flap states at the top right "BOOK-OF-THE-MONTH CLUB * SELECTION" and omits the $7.95. The bottom of the front flap states "*Trademark of Book-of-the-Month Club, Inc. / Reg. U.S. Pat. Off. and in Canada." The back flap states "BOOK-OF-THE-MONTH" at the top. The back flap of the first edition dust jacket states "JACKET DESIGN BY GUY FLEMING." This has been moved to the front flap of the BOMC dust jacket. At the bottom of the spine, is the number 1355 in white. Some BOMC copies state "First Printing" on the copyright page, and are distinguishable from true first printings only by the BOMC indentation on the back of the binding.

Section A.I - Descriptive Bibliography of First Editions

A.020 THE MATADOR WHO CONQUERED MEXICO [1965-66]

Title Page: THE MATADOR / WHO / CONQUERED / MEXICO / JAMES A. MICHENER / Author of 'Tales of the South Pacific,' 'Hawaii,' / 'The Bridge at Andau,' etc. / COLLEGE OF TECHNOLOGY, OXFORD

Copyright: None
Colophon page:

Designed and Composed by
A. C. Townsend
FIFTH YEAR COMPOSING STUDENT

and illustrated by
A. G. Walton
PRE-DIPLOMA STUDENT

SCHOOL OF ART, COLLEGE OF TECHNOLOGY
OXFORD 1965-6

Contents: [1] half title; [2] blank; [3] title; [4] blank; [5] prologue; [6] blank; [7-14] text; [15] blank; [16] colophon.

Collation: [1-16]; 5 7/16" x 8 5/16"

Binding: Heavy moderate red (15) paper wraps, stapled twice at centerfold. In the top third of the front cover, printed in black, is a circular woodblock abstract of a fighting bull with pics or banderillas in its back.

Dust Jacket: None.

Price: Not sold to the public.

Notes: The text is reprinted from an article by Michener in *Reader's Digest*, July, 1961, titled "Mexico's Mild-Mannered Matador." It is estimated that approximately 50 copies were printed.

Section A.I - Descriptive Bibliography of First Editions

A.021 ADICKES, A PORTFOLIO WITH CRITIQUE [1968]

Title Page: ADICKES / a portfolio with critique by / James A. Michener / and a critique in French by / Alessandra Cantey / DuBose Gallery, Houston / 1968

Copyright: PRINTED IN SPAIN EMPRESO EN ESPANA / Deposito Legal B. 21.337--1968 / I. G. Seix y Barral Hnos., S.A. - BARCELONA

Contents: [1] blank; [2] plate no. 1; [3] title; [4] copyright; [5-20] Michener's text and plate nos. 2-15; [21-55] plates nos. 16-47; [56] [artist's chronology]; [57-59] plate nos. 48-50; [51-59] French text and plate nos. 51-54, and a photograph of Adickes on page 55; [60-62] blank.

Collation: [1-62]; 8 1/4" x 9 7/8"

Binding: Strong red (12) cloth. Front: [black print] ADICKES. Spine: [vertical, from bottom to top, black print] ADICKES James A. Michener. Back: Blank.

Dust Jacket: Black. Front: [illustration by David Adickes titled "Harlequin With Birds," Plate no. 24 from the book] [at bottom, white print] ADICKES / Critique by James A. Michener. Spine: [vertical, from top to bottom, white print] ADICKES James A. Michener. Back: [photograph of the artist with a quotation from the text by Michener]. Front and back flaps: Blank.

Price: Not sold to the public.

Notes: The artist states that 1000 copies were printed for distribution to clients purchasing his art work.

Section A.I - Descriptive Bibliography of First Editions

A.022 IBERIA: Spanish Travels and Reflections [1968]

Title Page: [double title page] [on verso] JAMES A. MICHENER / PHOTOGRAPHS BY ROBERT VAVRA / [publisher's device] RANDOM HOUSE NEW YORK / [on recto] IBERIA / SPANISH TRAVELS AND REFLECTIONS / [across verso and recto] [illustration of silhouette outline of Spanish cathedrals]

Copyright: *First Printing / Copyright © 1968 by Random House, Inc. / All rights reserved under International and Pan-American Copyright Conventions. / Published in the United States by Random House, Inc., New York, and / simultaneously in Canada, by Random House of Canada Limited, Toronto. / Library of Congress Catalog Card Number: 67-22623 / Manufactured in the United States of America / Maps by Jean Paul Tremblay / Design by Betty Anderson*

Contents: [i-iii] blank; [iv] BOOKS BY James A. Michener [previous works]; [v] half title; [vi-vii] double title page; [viii] copyright; [ix-x] Acknowledgments; [xi] Contents; [xii] blank; [1] second half title; [2] photograph of dry bark on cork tree; [3-4] 5-24 [25] INTRODUCTION; [26] photograph of a cork harvester; [27-28] 29-794 [795] text; [796] blank; [797-798] 799-818 Index; [819-820] blank.

Collation: [i-xii] [1-4] 5-24 [25-28] 29-794 [795-798] 799-818 [819-820]; 6 1/2" x 9 1/4"

Binding: Strong orange yellow (68) cloth. All gold print. Front: [top right] [illustration of Spanish coat-of-arms]. Spine: [vertical] IBERIA / [calligraphy] Spanish Travels and Reflections / [publisher's device] RANDOM HOUSE / JAMES A. MICHENER. Back: Blank. Front end map: IBERIA. Back end papers: [Chronology of rulers of Spain]. Yellow orange top stain.

Dust Jacket: White and black. Front: [black print on top white panel] IBERIA / [within a vivid reddish orange (34) panel, across mid-front] [strong yellow (84) print] SPANISH TRAVELS AND REFLECTIONS / [three rows of alternating vivid reddish orange and dark purplish pink (251) checkerboard squares] / [strong yellow print] PHOTOGRAPHS BY ROBERT VAVRA / [black print on bottom white panel] JAMES A. / MICHENER. Spine: Black. [top-half] [vertical] [white print] IBERIA / [vivid reddish orange print] SPANISH TRAVELS AND REFLECTIONS / [bottom-half] [vertical] [dark purplish pink print] RANDOM / HOUSE / [publisher's device] / [vivid reddish orange print] JAMES A. / MICHENER. Back: [sideways] [full page photograph of the author and Robert Vavra]. Front flap: [top right] $10.00 / [blurb] / Jacket design Don Bolognese / [bottom right] 5/68. Back flap: [continuation of blurb from front flap] / RANDOM HOUSE, Inc. / [other imprints] / PRINTED IN U.S.A.

Price: $10.00

Notes: The history of Iberia, its role in shaping the Americas, and its rise and fall as a world power. A comprehensive travelog of Spain. The BOMC dust jacket omits the price at the top right and the date at the bottom right of the front flap and states "BOOK-OF-THE-MONTH CLUB * SELECTION / *Trademark of Book-of-the-Month Club, Inc. / Reg. U.S. Pat. Off. and in Canada." Top of the back flap states "BOOK-OF-THE-MONTH." At the base of the spine, is the number 0226.

Section A.I - Descriptive Bibliography of First Editions

A.023 PRESIDENTIAL LOTTERY:
  The Reckless Gamble in Our Electoral System [1969]

Title Page: [double title page] [on verso] [publisher's device] [decorative device of triangles] / RANDOM HOUSE, NEW YORK [on recto] PRESIDENTIAL LOTTERY / [decorative device of triangles] / *The Reckless Gamble in* / *Our Electoral System* / JAMES A. MICHENER

Copyright: FIRST PRINTING / Copyright © 1969 by RANDOM HOUSE, INC. / All rights reserved under International and / Pan-American Copyright Conventions. / Published in the United States / by Random House, Inc., New York, / and simultaneously in Canada / by Random House of Canada Limited, Toronto. / The quotations (in Chapter V and Appendix / C) from "One Man, 3.312 Votes: A Mathe- / matical Analysis of the Electoral College," by / John F. Banzhaf, III, are reprinted with per- / mission from *Villanova Law Review*, Vol. 13, / No. 2, pp. 314-315, 317, 329-332. Copyright / 1968 by Villanova University. / Library of Congress Catalog Card Number: 73-76278 / Manufactured in the United States of America / by H. Wolff, New York

Contents: [0] blank; [00] BOOKS BY / JAMES A. MICHENER [previous works]; [i] half title; [ii-iii] double title page; [iv] copyright; [v] dedication; vi blank; vii-viii Contents; [1] second half title; [2] blank; 3-194 text; [195] APPENDICES; [196] blank; 197-207 APPENDIX A; 208-219 APPENDIX B; 220-229 APPENDIX C; 230-233 APPENDIX D; 234-240 APPENDIX E; [241-246] blank.

Collation: [00-0] [i-vi] vii-viii [1-2] 3-194 [195-196] 197-240 [241-246]; 5 3/8" x 8"

Binding: Black cloth. Front: [silver print] $\mathcal{J}$ ∆ $\mathcal{A}$ ∆ $\mathcal{M}$. Spine: [vertical] [silver print] PRESIDENTIAL LOTTERY [gold print] JAMES A. MICHENER / RANDOM HOUSE / [horizontal silver publisher's device]. Back: Blank.

Dust Jacket: White. Front: [black print] Presidential / Lottery / [within vivid red (11) panel] The Reckless Gamble / [within bluish white (189) panel] in Our / [within strong blue (176) panel] Electoral System / [black print] JAMES A. / MICHENER. Spine: [black vertical print] Presidential Lottery JAMES A. MICHENER [horizontal] [vivid red publisher's device] [strong blue print] Random / House. Back: [strong blue print] Available from / RANDOM HOUSE / [vivid red rule] [author's previous works]. Front flap: [top right] $5.95 / [blurb]. Back flap: [continuation of blurb] / Jacket designed by Ronald Clyne / Random House, Inc., [publisher's address and imprints] / Printed in U.S.A. 4/69.

Price: $5.95

Notes: A careful analysis of the inherent dangers of the Electoral College system in our presidential election process and the potentially disasterous consequences which could be produced in a close election.

Section A.I - Descriptive Bibliography of First Editions

A.024 AMERICA VS. AMERICA:
The Revolution in Middle-Class Values [1969]

Title Page: JAMES A. MICHENER / America / vs. / America: / THE REVOLUTION IN / MIDDLE-CLASS VALUES / [publisher's device] / A SIGNET BOOK / Published by / THE NEW AMERICAN LIBRARY

Copyright: Copyright © 1968, 1969, by MARJAY PRODUCTIONS, INC. / All rights reserved / Library of Congress Catalog Card Number: 69-18320 / SIGNET TRADEMARK REG. U.S. PAT. OFF. AND FOREIGN COUNTRIES / REGISTERED TRADEMARK - MARCA REGISTRADA / HECHO EN CHICAGO, U.S.A. / *SIGNET BOOKS are published by / The New American Library, Inc., / 1301 Avenue of the Americas, / New York, New York 10019* / FIRST PRINTING, APRIL 1969 / PRINTED IN THE UNITED STATES OF AMERICA

Contents: [1] three quotations from the text; [2] SIGNET Specials of Related Interest [advertisement]; [3] title; [4] copyright; [5] Contents; [6] blank; [7] half title; [8] blank; [9] [chapter heading] 1. YOUNG AMERICA ATTACKS; [10] blank; 11-80 text.

Collation: [1-10] 11-80; 4 3/16" x 7"

Binding: Vivid reddish orange (34) wraps. Front: [black print] A SIGNET SPECIAL BROADSIDE #6 • P3819 • 60 ¢ / [vivid yellow (82) print] James A. / Michener / [black print] Author of / *Iberia, The Source, Hawaii* / [white print] AMERICA / VS. / AMERICA / [black print] THE REVOLUTION IN / MIDDLE-CLASS VALUES / "I am heartened by our young people, black and white. What some of their / elders see as rebellion, I see as the / proper assumption of responsibility / and a long-overdue attention to / problems requiring change." Spine: [horizontal black print] [publisher's device] / [rule] / P / 3819 [vertical vivid yellow print] AMERICA VS. AMERICA [horizontal black rule] [vertical] [white print] MICHENER [black print] 451-P3819-060. Back: [blurbs] / [black print] THE NEW AMERICAN LIBRARY PUBLISHES SIGNET, MENTOR, CLASSICS & NAL BOOKS.

Dust Jacket: None

Price: $.60

Notes: A reprint of an article Michener wrote for the *New York Times Magazine*, August 18, 1968, titled "Revolution in Middle-Class Values." This book comes only in paperback and all copies are first editions.

Section A.I - Descriptive Bibliography of First Editions

A.025 FACING EAST. [1970]

Title Page: FACING / EAST / I / text by / JAMES A. MICHENER / original lithographs / and woodcuts by / JACK LEVINE / II / sketchbook by / JACK LEVINE / MAECENAS PRESS [star] RANDOM HOUSE / NEW YORK 1970

Copyright: All rights reserved James A. Michener and Jack Levine

Colophon Page:

COLOPHON
THE 2500 DE LUXE PORTFOLIOS OF THIS LIMITED
EDITION, NUMBERED FROM 1 TO 2500, WERE INDIVID-
UALLY SIGNED BY THE AUTHOR AND THE ARTIST.
IN ADDITION, SIXTEEN PORTFOLIOS MARKED FROM
A TO P ARE THE PROPERTY OF THE AUTHOR AND
THE ARTIST. SEVERAL PORTFOLIOS MARKED H.C.
WERE PRINTED FOR THE PUBLISHERS AND THEIR
COLLABORATORS. * THE FOUR ORIGINAL LITHO-
GRAPHS, SIGNED IN THE STONE BY THE ARTIST,
WERE PULLED ON RIVES PAPER. * THE TEXT, HAND-
SET IN CASLON DE CORPS 24, AND THE ORIGINAL
WOODCUTS WERE PRINTED ON ARCHES PAPER.* THE
ORIGINAL "HORS-TEXT" WOODCUT WAS PULLED
ON KAWANAKA JAPANESE VELLUM PAPER. * THE
FIFTY-FOUR WATERCOLORS, GOUCHES, AND DRAW-
INGS FROM THE SKETCHBOOK BY JACK LEVINE
WERE PRINTED BY PHOTOTYPIE AND POCHOIR
PROCESSES ON INGRES PAPER. FROM TWO TO
FORTY COLORS WERE HAND-BRUSHED ON EACH.

Contents: [i] Portfolio number [number/2500] [handwritten signatures of Jack Levine and James A. Michener; [ii-iv] blank [an illustration of a Japanese woman serving tea laid in between pages ii and iii]; [v] half title with Japanese illustration; [vi] blank; [vii] title page; [viii] All rights reserved James A. Michener and Jack Levine; ix-xi [xii] xiii-xiv [xv] xvi [xvii] xviii-xxvii [xxviii] xxix-xxxi [xxxii] text; [xxxiii] Colophon; [xxxiv] Japanese illustration; [xxxv] Printing background; [xxxvi] blank.

Collation: [i-xii] xiii-xiv [xv] xvi [xvii] xviii-xxvii [xxviii] xxix-xxxi [xxxii-xxxvi]; 12 3/8"x18 7/8"

Binding: [This portfolio, a collection of original lithographs and woodcuts, and sketchbook by Jack Levine, is unbound consisting of large (12 1/2" x 10") pages of text by Michener with lithographs, woodcuts, and sketches laid in. The text, lithographs, and woodcuts are contained in folded and belted folio. The sketches are laid in loose in a separate black simulated leather folio. Both folios are contained in a foldover box signed on the inside front cover by Jack Levine and James A. Michener].

Dust Jacket: None

Price: Price not stated. Was sold retail for $600.00

Notes: Lithographs and woodcuts by Jack Levine, with text by Michener.

Section A.I - Descriptive Bibliography of First Editions

A.026 THE QUALITY OF LIFE   [1970]

Title Page: The / Quality / of Life / by James A. Michener / Paintings by James B. Wyeth / Written for and published by Girard Bank • February 1970

Copyright: JAMES A. MICHENER, distinguished American author, is a / long-time resident of the Philadelphia area.   He attended / Swarthmore College and after a number of successful / years in education and publishing, turned to the field of / writing where his books have met universal acclaim. His / books include TALES OF THE SOUTH PACIFIC, FIRES OF / SPRING, THE BRIDGES AT TOKO-RI, SAYONARA, / HAWAII, THE SOURCE and IBERIA. He has maintained a / continuing interest in state and local governmental affairs. / JAMES B. WYETH is the gifted young Pennsylvania artist / carrying on a family tradition of great American painting. / He is the son of the world renowned Andrew Wyeth and / grandson of noted illustrator N. C. Wyeth, who made / Chadds Ford the capital of the 20th century art world. In / 1969, James Wyeth won the honor of becoming - at 22 - / the youngest member in the history of the National / Academy of Arts and Letters. / Library of Congress catalog number: 71-116744 / Copyright © 1970 by the Girard Company / Paintings Copyright © 1967, 1970 by James B. Wyeth / Printed in the United States of America

Laid in Message: (3 5/16" x 7 13/16" folded over at top) states as follows: To Shareholders and Friends: / Good corporate citizenship takes / various forms. / We believe that among other things / it entails the stimulation of public / interest and concern for the major / issues and problems of our day. / The publication of a company's / annual report -- the yearly review of / its performance and goals -- is an / especially good time to seek widespread / involvement in the changing world / about us. / It is in this spirit that The Girard / Company takes pleasure and pride in / presenting this volume, "The Quality / of Life", by James A. Michener. In / commissioning him to write this / companion piece for our 1969 Annual / Report, Mr. Michener had complete / freedom to express his own views. / To enrich and give emphasis to the / text, we have added nine color / reproductions of paintings by / James B. Wyeth. / We are indebted to Messrs. / Michener and Wyeth for their unusual / contributions to this unique venture. / [signature] S S Gardner / Stephen S. Gardner / President / The Girard Company.

Contents: [i] half title; [ii] illustration LIFELINE; [iii] title; [iv] copyright; [v] CONTENTS; [vi] illustration THE TIN WOODSMAN; 1-9 Introduction; [10] 11-85 illustrations and text; [86] blank; [87] Acknowledgments; [88-90] blank.

Collation: [i-vi] 1-9 [10] 11-85 [86-90]; 5 1/2" x 8 1/4"

Binding: Dark yellowish green (137) paper covered boards. Front: [illustration titled "Buzz Saw" by James B. Wyeth pasted to top right corner] [to left of illustration in black print] The / Quality / of Life / by / James A. / Michener. Spine: [vertical black print] The Quality of Life by James A. Michener. Back: Blank.

Dust Jacket: None. Slipcase, color matches binding. [large horizontal print across top of front] THE QUALITY [vertical, at right edge] OF LIFE [horizontal, at bottom, small print] BY JAMES A. [large outline print] MICHENER.

Price: Not sold to the public.

Notes: Michener was commissioned by the Girard Bank to express his opinions on some of the issues of the day. An expanded trade edition was published by J. B. Lippincott Company in 1970.   It included an additional chapter titled "The Population Cancer." The trade edition omits the art work of James B. Wyeth.

Section A.I - Descriptive Bibliography of First Editions

A.027 KENT STATE: What Happened and Why [1971]

Title Page: [double title page] [on verso] RANDOM HOUSE [publisher's device] NEW YORK / A READER'S DIGEST [publisher's device] PRESS BOOK / [on recto] [rule] / KENT STATE / [rule] / WHAT HAPPENED AND WHY / JAMES A. MICHENER / [covering bottom two-thirds of verso and recto] [photograph of Kent State students with student throwing tear gas bomb]

Copyright: Copyright ©1971 by Random House, Inc., and / The Reader's Digest Association, Inc. / All rights reserved under International and Pan-American / Copyright Conventions. Published in the United States by / Random House, Inc., New York, and simultaneously in / Canada by Random House of Canada Limited, Toronto. / ISBN: 0-394-47199-7 / Library of Congress Catalog Card Number: 74-155822 / *Designed by Antonina Krass* / MANUFACTURED IN THE UNITED STATES OF AMERICA / FIRST EDITION

Contents: [i] blank; [ii] BOOKS BY JAMES A. MICHENER [previous works]; [iii] half title; [iv-v] double title page; [vi] copyright; [vii] viii foreword by James A. Michener; [ix] x Contents; [xi] xii ILLUSTRATIONS; [1] second half title; [2-5] oval framed photographs of Kent State personalities; [6] blank; [7] 8-554 text; [555] photograph; [556] 557-559 AFTERWORD by James A. Michener; [560-563] Kent State maps; [564] blank.

Collation: [i-vii] viii [ix] x [xi] xii [1-7] 8-554 [555-556] 557-559 [560-564]; 6" x 9 3/16"

Binding: Moderate blue (182) smooth cloth. Front: [thin black rule] / KENT STATE / [thin black rule]. Spine: [vertical between two horizontal silver rules in silver print] KENT STATE / JAMES A. MICHENER / [at bottom] [horizontal silver print] RANDOM / HOUSE [publisher's device] / [thin rule] READER'S / DIGEST / PRESS [publisher's device]. Back: Blank. Front end map: KENT, OHIO. Back end map: MONDAY, MAY 4, 1970. Black top stain.

Dust Jacket: Blackish blue (188). Front: [large white print] KENT / STATE / [small strong reddish orange (35) print] What Happened and Why / [white print] 'This could be your university. The students / and National Guardsmen could be you, or young / people of your neighborhood, or, if you are old / enough, your sons and daughters. The city of Kent could be your community. That is why you / need to know what happened to you, so that / you can prevent it from happening again.' / [large vivid yellow (82) print] JAMES A. / MICHENER. Spine: [vertical] [large white print at right edge] KENT STATE [small strong reddish orange print] What / Happened and Why / [large vivid yellow print at left edge] JAMES A. MICHENER [horizontal] [white print at bottom] [co-publishers' devices] / Random House. Back: [full page photograph of the author] / [bottom left] Photo: Ellen Levine [bottom right] 394-47199-7. Front flap: [top right] $10.00 / [blurb]. Back flap: [continuation of blurb] / Jacket design by Jay J. Smith Studio / Random House, Inc. [publisher's address and imprints] / Printed in U.S.A. / 4/71.

Price: $10.00

Notes: Michener's analysis of the tragedy at Kent State. Book-of-the-Month Club distributed copies marked "First Printing" which are only distinguishable by the small indented BOMC square at the bottom right of the back cover. The BOMC dust jacket is identical to the first edition dust jacket except the price ($10.00) is missing from the top right of the front flap and the ISBN number at the bottom of the bottom of the dust jacket is replaced with 1640.

Section A.I - Descriptive Bibliography of First Editions

A.028 THE DRIFTERS [1971]

Title Page: [right justified] *The* / DRIFTERS / *A* / *Novel* / *by* / JAMES / A. / MICHENER / [publisher's device] / RANDOM HOUSE / *New York*

Copyright: Copyright © 1971 by Random House, Inc. / All rights reserved under International and Pan-American Copyright Con- / ventions. Published in the United States by Random House, Inc., New York, / and simultaneously in Canada by Random House of Canada Limited, Toronto. / ISBN: 0-394-46200-9 TR. / Library of Congress Catalog Card Number: 75-117655 / Manufactured in the United States of America / by Kingsport Press, Inc., Kingsport, Tenn. / An extract from *The Lusiads of Luis de Camoes*, / Translated by Leonard Bacon, is reprinted by / permission of The Hispanic Society of America, / New York, 1966, p. 16. / 98765432 / First Edition / *Designed by Bernard Klein*

Contents: [i-iii] blank; [iv] Books by JAMES A. MICHENER [previous works]; [v] half title; [vi] blank; [vii] title; [viii] copyright; [ix] CONTENTS; [x] blank; [xi] author's note; [xii] blank; [1-3] 4-751 text; [752-756] blank.

Collation: [i-xii] [1-3] 4-751 [752-756]; 5 5/8" x 8 3/8"

Binding: Vivid red (11) cloth front with black cloth spine and back. Front: [red print stamped vertical at right edge] *The* / D R I F T E R S. Spine: [vivid red print] *The* / DRIFTERS / [copper print] *A Novel by* / JAMES A. / MICHENER / [publisher's device] / RANDOM HOUSE. Back: Blank. End maps: SPAIN, PORTUGAL, AND MOROCCO on verso; MOCAMBIQUE on recto. Grayish blue (186) top stain.

Dust Jacket: Black. Front: [large white print] James A. / Michener / [moderate yellow (87) print] A / Novel [strong reddish orange (35) print] The / Drifters. Spine: [vertical] [white print] James A. Michener / [strong reddish orange print] The Drifters [horizontal, moderate yellow] [publisher's device] / Random House. Back: [full page photograph of the author with inset list of previous works] [bottom right] 394-46200-9. Front flap: [top right] $10.00 / [blurb]. Back flap: [continuation of blurb] / A Book-of-the-Month Club selection /   Jacket design by Muriel Nasser / Random House, Inc. / [publisher's address and other imprints] Printed in U.S.A. / 4/71 [vertical at bottom right edge] Photo by Ellen Levine.

Price: $10.00

Notes: Six disenchanted and disillusioned young people from various parts of the world become free spirits in search of answers and meaning when they come together in the Spanish resort town of Torremolinos. The BOMC dust jacket omits the price at the top right of the front flap and states "BOOK-OF-THE-MONTH CLUB * SELECTION." At the bottom it states "*Trademark of Book-of-the-Month Club, Inc. / Reg. U.S. Pat. Off. and in Canada." The back flap omits "A Book-of-the-Month Club selection" and omits the publisher's identification, imprints, and date. The ISBN on the bottom right of the back cover is replaced with 0102.

Section A.I - Descriptive Bibliography of First Editions

A.029 A MICHENER MISCELLANY: 1950-1970 [1973]

Title Page: [double title page] [on verso] [rule] / Selected and edited / by Ben Hibbs / [publisher's device] A READER'S DIGEST PRESS BOOK / [on recto] A / Michener / Miscellany: / 1950-1970 / [rule] / James A. / Michener [decorative device] / [publisher's device] RANDOM HOUSE : NEW YORK

Copyright: [The top half of the copyright page is as follows] Copyright © 1973 by Random House, Inc., and The Reader's / Digest Association, Inc. / All rights reserved under International and Pan-American / Copyright Conventions. Published in the United States by / Random House, Inc., New York and simultaneously in Canada / by Random House of Canada Limited, Toronto. / Library of Congress Cataloging in Publication Data / Michener, James Albert, 1907- / A Michener miscellany: 1950 -1970. / "A Reader's Digest Press book." / Essays published in Reader's Digest, here largely revised. / I. Title. / PS3525.I19M5 814'.5'4 72-10926 / ISBN 0-394-47948-3 / Manufactured in the United States of America / First Edition / [The bottom half of the copyright page and the following page contain a list of acknowledgments of the articles and sources reproduced in this publication]

Contents: [i] blank; [ii] BOOKS BY JAMES A. MICHENER [previous works]; [iii] half title; [iv-v] double title page; [vi] top half, copyright; [vi] bottom half [vii] acknowledgments; [viii] blank; [ix] [dedication]; [x] blank; [xi-xii] CONTENTS; [1] second half title; [2] blank; [3] 4-9 BY WAY OF EXPLANATION; [10] blank; [11] 12-404 text.

Collation: [i-xii] [1-3] 4-9 [10-11] 12-404; 5 5/8" x 8 1/4"

Binding: Black cloth. Front: [moderate orange (53) print] J • A • M / [rule] / [decorative device]. Spine: [all silver print] [vertical at right edge] *A Michener Miscellany: 1950 - 1970* / [long narrow vertical rule] / James A. Michener [horizontal] [publisher's device] / RANDOM HOUSE / [publisher's device] / READER'S DIGEST PRESS. Back: Blank. Black top stain.

Dust Jacket: Black. Front: [white print] James A. / Michener / [light yellowish green (135) leafy decorative device] [strong yellow (84) print] A / [strong orange yellow (68) print] Michener / [moderate orange (53) print] Miscellany / [strong reddish orange (35) print] 1950 - 1970 / [deep purplish pink (248) print] Selected and edited by Ben Hibbs / from essays written during two decades. Spine: [vertical white print at right edge] James A. Michener / [vertical print at left edge] [strong yellow print] A [strong orange yellow print] Michener [moderate orange print] Miscellany: [strong reddish orange print] 1950 - 1970 [horizontal] [white print] [publisher's device] / Random House / [strong yellow print] READER'S / DIGEST / PRESS / [moderate orange print] [publisher's device]. Back: [full page photograph of the author] [white print] [bottom left] Photo: Ellen Levine [bottom right] 394-47948-3. Front flap: [top right] $8.95 / [blurb]. Back flap: Books by / James A. / MICHENER [previous works] / Jacket design by Muriel Nasser / Random House, Inc. [publisher's address and other imprints] / Printed in U.S.A. / 4/73.

Price: $8.95

Notes: Twenty-five essays on a variety of subjects including travel, politics, fine and popular arts, education, censorship, sports, and rock music. New prefatory notes were written by the author for the fourteen categories in which he arranged the essays.

Section A.I - Descriptive Bibliography of First Editions

A.030 FIRSTFRUITS: A Harvest of Twenty-five Years of Israeli Writing [1973]

Title Page: [double title page] [on recto] edited and with an introduction by / James A. Michener / [across verso and recto] FIRSTFRUITS / a harvest of 25 years of Israeli writing / [on recto] with a foreword by Chaim Potok / [on verso] The Jewish Publication Society of America / Philadelphia   5733 • 1973 [publisher's device]

Copyright: *Copyright © 1973 by The Jewish Publication Society of America / First edition / All rights reserved / All of these stories originally appeared in Hebrew / Library of Congress Catalog Card Number 72-14199 / ISBN: 0-8276-0018-6 / Manufactured in the United States of America / Designed by Adrianne Onderdonk Dudden*

Contents: [i] half title; [ii-iii] double title page; [iv] copyright; [v] Contents; [vi] blank; [vii] viii Foreword; [ix] x-xxv Introduction; [xxvi] blank; [1] 2-344 text; [345] 346 About the Writers; [347] Acknowledgments; [348-350] blank.

Collation: [i-vii] viii [ix] x-xxv [xxvi] [1] 2-344 [345] 346 [347-350]; 5 1/2" x 8 1/4"

Binding: Pale orange yellow (73) cloth. Front: Blank. Spine: [vertical at right edge] [moderate brown (58) print] Michener   Jewish Publication Society / [vertical moderate green (145) print at left edge] FIRSTFRUITS. Back: Blank.

Dust Jacket: Covering front and spine in multiple brown tones ranging from grayish red (19) to brownish pink (33) is an illustration of rocky terrain with plant growing from crack. Front: [moderate green (145) print] edited and with an introduction by / [white print] James A. Michener / Firstfruits / [moderate green print] a harvest of 25 years of Israeli writing / with a foreword by [white print] Chaim Potok. Spine: [vertical, moderate green print, top left edge] Michener [vertical white print, at right edge, mid-spine] Firstfruits / [vertical, moderate green print, centered at bottom] JPS. Back: [list of prior publications by the publisher]. Front flap: [top right] $6.95 / [blurb and biographical sketch of editor]. Back flap: [continuation of biographical sketch of editor and Chaim Potok] / Jacket design by / Adrianne Onderdonk Dudden / ISBN 0-8276-0018-6.

Price: $6.95

Notes: Twenty-five years of Israeli short fiction, edited and with an introduction by Michener.

Section A.I - Descriptive Bibliography of First Editions

A.031 CENTENNIAL [1974]

Title Page: [framed within half circle] [illustration of eagle clutching shield, arrows, and olive branch] / CENTENNIAL / [rule] / JAMES A. / MICHENER / *Random House* [publisher's device] *New York*

Copyright: Copyright © 1974 by Random House, Inc. / All rights reserved under International and Pan- / American Copyright Conventions. Published in the / United States by Random House, Inc., New York, / and simultaneously in Canada by Random House / of Canada Limited, Toronto. / Lyrics from "The Buffalo Skinners" on page 858, / collected, adapted and arranged by John A. Lomax / and Alan Lomax. TRO ---- © Copyright 1934 and / renewed 1962 LUDLOW MUSIC, INC. New / York, N.Y. Used by permission. / Library of Congress Cataloging in Publication Data / Michener, James Albert, 1907- / Centennial. / I. Title. / PZ3.M583Ce 813'.5'4 74-5164 / ISBN 0-394-47970-X / ISBN 0-394-49345-1 (limited edition) / Designed by Antonina Krass / Manufactured in the United States of America / First Edition

Contents: [i] blank; [ii] BOOKS BY JAMES A. MICHENER [previous works]; [iii] half title; [iv] blank; [v] title; [vi] copyright; [vii] viii-x acknowledgment; [xi] dedication; [xii] blank; [xiii] author's note; [xiv] blank; [xv] Contents; [xvi] blank; [1] [chapter heading] THE COMMISSION; [2] blank; [3] 4-909 text; [910-912] blank.

Collation: [i-vii] viii-x [xi-xvi] [1-3] 4-909 [910-912]; 5 5/8" x 8 1/4"

Binding: Dark red (16) cloth. All copper print. Front: [within lined semi-circle] [eagle clutching shield, arrows, and olive branch]. Spine: CENTENNIAL / [row of four leaflike decorative devices] / JAMES A. / MICHENER / [publisher's device] *Random House*. Back: Blank. Front end map: THE SETTING. Back end map: CENTENNIAL, COLORADO, 1973. Dark greenish blue top stain.

Dust Jacket: Black. Front: [moderate yellow (87) print] Centennial / [strong red (11) print] James A. / Michener / [within strong blue (178) semi-circle, lined in white] [white outline of eagle clutching shield, arrows, and olive branch] / [white print] A Random House Novel. Spine: [vertical moderate yellow print, at right edge] Centennial / [vertical strong red print, at left edge] James A. Michener [horizontal blue print] [publisher's device] / RANDOM / HOUSE. Back: [full page photograph of the author] [bottom left] Photo: Tessa J. Dalton. [bottom right] 394-47970-X. Front flap: [top right] $10.95 / [blurb]. Back flap: [continuation of blurb] / Random House Inc. / [publisher's address and other imprints] / Printed in the U.S.A. / 9/74.

Price: $10.95

Notes: A fictional account of a Colorado town called Centennial and characters illustrating the historical development of Colorado, nicknamed the Centennial State when admitted to the Union in the Centennial year of the Republic.

Section A.I - Descriptive Bibliography of First Editions

A.032 ABOUT CENTENNIAL: Some Notes on the Novel [1974]

Title Page: ABOUT / *Centennial* / SOME NOTES ON THE NOVEL / [two leaflike decorative devices] / *James A. Michener* / RANDOM HOUSE [publisher's device] NEW YORK

Copyright: Copyright © 1974 by Random House, Inc. / All rights reserved under International and Pan-American / Copyright Conventions. Published in the United States / by Random House, Inc., New York, and simultaneously / in Canada by Random House of Canada Limited, / Toronto. / **Library of Congress Cataloging in Publication Data** / Michener, James Albert, 1907- / About Centennial. / 1. Michener, James, Albert, 1907- Centennial. / I. Title. / PS3525.I19C435 813'.5'4 74-9770 / ISBN 0-394-45937-3 / Manufactured in the United States of America.

Contents: [1-2] blank; [3] half title; [4] blank; [5] title; [6] copyright; [7] PUBLISHER'S NOTE; [8] blank; [9] second half title; [10] blank; 11-57 text; [58-64] blank.

Collation: [1-10] 11-57 [58-64]; 5 5/8" x 8 3/8"

Binding: Yellowish white (92) cloth. Front: [within silver lined semi-circle] [eagle clutching shield, arrows, and olive branch]. Spine: [vertical copper print] ABOUT *Centennial* : SOME NOTES ON THE NOVEL [two leaflike decorative devices] JAMES A. MICHENER *Random House*. Back: Blank. Front end map: THE SETTING. Back end map: CENTENNIAL, COLORADO, 1973. Dark blue top stain.

Dust Jacket: Black. Front: [moderate yellow (87) print] About *Centennial* / [strong blue (178) print] James A. / Michener / [within strong red (11) semi-circle, lined in white] [white outline of eagle clutching shield, arrows, and olive branch] / [white print] Some Notes on the Novel. Spine: [vertical] [moderate yellow print] ABOUT *CENTENNIAL* [strong blue print] James A. Michener [horizontal] [publisher's device] [vertical] RANDOM HOUSE. Back: [bottom right, white print] 394-49537-3. Front flap: [publisher's note]. Back flap: Blank.

Price: Not sold.

Notes: From the front flap: "The editors of Random House, having heard Mr. Michener relate the circumstances that led to the writing of Centennial, and his experiences during his long preparation for the task, felt that an account of these matters would be of particular interest to those who are concerned with the making and dissemination of books. In response to the editors' request, Mr. Michener wrote the notes which follow in this book, which has been especially produced for the librarians and booksellers of the United States. Only 3200 copies of this book have been made and no more will be printed. No copies are for sale."

Section A.I - Descriptive Bibliography of First Editions

A.033 THE MICHENER TRIO [1974]

Titles: THE DRIFTERS / THE SOURCE / HAWAII
This 3-volume set was prepared exclusively for the Book-of-the-Month Club.

Binding: Specially bound matched set issued without dust jacket or slipcase. Grayish yellow (90) cloth with grayish red (19) cloth spine. Front and back covers blank. Spine stamped in gold:
      1. [within dark reddish gray (23) panel] [triple rule] / THE DRIFTERS / [decorative device] /   JAMES   / A. / MICHENER / [triple rule] / [at bottom of spine, outside of   panel] [publisher's device] / RANDOM HOUSE
      2. [within dark reddish gray panel] [triple rule] / THE SOURCE / [decorative device] / JAMES   / A. / MICHENER / [triple rule] / [at bottom of spine, outside of panel] [publisher's device] / RANDOM HOUSE
      3. [within dark reddish gray panel] [triple rule] / HAWAII / [decorative device] / JAMES /   A. / MICHENER / [triple rule] / [at bottom of spine, outside of panel] [publisher's device] / RANDOM HOUSE
5 3/4" x 8 1/4"

Dust Jacket: None

Price: [November, 1974, dividend for 3 credits plus $7.50]

Notes: The Book-of-the-Month Club identifying square is indented at the bottom right corner on the back of each book. This 3-volume set was later reissued, with another 3-volume Michener set (A.039 SAYONARA / RETURN TO PARADISE / CARAVANS) as a Christmas dividend in 1980, in a special 6-volume set.

Section A.I - Descriptive Bibliography of First Editions

A.034 SPORTS IN AMERICA [1976]

Title Page: James A. / Michener / [thick rule] [thin rule] Sports in / America / Random House [publisher's device] New York

Copyright: Copyright ©1976 by Random House, Inc., / All rights reserved under International and Pan-American Copyright Conventions. / Published in the United States by Random House, Inc., New York, and simultane- / ously in Canada by Random House of Canada Limited, Toronto. / Library of Congress Cataloging in Publication Data / Michener, James Albert, 1907- / Sports in America. / 1. Sports -- United States. 2. Physical education and / training -- United States. I. Title. / GV583.M5 796'.0973   75-40549 / ISBN 0-394-40646-X / Manufactured in the United States of America / 98765432 / First Edition / [acknowledgments begin on bottom half of copyright page]

Contents: [i] half title; [ii] BOOKS BY JAMES A. MICHENER [previous works]; [iii] title; [iv] copyright and acknowledgments; [iv-viii] continuation of acknowledgments; [ix] dedication; [x] blank; [xi] Contents; [xii] blank; [xiii] Author's Note; [xiv] blank; [1] second half title; [2] blank; [3] 4-443 text; [444] 445-451 Epilogue; [452] 453-466 Index.

Collation: [i-xiv] [1-3] 4-443 [444] 445-451 [452] 453-466; 6" x 9 1/4"

Binding: Light purplish blue (199) paper covered boards with black cloth spine that wraps around and covers left one-third of front and right one-third of back.   Front: [horizontal strong red (11) double rule on the black cloth].   Spine: [vertical gold print at top] James A. / Michener / [horizontal strong red double rule continued from front] / [vertical gold print at mid-spine] Sports in / America / [horizontal gold print] [publisher's device] / *Random* / *House*.   Back: Blank.

Dust Jacket: Black. Front: [strong red print] James A. / Michener / [gold thick wavy horizontal double lines] / [strong blue (178) print] Sports in / America.   Spine: [vertical strong red print] James A. Michener / [vertical strong blue print] Sports in America / [gold wavy double lines] [horizontal] [white publisher's device] / [strong blue print] RANDOM / HOUSE.   Back: [photograph of the author within gold lined frame] [at top right of photograph] Photo: Tessa J. Dalton / [below photograph in strong blue print] Books by / [strong red print] James A. Michener / [double column of author's previous works] / [bottom right,   white print] 394-40646-X.   Front flap: [top right] $12.50 /   [blurb].   Back flap: [continuation of blurb] / [at bottom] Jacket design: Robert Aulicino / Random House, Inc. [publisher's address and other imprints] / Printed in the U.S.A. / 6/76.

Price: $12.50

Notes: An analysis of the phenomena of sports in America as they involve and affect youth, genders, and minorities. Michener concludes that we create too much stress on our young athletes, and fail to provide equal opportunities to women. He analyzes the role of sports in creating opportunities for minorities. Michener would prefer to reduce the emphasis on spectator sports and increase the emphasis on promoting lifetime participation.

Section A.I - Descriptive Bibliography of First Editions

A.035 JAMES A MICHENER: THE SOURCE, THE BRIDGES AT TOKO-RI, CARAVANS, SAYONARA [1976]

Title Page: [superimposed on full page photograph of cloudy blue skies] JAMES • A / MICHENER / THE SOURCE / • / THE BRIDGES / AT TOKO-RI / • / CARAVANS / • / SAYONARA / • / Secker & Warburg / Octopus

Copyright: *The Source* first published in Great Britain in 1965 / *The Bridges at Toko-Ri* first published in Great Britain in 1953 / *Caravans* first published in Great Britain in 1964 / *Sayonara* first published in Great Britain in 1954 / This edition first published in 1976 by / Secker & Warburg Limited / 14 Carlisle Street, Soho Square, London W1 / in association with / Octopus Books Limited / 59 Grosvenor Street, London, W1 / *The Source* Copyright © 1965 by Random House Inc. / *The Bridges at Toko-Ri* Copyright © 1953 by James A. Michener / *Caravans* Copyright © 1963 by Random House Inc. / *Sayonara* Copyright © 1953-4 by James A. Michener / ISBN 0 7064 0576 5 / Printed in Great Britain by / Jarrold & Sons Ltd., Norwich.

Contents: [1] half title; [2] blank; [3] title; [4] copyright; [5] CONTENTS; [6] blank; [7-13] 14-734 text of *The Source*; [735-736] blank; [737-741] 742-790 text of *The Bridges at Toko-ri;* [791-792] blank; [793-797] 798-990 text of *Caravans;* [991-992] blank; [993-995] 996-1113 text of *Sayonara;* [1114-1120] blank.

Collation: [1-13] 14-734 [735-741] 742-790 [791-797] 798-990 [991-995] 996-1113 [1114-1120] ; 5 3/4" x 9 1/4"

Binding: Grayish red (19) leatherette. Front: [gold print] JAMES • A / MICHENER. Spine: [vertical gold print] JAMES • A • MICHENER [horizontal at bottom] Secker & Warburg / Octopus. Back: Blank.

Dust Jacket: Shades of brownish orange fading to light orange. Front: [light yellowish brown print] JAMES / MICHENER / [horizontal, narrow light blue panel between two thick light yellowish brown stripes] [white print] THE SOURCE / [thick rule] / THE BRIDGES AT TOKO-RI / [thick rule] CARAVANS / [thick rule] / SAYONARA / [thick rule] / [color photograph of young girl sitting at site of archeological dig]. Spine: [light orange tan print] JAMES / MICHENER / [stripes continuing from front] / [white print] THE SOURCE / THE BRIDGES AT / TOKO-RI / CARAVANS / SAYONARA / Secker & Warburg / Octopus. Back: [large photograph of the author, centered and superimposed over continuation of stripes from front and spine]. Front flap: JAMES / MICHENER / [blurb] / [angled below diagonal line crossing bottom right corner] £3.95. Back flap: [continuation of blurb from front flap] [list of other titles from Heinemann/Octopus and Secker & Warburg/Octopus] / Front Jacket: Camera and Pen International; Rex Features.

Price: £3.95

Notes: Four volumes in one.

Section A.I - Descriptive Bibliography of First Editions

A.036 CHESAPEAKE [1978]

Title Page: [double title page] [across verso and recto] [illustration of marshlands and geese in flight] [on recto] CHESAPEAKE / James A. Michener / [publisher's device] Random House New York

Copyright: Copyright ©1978 by Random House, Inc., / All rights reserved under International and Pan-American / Copyright Conventions. Published in the United States by / Random House, Inc., New York, and simultaneously in Canada / by Random House of Canada Limited, Toronto. / Library of Congress Cataloging in Publication Data / Michener, James Albert, 1907- / Chesapeake. / 1. Eastern Shore, Md.-- History -- Fiction. I. Title. / PZ3.M583Ch [PS3525.119] 813'.5'4 78-2892 / ISBN 0-394-50079-2 / ISBN 0-394-50202-7 lim. ed. / ISBN 0-394-50312-0 deluxe ed. / *Manufactured in the United States of America* / 24689753 / FIRST EDITION / *Designed by Carole Lowenstein.*

Contents: [i] blank; [ii] BOOKS BY JAMES A. MICHENER [previous works]; [iii] half title; [iv-v] double title page; [vi] copyright; [vii] viii-x Acknowledgments; [xi] dedication; [xii-xiii] Contents; [xiv] author's note; [1] second half title; [2] blank; [3] 4-865 text; [866] blank.

Collation: [i-vii] viii-x [xi-xiv] [1-3] 4-865 [866]; 5 3/16" x 8 3/16"

Binding: Moderate greenish blue (173) cloth. Front: [copper print] [illustration of swamp grass and cattails]. Spine: [vertical at right edge] CHESAPEAKE / [thin vertical rule] [at left edge] / James A. Michener [publisher's device] *Random / House*. Back: Blank. Front end map: CHOPTANK AREA. Back end map: THE CHESAPEAKE BAY REGION.

Dust Jacket: Black. Front: [strong reddish orange (35) print] Chesapeake / [pale blue (185) print] A Novel by / [white print] James A. / Michener / [within oval bordered by thin moderate green outline, illustration of geese in flight over the bay]. Spine: [vertical reddish orange print] Chesapeake / [white print] James A. Michener [horizontal] [pale blue print] [publisher's device] / Random / House. Back: [full page photograph of the author] / [bottom left] PHOTO: FRANK E. SCHRAMM III. [bottom right] 394-50079-2. Front flap: [top right] $12.95 / [blurb]. Back flap: [continuation of blurb] / Jacket design: R. Adelson / Jacket illustration: Peter Cox / Random House, Inc., New York, N. Y. 10022 / Printed in U.S.A. 7/78.

Price: $12.95

Notes: Flora, fauna, and fictionalized accounts of the history of the people of the Chesapeake Bay region and Maryland's eastern shore.

Section A.I - Descriptive Bibliography of First Editions

A.037 THREE FAMOUS BEST SELLERS [1978]

Titles: THE SOURCE / CENTENNIAL / HAWAII
A three volume set of paperbacks published by Fawcett-Crest.

Binding: Normal paperback wraps.

1. THE SOURCE; 0-449-23859-8; $2.95

2. CENTENNIAL; 0-449-23494-0; $2.95

3. HAWAII; 0-449-23761-3; $2.95

Dust Jacket: None. Thin cardboard strong green (141) slipcase; 4 5/8" x 7 1/8" x 4 1/4" [on sides and back, top left, within moderate pink (5) double circle] THE / SOURCE / [rule] / CENTENNIAL / [rule] / HAWAII / [below double circle, on angle from bottom left to top right] [white print with dark green (146) shadow] James A. / Michener / [black print] THREE FAMOUS / BESTSELLERS / [centered at bottom of back] 2-3741-9; [top] [centered within geometric design consisting of 4 black ruled trapezoids in black print] FAWCETT.

Price: [Box price-$8.85]

Notes: Slipcased set of three volumes.

Section A.I - Descriptive Bibliography of First Editions

A.038 THE WATERMEN [1979]

Title Page: THE / WATERMEN / [rule] [decorative rule] / *Selections from* Chesapeake *by* / JAMES A. MICHENER / *With drawings made for this book by* / JOHN MOLL / [publisher's device] / RANDOM HOUSE   NEW YORK

Copyright: *Copyright © 1978, 1979 by Random House, Inc., / All rights reserved under International and Pan-American / Copyright Conventions. Published in the United States by / Random House, Inc., New York, and simultaneously in Canada / by Random House of Canada Limited, Toronto. / Library of Congress Cataloging in Publication Data / Michener, James Albert, 1907- / The watermen. / A narrative consisting of excerpts from the / author's Chesapeake. / 1. Eastern Shore, Md. -- History -- Fiction. / I. Moll, John   II. Title. / PZ3.M583Wat [PS3525.I19] 813'.5'4 79-14119 / ISBN 0-394-50660-X / Manufactured in the United States of America / 24689753 / First Edition*

Contents: [i-ii] blank; [iii] half title; [iv] illustration of skipper at ship's helm; [v] title; [vi] copyright; vii Contents; [viii] blank; ix-xi Foreword by James A. Michener; [xii] blank; [1] [chapter heading] The Geese [illustration of geese in flight]; [2] blank; 3-193 text and illustrations; [194-196] blank.

Collation: [i-vi] vii [viii] ix-xi [xii] [1-2] 3-193 [194-196]; 7" x 9 15/16"

Binding: Dark blue (183) cloth. Front: [blind stamped imprint of three geese in flight]. Spine: [vertical brilliant green (144) print] THE WATERMEN   JAMES A. MICHENER / *Drawings by* JOHN MOLL [horizontal publisher's device] / Random / House. Back: Blank. Front end map: CHESAPEAKE BAY. Back end papers: [drawing of Skipjack and ship gear}.

Dust Jacket: Yellowish blue (92) at top, fading to pale blue (185) at bottom. Front: [grayish red (10) print] THE / [thin black rule] / [grayish red print] WATERMEN / [thin black rule] / [black and white illustration of three geese in flight] / [thin black rule] [grayish red print] Selections from CHESAPEAKE by / [moderate green (145) print] JAMES A. MICHENER / [grayish red print] With drawings made for this book by / [moderate green print] JOHN MOLL / [thin black rule]. Spine: [vertical grayish red print between two vertical thin parallel black rules] THE WATERMEN [moderate green print] JAMES A. MICHENER / Illustrated by JOHN MOLL [horizontal at bottom] [white publisher's device outlined in black] / [grayish red print] Random / House. Back: [drawings of ships and watermen] [bottom right] 394-50660-X. Front flap: [top right] $12.95 / [blurb, including quote from author's foreword.] Back flap: [continuation of author's quote] / [drawing of a water bird] / Jacket illustration: John Moll / Random House, Inc., New York, N.Y. 10022 / Printed in U.S.A. 7/79.

Price: $12.95

Notes: Selections from **Chesapeake** combined with topical sketches by John Moll, fulfilling Michener's dream of having his work appear in an illustrated publication.

Section A.I - Descriptive Bibliography of First Editions

A.039 MICHENER SET [1979]

Titles: SAYONARA / RETURN TO PARADISE / CARAVANS
This 3-volume set was prepared exclusively for the Book-of-the-Month Club.

Binding: A specially bound matched set issued without dust jacket or slipcase. Grayish yellow (90) cloth with grayish red (19) cloth spine. Front and back covers blank. Spine stamped in gold:
    1. [within dark reddish gray (23) panel] [triple rule] / SAYONARA / [decorative device] /   JAMES / A. / MICHENER / [triple rule] / [at bottom of spine, outside of panel] [publisher's device] / RANDOM HOUSE
    2. [within dark reddish gray panel] [triple rule] / RETURN TO PARADISE / [decorative device] /   JAMES / A. / MICHENER / [triple rule] / [at bottom of spine, outside of panel] [publisher's device] / RANDOM HOUSE
    3. [within dark reddish gray panel] [triple rule] / CARAVANS / [decorative device] / JAMES / A. / MICHENER / [triple rule] / [at bottom of spine, outside of panel] [publisher's device] / RANDOM HOUSE
5 3/4" x 8 1/4"

Dust Jacket: None

Price: [April, 1979, dividend for credits plus $7.50]

Notes: The Book-of-the-Month Club identifying square is indented at the bottom right of the back of each book. This 3-volume set was later reissued, with another 3-volume Michener set (A.033 THE DRIFTERS / THE SOURCE / HAWAII) as a Christmas dividend in 1980, in a special 6-volume set.

Section A.I - Descriptive Bibliography of First Editions

A.040 THREE FAMOUS BESTSELLERS [1979]

Titles: CHESAPEAKE / HAWAII / CENTENNIAL
A three volume set of paperbacks published by Fawcett-Crest. Also includes a white thin booklet of blank pages titled *THE MICHENER NOTE PAD FOR THOSE DAY TO DAY IDEAS*

Binding: Normal paperback wraps.

1. CHESAPEAKE; 0-449-24163-7; $3.95

2. HAWAII; 0-449-23761-3; $2.95

3. CENTENNIAL; 0-449-23494-0; $2.95

Dust Jacket: None. Thin cardboard black slipcase; 5 1/8" x 7 1/8" x 4 1/4". [on sides and back] [strong reddish orange (35) print] James A. / Michener / [white heavy rule] [white print] Three Famous Bestsellers / [within a moderate greenish blue (173) centered oval frame] [illustration of geese in flight over water] / [in white print] CHESAPEAKE / HAWAII • CENTENNIAL / [centered at bottom of back] 5-4226 / [top] [centered within geometric design consisting of 4 white ruled trapezoids in strong reddish orange print] FAWCETT

Price: [Box price-$9.85]

Notes: Slipcased set of three volumes. A later boxed set with the same titles and with a similar black slipcase did not include the Michener note pad. The top geometric design and blank bottom were replaced with strong reddish orange print "James A. Michener" above a white rule and white print "Three Famous Bestsellers." The number at the bottom center of the back is 6-4226. The price of **Centennial** was increased from $2.95 to $3.95 for a total box price of $10.85.

Section A.I - Descriptive Bibliography of First Editions

A.041 THE COVENANT [1980]

Title Page: [decorative rule] The First Edition Society / The Covenant / [decorative device] / James A. Michener / ILLUSTRATED BY JERRY PINKNEY / THE FRANKLIN LIBRARY / Franklin Center, Pennsylvania / 1980 / [rule]

Copyright: The drawings of African animals that appear at the opening of each chapter are / the work of Lois Lowenstein, and were inspired by Bushman cave paintings: / page 3, Eland; page 33, Rhinoceros; page 79, Hippopotamus; page 177, Leopard; / page 265, Hyena; page 359, Wildebeest; page 453, Lion; page 505, Sable Antelope; / page 611, Zebra; page 691, Basuto Pony; page 779, Springbok; page 851, Elephant; / page 903, Cape Buffalo; and page 969, Giraffe. / Cartography by Jean Paul Tremblay / This limited first edition / has been published by special arrangement with / Random House, Inc. / Copyright © 1980 by James A. Michener / All Rights Reserved / Special contents copyright © 1980 Franklin Mint Corporation / Printed in the United States of America

Contents: [i-iii] blank; [iv-v] [map] The Nations of South Africa and Surrounding Lands; [vi] blank; [vii] [statement of limited first edition]; [viii] blank; [ix] OTHER BOOKS BY JAMES A. MICHENER [previous works]; [x] blank; [xi] half title; [xii-xiii] A special message to the members of THE FIRST EDITION SOCIETY [by James A. Michener]; [xiv] blank; [xv] title; [xvi] copyright; [xvii] NOTE [by James A. Michener]; [xviii] blank; [xix] xx-xxii ACKNOWLEDGEMENTS; [xxiii] author's explanatory note; [xxiv] blank; [xxv] Contents; [xxvi-xxvii] [map] Travels and Treks; [xxviii] blank; [xxix] second half title; [xxx] blank; [1-2] 3-1068 text; [1069-1070] 1071-1073 glossary; [1074-1077] genealogies; [1078-1082] blank.

Laid in message: [note from the editors, printed on long horizontal sheet folded twice vertically to create eight pages. The note includes a portrait of the author by Gail Dolphin, especially for the First Edition Society]

Collation: [i-xix] xx-xxii [xxiii-xxx] [1-2] 3-1068 [1069-1070] 1071-1073 [1074-1082]; 7" x 9 15/16"

Binding: Moderate brown (58) leather with ornate gold design rectangles on front, back, and spine. Spine stamped in gold: [double rule] / FIRST EDITION / [double rule] / [within gold rule frame] THE / COVENANT / [three small diamonds] / JAMES A. / MICHENER / [ornate decorative gold frame] / [double rule] / THE / FRANKLIN / LIBRARY / [double rule] / [double rule]. Moderate brown attached ribbon marker. Three raised ribs on spine. Pages trimmed in gold. Brown moire end papers.

Dust Jacket: None

Price: Subscription price unknown.

Notes: From the bushmen of 15,000 years ago to the apartheid policies of modern South Africa, Michener traces natives and foreigners in social, religious, and economic confrontations. A first trade edition was published by Random House, following publication of this Franklin Library First Edition. In preparing the trade edition, multiple printers were necessary to meet publication deadlines, and the printers were identified by small geometric marks embossed on the bottom right corner of the back cover. These indentations are not Book-of-the-Month Club markings. Copies have been noted with circular, triangular, and square marks. All genuine first editions will have such a mark.

46

Section A.I - Descriptive Bibliography of First Editions

A.042 THE QUALITY OF LIFE, INCLUDING THE PRESIDENTIAL LOTTERY [1980]

Title Page: JAMES A. MICHENER / THE QUALITY OF LIFE / including *Presidential Lottery* / CORGI BOOKS / A DIVISION OF TRANSWORLD PUBLISHERS LTD

Copyright: THE QUALITY OF LIFE / A CORGI BOOK 0 552 11416 2 / Originally published separately by / Martin Secker & Warburg Ltd. / PRINTING HISTORY / *The Quality of Life* / Secker & Warburg edition published 1971 / Corgi edition published 1973 / Corgi edition reissued 1980 / Copyright © 1970 J. B. Lippincott Company / *Presidential Lottery* / Secker & Warburg published 1969 / Corgi edition published 1971 / Corgi edition reissued 1980 / Copyright ©, 1969, by Random House Inc. / The quotations (in Chapter V and Appendix) © from 'One / Man, 3,312 Votes: A MATHEMATICAL ANALYSIS OF THE ELECTORAL COLLEGE,' by John F. Banzhaf, III, are reprinted with permission / from *Villanova Law Review,* Vol. 13, No. 2, pp. 314-315, 317, / 329-332. / Copyright © 1968 by Villanova University / Conditions of sale / 1: This book is sold subject to the condition that it shall not / by way of trade *or otherwise* be lent, re-sold, hired out or / otherwise *circulated* without the publisher's prior consent in / any form of binding or cover other than that in which it is / published *and without a similar condition including this / condition being imposed on the subsequent purchaser.* / 2: This book is sold subject to the Standard Conditions of / Sale of Net Books and may not be re-sold in the UK below the net price fixed by the publishers for the book. / This book is set in Baskerville / Corgi Books are published by / Transworld Publishers Ltd, / Century House, 61-63 Uxbridge Road, / Ealing, London W5 5SA / Printed and bound in Great Britain by / Cox & Wyman Ltd., Reading

Contents: [i] editor's note; [ii] Also by James A. Michener [previous works] And published by Corgi Books; [iii] title; [iv] copyright; [v-viii] 1-89 [90] text of *The Quality of Life;* [The text of *Presidential Lottery* follows and is independently numbered beginning after page 90]; [i-vi] 1-183 [184] text of *Presidential Lottery.*

Collation: [i-viii] 1-89 [90]; [i-vi] 1-183 [184]; 4 3/8" x 7"

Binding: White wraps. Front: [vertical, at edge of top left, black print, reading from bottom to top] 0 552 11416 2 [horizontal, at top left, with O filled in with red and yellow design] CORGI / JAMES A. / MICHENER / [black rule] / [moderate red (15) print] THE QUALITY / OF LIFE / [illustration of rural setting] / including / 'THE PRESIDENTIAL LOTTERY' / by bestselling author of / HAWAII, CENTENNIAL and CHESAPEAKE. Spine: [horizontal black print] 0 552 / 11416 / 2 / GENERAL / [black outline of circle] / [vertical] [moderate red print] THE QUALITY OF LIFE [black print] JAMES A. MICHENER [horizontal black print with the O filled in with red and yellow] CORGI. Back: JAMES A. / MICHENER / [black rule] / [moderate red (15) print] THE QUALITY / OF LIFE / THIS EDITION / ALSO INCLUDES / 'THE PRESIDENTIAL / LOTTERY' / [illustration of rural setting] / [blurb from The Times Literary Supplement] / [recommended prices.]

Dust Jacket: None

Price: Issue price not known.

Notes: Two volumes in one.

47

Section A.I - Descriptive Bibliography of First Editions

A.043 SPACE [1982]

Title Page: [double title page] [background illustration of galaxy covering verso and recto] [on verso] [all white print] [publisher's device] / Random House / New York / [on recto] SPACE / JAMES A. / MICHENER

Copyright: Copyright ©1982 by James A. Michener / All rights reserved under International and Pan-American / Copyright Conventions. Published in the United States by / Random House, Inc., New York, and simultaneously in Canada / by Random House of Canada Limited, Toronto. / Library of Congress Cataloging in Publication Data / Michener, James A. (James Albert), 1907- / Space. / I. Title. / PS3525.I19S6 1982 813'.54 82-40127 / ISBN 0-394-50555-7 / ISBN 0-394-52764-X (lim. ed.) / *Manufactured in the United States of America* / 24689753 / FIRST EDITION / *Cartography by Jean Paul Tremblay* / *Book design by Carol Lowenstein*

Contents: [i] blank; [ii] BOOKS BY JAMES A. MICHENER [previous works]; [iii] half title; [iv-v] double title page; [vi] copyright; [vii] iii-x ACKNOWLEDGMENTS; [xi] CONTENTS; [xii] author's note; [1] second half title; [2] blank; [3] 4-622 text; [623-624] cast of characters; [625-626] blank.

Collation: [i-vii] viii-x [xi-xii] [1-3] 4-622 [623-626]; 6" x 9 3/16"

Binding: Dark blue (183) cloth. All gold print. Front: [within thin and thick double ruled frame] J • A • M. Spine: [within thin and thick double ruled frame] SPACE / JAMES A. / MICHENER [at bottom] [publisher's device] / Random / House. Back: Blank. Front end map: NASA OPERATIONS. Back end map: APOLLO 18.

Dust Jacket: Black. Front: [large white print] SPACE / [brilliant greenish blue (169) print] A Novel by / [moderate yellow (87) print] James A. / Michener / [within concentric strong reddish orange (35), black, and white ovals] [illustration of galaxy]. Spine: [vertical white print at right edge] SPACE / [moderate yellow print at left edge] James A. Michener [horizontal] [white publisher's device] / [brilliant greenish blue print] Random / House. Back: [full page photograph of author at NASA launch site] [bottom left of photograph, vertical, bottom to top] PHOTO: JACK REIFERT [bottom right] 394-50555-7. Front flap: [top left] FPT [top right] $17.95 / [blurb]. Back flap: [continuation of blurb] / Jacket photograph, courtesy U. S. Naval Observatory / Jacket design: Richard Adelson / Random House, Inc., New York, N.Y. 10022 / Printed in U.S.A. 10/82 / ©1982 Random House, Inc.

Price: $17.95

Notes: The lives of politicians and astronauts are intertwined in this story of the development of the American space program and man's approach to the final frontier. Because multiple printers were necessary to meet publication deadlines, the printers were identified by small geometric marks embossed on the bottom right corner of the back cover. These indentations are not Book-of-the-Month Club markings. Copies have been noted with circular and square marks. All genuine first editions will have such a mark.

A.044 COLLECTORS, FORGERS —AND A WRITER: A Memoir [1983]

Title Page: Collectors, Forgers -- / And A Writer: / *A MEMOIR* / By James A. Michener / FOREWORD BY JOHN F. FLEMING / [illustration of antiquated desktop, with quill pens, globe, maps and books] / Targ Editions • New York City • 1983 [on verso] [publisher's device] / Random House / New York

Copyright: Copyright ©1983 by James A. Michener

Colophon Page:

Collectors, Forgers, —And a Writer:
A Memoir by James A. Michener

is Number Nineteen of the Targ Editions, published in Greenwich
Village, New York, by William Targ. The book was designed
by Ronald Gordon at The Oliphant Press, New York, and
printed by letterpress at The Anthoensen Press,
Portland, Maine. The types are Monticello and
Bell; the paper is Frankfurt White Laid.
The binding is by Spink & Gaborc. This
first edition is limited to 250 copies,
each signed by James A. Michener.

[illustration of open book with red T on left page and a red E on right page]
[autograph of author]

Contents: [i-iv] blank; [1] title; [2] copyright; [3] dedication FOR JANE ENGELHARD; [4] blank; 5-7 Foreword; [8] blank; [9] half title; [10] blank; 11-64 text; [65] colophon; [66-68] blank.

Collation: [i-iv] [1-4] 5-7 [8-10] 11-64 [65-68]; 5 7/8" x 9 1/4"

Binding: Dark red (16) cloth and yellow white (92) cloth spine. Front: White pasted-on label [within a black ruled frame] Collectors, Forgers - / And A Writer : / A Memoir / *James A. Michener.* Spine: [vertical] [gold print] Collectors, Forgers - And A Writer: A Memoir • James A. Michener Targ Editions. Back: Blank.

Dust Jacket: None. Bluish white (189) slipcase.

Price: [$90.00]

Notes: Autobiographical commentary on early influences on Michener's life. Previously referred to as "Book Collecting, Forgeries, and Other Amenities."

Section A.I - Descriptive Bibliography of First Editions

A.045 POLAND [1983]

Title Page: [all within a rectangular red ruled frame] [black rule] / [white print within a black rectangular panel] POLAND / [black rule] [large red decorative device] / [black rule] / [white print within a black rectangular panel] James A. / Michener / [black rule] [below red ruled frame] [red publisher's device on red rule] / RANDOM HOUSE • NEW YORK

Copyright: Copyright © 1983 by James A. Michener / Cartography © 1983 by Jean Paul Tremblay / All rights reserved under International and Pan-American / Copyright Conventions. Published in the United States by / Random House, Inc., New York, and simultaneously in Canada / by Random House of Canada Limited, Toronto. / Library of Congress Cataloging in Publication Data / Michener, James A. (James Albert), 1907- / Poland. / 1. Poland--History--Fiction. I. Title. / PS3525.I19P6 1983 813'.54 83-4477 / ISBN 0-394-53189-2 / ISBN 0-394-53388-7 (lim. ed.) / *Manufactured in the United States of America* / 24689753 / FIRST EDITION / *Book design by Carol Lowenstein*

Contents: [i] blank; [ii] BOOKS BY JAMES A. MICHENER [previous works]; [iii] half title; [iv] blank; [v] title; [vi] copyright; [vii] viii-ix ACKNOWLEDGMENTS; [x] blank; [xi] CONTENTS; [xii] blank; [xiii] xiv EXPLANATION; [xv] xvi-xviii THE PEOPLE OF POLAND; [1] second half title; [2] blank; [3] 4-556 text; [557-558] blank.

Collation: [i-vii] viii-ix [x-xiii] xiv [xv] xvi-xviii [1-3] 4-556 [557-558]; 6" x 9 1/8"

Binding: Moderate red (15) cloth. All gold print. Front: [within square gold frame] [rule] [decorative design] [rule]. Spine: [within thick square ruled frame] [thick rule] / POLAND / [double thick rule] / James A. / Michener / [thick rule] [below square] [publisher's device on thin rule] / RANDOM HOUSE. Back: Blank. Front end map: Scene of the Novel. Back end map: The Polish State.

Dust Jacket: Black. Front: [white print outlined in vivid red (11)] POLAND / [light orange (52) print] A Novel by / [vivid red print] James A. / Michener / [within concentric vivid red, black, and white ovals] [illustration of castle on a promontory]. Spine: [vertical, white print outlined in vivid red, at right edge] POLAND / [vertical, vivid red print at left edge] James A. Michener / [horizontal light orange print] [publisher's device] / Random House. Back: [half page photograph of author] [vertical white print at right of photograph, from bottom to top] PHOTO: JOHN KINGS [bottom right] 394-53189-2. Front flap: [top left] FPT [top right] $17.95 / [blurb]. Back flap: [continuation of blurb] / Jacket design: Richard Adelson / Jacket illustration: Peter Cox / Random House, Inc., New York, N.Y. 10022 / Printed in U.S.A. 9/83 / © 1983 Random House, Inc.

Price: $17.95

Notes: A review of eight important periods of Polish history, from the thirteenth century to the present, through the perspectives of successive generations of three fictional family histories. Sweeping fictionalized saga of Poland's history. Because multiple printers were necessary to meet publication deadlines, the printers were identified by small geometric marks embossed on the bottom right corner of the back cover. These indentations are not Book-of-the-Month Club markings. Copies have been noted with circular and square marks. All genuine first editions will have such a mark.

Section A.I - Descriptive Bibliography of First Editions

A.046 TESTIMONY [1983]

Title Page: Testimony / James A. Michener / [small illustration of a Colonial man holding sword] / The WHITE KNIGHT PRESS / Honolulu, Hawaii: 1983

Copyright: Copyright ©1983 by James A. Michener
Colophon Page:

Colophon
Of this keepsake, two hundred copies in hand-set
Goudy Oldstyle were printed by A. Grove Day before the type was distributed. Copies 1-100 were
signed by the author and issued to friends. Copies
101-200 were issued to friends of the publisher.
This is Copy No. [handwritten number]

[on copies 1-100, handwritten inscription, and autograph of the author]
[on copies 101-200, handwritten inscription, and autograph of the publisher]

Contents: [i] blank; [ii] BOOKS [previous works of James A. Michener]; [iii] title; [iv] copyright; 1 Rondeau of a writer on attaining age seventy-five; 2-4 Credo; 5-18 A Faithful Remembrance; 19 Rondeau of a compulsive worker on his eightieth birthday; [20] Colophon.

Collation: [i-iv] 1-19 [20]; 5 1/2" x 8 1/2"

Binding: Copies 1-100 are moderate orange yellow (71) heavy paper wraps and 101-200 are light yellow green (119) heavy paper wraps. Stapled twice at centerfold. Black print. Front: Testimony / James A. Michener / The WHITE KNIGHT PRESS / Honolulu, Hawaii: 1983. Back: [publisher's device (an illustration with "The White Knight Press" in an arch over a Knight chess piece)] / A WHITE KNIGHT CHAPBOOK.

Dust Jacket: None.

Price: Not sold to the public.

Notes: **Testimony** reveals the development of Michener's credo of writing. The WHITE KNIGHT PRESS was the private press of A. Grove Day begun in 1940 at Stanford.

Section A.I - Descriptive Bibliography of First Editions

A.047 TEXAS [1985]

Title Page: [double title page] [covering verso and recto is a Texas state flag bordered in black] [on recto] TEXAS / JAMES A. / MICHENER / [publisher's device] / RANDOM HOUSE NEW YORK

Copyright: Copyright © 1985 by James A. Michener / Cartography © 1985 by Jean Paul Tremblay / All rights reserved under International and Pan-American / Copyright Conventions. Published in the United States by / Random House, Inc., New York, and simultaneously in Canada / by Random House of Canada Limited, Toronto. / Library of Congress Cataloging in Publication Data / Michener, James A. (James Albert), 1907- / Texas. / 1. Texas--History--Fiction. I. Title. / PS3525.I19T48 1985 813'.54 85-8248 / ISBN 0-394-54154-5 / *Manufactured in the United States of America* / 24689753 / FIRST EDITION / *Book design by Carol Lowenstein*

Contents: [i] blank; [ii] BOOKS BY JAMES A. MICHENER [previous works]; [iii] half title; [iv-v] double title page; [vi] copyright; [vii] viii-xiii ACKNOWLEDGMENTS; [xiv] blank; [xv] dedication; [xvi] blank; [xvii] xviii FACT AND FICTION; [xix] CONTENTS; [xx] blank; [1] [chapter heading] THE GOVERNOR'S TASK FORCE; [2] blank; [3] 4-1096 text; [1097-1098] blank.

Collation: [i-vii] viii-xiii [xiv-xvii] xviii [xix-xx [1-3] 4-1096 [1097-1098]; 6" x 9 1/8"

Binding: Moderate blue (182) cloth. Front: [copper outline of five-point star]. Spine: [deep purplish blue (197) rule below longhorns] / [copper print] TEXAS / [deep purplish blue rule] / [copper print] JAMES A. / MICHENER / [publisher's device] / RANDOM HOUSE. Back: Blank. Front end map: THE PLACES OF THE STORY. Back end map: TEXAS TODAY.

Dust Jacket: Black. Front: [large white print shadowed by strong blue (178)] TEXAS / [with same colored rule to each side, in pale yellowish pink (31) print] *A Novel* / [vivid red (11) print] James A. / Michener / [within concentric vivid red, black, and white ovals] [illustration of vivid red, white, and strong blue Texas state flag]. Spine: [multi-toned browns, illustration of The Alamo] / [white print shadowed by strong blue] TEXAS / [pale yellowish pink rule] / [vivid red print] James A. / Michener / [pale yellowish pink print] [publisher's device] / RANDOM HOUSE. Back: [full page photograph of author wearing Stetson hat] [bottom left corner, from bottom to top] PHOTO: JOHN KINGS [bottom right] 0-394-54154-5. Front flap: [top left] FPT [top right] $21.95 / [blurb]. Back flap: [continuation of blurb] / Front of jacket illustration is based on an early Texas battle / flag in the Star of the Republic Museum, Washington-on- / the-Brasos, Texas. / Jacket art and typography: Wendell Minor / Random House, Inc., New York, N.Y. 10022 / Printed in U.S.A. 10/85 / © 1985 Random House, Inc.

Price: $21.95

Notes: Major events of Texas history, including the struggle for independence from Mexico and the battles of the Alamo, Goliad, and San Jacinto, are the background of fictional characters who illustrate the migrations of the Spanish, Europeans, and Americans to Texas. Michener examines the economic catalysts of cotton, cattle, oil, and high school football. Because multiple printers were necessary to meet publication deadlines, the printers were identified by small geometric marks embossed on the bottom right corner of the back cover. These indentations are not Book-of-the-Month Club markings. Copies have been noted with circular and square marks. All genuine first editions will have such a mark.

Section A.I - Descriptive Bibliography of First Editions

A.048 LEGACY [1987]

Title Page: LEGACY / [decorative rule with stars] / [calligraphy] JAMES A. / MICHENER / [publisher's device] / [calligraphy] Random House / New York

Copyright: Copyright © 1987 by James A. Michener / All rights reserved under International and Pan-American Copyright Conventions. / Published in the United States by Random House, Inc., New York, and / simultaneously in Canada by Random House of Canada Limited, Toronto. / Library of Congress Cataloging in Publication Data / Michener, James A. (James Albert), 1907- / Legacy. / I. Title. / PS3525.I19L4 1987 813'.54 87-42644 / ISBN 0-394-56432-4 / *Manufactured in the United States of America* / 98765432 / FIRST EDITION / *Book design and calligraphy by Carol Lowenstein*

Contents: [i] blank; [ii] BOOKS BY JAMES A. MICHENER [previous works]; [iii] half title; [iv] blank; [v] title; [vi] copyright; [vii] Contents; [viii] blank; [1] [chapter heading] The Starrs; [2] blank; 3-149 text; [150] blank; [151-152] 153-176 The Constitution of the United States.

Collation: [i-viii] [1-2] 3-149 [150-152] 153-176; 5 5/8" x 8 1/4"

Binding: Strong red (12) cloth. All gold print. Front: [broken starred ribbon rule] *J* [ribbon rule] *A* [ribbon rule]   *M* [ribbon rule].   Spine: [vertical] [broken starred ribbon rule] [calligraphy] *James A. / Michener* [ribbon rule] LEGACY [ribbon rule] [publisher's device] [calligraphy] *Random / House* [ribbon rule].   Back: Blank.   End papers: [facsimile of portion of The Constitution].

Dust Jacket: Black.   Front: [light olive (106) print, outlined in white] LEGACY / [vivid red (11) rule] / [white print] *A Novel* / [vivid red rule] / [white print, outlined in vivid red] James A. / Michener / [within concentric red, black, and white ovals] [illustration of military hats from the Revolutionary, Civil, and World Wars, set on parchment Preamble to the Constitution, and red quill pen].   Spine: [vertical] [light olive print, outlined in white] LEGACY [white print, outlined in vivid red] James A. Michener [horizontal, light olive print] [publisher's device] / RANDOM / HOUSE.   Back: [full page photograph of the author] / [bottom left from bottom to top] PHOTO: JOHN KINGS [bottom right] [bar codes] / ISBN 394-56432-4.   Front flap: [top left] FPT [top right] $16.95 / [blurb].   Back flap: [continuation of blurb] / Jacket design and illustration: Wendell Minor / Random House, Inc., New York, N. Y. 10022 / Printed in U.S.A. 9/87 / © 1987 Random House, Inc.

Price: $16.95

Notes: Reminiscent of Congressional hearings regarding the Iran-Contra scandal, Michener reflects on the inherent dangers to a constitutional democracy when its leaders put themselves above the law.

Section A.I - Descriptive Bibliography of First Editions

A.049 ALASKA [1988]

Title Page: [double title page] [covering verso and recto is an illustration of an Alaskan lake and mountain range] [on recto] ALASKA / [rule] / JAMES A. / MICHENER / RANDOM HOUSE [publisher's device]/ NEW YORK

Copyright: Copyright © 1988 by James A. Michener / Cartography © 1988 by Jean Paul Tremblay / All rights reserved under International and Pan-American / Copyright Conventions. Published in the United States by / Random House, Inc., New York, and simultaneously in Canada / by Random House of Canada Limited, Toronto. / Library of Congress Cataloging-in-Publication Data / Michener, James A. (James Albert), 1907- / Alaska. / 1. Alaska--History--Fiction. I. Title. / PS3525.I19A79 1988 813'.54 87-43232 / ISBN 0-394-55154-0 / ISBN 0-394-56981-4 (lim. ed.) / *Manufactured in the United States of America* / 24689753 / FIRST EDITION / FG / *Book design and calligraphy by Carol Lowenstein*

Contents: [i] blank; [ii] BOOKS BY JAMES A. MICHENER [previous works]; [iii] half title; [iv-v] double title page; [vi] copyright; [vii] viii ACKNOWLEDGMENTS; [ix] x FACT AND FICTION; [xi] CONTENTS; [xii] blank; [1] second half title; [2] blank; [3] 4-868 text.

Collation: [i-vii] viii [ix-x] xi [xii] [1-3] 4-868; 6" x 9 3/16"

Binding: Moderate orange yellow (71) cloth. All copper print. Front: [illustration of an Alaskan bay and mountains].   Spine: [thick vertical calligraphic rule] / [horizontal] JAMES A. / MICHENER / [calligraphic rule] / ALASKA / [calligraphic rule] / RANDOM HOUSE / [publisher's device] / [thick vertical calligraphic rule].   Back: Blank. Front end map: [Soviet Union, Alaska, and Northwestern Canada]. Back end map: [North Pole surrounded by Soviet Union, Alaska, and Canada].

Dust Jacket: Black. Front: [large gold print, lined in white] ALASKA / [white rule] *A Novel* [white rule] / [vivid red (11) print] James A. / Michener / [within concentric gold, black, and white ovals] [illustration of iceberg in a glacier bay].   Spine: [smaller illustration from front cover] / [gold print] ALASKA / [white rule] / [vivid red print] James A. / Michener / [white print] [publisher's device] / RANDOM HOUSE.   Back: [full page photograph of author] [bottom right] [bar code] / ISBN 0-394-55154-0.   Front flap: [top left] FPT [top right] $22.50 / [blurb].   Back flap: [continuation of blurb] / Jacket design and illustration: Wendell Minor / Back of jacket photo: Michael A. Lewis, / Sheldon Jackson College, Sitka, Alaska / Random House, Inc., New York, N.Y. 10022 / Printed in U.S.A.   6/88 / © 1988 Random House, Inc.

Price: $22.50

Notes: Michener traces the prehistoric migrations of Asians and animals across the Bering Straits. He focuses on the early Russian explorations, the 1867 sale of Alaska to the United States, the 1890's gold rush, the ALCAN highway and statehood.

Section A.I - Descriptive Bibliography of First Editions

A.050 JOURNEY [1988]

Title Page: JOURNEY / James A. / Michener / [publisher's device]

Copyright: Copyright © 1988 James A. Michener / All rights reserved. The use of any part of this publication reproduced, / transmitted in any form or by any means, electronic, mechanical, / photocopying, recording, or otherwise, or stored in a retrieval system, / without the prior consent of the publisher is an infringement of the / copyright law. / Canadian Cataloguing in Publication Data / Michener, James A. (James Albert), 1907- / Journey / ISBN 0-7710-5866-7 / I. Title. / PS3525.I19J68 1988 813'.54 C88-094542-7 / Design by T. M. Craan / Maps by James Loates / Illustrations by Mark Summers / McClelland and Stewart / *The Canadian Publishers* / 481 University Avenue / Toronto, Ontario / M5G 2E9

Contents: [1] half title; [2] blank; [3] antique photograph, Mrs. Garner, 1897; [4] blank; [5] title; [6] copyright; [7] CONTENTS; [8] blank; [9] MAPS [index]; [10-11] [map] The Journey; [12] blank; [13] [chapter heading] HOPE; [14-15] [map] The Railway; [16] blank; 17-202 [203-204] 205-218 text; 219-240 Reflections.

Collation: [1-16] 17-202 [203-204] 205-240; 6" x 9"

Binding: Medium gray (265) cloth. Front: Blank. Spine: [vertical silver print] JAMES A. / MICHENER JOURNEY [horizontal silver publisher's device]. Back: Blank. End papers: [Pen and ink sketches of goldseekers].

Dust Jacket: Black. Front: [silver print, shadowed in light blue (181)] JAMES A. / MICHENER / [illustration of goldseekers navigating Canadian waters by lamplight] / [light blue rule] [white print] *a novel* [light blue rule] / [white print] *JOURNEY* / [light blue print] A QUEST FOR CANADIAN GOLD. Spine: [vertical] [light blue print] JAMES A. / MICHENER [white print] *JOURNEY* [continuation of illustration and rule from front] [horizontal light blue publisher's device with white print M & S]. Back: [light blue print] A QUEST FOR CANADIAN GOLD / [white print] [blurb] / [continuation of illustration and rule from front and spine] / [within white panel] ISBN 0-7710-5865-9 / [bar codes]. Front flap: [top right] $24.95 / [blurb]. Back flap: [photograph and biographical sketch of author] / Jacket design by T. M. Craan / Jacket art by Mark Summers / Author photograph © Jimm Roberts / [publisher's device] / McClelland and Stewart / *The Canadian Publishers*.

Price: $24.95

Notes: Five Englishmen respond to the Klondike gold fever of 1897. Stubborn misguided British pride leads them in a journey to reach the gold fields over British soil, and not by way of American territory. Their misplaced nationalistic pride leads to disastrous consequences. The Canadian publication is the First Edition, published one year earlier than the American edition.

Section A.I - Descriptive Bibliography of First Editions

A.051 CARIBBEAN [1989]

Title Page: [double title page] [across verso and recto is an illustration of a Caribbean cove, palm trees, and huts] [on recto] CARIBBEAN / [rule] / JAMES A. MICHENER / RANDOM HOUSE [tropical style publisher's device] NEW YORK

Copyright: Copyright ©1989 by James A. Michener / Cartography © 1989 by Jean Paul Tremblay / Illustrations © 1989 by Franca Nucci Haynes / All rights reserved under International and Pan-American / Copyright Conventions. Published in the United States by / Random House, Inc., New York, and simultaneously in Canada / by Random House of Canada Limited, Toronto. / Library of Congress Cataloging-in-Publication Data / Michener, James A. (James Albert) / Caribbean / James A. Michener. / p. cm. / ISBN 0-394-56561-4 / 1. Caribbean Area--History--Fiction. I. Title. / PS3525.I19C38 1989 / 813'.54--dc20   89-42785 / *Manufactured in the United States of America* / 24689753 / FIRST EDITION / *Book design by Carol Lowenstein*

Contents: [i] blank; [ii] BOOKS BY JAMES A. MICHENER [previous works]; [iii] half title; [iv-v] double title page; [vi] copyright; [vii] dedication; [viii] blank; [ix] x FACT AND FICTION; [xi] CONTENTS; [xii] blank; [1] second half title; [2] blank; [3] 4-667 text; [668] blank; [669] 670-672 FURTHER READING; [673] THE SETTING; [674-676] blank.

Collation: [i-ix] x [xi-xii] [1-3] 4-667 [668-669] 670-672 [673-676]; 6" x 9 3/16"

Binding: Moderate reddish orange (35) cloth. Front: [copper print] [croton plant]. Spine: [all gold print] [horizontal] JAMES A. / MICHENER / [vertical rule] / CARIBBEAN / [vertical rule] [horizontal] [tropical style publisher's device] / RANDOM HOUSE. Back: Blank. Front end map: THE CARIBBEAN. Back end map: JAMAICA; HISPANIOLA; AND PORT ROYAL.

Dust Jacket: White. Front: [shades of yellow orange print] Caribbean / [black rule] *A Novel* [black rule] / [strong greenish blue (169) print] James A. / Michener / [within concentric gold, white, and blue ovals] [illustration of cruise ship crossing bay of lush tropical Caribbean island in hues of blue, green, and orangish yellow]. Spine: [shades of yellow orange print] Caribbean / [strong greenish blue (169) print] James A. / Michener / [smaller copy of illustration from front] / [gold publisher's device] / [strong greenish blue print] RANDOM HOUSE. Back: [color photograph, lined in gold, of author in island dress] [to right of photograph, vertical, from bottom to top] PHOTO: ELFRIEDE RILEY / [at bottom] [bar codes] / ISBN 0-394-56561-4. Front flap: [top left] FPT [top right] $22.95 / [blurb]. Back flap: [continuation of blurb] / Jacket design and illustration: Wendell Minor / Random House, Inc., New York, N.Y. 10022 / Printed in U.S.A. 11/89 / © 1989 Random House, Inc.

Price: $22.95

Notes: Ancient Caribbean Indian civilizations are decimated by European explorations and struggles for empire in this semi-historical tale of slavery, dictatorships, politics, and economics leading up to modern Caribbean life. Michener explains the alternate pronunciations of the word Caribbean: "I found that most islanders pronounce this Car-ib-*bee*-an, and dictionaries give that as preferred, with Ca-*rib*-eean in second place as acceptable. A wag explained: 'The hoi polloy use the first, but intellectual snobs prefer the second.' And so do I."

Section A.I - Descriptive Bibliography of First Editions

A.052 SIX DAYS IN HAVANA [1989]

Title Page: SIX DAYS IN HAVANA / by James A. Michener / and John Kings / [publisher's device] UNIVERSITY OF TEXAS PRESS / AUSTIN

Copyright: [left half of copyright page] Copyright © 1989 by James A. Michener / and John Kings / All rights reserved / Printed in Japan / First Edition, 1989 / Requests for permission to reproduce material / from this work should be sent to / Permissions, University of Texas Press, / Box 7819, Austin, Texas 78713-7819. / LIBRARY OF CONGRESS / CATALOGING-IN-PUBLICATION DATA / Michener, James A. (James Albert), 1907- / Six days in Havana / by James A. Michener and / John Kings.--1st ed. / p. cm. / ISBN 0-292-77629-2 / 1. Havana (Cuba) -- Description, 2. Havana / (Cuba)-- Description --Views. 3. Cuba -- Description / and travel--1981-- 4. Cuba -- Description / and / travel -- 1981 --- Views. 5. Michener, James A. / (James Albert), 1907-. 6. Kings, John, 1923-. / I. Kings, John, 1923--. II. Title. III. Title: 6 days / in Havana. / F1799.H34M5 1989 / 972.91'23064--dc19 89-31091 / CIP / James A. Michener and John Kings / gratefully acknowledge research and / photographic assistance extended by the / United States Information Agency, / Havana, Cuba. / The photographs on pages 6-16 / are reproduced courtesy of / The Special Collections / University of Miami Library, / Coral Gables, Florida. [the right half of the copyright page] BOOKS BY / JAMES A. MICHENER / [previous works by James A. Michener, A. Grove Day, and John Kings]

Contents: [1] half title, with small color photograph of James A. Michener; [2] [photograph of a Cuban public bulletin board with miscellaneous notices and a poster of Fidel Castro]; [3] title; [4] [left half] copyright; [right half] BOOKS BY JAMES A. MICHENER [previous works]; [5] Contents; 6 [photograph of Teddy Roosevelt and the Rough Riders in Cuba]; 7-144 text and photographs.

Collation: [1-5] 6-144; 7" x 9 7/8"

Binding: Moderate blue (182) cloth. Front: Blank. Spine: [all silver print] [vertical] Michener and Kings SIX DAYS IN HAVANA [horizontal publisher's device]. Back: Blank. Front end map: [La Habana]. Back end map: [detail of La Habana].

Dust Jacket: Moderate greenish blue (173). Front: [full page color photograph of Bahia de la Habana and the Castillo de Morrow] [white print] James A. Michener / and John Kings / [yellow rule] / [vivid red (11) print] SIX DAYS / IN HAVANA. Spine: [vertical] [white print] Michener and Kings [vivid red print] SIX DAYS IN HAVANA [horizontal] [vivid red publisher's device] / [white print] TEXAS. Back: [color photograph of photographer taking Michener's photo with Cuban] / [vivid red print] UNIVERSITY OF TEXAS PRESS / Post Office Box 7819 Austin, Texas 78713-7819 / [white print] ISBN 0-292-77629-2. Front flap: [blurb]. Back flap: [continuation of blurb with biographical notes about authors] / University of Texas Press, Austin / Printed in Japan.

Price: No price stated, but sold retail for $24.95

Notes: Contemporary Cuba through the eyes of Michener and photographer John Kings.

Section A.I - Descriptive Bibliography of First Editions

A.053 THE EAGLE AND THE RAVEN [1990]

Title Page: [double title page] [across verso and recto are illustrations of Santa Anna, Sam Houston, and Mexican and Texan soldiers] [on recto] THE EAGLE AND THE RAVEN / [calligraphy] James A. Michener / Drawings by Charles Shaw / State House Press / Austin, Texas

Copyright: Copyright © 1990 by James A. Michener / All rights reserved / First edition / Requests for permission to reproduce material from this work / should be sent to Permissions, State House Press, Box 15247, / Austin, Texas 78761 / *Library of Congress Cataloging-in-Publication Data* / Michener, James A. (James Albert), 1907- / The Eagle and the Raven / by James A. Michener: illustrated / by Charles Shaw. --1st ed. / p. cm. / ISBN 0-938349-57-0 / 1. Santa Anna, Antonio Lopez de. 1794-1876-- / Fiction. 2. Houston, Sam, 1793-1863--Fiction. / 3. Mexico--History--1821 -- 1861 --- Fiction. / 4. Texas -- History--Fiction. I. Title. / PS3525.I19E16 1990 / 813'.54--dc20   90-9684 / Printed in the United States of America

Contents: [i] blank; [ii] Books by James A. Michener [previous works]; [iii] half title; [iv-v] double title page; [vi] copyright; [vii] Acknowledgments; [viii] blank; [ix] Illustrations; [x] blank; [1-2] 3-32 PROLOGUE; [33] second half title; [34] blank; 35-210 text; [211] Chronology / SANTA ANNA SAM HOUSTON; [212] blank; 213-214 Suggested Reading.

Collation: [i-x] [1-2] 3-32 [33-34] 35-210 [211-212] 213-214; 5 3/8" x 8 1/2"

Binding: Grayish red (19) cloth. Front: Blank. Spine: [all gold vertical print] James A. / MICHENER / The Eagle and The Raven [horizontal] State / House / Press. Back: Blank. Front end map: The Eagle's World. Back end map: The Raven's World.

Dust Jacket: Brownish black at top fading into tones of yellow red at bottom. Front: [moderate orange yellow (71) print] THE EAGLE / AND / THE RAVEN / [white print] James A. / Michener / [colored illustrations of Santa Anna and Sam Houston]. Spine: [vertical] [moderate orange yellow print] James A. / MICHENER   [white print] The Eagle and The Raven [horizontal black print] State / House / Press. Back: [full page color illustration of the author] [at bottom in white panel] ISBN 0-938349-57-0 [bar codes]. Front flap: [top right] $19.95 / [author's quote from the text] / [blurb]. Back flap: [continuation of blurb] / STATE HOUSE PRESS / P. O. Box 15247 / Austin, Texas 78761 / Cover illustration and map / endpapers by Charles Shaw.

Price: $19.95

Notes: Parallel historical characterizations of Santa Anna and Sam Houston, leading to their confrontation at the Battle of San Jacinto. The first 5,000 copies, missing an accent mark over the word "Yucatán," were printed on a sheet fed press, case bound, sewn and shrink-wrapped. All later copies were printed on a web press and case bound only - not sewn or shrink-wrapped - and the accent mark was added to "Yucatán."

Section A.I - Descriptive Bibliography of First Editions

A.054 PILGRIMAGE, A MEMOIR OF POLAND & ROME [1990]

Title Page: PILGRIMAGE / A Memoir of Poland and Rome / by / JAMES A. / MICHENER / [publisher's device] / Rodale Press, Emmaus, Pennsylvania

Copyright: Copyright © 1990 by James A. Michener / All rights reserved. No part of this publication may be reproduced or / transmitted in any form or by any means, electronic or mechanical, / including photocopy, recording, or any other storage and retrieval system, / without the written permission of the publisher. / Printed in the United States of America on acid-free paper [symbol] / Cover and book design by Anita G. Patterson / If you have any questions or comments concerning this book, please write: / Rodale Press / Book Reader Service / 33 East Minor Street / Emmaus, PA 18098 / **Library of Congress Cataloging-in-Publication Data** / Michener, James A. (James Albert), 1907 - / Pilgrimage: a memoir of Poland and Rome / James A. Michener. / p. cm. / ISBN 0-87857-910-9 hardcover / 1. Poland--Description and travel --1981-- 2. Rome (Italy)--/ Description --1975-- 3. Michener, James A. (James Albert), 1907- / --Journeys. I. Title. / DK4081.M53 1990 / 914.3804'56--dc20 90-43039 / CIP / **Distributed in the book trade by St. Martin's Press** / 2 4 6 8 10 9 7 5 3 1 hardcover

Contents: [i] title; [ii] copyright; iii CONTENTS; [iv] blank; v-vi INTRODUCTION Lech Walesa; vii PREFACE; [viii] blank; [1] half title; 2-119 text; [120] blank.

Collation: [i-ii] iii [iv] v-vii [viii] [1] 2-119 [120]; 6 1/8" x 9 3/16"

Binding: Yellow white (92) paper covered boards. Front: Blank. Spine: [vertical metallic red print] PILGRIMAGE Michener [horizontal] [publisher's device] / RODALE. Back: Blank.

Dust Jacket: Mottled moderate yellow (87) and dark red (16). Front: [narrow decorative tile design borders at top and bottom] / [dark red print] PILGRIMAGE / [tile mosaic of Europe in shades of blue, green, and yellow within framed decorative tile square] / [dark red calligraphy] a Memoir of / Poland & Rome / [brilliant bluish green (159) print] James A. / Michener / [black calligraphy] Introduction by Lech Walesa. Spine: [vertical] [dark red print] PILGRIMAGE [brilliant bluish green print] Michener [horizontal black print] [publisher's device] / RODALE. Back: [narrow decorative tile design borders at top and bottom] / [within black double ruled frame with thick black corners] [quote from Introduction by Lech Walesa] / [bottom right] [bar codes] ISBN 0-87857-910-9. Front flap: [top right] $14.95 / [blurb]. Back flap: [continuation of blurb] / [photograph of author and Pope John Paul II] / Cover design by Anita G. Patterson / Cover illustration by Patti Rutman.

Price: $14.95

Notes: Two weeks with Michener on a trip to Poland, and his visit with the Pope in Rome. All royalties go to the Young Polish Writers Fund to help the development of literature in Poland.

Section A.I - Descriptive Bibliography of First Editions

A.055 JAMES A. MICHENER ON THE SOCIAL STUDIES [1991]

Title Page: [outline type] **JAMES A.** / [normal type] **MICHENER** / [outline type] **ON THE SOCIAL STUDIES** / [rule] / [within rectangular ruled frame] [large photograph of James A. Michener in meditative pose, with hands clasped] [at bottom right of photograph, vertical, from bottom to top] ©1991 by John Kings

Copyright: National Council for / the Social Studies / [three columns listing the officers, directors, publications committee, and ex-officio members] / ISBN 0-87986-060-X / Copyright © 1991 by / NATIONAL COUNCIL FOR THE SOCIAL STUDIES / 3501 Newark Street N.W. / Washington, D.C. 20016-3167

Contents: [i] title; [ii] copyright; [iii] Table of Contents; [iv] blank; v-vii Preface; [viii] blank; ix-xiv Michener's Early Work: The Foundation Years; [1] [chapter heading] Music and the Social Studies [citation and quotation from the text]; [2] blank; 3-110 text of writings in publications of National Council for the Social Studies from 1938 to 1987; [111-112] 113-118 James A. Michener: Reaffirmations of a Permanent Liberal by Cleta Galvez-Hjornevik [includes a chronological list of Michener's writings on the social studies]; [119] Books by James A. Michener; [120-126] blank.

Collation: [1-iv] v-vii [viii] ix-xiv [1-2] 3-110 [111-112] 113-118 [119-126]; 7" x 10"

Binding: Glossy dark purplish red (259) wraps glued at spine. Strong yellow (84) print. Front: [strong yellow outline print] JAMES A. / [solid white print] MICHENER / [strong yellow outline print] ON THE SOCIAL STUDIES / [rule] [solid strong yellow print] His writings in publications of / National Council for the Social Studies / from 1938 to 1987 / [white publisher's device containing circular global map centered at North Pole circled by National Council for / the Social Studies] / [strong yellow print] Bulletin No. 85. Spine: [all strong yellow vertical print] JAMES A. MICHENER ON THE SOCIAL STUDIES [at bottom] NCSS. Back: [within large vertical white mailing panel with concave corners, bordered by thin white rule] [vertical at top right] National Council for the Social Studies / 3501 Newark Street N.W. / Washington, D.C. 20016-3167 / [vertical at bottom right] [Non-Profit Org. permit stamp] Inside front cover: Blank. Inside back cover: Bulletins in Print / [price list for current NCSS publications} / ORDERING INFORMATION / [instructions and charges for ordering bulletins] / NCSS Publications • c/o Maxway Data Corp. • Suite 1105 • 225 West 34th St. • New York, NY 10001.

Dust Jacket: None.

Price: [$14.95]

Notes: A compilation of Michener's writings on the Social Studies from 1938 to 1987.

Section A.I - Descriptive Bibliography of First Editions

A.056 THE NOVEL [1991]

Title Page: [illustration of Pennsylvania Dutch fraktur] [superimposed on the fraktur design is the following] THE / NOVEL / [rule] / James A. Michener / [publisher's device] / RANDOM HOUSE NEW YORK

Copyright: *The Novel* is a work of fiction. The characters in it have been / invented by the author, and any resemblance to actual persons, / living or dead, is purely coincidental. The story / is also fictitious. / Copyright © 1991 by James A. Michener / Cartography ©1991 by Jean Paul Tremblay / All rights reserved under International and Pan-American / Copyright Conventions. Published in the United States by / Random House, Inc., New York and simultaneously in Canada / by Random House of Canada Limited, Toronto. / Library of Congress Cataloging-in-Publication Data / Michener, James A. (James Albert). / The novel / James Michener. / p. cm. / ISBN 0-679-40133-4 / I. Title. / PS3525.I19N68 1991 / 813'.54--dc20 90-53489 / *Manufactured in the United States of America* / 24689753 / FIRST EDITION / *Book design by Carol Lowenstein*

Contents: [i-iii] blank; [iv] BOOKS BY JAMES A. MICHENER [previous works]; [v] half title; [vi] blank; [vii] title; [viii] copyright; [ix] dedication; [x] blank; [xi] Contents; [xii] blank; [1] second half title; [2] blank; [3] 4-446 text; [447-450] blank.

Collation: [i-xii] [1-3] 4-446 [447-450]; 6 1/8" x 9 3/16"

Binding: White ribbed paper covered boards, black cloth spine which covers left quarter of front and right quarter of back. Front: [vivid red (11) illustration of floral Pennsylvania Dutch fraktur]. Spine: [all copper print] James A. / Michener / [rule] / THE / NOVEL / [rule] / [publisher's device] / Random / House. Back: Blank. Front end map: THE LOCALE OF THE NOVEL. Back end map: THE GRENZLER REGION.

Dust Jacket: White and black. Front: [black print on white upper half] THE / NOVEL / [vivid red (11) print on black lower half] James A. / Michener. Spine: [vertical] [vivid red print on white upper half] James A. Michener [white print on black lower half] THE NOVEL [horizontal] [vivid red publisher's device] / [white print] RANDOM / HOUSE. Back: [centered photograph of pensive author] [vertical black print from bottom to top at bottom right edge of photograph] PHOTO: © JOHN KINGS [bottom right] [bar codes] / ISBN 0-679-40133-4. Front flap: [top left] FPT [top right] U.S.A. $23.00 / Canada $30.00 / [blurb]. Back flap: [biographical sketch of the author] / Jacket design: Wendell Minor / Random House, Inc., New York, N. Y. 10022 / Printed in U.S.A. 3/91 / © 1991 Random House, Inc.

Price: U.S.A. $25.00 / Canada $30.00

Notes: The world of publishing as seen through the writer, the publisher, the critic and the reader.

Section A.I - Descriptive Bibliography of First Editions

A.057 THE WORLD IS MY HOME: A MEMOIR [1992]

Title Page: [double title page] [illustration of Old World map covers both verso and recto] [on recto, within ruled border, superimposed over map] The / World Is / My Home: / A Memoir / James A. / Michener / [publisher's device] RANDOM HOUSE / NEW YORK

Copyright: The names and identifying details of a few individuals / and some place names have been changed to protect / the privacy of those involved. / Copyright © 1992 by James A. Michener / Maps Copyright © 1992 by Jean Paul Tremblay / All rights reserved under International and Pan-American / Copyright Conventions. Published in the United States / by Random House, Inc., New York and simultaneously / in Canada by Random House of Canada Limited, / Toronto. / Grateful acknowledgment is made to / Sterling Lord Literistic, Inc., / for permission to reprint excerpts from *Ross and Tom,* / by John Leggett (Simon and Schuster, 1974.) / Copyright © 1974 by John Leggett. Reprinted by / permission of Sterling Lord Literistic, Inc. / Library of Congress Cataloging-in-Publication Data / Michener, James A. (James Albert). / The world is my home: a memoir / James A. / Michener.--1st ed. / p. cm. / ISBN 0-679-40134-2 / 1. Michener, James A. (James Albert), 1907- / -- Biography. / 2. Authors, American--20th century--Biography. / I. Title. / PS3525. I19Z476 1992 / 813'.54--dc20 / [B] 91-18447 / *Manufactured in the United States of America* / 24689753 / FIRST EDITION / This book was set in 10.5/13 Times Roman. / *Book design by Carol Lowenstein*

Contents: [i] blank; [ii] BOOKS BY JAMES A. MICHENER [previous works]; [iii] half title; [iv-v] double title page; [vi] copyright; [vii] Contents; [viii] blank; [1] second half title; [2] blank; [3] 4-512 text; [513] 514-519 Index; [520] editor's note.

Collation: [i-viii] [1-3] 4-512 [513] 514-519 [520]; 6" x 9 3/8"

Binding: White fiber-flecked paper covered boards, moderate blue (182) cloth spine which covers left quarter of front and right quarter of back. All gold print. Front: J • A • M / [thick decorative rule]. Spine: James A. / Michener / [thick decorative rule] / The / World / Is My / Home: / A / Memoir / [thick decorative rule] / [publisher's device] / RANDOM / HOUSE. Back: Blank. Front end map: THE WRITER'S WORLD [Pacific area]. Back end map: THE WRITER'S WORLD [Atlantic area]. [Various copies have been noted with identical end papers at front and back instead of Pacific area at front and Atlantic area at back.]

Dust Jacket: [Covering the front, spine, and back is a color photograph of the author sitting on a stone outcrop against a suburban background in tones of blue, gray, and green] [all white print]. Front: THE WORLD / IS MY HOME / A MEMOIR / James A. / Michener. Spine: [vertical] James A. / Michener THE WORLD / IS MY HOME [horizontal] [publisher's device] / RANDOM / HOUSE. Back: [within white panel at bottom] [bar-codes] / ISBN 0-679-40134-2. Front flap: [top left] FPT [top right] U.S.A. $25.00 / Canada $30.00 / [blurb]. Back flap: [biographical sketch of the author] / Photo by Kelly Campbell / Jacket design by Wendell Minor / Random House, Inc., New York, N.Y. 10022 / Printed in the U.S.A. 1/92 / ©1991 Random House, Inc.

Price: U.S.A. $25.00; Canada $30.00

Notes: Autobiography.

Section A.I - Descriptive Bibliography of First Editions

A.058 JAMES A MICHENER'S WRITER'S HANDBOOK:
Explorations in Writing and Publishing [1992]

Title Page: [wide rule at top] / [all within a single frame rule] JAMES A. / MICHENER'S / [light gray illustration of pen point extended into rule] / WRITER'S HANDBOOK / [light gray rule] / Explorations in / Writing and / Publishing / RANDOM HOUSE / [publisher's device] / NEW YORK / [wide rule at bottom]

Copyright: [wide rule at top] Copyright ©1992 by James A. Michener / All rights reserved under International and Pan-American Copyright Conventions. / Published in the United States by Random House, Inc., New York and / simultaneously in Canada by Random House of Canada Limited, Toronto. / Grateful acknowledgment is made to Random House Inc., / and McClelland & Stewart, Inc., for permission to reprint / excerpts from *Journey* by James A. Michener / Copyright © 1988, 1989, by James A. Michener. Rights / throughout Canada are controlled by McClelland & Stewart, Inc. / Reprinted by permission of Random House, Inc., / and McClelland & Stewart, Inc. / Library of Congress Cataloging-in-Publication Data / Michener, James A. (James Albert) / [Writer's handbook] / James A. Michener's writer's handbook: explorations in writing / and publishing. --1st ed. / p. cm. / ISBN 0-679-74126-7 / 1. Michener, James A. [James Albert] -- Authorship / 2. Authors and publishers -- United States. 3. Authorship. / I. Title / PS3525.I19Z477 1992 / 808'.02--dc20 92-22120 / *Manufactured in the United States of America* / 24689753 / FIRST EDITION / *Book design by Carol Lowenstein* / [wide rule at bottom]

Contents: [i] blank; [ii] BOOKS BY JAMES A. MICHENER [previous works]; [iii] half title; [iv] blank; [v] title; [vi] copyright; [vii] Contents; [viii] blank; ix A Word of Explanation; [x] blank; [1] [chapter heading] JOURNEY / A Canadian Novella; [2] blank; 3-180 text; [181] ABOUT THE AUTHOR; [182] ABOUT THE TYPE.

Collation: [i-viii] ix [x] [1-2] 3-180 [181-182]; 8 1/2" x 11"

Binding: Glossy white and light yellow (86) illustrated wraps glued at spine. All black print. Front: [facsimile of yellow-lined legal page covered with the following: small photographs, audio Hawaii, The Novel. Also illustrating the front are: the author's hand-drawn maps of Alaska, Canada, and South Sea islands, a crumpled page from the author's working papers, a pencil and paper clips] James A. / Michener's / Writer's / Handbook / *Explorations in Writing and Publishing*. Spine: [vertical] James A. Michener's Writer's Handbook [horizontal publisher's device] [vertical] RANDOM HOUSE. Back: [top left] WRITING REFERENCE / [top right] U.S.A. $15.00 / Canada $19.00 / [blurb] / [bottom left] Cover design: Wendell Minor / Cover photo of James Michener (inset): Kelly Campbell / Random House, Inc., New York, N.Y. 10022 / Printed in U.S.A. 8/92 © 1992 Random House, Inc. [bottom right] [bar codes] / ISBN 0-679-74126-7.

Dust Jacket: None.

Price: U.S.A. $15.00 / Canada $19.00

Notes: Michener's informative guide for writers, editors, and book lovers of both fiction and nonfiction. The first edition exists only in wraps. A hard cover edition with dust jacket similar to the wraps was distributed by The Literary Guild.

Section A.I - Descriptive Bibliography of First Editions

A.059 SOUTH PACIFIC, AS TOLD BY JAMES A. MICHENER [1992]

Title Page: SOUTH PACIFIC / as told by / James A. Michener / ILLUSTRATED BY / Michael Hague / [framed within illustration of World War II bomber flying over South Sea islands bordered by palm trees] BASED ON / RODGERS AND HAMMERSTEIN'S *South Pacific* / GULLIVER BOOKS / HARCOURT BRACE JOVANOVICH, PUBLISHERS / San Diego New York London

Copyright: HBJ / Text copyright © 1992 by James A. Michener, / The Beneficiaries of the Estate of Richard Rodgers / and the Estate of Oscar Hammerstein II / Illustrations copyright © 1992 by Michael Hague / All rights reserved. No part of this publication / may be reproduced or transmitted in any form or / by any means, electronic or mechanical, including / photocopy, recording, or any information storage / and retrieval system, without permission in / writing from the publisher. / Requests for permission to make copies of / any part of the work should be mailed to: / Permissions Department, / Harcourt Brace Jovanovich, Publishers, / 8th Floor, Orlando, Florida 32887. / Library of Congress Cataloging-in-Publication Data / Michener, James A. (James Albert), 1907- / South Pacific / as told by James A. Michener; / illustrated by Michael Hague. --1st ed. / p. cm. / "Gulliver books." / "Based on Rodgers and Hammerstein's South Pacific." / Summary: A retelling of the story of the musical "South Pacific," / concerning the lives of officers, nurses, a French expatriate, / and natives on the islands of the South Pacific during World War II. / Includes discussion of the original Broadway production and its cast. / ISBN 0-15-200618-4 / ISBN 0-15-200615-X (Ltd. ed.) / [1. World War, 1939-1945-- Campaigns--Pacific Area--Fiction. / 2. South Pacific Ocean-- Fiction. 3. Musicals--Stories, plots, etc.] / I. Hague, Michael, ill. II. Rodgers, Richard, 1902-1979--South Pacific. / III. Title. / PZ7.M581917So 1992 / [Fic]--dc20 91-28934 / First edition / ABCDE / The illustrations in this book were done in pen-and-ink / and water color on Crescent cold-press watercolor board. / The display type was set in Florentine and the text type / in Linotype Walbaum by Thompson Type, San Diego, California. / Color separations were made by Bright Arts Ltd., Singapore / Printed and bound by Tien Wah Press, Singapore. / Production supervision by Warren Wallerstein and Ginger Boyer / Designed by Michael Farmer

Contents: [1] title; [2] copyright; [3] dedication; [4] illustration; [5-62] text and illustrations; [63-64] STORYTELLER'S NOTE.

Collation: [1-64]; 10" x 11"

Binding: Strong greenish blue (169) paper covered boards, moderate blue (182) cloth spine which covers edge of front and back. All gold print. Front: SOUTH PACIFIC. Spine: [vertical] Michener/Hague SOUTH PACIFIC [horizontal publisher's device] [vertical] Gulliver/HBJ. Back: Blank. End papers: [vivid colored illustrations by Michael Hague of a South Sea island].

Dust Jacket: Front, spine, and back is a continuous illustration of Nellie Forbush leaning against a palm tree at sunset on remote South Sea island. All white print. Front: James A. Michener / RETELLS / SOUTH PACIFIC / Based on Rodgers and Hammerstein's award-winning musical / WITH ILLUSTRATIONS BY / Michael Hague. Spine: [vertical] Michener/Hague SOUTH PACIFIC [horizontal publisher's device] [vertical] Gulliver/HBJ. Back: [small inset illustration of Emile de Becque with two children] / [at bottom in white panel] ISBN 0-15-200618-4 / [bar codes]. Front flap: [top right] >$16.95 / (HIGHER IN CANADA) / [brief history of the original musical]. Back flap: [biographical sketches of the author and the illustrator] / Reinforced binding / Printed in Singapore / Gulliver Books / Harcourt Brace Jovanovich, Publishers / 1250 Sixth Avenue, San Diego, CA 92101 / 111 Fifth Avenue, New York, NY 10003.

Price: $16.95 / [HIGHER IN Canada]

Notes: A retelling of the story of the musical "South Pacific" for children.

Section A.I - Descriptive Bibliography of First Editions

A.060 MEXICO [1992]

Title Page: JAMES A. / MICHENER / [thick rule] / [wide Aztec style decorative device] [white on black rectangular panel] MEXICO / [wide Aztec style decorative device] / [thick rule] / RANDOM HOUSE / NEW YORK / [publisher's device]

Copyright: *This book / is / dedicated to / Conchita Cintron / La Superba* / [rule] / Copyright © 1992 by James A. Michener / Maps © 1992 by Jean Paul Tremblay / All rights reserved under International and Pan-American Copyright Conventions. / Published in the United States by Random House, Inc., New York, and / simultaneously in Canada by Random House of Canada Limited, Toronto. / Library of Congress Cataloging-in-Publication Data / Michener, James A. (James Albert) / Mexico / by James Michener.--1st ed. / p. cm. / ISBN 0-679-41649-8 / 1. Mexico--History--Fiction. I. Title. / PS3525.I19M48 1992 / 813'.54--dc20 92-50151 / *Manufactured in the United States of America / on acid-free paper using partially recycled fibers* / 24689753 / FIRST EDITION / *Book design by Carol Lowenstein*

Contents: [i] blank; [ii] BOOKS BY JAMES A. MICHENER [previous works]; [iii] half title; [iv] blank; [v] title; [vi] dedication and copyright; vii CONTENTS; [viii] blank; ix AUTHOR'S NOTE; [x] blank; xi-xiii CHRONOLOGY; [xiv] blank; [1] second half title; [2] blank; 3-625 text; [626] ABOUT THE TYPE.

Collation: [i-vi] vii [viii] ix [x] xi-xiii [xiv] [1-2] 3-625 [626]; 6" x 9 3/8"

Binding: Moderate orange yellow (71) paper covered boards, dark grayish red (20) cloth spine which covers the left third of front and right third of back. All copper print. Front: [Aztec decorative device] [rule] J • A • M / [rule] [Aztec decorative device]. Spine: JAMES A. / MICHENER / [rule] / [Aztec decorative device] / [inverse print on gold rectangular panel] MEXICO / [Aztec decorative device] [rule] [publisher's device] / RANDOM / HOUSE. Back: Blank. Front end map: MEXICO. Back end map: [verso] ENVIRONS OF TOLEDO; [recto] PLAZA DE TOLEDO.

Dust Jacket: White. Front: [light olive (106) rule] / [to left] [illustration of Aztec carving] [to right, dark red (16) print] James A. / Michener / [light olive rule] / [light greenish blue (172) print] A NOVEL / [light olive print] Mexico / [light olive rule]. Spine: [continuation of illustration from front] / [dark red print] James A. / Michener / [light greenish blue rule] / [light olive print] Mexico / [light greenish blue rule] / [light olive] [publisher's device] / RANDOM / HOUSE. Back: [large photograph of the author] [bottom right edge of photograph, from bottom to top] PHOTO: © STEVEN PUMPHREY [bottom right] ISBN 0-679-41649-8 / [bar codes]. Front flap: [top left] FPT [top right] U.S.A. $25.00 / In Canada $31.50 / [blurb]. Back flap: [biographical sketch of the author] / Jacket art: © Wendell Minor / Random House, Inc., New York, N.Y. 10022 / ISBN 0-679-41649-8 / [bar codes].

Price: U.S.A. $25.00 / Canada $31.50

Notes: Mexico's history, past and present, from fictional pre-Columbian Indians to modern Mexico through the eyes of an American reporter. The fictional characters portrayed by the two primary bullfighters epitomize the continuing cultural conflict between Spaniard and Indian. Begun by Michener in the 1950's, and set aside because of negative comments by his publisher, this novel was lost, rediscovered in 1992, and then completed.

Section A.I - Descriptive Bibliography of First Editions

A.061 MY LOST MEXICO [1992]

Title Page: MY LOST MEXICO / by / JAMES A. / MICHENER / [Aztec serpent decorative device] *with photographs by the author* / STATE / HOUSE PRESS / 1992

Copyright: Copyright © 1992 James A. Michener / All rights reserved / *Library of Congress Cataloging-in-Publication Data* / Michener, James A. (James Albert), 1907- / My lost Mexico / by James Michener; with photographs / by the author. / p. cm. / ISBN 0-938349-93-7 (acid free paper). / ISBN 0-938349-94-5 (limit ed.) (acid free paper) / 1. Michener, James A. (James Albert), 1907- Mexico. 2. / Michener, James A. (James Albert) 1907- --Authorship. / 3. Bullfights in literature. 4. Mexico in literature. 5. / Fiction--Authorship. / PS3525.I19M48 1992c / 813'.54--dc20 92-26953 / *Printed in the United States of America* / First Edition / STATE HOUSE PRESS / P.O. Box 15247 / Austin, Texas 78761

Contents: [i] half title; [ii] BOOKS BY JAMES A. MICHENER [previous works]; [iii] title; [iv] copyright; [v] CONTENTS; [vi] blank; [vii] quote by Walt Whitman; [viii] blank; [ix] second half title; [x] blank; [1] 2-165 text; [166] blank.

Collation: [i-x] [1] 2-165 [166]; 7" x 10"

Binding: Grayish red (19) cloth. All gold print. Front: Blank. Spine: [vertical] MICHENER [Aztec serpent decorative device] MY LOST MEXICO [horizontal] STATE / HOUSE / PRESS. Back: Blank.

Dust Jacket: White. Front: [grayish red (19) print] JAMES A. / MICHENER / [moderate greenish blue (173), light grayish red (18), and moderate yellowish pink (29) Aztec serpent decorative device] / [a single large M for both My and Mexico] My LOST / MEXICO / [grayish red] The Δ Making Δ of Δ a Δ Novel. Spine: [vertical grayish red print] MICHENER [moderate greenish blue Aztec serpent decorative device] [vertical black print] MY LOST MEXICO [horizontal grayish red print] STATE / HOUSE / PRESS. Back: [two small photographs] [top: Michener attending a bullfight researching novel in the 1950's] [bottom: Michener at time he rediscovered lost manuscript in 1992] / [below photo] *photo by George Holmes, Archer M. Huntington Art Gallery* / ISBN 0-938349-7 [bar codes]. Front flap: [quotation by the author] / [blurb] / *Jacket design by David Timmons.* Back flap: [continuation of blurb] / Also published / by State House Press: / THE EAGLE AND THE RAVEN / *by James A. Michener* / [blurb from Publisher's Weekly] / STATE HOUSE PRESS / PO Box 15247 / Austin, Texas 78761.

Price: No price stated, but sold retail for $24.95

Notes: The incomplete manuscript of the novel **Mexico** was set aside and lost for three decades because of Michener's reactions to the publisher's critical comments. It was rediscovered and published by Random House in 1992. In **My Lost Mexico** Michener concludes, "Sometimes it is the writer, not the publisher, who knows what makes a viable book."

66

Section A.I - Descriptive Bibliography of First Editions

A.062 JAMES A MICHENER, TWO COMPLETE NOVELS [1993]

Title Page: JAMES A. / MICHENER / TWO COMPLETE NOVELS / [rule] / ALASKA / [rule] / HAWAII / [rule] / WINGS BOOKS / New York • Avenel, New Jersey

Copyright: This edition contains the complete and unabridged texts of the original editions. / They have been completely reset for this volume. / This omnibus was originally published in separate volumes under the titles: / *Alaska,* copyright © 1959 by James A. Michener. / *Hawaii,* copyright © 1988 by James A. Michener, / cartography © 1988 by Jean Paul Tremblay. / All rights reserved. / This 1993 edition is published by Wings Books, / distributed by Outlet Book Company, Inc., A Random House Company, / 40 Engelhard Avenue, Avenel, New Jersey 07001, / by arrangement with Ballantine Books. / Random House / New York • Toronto • London • Sydney • Auckland / Printed and bound in the United States of America / Library of Congress Cataloging-in-Publication Data / Michener, James A. (James Albert), 1907- [Alaska] / Two complete novels / James A. Michener / p. cm. / Contents: Alaska - Hawaii. / ISBN 0-517-09151-8 / 1. Alaska--History--Fiction. 2. Hawaii--History--Fiction. I. Michener, James A. (James Albert), 1907- Hawaii, 1993. / II. Title. / PS3525.I19A6 1993 / 813'.54-- dc20 92-42529 / CIP / 87654321

Contents: [i-ii] blank; [iii] half title; [iv] blank; [v] title; [vi] copyright; [vii] CONTENTS; [viii] blank; [1-5] 6-774 text of Alaska; [775-783] 784-1528 [1529-1537] text and genealogy of Hawaii; [1538] blank; [1539] ABOUT THE AUTHOR; [1540-1544] blank.

Collation: [i-viii] [1-5] 6-774 [775-783] 784-1528 [1529-1544]; 6" x 9 1/8"

Binding: Black paper covered boards, strong blue (178) cloth spine covering edges of front and back. All gold print. Front: Blank. Spine: JAMES A. / MICHENER / [rule] / TWO COMPLETE / NOVELS / [rule] / ALASKA / HAWAII / WINGS / BOOKS. Back: [vertical at bottom right edge] ISBN 0-517-09151-8.

Dust Jacket: Black. Front: [top half - Alaskan peaks in tones of blue] [bottom half - Hawaiian sunset in tones of red] [white print] ALASKA / [white print edged in gold] JAMES A. / MICHENER / [moderate orange (53) print] TWO COMPLETE NOVELS / [white print] HAWAII. Spine: [moderate orange print] JAMES A. / MICHENER / TWO COMPLETE NOVELS / [small copy of illustrations from front] [white print] [at top of illustration] ALASKA / [at bottom of illustration] HAWAII / [white print] WINGS / BOOKS. Back: [blurbs] / [bottom right, within white panel] [bar codes] / ISBN 0-517- 09151-8. Front flap: [top right] Originally published / in two volumes / at $62.95 / [diagonal broken line across corner] [blurbs]. Back flap: [continuation of blurbs] / [biographical sketch of the author] / *Jacket design by Don Bender / Photography courtesy of Colour Library Books, Ltd.* / WINGS BOOKS / Distributed by Outlet Book Company, Inc. / A Random House Company / 40 Engelhard Avenue / Avenel, New Jersey 07001.

Price: Price not stated, but sold retail for $14.99.

Notes: Two volumes in one.

Section A.I - Descriptive Bibliography of First Editions

A.063 CREATURES OF THE KINGDOM: Stories of Animals and Nature [1993]

Title Page: [double title page] [across verso and recto within ruled border, illustration of various animals which are described in the text] [on verso] ILLUSTRATIONS BY KAREN JACOBSEN / [publisher's device] / RANDOM HOUSE / NEW YORK / [on recto] [superimposed on bottom right of illustration between vertical rules] JAMES A. / MICHENER / [rule] / CREATURES / OF THE / KINGDOM / [rule] / STORIES OF / ANIMALS AND NATURE

Copyright: Copyright © 1993 by James A. Michener / Illustrations copyright © 1993 by Karen Jacobsen / All rights reserved under International and Pan-American Copyright / Conventions. Published in the United States by Random House, Inc., / New York, and simultaneously in Canada by Random House / of Canada Limited, Toronto. / Portions of this work were originally published in *Alaska, / Centennial, Chesapeake, The Covenant, Hawaii,* and *Texas,* / all by James A. Michener. / Library of Congress Cataloging-in-Publication Data / Michener, James A. (James Albert) / Creatures of the kingdom / James A. Michener.--1st ed. / p. cm. / 1. Animals--Fiction. I. Title. / PS3525.I19C74 1993 / 813'.54--dc20 92-46075 / *Manufactured in the United States of America* / 24689753 / FIRST EDITION / *Book design by Carol Lowenstein*

Contents: [i] blank; [ii] BOOKS BY JAMES A. MICHENER [previous works]; [iii] half title; [iv-v] double title page; [vi] copyright; [vii] dedication; [viii] blank; [ix] CONTENTS; [x] blank; [xi] xii-xvi FOREWORD; [1] second half title; [2-3] [two page illustration of Hawaii and chapter heading] FROM THE BOUNDLESS DEEP; [4] blank; [5] 6-281 text; [282] blank; [283] ABOUT THE TYPE; [284-288] blank.

Collation: [i-xi] xii-xvi [1-5] 6-281 [282-288]; 6" x 9 3/16"

Binding: Grayish red (19) paper covered boards, dark grayish red (20) cloth spine covering edges of front and back. All copper print. Front: [two long parallel vertical rules broken mid-cover by two horizontal parallel rules] [between horizontal parallel rules] *J* [diamond] *A* [diamond] *M.* Spine: [two vertical parallel rules broken by two horizontal parallel rules, similar to those on the front] [vertical, between the top rules] JAMES A. MICHENER [vertical, between the horizontal rules] CREATURES / OF THE / KINGDOM [vertical, between the bottom rules] [publisher's device] RANDOM HOUSE. Back: Blank.

Dust Jacket: Speckled yellowish white (92). Front: [grayish red print shadowed in gold] JAMES A. / MICHENER / [multi-colored illustration of animals memorialized in the author's writings] [grayish red print shadowed in gold] CREATURES / [gold rule] OF THE [gold rule] / KINGDOM / [black print] *Stories of Animals and Nature.* Spine: [vertical grayish red print shadowed in gold] JAMES A. / MICHENER [continuation of illustration from front] [vertical grayish red print shadowed in gold] CREATURES / [gold rule] OF THE [gold rule] / KINGDOM [horizontal] [grayish red publisher's device] / [black print] RANDOM / HOUSE. Back: [small photograph of author with black bird perched on his hat] [vertical at right, bottom to top] PHOTO: © JOHN KINGS / [photograph is partially superimposed over illustration which continues from front and spine] / [within white panel at bottom] ISBN 0-679-41367-7 / [bar codes]. Front flap: [top left] FPT [top right] U.S.A. $22.00 / Canada $29.00 / [blurb]. Back flap: [biographical sketch of the author] / Jacket painting and design: ©1993 Wendell Minor / Random House, Inc. / New York, N.Y. 10022 11/93 ©1993 Random House, Inc. / Printed in U.S.A. / [bar codes].

Price: U.S.A. $22.00; Canada $29.00

Notes: Sixteen tales of Michener's animals and of his love affair with nature. Contains two original new stories with a collection of earlier writings.

Section A.I - Descriptive Bibliography of First Editions

A.064 LITERARY REFLECTIONS:
Michener on Michener, Hemingway, Capote, & Others [1993]

Title Page: [all within a double ruled frame with small black squares superimposed at each corner] LITERARY / REFLECTIONS / MICHENER ON MICHENER / HEMINGWAY, CAPOTE, & OTHERS / by / JAMES A. MICHENER / State House Press / 1993

Copyright: Copyright © 1993 James A. Michener / All Rights Reserved / *Library of Congress Cataloging-in-Publication Data* / Michener, James A. (James Albert), 1907- / Literary reflections: Michener on Michener, Hemingway, / Capote, and others / by James A. Michener. / p. cm. / ISBN 1-880510-06-5 : / ISBN 1-880510-07-3 (limited ed.) / 1. Michener, James A. (James Albert), 1907- -- Authorship. / 2. American fiction--20th century--History and criticism. / I. Title. / PS3525.I19Z469 1993 / 810.9'005--dc20 93-32356 / *Printed in the United States of America* / STATE HOUSE PRESS / P.O. Box 15247 / Austin, Texas 78761

Contents: [i] half title; [ii] BOOKS BY JAMES A. MICHENER [previous works]; [iii] title; [iv] copyright; [v] Table of Contents; [vi] photograph of James A. Michener by Tim Boole; vii-x Introduction; [1] [chapter heading] AN EMERGING WRITER; [2] blank; [3-4] 5-68 COLLECTORS, FORGERS--AND A WRITER: A MEMOIR; [69-70] 71-96 TESTIMONY; [97] 98-110 WHO IS VIRGIL T. FRY?; 111-213 remaining text; [214] blank.

Collation: [i-vi] vii-x [1-4] 5-68 [69-70] 71-96 [97] 98-213 [214]; 5 1/2" x 8 3/8"

Binding: Yellowish white (92) cloth. All black print. Front: Blank. Spine: [vertical] Michener [diamond decorative device] LITERARY REFLECTIONS [diamond decorative device] [horizontal] STATE / HOUSE / PRESS. Back: Blank.

Dust Jacket: Brownish pink (33). Front: [full page color photograph of a barefoot Michener standing on a sandy tropical beach, watching a sunset] [moderate red (15) print] LITERARY REFLECTIONS / [grayish red (19) print] JAMES A. / MICHENER / [pinkish white (9) print] MICHENER ON MICHENER, / HEMINGWAY, / CAPOTE & OTHERS. Spine: [vertical grayish red print] Michener [white diamond decorative device] [vertical moderate red print] LITERARY REFLECTIONS [white diamond decorative device] [horizontal grayish red print] STATE / HOUSE / PRESS. Back: [full page color photograph of author walking away with a cane, along a sandy tropical beach] [within a white panel at bottom right] ISBN 1-880510-06-5 / [bar codes]. Front flap: [top right] $21.95 / [quote by the author] / [blurb] / cover photographs by Tim Boole. Back flap: [continuation of blurb] / [list of other Michener titles by State House Press] / STATE HOUSE PRESS / P. O. Box 15247 / Austin, Texas 78761.

Price: $21.95

Notes: Includes reprints of rare earlier limited printings of **Collectors, Forgers—And A Writer** (A.044) and **Testimony** (A.046) with insightful commentaries on other authors. Michener has written two new poems titled "Sonnet To A Weathered Wanderer," and "Verses To A Writer Heading For Ninety," especially for this book.

Section A.I - Descriptive Bibliography of First Editions

A.065 JAMES A. MICHENER'S AMERICANA [1993]

Titles: TEXAS / ALASKA / CHESAPEAKE
A three volume set of paperbacks published by Fawcett-Crest.

Binding: Normal paperback wraps.

    1. TEXAS; 0-449-21092-8; U.S. $6.99; CANADA $7.99

    2. ALASKA; 0-449-21726-4; U.S. $6.99; CANADA $7.99

    3. CHESAPEAKE; 0-449-21158-4; U.S. $6.95; CANADA $7.95

Dust Jacket: None; Thin white cardboard slipcase; 5 1/8" x 7 1/8" x 4 1/4" [on sides and back] [black print] COLLECTORS' EDITIONS / [vivid red (11) print] James A. Michener's / Americana / [vivid red rule with centered vivid red star emitting light rays] / [deep blue (179) print] Texas / Alaska / Chesapeake / [centered at top of back] [publisher's device] / Fiction; [top and bottom] [vivid red print] James A. / Michener's / Americana. [within white label affixed to shrink-wrap] COLL. ED. AMERICANA / BOXED SET 449-22263-2 / [bar codes] / ISBN 0-449-22263-2 / US $20.93/CAN $23.89.

Price: U.S. $20.93 - CANADA $23.89

Notes: Slipcased set of three volumes.

Section A.I - Descriptive Bibliography of First Editions

A.066 RECESSIONAL [1994]

Title Page: [double title page] [across verso and recto is an illustration of a Florida retirement community with palm tree lined entrance way] [on bottom of recto] RECESSIONAL / [rule broken in middle by leaf-like decorative device] / JAMES A. MICHENER / FIRST EDITION / THE FRANKLIN LIBRARY / FRANKLIN CENTER, PENNSYLVANIA / 1994

Copyright: *This signed, limited first edition has been published by special arrangement / with Random House, Inc. / Copyright © 1994 by James A. Michener / Maps © 1994 by Anita Karl and Jim Kemp / Interior illustrations © 1994 by Franca Nucci Haynes / Special contents copyright © 1994 by The Franklin Library. / The frontispiece by Rafal Olbinski was specially commissioned by / The Franklin Library. / All rights reserved under International and Pan-American / Copyright Conventions. / The acid-free paper used in this book conforms with the guidelines for / permanence and durability set by the Council of Library Resources and / the American National Standards Institute. / Printed in the United States of America.*

Contents: [i] [signed limitation page]; [ii] blank; [iii] half title; [iv] blank; [v] ALSO BY JAMES A. MICHENER [previous works]; [vi-ix] A special message for the first edition from James A. Michener; [x] blank; [xi] frontispiece; [xii-xiii] double title page; [xiv] copyright; [xv] [definition of recessional]; [xvi] blank; [xvii] second half title; [xviii] [1] [two page illustration of a retiree fishing in Florida marsh] [chapter heading] ARRIVALS; [2] blank; [3] 4-484 text; [485] ABOUT THE AUTHOR; [486] blank; [487] [colophon]; [488] blank.

Laid in message: [on front and back of a heavy slick white card addressed to members of the THE SIGNED FIRST EDITION SOCIETY] [picture of Michener] [blurbs regarding Recessional] [message from the Chairman of the society, Stewart Resnick]

Collation: [i-xviii] [1-3] 4-484 [485-488]; 7" x 9 15/16"

Binding: Strong brown (55) leather with ornate gold design rectangles on front, back, and spine. Front: [within double rule framed border] [silhouette outline of wrought iron gates enclosing palm trees, blue herons, and marshy area]. Spine: [within ruled frame at top, bordered at top and bottom by five horizontal touching circles] [horizontal, in gold print] RECESSIONAL / JAMES A. / MICHENER / [within ruled frame covering middle of spine, bordered at top and bottom by five horizontal touching circles] [same as left one-half of front] / [within ruled frame at bottom, bordered at top and bottom by five horizontal touching circles] SIGNED / FIRST / EDITION / THE / FRANKLIN / LIBRARY. Back: [same as front]. Light grayish brown (60) attached ribbon marker. Two raised ribs on spine. Pages trimmed in gold. End papers: The PALMS [schematic layout of the buildings and grounds].

Dust Jacket: None

Price: Subscription price unknown.

Notes: This fictional novel depicts the challenges and rewards faced by the elderly and their families in a Florida retirement community. A first trade edition was published by Random House, following publication of this Franklin Library Signed First Edition.

Section A.I - Descriptive Bibliography of First Editions

A.067 WILLIAM PENN [1994]

Title Page: [thick rule] / [thin rule] WILLIAM PENN / by / James A. Michener / Illustrations by / Violet Oakley / [publisher's device] / The Pennsbury Society / [narrow rule] / [thick rule]

Copyright: Copyright ©1994 by The Pennsbury Society / All rights reserved. No part of this book may be reproduced in any form / without written permission from The Pennsbury Society. / Pennsbury Manor is administered by the Pennsylvania Historical / and Museum Commission with the assistance of the Pennsbury Society, / a non-profit support organization. / The Pennsbury Society is grateful to the PHMC for permission to reproduce / Violet Oakley's engravings in this book. / *Book design* / Gretchen Leahy and Jeannine Vannais / [recycle symbol] Printed on recycled papers by MPI Commercial Printing, Inc.

Acknowledgment Page:

The Pennsbury Society
gratefully acknowledges the generosity of
James A. Michener
for donating this tract on William Penn
in commemoration of the 350th birthday of
the first governor and proprietor of
Pennsylvania.

Contents: [i-ii] blank; [iii] title; [iv] copyright; 1-14 text; 15 illustration of Penn's vision; [16] blank; [17] acknowledgment; [18] biographical sketch of Violet Oakley; [19] Illustrations; [20] history of Pennsbury Manor.

Collation: [i-iv] 1-15 [16-20]; 7 1/2" x 9 1/4"

Binding: Very pale green (148) heavy paper wraps. Stapled twice at centerfold. Front: [thick and thin black double rule] / [moderate red (15) print] WILLIAM PENN / [large illustration of mural by Violet Oakley depicting William Penn, student at Christ Church, Oxford. 1660.] / [moderate red print] by / JAMES A. MICHENER / [thin and thick black double rule]. Back: Blank. Front and back flaps are blank.

Dust Jacket: None.

Price: [$7.00].

Notes: Michener reminisces about lessons learned at the age of seven which led him to believe that William Penn had great and noble qualities, only to discover in later life that Penn was less than the hero that Michener had been taught. Nevertheless, Michener arrives at a respect and appreciation for Penn as a Quaker and as a person who established beneficial principles of education, liberty, and good government for his commonwealth. 2500 copies were printed and sold by the Pennsbury Society, 400 Pennsbury Memorial Lane, Morrisville, PA 19067. The book includes 10 illustrations from engravings included in a book published to commemorate William Penn's 300th birthday titled *The Holy Experiment: Our Heritage from William Penn.*

Section A.I - Descriptive Bibliography of First Editions

A.068 MIRACLE IN SEVILLE. [1995]

Title Page: [all within a rectangular ruled frame] [large illustration depicting gypsy woman Magdalena Lopez at left, and the Virgin Mary at right of ornate circular inset of La Giralda, a church built in 1172 a.d. by the Moors]] [below inset] [JAMES A. / MICHENER / [rule] / MIRACLE / IN SEVILLE [below rectangular ruled frame] / ILLUSTRATIONS BY JOHN FULTON / [publisher's device] / RANDOM HOUSE / NEW YORK

Copyright: Copyright © 1995 by James A. Michener / Illustrations: copyright © by John Fulton / All rights reserved under International and Pan-American / Copyright Conventions. Published in the United States by Random House, / Inc., New York, and simultaneously in Canada by Random House / of Canada Limited, Toronto. / *The illustration of Matt Carney was based on / a photograph by Jim Hollander.* / Library of Congress Cataloging-in-Publication Data / Michener, James A. (James Albert) / Miracle in Seville [/] by James A. Michener : / illustrations by John Fulton. --1st ed. / p. cm. / 1. Americans--Travel--Spain--Seville--Fiction. / 2. Bulls -- Spain -- Seville -- Breeding -- Fiction. / 3. Bullfighters -- Spain -- Seville -- Fiction. / 4. Seville (Spain) -- Fiction. 5. Miracles -- Fiction. / I. Title. / PS3525.I19M56 1995 / 813'.54--dc20 94-10187 / *Manufactured in the United States of America on acid-free paper* / 24689753 / FIRST EDITION / *Book design by Carol Lowenstein*

Contents: [i-iii] blank; [iv] BOOKS BY JAMES A. MICHENER [previous works]; [v] half title; [vi] blank; [vii] title page; [viii] copyright; [ix] dedication [illustration of Matt Carney based on a photograph by Jim Hollander]; [x] blank; [1] second half title; [2] blank; 3-107 text; [108] [blank]; [109] ABOUT THE AUTHOR; ABOUT THE ILLUSTRATOR; [110] [blank]; [111] ABOUT THE TYPE; [112-118] blank. [26 two-color illustrations throughout]

Collation: [i-x] [1-2] 3-107 [108-118]; 7 3/8" x 9 1/4"

Binding: White paper covered boards, black cloth spine covering edges of front and back. Front: [within thick and thin double gold rectangles with concave corners] J · A · M. Spine: [all gold print] [vertical from top to bottom] James A. Michener [within single gold rectangle with concave corners] MIRACLE IN SEVILLE [horizontal publisher's device] [vertical] RANDOM / HOUSE. Back: Blank.

Dust Jacket: White. Front: [black print]. JAMES A. MICHENER / [multicolored illustration similar to illustration on title page] / MIRACLE / [decorative device] IN [/ decorative device] / SEVILLE / ILLUSTRATIONS BY JOHN FULTON. Spine: [black print] [vertical] JAMES A. MICHENER [decorative device] MIRACLE IN SEVILLE [horizontal] [publisher's device] / Random / House. Back: [repeat of illustration from front jacket] [bottom right] ISBN 0-679-41822-9 / [bar codes]. Front flap: [top left] FPT [top right] U.S.A. $23.00 / Canada $32.00 / [blurb]. Back flap: [photograph of Michener by Steven Pumphrey] / [notes on James A. Michener and John Fulton] / Jacket design: Susan Shapiro / Jacket Illustration: John Fulton / Random House, Inc., New York, N.Y. 10022 / Printed in U.S.A. 10/95 / © 1995 Random House, Inc. / ISBN 0-679-41822-9 / [bar codes].

Price: U.S.A. $23.00; Canada $32.00

Notes: A dual between matador and fighting bull. A gypsy's spell is cast in aid of the matador. Prayers to the Virgin Mary are invoked to revive the proud reputation of the fighting bull. Illustrated by John Fulton, Matador de Toros. A private deluxe edition of 100 numbered copies and 26 lettered subscribers' copies, published in Seville, boxed with folding cover that includes hand bound text, two numbered and signed dry point etchings, a lithographic portrait of Michener as "the Universal Story Teller" signed and stamped by Michener and numbered and signed by Fulton.

Section A.I - Descriptive Bibliography of First Editions

A.069 VENTURES IN EDITING [1995]

Title Page: **Ventures in Editing** / James A. Michener / James Cahill Publishing / Huntington Beach, CA / 1995

Copyright: © 1995 by James A. Michener / Copyright Protected / First Edition / Book Design by / James Cahill / Book Layout and Typesetting by / J. F. Gonzalez / James Cahill Publishing / 9932 Constitution Dr. / Huntington Beach, CA / 92646

Colophon Page:

This is letter ___ of 26 copies
of Ventures In Editing. The edition
is limited to two hundred seventy-four
numbered copies, and twenty-six deluxe
copies lettered A to Z. All copies are
personally signed by the author.

[author's signature]

[author's hand stamp]

James A. Michener

[the limitation page for the numbered copies differs]

Contents: [i] limitation signature page; [ii] blank; [iii] title page; [iv] copyright; [v] Table of Contents; [vi] blank; vii-xi [introduction] An Editing Problem; [xii] blank; [1] half title page; [2] blank; 3-95 text; [96-98] blank.

Collation: [i-vi] vii-xi [xii] [1-2] 3-95 [96-98]; 4 7/8" x 7 1/2"

Binding: 26 lettered copies are bound in bluish gray (191) cloth. 148 numbered copies are bound in pale blue (185) cloth. 50 proof copies have been prepared and bound in grayish red (19) cloth. Front: [horizontal silver print] Ventures / in / Editing. Spine: [vertical silver print] Michener Ventures in Editing Cahill Publishing. Back: Blank.

Dust Jacket: None. Clamshell slipcase for lettered copies. Slipcase for numbered copies matches binding.

Price: Lettered copies: $250.00
Numbered copies: $125.00

Notes: A critical analysis of the steps taken by a writer in submitting his original manuscript and then watching it progress through editorial cutting, rewriting, and ultimately, publication. Although the limitation signature page indicates 274 numbered copies, only 148 numbered copies were produced. [The bibliographer has not examined the published copies. Information has been provided by the publisher. Not yet released for public sale.]

A.II
First Printings
and
Subsequent Publications

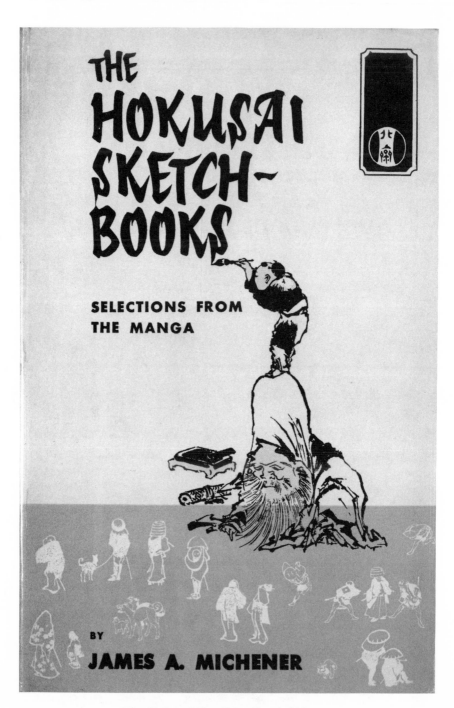

THE HOKUSAI SKETCH-BOOKS

SELECTIONS FROM THE MANGA

BY

JAMES A. MICHENER

The Hokusai Sketchbooks. A.013.

Section A.II - First Printings and Subsequent Publications

A.001   **THE FUTURE OF THE SOCIAL STUDIES.**
("THE PROBLEM OF THE SOCIAL STUDIES").

Cambridge: National Council for Social Studies, 1939, pages 1-5.   ***First Edition.***
Paperback. Edited by Michener, who wrote the first article. Curriculum Series number one. Proposals for a social studies curriculum.

A.002   **THE UNIT IN THE SOCIAL STUDIES.**

Cambridge: Harvard University, 1940, 108 pages. Paperback.   ***First Edition.***
Written with Harold M. Long. Harvard Workshop Series No. 1.
Published by the Graduate School of Education.

A.003   **TALES OF THE SOUTH PACIFIC.**

a   New York: Macmillan, 1947, 326 pages.   ***First Edition.***
Pulitzer Prize Winner, Michener's first published novel.

b   New York: Editions for the Armed Services, 1947/04, 448 pages. Paperback.

c   New York: [Literary Guild], [1947], 326 pages.
"Book Club Edition" noted at bottom of front dust jacket flap.

d   Rockefeller Center, N.Y.: Pocket Books, 1948/04, 312 pages.
Paperback. Abridged. Does not include *"Mutiny," "Our Heroine," "Dry Rot," "Passion,"* and *"The Airstrip at Konora."*

e   New York: Macmillan, 1950, 316 pages.
Limited Edition, Signed, 1500 copies, issued without dust jacket.
The American Bookseller's Association Golden Anniversary Edition.

f   London: Collins, 1951, 320 pages.

g   Sydney, Australia: Dymock's Book Arcade, 1951.

h   New York: Pocket Books, Cardinal Ed., 1957/04, 375 pages. Paperback.
The second printing has movie tie-in to "South Pacific," with photographs from the movie starring Mitzi Gaynor and Rossano Brazzi.

i   London: Collins, Fontana Books, 1958, Paperback.

j   London: Corgi Books, 1964, 351 pages. Paperback.

k   New York: Macmillan, [1967?], 325 pages. Large Print Edition.

l   New York: Bantam Books, 1967/12, 371 pages. Paperback.

m   Greenwich: Fawcett Crest, 1973/02, 384 pages. Paperback.

n   Franklin Center, Pa.: Franklin Library, 1975, 413 pages.
Illustrated by William F. Draper. Limited Edition. Leather bound.
Exclusively for subscribers to Pulitzer Prize Series. Pulitzer Prize winner for 1948.

Section A.II - First Printings and Subsequent Publications

o   Garden City: International Collectors Library, [1977?], 362 pages. Leather bound.

p   Boston: G. K. Hall, 1981, 635 pages. ISBN 0-8161-3263-1. Large Print Edition.

q   Franklin Center, Pa.: Franklin Library, 1982, 413 pages.
Illustrated by Dwight C. Shepler. Limited Edition. Leather bound.
Exclusively for subscribers to the Collected Stories of the World's Greatest Writers.

r   New York: Ballantine Books, 1983/03, 384 pages. Paperback. A later printing
erroneously indicates a first Ballantine printing date of 1984/11.

s   Franklin Center, Pa.: Franklin Library, 1986, 415 pages. Illustrated by Philippe
Weisbecker. Limited Edition. Leather bound. Exclusively for subscribers to The
Franklin Library of Pulitzer Prize Classics.

t   New York: Macmillan, 1986, 326 pages. ISBN 0-02-584540-3. Hudson River
Edition. A series of reprints of outstanding titles, classical works of fiction, etc.

u   New York: [Book-of-the-Month Club], [1990/10], 326 pages.
Special Edition. There are various BOMC editions. Some state BOMC on the
copyright page. Some have nothing. No price stated on dust jacket.

v   New York: [Book-of-the-Month Club], [1991/11], 326 pages.
HBC "World War II Issue." No price stated on dust jacket.

w   Pleasantville: Reader's Digest Association, 1995, 360 pages. ISBN 0-89577-697-9.
Illustrations by James Barkley. Afterword by Orville Prescott.

A.004   **THE FIRES OF SPRING.**

a   New York: Random House, 1949, 495 pages.   *First Edition*
Semi-autobiographical. Michener originally planned to title this
"The Homeward Journey."

b   New York: Random House, 1949, 495 pages.
Presentation Edition, issued without dust jacket.

c   New York: Bantam Books, 1951/04, 436 pages. Paperback. Bantam Giant Edition.

d   Sydney, Australia: Dymock's Book Arcade, 1952, 495 pages.

e   New York: Bantam Books, 1955/08, 436 pages. Paperback. Bantam Fifty Edition.

f   New York: Ballantine Books, 1960, 446 pages. Paperback.

g   London: Corgi Books, 1960, 446 pages. Paperback.

h   New York: Bantam Books, 1961/01, 436 pages. Paperback. Bantam Sixty Edition.

i   Greenwich: Fawcett Crest, 1972, 480 pages. LC 63-16152. Paperback.

j   London: Secker & Warburg, 1972, 495 pages.

k   New York: [Book-of-the-Month Club], [1978/12], 495 pages. BOMC Edition has a small square indentation at bottom right of back cover and the price is not stated on the dust jacket.

A.005   **RETURN TO PARADISE.**

a   New York: Random House, 1951, 437 pages.   *First Edition.*

b   New York: Random House, 1951, 437 pages.
Presentation Edition. Issued without dust jacket. "Presentation Edition" noted on front cover. Tipped-in limitation page precedes half-title page and states: "This is number [handwritten number] of a limited edition specially made for presentation to the Booksellers of America." The number distributed is unknown.

c   London: Secker & Warburg, 1951, 437 pages.

d   New York: [Book-of-the-Month Club], [1951/05], 437 pages.
Selection. BOMC editions may state "First Printing" on copyright page, but have a green dot at bottom right of back cover. Price not stated on dust jacket.

e   New York: Bantam Books, 1952/04, 499 pages. Paperback.
A Bantam Giant Edition.

f   Harmondsworth, Middlesex: Penguin Books, 1957, 372 pages. Paperback.

g   New York: Bantam Books, 1957/10, 371 pages.
Paperback. A Bantam Fifty Edition. The cover provides a tie-in for the movie, "*Until They Sail*," starring Paul Newman and Jean Simmons.

h   London: Corgi Books, 1967, 371 pages. Paperback.

i   Greenwich: Fawcett Crest, 1974/02, 416 pages. Paperback.

j   New York: Ballantine Books, 1982/07, 416 pages. Paperback.

k   London: Mandarin Paperbacks, 1993, 371 pages. Paperback.

A.006   **THE VOICE OF ASIA.**

a   New York: Random House, 1951, 338 pages.   *First Edition.*

b   New York: Bantam Books, 1951/11, 331 pages. Paperback. A Bantam Giant.
The Overseas Bantam Edition Published November, 1951 is the "1st [paperback] Printing......September, 1951"

c   Retitled **Voices of Asia**. London: Secker & Warburg, 1952, 291 pages.

d   New York: [Literary Guild], [1952/02], 245 pages. "Book Club Edition" noted at bottom of front dust jacket flap. Family Reading Club - Literary Guild edition.

e   New York: Bantam Books, 1952/10, 331 pages. Paperback. A Bantam Giant.
The Regular Bantam Edition Published November, 1951 is the "2nd [paperback] Printing.......September, 1952"

    f   Greenwich: Fawcett Crest, 1973. Paperback.

A.007   **THE BRIDGES AT TOKO-RI.**

    a   New York: Random House, 1953. Long galleys, printed on rectos only.

    b   New York: Random House, 1953, 150 pages. LC 52-7129.   *First Edition.*

    c   London: Secker & Warburg, 1953, 136 pages.

    d   London: Reader's Digest Association, 1954.

    e   New York: Bantam Books, 1955/12, 106 pages. Paperback.

    f   London: Viking Press, 1957, 157 pages. Paperback.

    g   New York: Globe Book Company, 1960, 176 pages.
           School Edition, photographs from the motion picture with William Holden,
           Grace Kelly, Mickey Rooney, and Frederick March.

    h   London: Bantam Books, 1962. Paperback.

    i   London: Corgi Books, 1963, 106 pages. Paperback.

    j   New York: Bantam Books, 1963/02, 106 pages. Paperback.
           Bantam Pathfinder Edition.

    k   Greenwich: Fawcett Crest, 1973/04, 126 pages. Paperback.

    l   Boston: G.K. Hall, 1981, 165 pages. ISBN 0-8161-3262-3. Large Print Edition.

    m   New York: Ballantine Books, 1982/06, 127 pages. Paperback.

    n   Norwalk: Easton Press, 1991, 147 pages. With a special introduction by Michener.
           Illustrated by Kent Bash. Collector's Edition. Leather bound.

    o   London: Mandarin Paperbacks, 1993, 136 pages. Paperback.

A.008   **SAYONARA.**

    a   New York: Random House, 1954, 245 pages. LC 54-5953.   *First Edition.*
           First published under title "Sayonara Means Goodbye," *McCalls*, 81:1
           (1953/10) 30-31; 81:2 (1953/11) 30-31; 81:3 (1953/12) 38-39.

    b   London: Secker & Warburg, 1954, 234 pages.

    c   New York: [Book-of-the-Month Club], [1954/02], 243 pages.
           Alternate Selection. Binding on BOMC edition is black and gray with Japanese
           characters and green print, with a gray dot at bottom right of back cover.

    d   Tokyo: Charles E. Tuttle, 1954/04, 245 pages. A special edition sold in Japan,
           Okinawa & Korea only. Photo offset reproduction of the first American edition.

e   New York: Bantam Books, 1955/03, 214 pages. Paperback. A Bantam Giant.

f   London: Corgi Books, 1957, 214 pages. Paperback.

g   New York: Bantam Books, 1957/08, 214 pages. Paperback. New Bantam Edition. Movie tie-in with picture of Marlon Brando on back of cover.

h   Greenwich: Fawcett Crest, 1974/04, 214 pages. ISBN 0-449-20414-6. Paperback.

i   Bath, England: Chivers, 1978, 349 pages. Large Print Edition. British.

j   Boston: G.K. Hall, 1981, 395 pages. ISBN 0-8161-3260-7. Large Print Edition.

k   New York: Ballantine Books, 1983/02, 208 pages. ISBN 0-449-20051-1. Paperback.

l   London: Mandarin Paperbacks, 1993, 234 pages. Paperback.

A.009   THE FLOATING WORLD.

a   New York: Random House, 1954, 404 pages. LC 54-7812.   ***First Edition.***

b   London: Secker & Warburg, 1955, 404 pages.

c   Honolulu: University of Hawaii Press, 1983/10, 471 pages. ISBN 0-8248-0873-8. Paperback. Commentary by Howard A. Link.

A.010   THE BRIDGE AT ANDAU.

a   New York: Random House, 1957, 273 pages. LC 57-8158.   ***First Edition.*** Also a selection of the Catholic Digest Book Club (1957/07), and the Christian Herald Family Bookshelf (1957/06).

b   London: Secker & Warburg, 1957, 259 pages.

c   New York: Random House, 1957, 271 pages. Special Deluxe Edition (noted on top front cover flap), with new foreword, with minor changes to the text, and photographs of escapees. Reddish-brown cloth binding. (It is believed that this edition was distributed by Book-of-the-Month Club.)

d   New York: Bantam Books, 1957/09, 241 pages. Paperback. A Bantam Giant.

e   London: Corgi Books, 1958, 254 pages. Paperback.

f   New York: Bantam Books, 1963, 241 pages. Paperback. A Bantam Pathfinder Edition.

g   Greenwich: Fawcett Crest, 1973/12, 224 pages. Paperback.

h   New York: Ballantine Books, 1983/11, 224 pages. Paperback.

Section A.II - First Printings and Subsequent Publications

A.011   **RASCALS IN PARADISE.**
Written with A. Grove Day.

a   New York: Random House, 1957, 376 pages. LC 57-5364.   *First Edition.*

b   New York: [Literary Guild], [1957?], 342 pages.

c   London: Secker & Warburg, 1957, 383 pages.

d   New York: Bantam Books, 1958/10, 325 pages. Paperback.

e   London: Corgi Books, 1960. Paperback.

f   Greenwich: Fawcett Crest, 1974/07, 384 pages. Paperback.

g   New York: Ballantine Books, 1983/04, 384 pages. ISBN 0-449-20441-3. Paperback.

h   London: Mandarin Paperbacks, 1993, 325 pages. Paperback.

A.012   **SELECTED WRITINGS OF JAMES A. MICHENER;**
With a Special Foreword by the author.

New York: Random House, Modern Library, 1957, 434 pages.   *First Edition.*
LC 57-6493. Includes selections from **"Tales of the South Pacific,"** **"Return to
Paradise,"** and **"The Voice of Asia,"** and **"The Bridges at Toko-ri"** in its entirety.

A.013   **THE HOKUSAI SKETCHBOOKS: SELECTIONS FROM THE MANGA.**

Tokyo: Charles E. Tuttle, 1958, 286 pages. LC 58-9983.   *First Edition.*
Edited by Michener. Based on the *"Hokusai Manga,"* or *"Hokusais Sketched
from Life."* Woodblock Prints (1814-78).

A.014   **HAWAII.**

a   New York: Random House, 1959. LC 59-10815. Uncorrected galley sheets printed
on recto only. Issued in spiral bound, printed, blue wraps.

b   New York: Random House, 1959, 949 pages. LC 59-10815   *First Edition.*

c   New York: Random House, 1959, 949 pages.
Limited Edition, Signed, in slipcase, 400 copies.

d   New York: [Book-of-the-Month Club], [1959/12], 937 pages. Selection.
BOMC editions may state "First Printing" on copyright page, but have a small
square at bottom right of back cover. No price stated on dust jacket.

e   London: Secker & Warburg, 1960, 1011 pages.

f   New York: Bantam Books, 1961/01, 905 pages. Paperback.

g   London: Corgi Books, 1962, 1138 pages. Paperback.

h   London: Bantam Books, 1962. Paperback.

Section A.II - First Printings and Subsequent Publications

i   New York: Knopf & Random House, n.d., 937 pages. Paperback. A Vintage Giant. Probably published in 1963 following "**Caravans**," but prior to "**The Source**."

j   New York: Random House, n.d., 937 pages. Paperback. Probably published in 1963 following "**Caravans**," but prior to "**The Source**."

k   New York: Bantam Books, 1966/09, 1130 pages. Paperback. New Bantam Edition. "Special Souvenir Edition" with 16 pages of color photographs from the movie.

l   Greenwich: Fawcett Crest, 1973/02, 1130 pages. LC 63-16152. Paperback.

m   New York: Ballantine Books, 1982/11, 1130 pages. Paperback.

n   Norwalk: Easton Press, 1988, 937 pages. With a special introduction by Michener. Illustrated by Richard Powers. Limited Edition. 5,000 sets. 2 volumes, leather bound.

o   **FROM THE BOUNDLESS DEEP.**
Wailea, Maui: Four Seasons Resort, [1989], 28 pages.
Paperback. Opening chapter from "**Hawaii**." A complimentary keepsake announcing the new resort. 80,000 copies, in slipcase, message card laid in.

p   **FROM THE BOUNDLESS DEEP.**
Wailea, Maui: Four Seasons Resort, [1989], 28 pages.
Same as A.014.o, but leather bound, for VIPs attending Resort opening ceremony.

q   London: Mandarin Paperbacks, 1993, 1139 pages. Paperback.

A.015   **JAPANESE PRINTS: FROM THE EARLY MASTERS TO THE MODERN.**

a   Tokyo: Charles E. Tuttle, 1959, 287 pages.   *First Edition.*
With notes on the Prints by Richard Douglas Lane. LC 59-10410.

b   Tokyo: Charles E. Tuttle, 1959, 287 pages. Limited Edition, 510 copies.

A.016   **REPORT OF THE COUNTY CHAIRMAN.**

a   New York: Random House, 1961, Uncorrected proof in spiral bound, printed wraps.

b   New York: Random House, 1961, 311 pages. LC 61-10872.   *First Edition.*

c   London: Secker & Warburg, 1961, 310 pages.

d   New York: Bantam Books, 1961/11, 214 pages. Paperback.

A.017   **THE MODERN JAPANESE PRINT: AN APPRECIATION.**
Illustrated.

a   Tokyo: Charles E. Tuttle, 1962, 55 pages. Limited Edition.   *First Edition.*
LC 62-17555.

b   Tokyo: Charles E. Tuttle, 1968, 57 pages.   *First Popular Edition.*
ISBN 0-8048-0405-2.

Section A.II - First Printings and Subsequent Publications

A.018   **CARAVANS.**

a   New York: Random House, 1963. Uncorrected galley sheet printed on rectos. Issued in spiral bound, printed, blue wraps.

b   New York: Random House, 1963. Uncorrected proof copies in tall gray wraps.

c   New York: Random House, 1963, 341 pages. LC 63-16152.   *First Edition.*

d   New York: Random House, 1963, 341 pages. Special autographed Edition for The First Edition Circle, with signature page tipped in. This edition is accompanied by a laid in card that reads: A FIRST EDITION, AUTOGRAPHED BY THE AUTHOR ESPECIALLY FOR THE MEMBERS OF THE FIRST EDITION CIRCLE KROCH'S & BRENTANO'S. THE WORLD'S LARGEST BOOKSTORE CHICAGO 3.

e   London: Companion Book Club, 1963.

f   New York: [Book-of-the-Month Club], [1963/08], 341 pages. Selection. BOMC edition has a small circle indentation at bottom right of back cover.

g   London: Secker & Warburg, 1964, 384 pages.

h   New York: Bantam Books, 1964/09, 370 pages. Paperback.

i   London: Corgi Books, 1966, 370 pages. Paperback.

j   New York: Bantam Books, 1968/10, 438 pages. Paperback. New Bantam Edition.

k   Greenwich: Fawcett Crest, 1973/09, 438 pages. Paperback.

l   Boston: G.K. Hall, 1981, 525 pages. ISBN 0-8161-32615-5. Large Print Edition.

m   New York: Ballantine Books, 1982/11, 438 pages. Paperback. Movie tie-in with picture of Anthony Quinn on front cover.

n   London: Mandarin Paperbacks, 1993, 370 pages. Paperback.

A.019   **THE SOURCE.**

a   New York: Random House, 1965, 916 pages. LC 65-11255.   *First Edition.*

b   New York: Random House, 1965, 916 pages. Limited Edition, Signed, in slipcase, 500 copies.

c   New York: Random House, 1965, 916 pages. Limited Edition. Signed. 300 copies were specially prepared from the first trade edition to benefit the Israeli Museum, Jerusalem. The limitation page is tipped in before the title page and the edition was issued before the trade edition.

d   London: Secker & Warburg, 1965, 913 pages.

e   New York: [Book-of-the-Month Club], [1965/06], 916 pages. Selection. BOMC edition has a small square indentation at bottom right corner of back cover.

Section A.II - First Printings and Subsequent Publications

f   London: Corgi Books, 1966, 1037 pages. Paperback.

g   London: The Reprint Society, 1966, 916 pages.

h   Greenwich: Fawcett Crest, 1967/01, 1088 pages. Paperback.

i   New York: Ballantine Books, 1983/04, 1088 pages. ISBN 0-449-20314-X. Paperback.

j   Norwalk: Easton Press, 1989, 909 pages. With a special introduction by Michener. Illustrated by Richard Sparks. Special Edition. 2 volumes, leather bound.

k   London: Mandarin Paperbacks, 1993, 1037 pages. Paperback.

A.020   **THE MATADOR WHO CONQUERED MEXICO.**

Oxford, England: College of Technology, 1965-66, 14 pages.   *First Edition.*
A project of A.C. Townsend, 5th year student. Illustrated by A.G. Walton.
Paperback. From "Mexico's Mild Mannered Matador," *Reader's Digest*, 79:471 (1961/07) 202-6.

A.021   **ADICKES, A PORTFOLIO WITH CRITIQUE.**

Houston: Dubose Gallery, 1968, 59 pages.   *First Edition.*
A critique of the artwork of David Adickes by James A. Michener. Also includes French commentary by Allesandra Cantey. 54 Plates by the Artist. 1000 copies.

A.022   **IBERIA: SPANISH TRAVELS AND REFLECTIONS.**

a   New York: Random House, 1968, 818 pages.   *First Edition.*
Photography by Robert Vavra. LC 67-22623.

b   New York: Random House, 1968, 818 pages. Limited Edition, Signed, special illustrated black and white dust wrapper and in slipcase, 500 copies.

c   London: Secker & Warburg, 1968, 818 pages.

d   New York: [Book-of-the-Month Club], [1968/05], 818 pages. Selection. BOMC edition has a small square indentation at bottom right corner of back cover.

e   London: Corgi Books, 1971, 818 pages. 2 volumes. Paperback.

f   Greenwich: Fawcett Crest, 1969/09, 960 pages. Paperback.

g   New York: Bantam Books, 1973. Paperback.

h   New York: Ballantine Books, 1982/11, 960 pages. Paperback.

A.023   **PRESIDENTIAL LOTTERY: THE RECKLESS GAMBLE IN OUR ELECTORAL SYSTEM.**

a   New York: Random House, 1969, 240 pages. LC 73-76278.   *First Edition.*

Section A.II - First Printings and Subsequent Publications

b   Lancaster, N.Y.: Associated Reprinting, 1969, 240 pages. Large Print Edition.

c   London: Secker & Warburg, 1969, 240 pages. Published under the title
"Presidential Lottery: The Reckless Gamble in the American Electoral System."

d   New York: [Book-of-the-Month Club], [1969/07], 240. Rec. Bk.

e   Greenwich: Fawcett World Library, 1969/11, 192 pages. Paperback.

f   Buffalo: Associated Reprinting, 1970, 240 pages. Large Print Edition.

g   London: Corgi Books, 1971, 190 pages. Paperback. Published under the title
"Presidential Lottery: The Reckless Gamble in the American Electoral System."

A.024   **AMERICA VS. AMERICA: THE REVOLUTION IN MIDDLE-CLASS
VALUES.**

a   New York: New American Library, 1969/04, 80 pages.   *First Edition.*
LC 69-18320. Paperback. First Printing, April, 1969, noted on copyright page.
Issued only in paperback. A Signet special broadside #6, P3819.

b   Tokyo: Nan'un-do, 1971. Paperback. Issued only in paperback. Text in English;
Preface and notes in Japanese.

A.025   **FACING EAST**

New York: Maecenas Press, Random House, 1970, 35 pages.   *First Edition.*
Text by James A. Michener. Original lithographs and woodcuts by Jack Levine.
Sketchbook by Jack Levine.

A.026   **THE QUALITY OF LIFE.**

a   Philadelphia: Girard Bank, 1970, 87 pages.   *First Edition.*
Paintings by James B. Wyeth. LC 71-116744. Commissioned by the Girard Bank of
Philadelphia for their 1969 annual report. In slipcase, with message card laid in.
The later trade edition includes a chapter titled "The Population Cancer,"
which was initially omitted by Michener from the Girard Bank edition.

b   Philadelphia: J.B. Lippincott, [1970]. Uncorrected proof in pad bound printed wraps.

c   Philadelphia: J.B. Lippincott, [1970], 127 pages.   *First Popular Edition.*
LC 76-129673. Longer and unillustrated. Also a selection of the Christian Herald
Family Bookshelf (1971/01). This edition includes a chapter titled "The Population
Cancer," which was intentionally omitted by Michener from the earlier private
printing. He states, "I foresee such a rapid increase of population throughout the world
that it must become like a cancer, multiplying fantastically and eating up all available
sustenance to no constructive purpose. If allowed to proceed unchecked, it has got to
produce catastrophe." (at pp. 91-92).

d   Philadelphia: J.B. Lippincott, [1970], 127 pages. "Third Printing" noted on copyright
page. "Second Printing" noted on bottom of front dust jacket flap.
Special Presentation Edition for the membership of the Million Dollar Round Table.
Inscription on the half-title page: "To the Membership of the Million Dollar Round

Table, whose life work is aimed at improving the quality of life of countless numbers of men, women and children throughout the world." James A. Michener

e Boston: G.K. Hall, 1971, 169 pages. Large Print Edition.

f London: Secker & Warburg, 1971, 127 pages.

g Greenwich: Fawcett Crest, 1971/07, 128 pages. Paperback.

h Tokyo: Kinseido, 1972. Paperback.
Text in English with introduction and notes in Japanese.

i London: Corgi Books, 1973, 184 pages. ISBN 0-552-11416-2. Paperback.

j Tokyo: Nan'un-do, n.d. Paperback. Text in English with foreword in Japanese.

A.027 **KENT STATE: WHAT HAPPENED AND WHY**.

a New York: Random House & Reader's Digest, 1971.
Uncorrected proof in spiral bound, printed wraps.

b New York: Random House & Reader's Digest, 1971, 563 pages.   *First Edition.*
ISBN 0-394-47199-7; LC 74-155822.

c London: Secker & Warburg, 1971, 563 pages.

d New York: [Book-of-the-Month Club], [1971/08], 563 pages. Alternate Selection.
BOMC edition may state "First Edition," but has a small square indentation at bottom of back cover.

e Greenwich: Fawcett Crest, 1971/11, 512 pages. ISBN 0-449-23869-5. Paperback.

f Reader's Digest Association, 1973, 65 pages.
Paperback. Reader's Digest Press Book. Reprinted from Reader's Digest, 98:588 (1971/04) 217-20. Kent State University seal embossed on cover.

g London: Corgi Books, 1973, 563 pages. Paperback.

h New York: Ballantine Books, 1982/10, 512 pages. ISBN 0-449-20273-9. Paperback.

A.028 **THE DRIFTERS.**

a New York: Random House, 1971. Uncorrected proof copy in printed green pad wraps.

b New York: Random House, 1971, 751 pages.   *First Edition.*
ISBN 0-394-46200-9; LC 75-117655.

c New York: Random House, 1971, 751 pages.
Limited Edition, Signed, in slipcase, 500 copies.

d London: Secker & Warburg, 1971, 751 pages. SBN 436 27957 6.

e Greenwich: Fawcett Crest, 1972/05, 768 pages. Paperback.

f   New York: [Book-of-the-Month Club], [1972/07], 751 pages.
Selection. BOMC edition has a small square indentation at bottom of back cover.

g   London: Corgi Books, 1972, 830 pages. ISBN 0-552-09240-1. Paperback.

h   New York: Ballantine Books, 1982/11, 768 pages. Paperback.

i   London: Mandarin Paperbacks, 1993, 830 pages. Paperback.

A.029   **A MICHENER MISCELLANY: 1950-1970.**

a   New York: Random House, 1973 "Uncorrected first proof" in printed red wraps. Copyright page blank. Titled "**Michener Miscellany: 1950-1970.**"

b   New York: Random House and Readers Digest Press, 1973.   *First Edition.*
404 pages. ISBN 0-394-47948-3; LC 72-10926. Ben Hibbs, editor.

c   London: Corgi Books, 1975, 383 pages. ISBN 0-552-09733-0. Paperback.

d   Greenwich: Fawcett Crest, 1975/08, 383 pages. Paperback.

A.030   **FIRSTFRUITS, A HARVEST OF TWENTY-FIVE YEARS OF ISRAELI WRITING.**

a   Philadelphia: The Jewish Publication Society of America, 1973.   *First Edition.*
347 pages. SBN 0-8276-0018-6; LC 72-14199. Edited by and with an introduction by James A. Michener at pages ix-xxv.

b   Greenwich: Fawcett Crest, 1974/07, 432 pages. Paperback.
Edited by and with an introduction by James A. Michener at pages 2-30.

A.031   **CENTENNIAL.**

a   New York: Random House, 1974. Uncorrected proof in pad bound, printed wraps.

b   New York: Random House, 1974, 909 pages.   *First Edition.*
ISBN 0-394-47970-X; LC 74-5164. Also a selection of Playboy Book Club.

c   New York: Random House, 1974, 909 pages. ISBN 0-394-49345-1.
Limited Edition, Signed, in slipcase, 500 copies.

d   London: Secker & Warburg, 1974, 909 pages.

e   New York: [Book-of-the-Month Club], [1974/09], 909 pages.
Selection. BOMC edition has a small indentation at bottom of back cover.

f   London: Corgi Books, 1975, 1100 pages. ISBN 0-552-09945-7. Paperback.

g   Greenwich: Fawcett Crest, 1975/11, 1086 pages. Paperback.

h   Leicester, England: Ulverscroft, 1976, 405 pages. Large Print Edition.
A condensed version by the Editors of Reader's Digest Condensed Books.

Section A.II - First Printings and Subsequent Publications

i   New York: Ballantine Books, 1983/06, 1086 pages. Paperback.

j   Norwalk: Easton Press, 1988, 909 pages. With a special introduction by Michener. Illustrated by Jeff Fisher. Limited Edition. 5,000 sets. 2 volumes, leather bound.

A.032   **ABOUT CENTENNIAL: SOME NOTES ON THE NOVEL.**

New York: Random House, 1974, 57 pages.   ***First Edition.***
ISBN 0-394-45937-3; LC 74-9770. 3200 copies printed for librarians and booksellers. None was offered for sale.

A.033   **THE MICHENER TRIO - THE DRIFTERS / THE SOURCE / HAWAII.**

New York: Random House, BOMC, 1974.   ***Special Collection.***
A specially bound three volume set with light and dark brown binding and without dust jackets. Later offered as part of a six volume set with A.039.

A.034   **SPORTS IN AMERICA.**

a   New York: Random House, n.d. Uncorrected proof in pad bound, red paper wraps.

b   New York: Random House, 1976, 466 pages.   ***First Edition.***
ISBN 0-394-40646-X; LC 75-40549.

c   New York: Random House, 1976, 466 pages. Limited Edition, 500 copies.
Black cloth boards with James A. Michener's signature and logo for the Copernicus Society of America embossed in gold on the front cover. The normal half-title page is replaced with a personal comment from Edward J. Piszek, President of Mrs. Paul's Kitchens, Inc., which explains that the book was conceived from the mutual interests and convictions of Piszek and Michener in Sports in America and a strong belief in their importance to our nation. A corporate cultural project of Mrs. Paul's Kitchens. This special presentation copy, without dust jacket or slipcase, was produced for and distributed to employees of Mrs. Paul's Kitchens, Inc.

d   Retitled **Michener on Sport**. London: Secker & Warburg, 1976, 466 pages.

e   New York: [Book-of-the-Month Club], [1976/09], 466 pages.
Featured Alternate and also SIBC selection.

f   Retitled **Michener on Sport**. London: Corgi Books, 1977, 635 pages. Paperback.

g   Greenwich: Fawcett Crest, 1977/06, 576 pages. ISBN 0-449-23204-2. Paperback.

h   New York: Ballantine Books, 1983/03, 576 pages. Paperback.

A.035   **JAMES A. MICHENER:**
              THE SOURCE, THE BRIDGES AT TOKO-RI, CARAVANS, SAYONARA.

London: Secker & Warburg/Octopus, 1976, 1113 pages.   ***Special Collection.***
ISBN 0-7064-0576-5. A collection of four reprints published in one volume.

Section A.II - First Printings and Subsequent Publications

A.036   **CHESAPEAKE.**

a   New York: Random House, 1978. Advance uncorrected proof, in red printed wraps.

b   New York: Random House, 1978, 865 pages.   *First Edition.*
ISBN 0-394-50079-2; LC 78-2892.

c   New York: Random House, 1978, 865 pages.
Limited Edition, Signed, in slipcase, 500 copies.

d   New York: Random House, 1978, 865 pages. ISBN 0-394-50312-0.
Deluxe Edition noted on copyright page. Red slipcase says Presentation Edition.
Navy boards with gold letters.

e   New York: Random House, 1978, 865 pages.
Deluxe Edition noted on copyright page. White slipcase. Navy boards with gold letters.

f   New York: Random House, 1978, 865 pages. It is believed that a special autographed
edition was prepared for The First Edition Circle, with signature page tipped in.
See note at A.018.d.

g   London: Secker & Warburg, 1978, 865 pages.

h   New York: [Book-of-the-Month Club], [1978/08], 865 pages. Selection.

i   London: Corgi Books, 1979, 1132 pages. ISBN 0-552-11320-4. Paperback.

j   New York: Ballantine Books, 1983/04, 1001 pages. Paperback.

k   Norwalk: Easton Press, 1989, 865 pages. With a special introduction by Michener.
Illustrated by Alan Phillips. Special Edition. 2 volumes, leather bound.

l   London: Mandarin Paperbacks, 1991, 1132 pages.
ISBN 0-7493-1162-2. Paperback.

m   Greenwich: Fawcett Crest, n.d., 1083 pages. Paperback.

A.037   **THREE FAMOUS BESTSELLERS.**

New York: Fawcett Crest, [1978/12?]. Paperback.   *Special Collection.*
A boxed set of three paperback works by James A. Michener. Includes
"The Source," **"Centennial,"** and **"Hawaii."**

A.038   **THE WATERMEN.**

a   New York: Random House, 1979, 193 pages.   *First Edition.*
Illustrated by John Moll. ISBN 0-394-50660-X; LC 79-14119.
Selections from **"Chesapeake."**

b   New York: [Book-of-the-Month Club], [1979/10], 193 pages. No price stated on dust
jacket. The BOMC edition may state "First Edition" on the copyright page.
No mark on back cover.

Section A.II - First Printings and Subsequent Publications

A.039 **MICHENER SET - SAYONARA / RETURN TO PARADISE / CARAVANS.**

New York: Random House, BOMC, 1979 pages. *Special Collection.*
A specially bound three volume set with light and dark brown binding and without
dust jackets. Later offered as part of a six volume set with A.033.

A.040 **THREE FAMOUS BESTSELLERS.**

New York: Fawcett Crest, [1979/11?]. Paperback. *Special Collection.*
Boxed set of three paperback works. **"Chesapeake," "Hawaii,."** and **"Centennial."**
Also includes "The Michener Note Pad."

A.041 **THE COVENANT.**

a Franklin Center, Pa.: Franklin Library, 1980, 1077 pages. *First Edition.*
With a special introduction by Michener to the members of THE FIRST EDITION
SOCIETY. Illustrated by Jerry Pinkney. Limited edition. Leather bound.

b New York: Random House, 1980. Uncorrected first proof in red printed wraps.

c New York: Random House, 1980, 873 pages. *First Trade Edition.*
ISBN 0-394-50505-0; LC 80-5315.
Book Club rights were sold to Literary Guild for $1,750,000.

d New York: Random House, 1980, 873 pages. ISBN 0-394-51400-9.
Limited Edition, Signed, in slipcase, 500 copies.

e London: Secker & Warburg, 1980, 881 pages.

f New York: [Literary Guild], [1980], 1125 pages.
2 volumes. "Book Club Edition" noted at bottom of front dust jacket flap.

g New York: [Literary Guild], 1980. Large Print Edition. 2 volumes.
"Book Club Edition" noted at bottom of front dust jacket flap.

h London: Corgi Books, 1981, 1086 pages. ISBN 0-552-11755-2. Paperback.

i New York: Fawcett Crest, 1982/03, 1238 pages. Illustrated by Lois Lowenstein.
ISBN 0-449-24474-1. Paperback.

j Garden City: International Collectors Library, [1983?], 976 pages.
Leather bound. 2 volumes.

k New York: Ballantine Books, 1987/02, 1238 pages. Paperback.
First Canadian Edition. (1984/02).

l Norwalk: Easton Press, 1990, 873 pages. With a special introduction by Michener.
Illustrated by Richard Sparks. Collector's Edition. 2 volumes, leather bound.

m London: Mandarin Paperbacks, 1992, 1087 pages. Paperback.

Section A.II - First Printings and Subsequent Publications

A.042   THE QUALITY OF LIFE, INCLUDING THE PRESIDENTIAL LOTTERY.

London: Corgi Books, 1980, 90 pages and 184 pages.   *Special Collection.*
ISBN 0-552-11416-2. Paperback.
This edition combines the two works previously published separately by Corgi.

A.043   SPACE.

a   New York: Random House, 1982. Uncorrected proof, in red printed paper wraps.

b   New York: Random House, 1982, 624 pages.   *First Edition.*
ISBN 0-394-50555-7; LC 82-40127.

c   New York: Random House, 1982, 624 pages. ISBN 0-394-52764-x.
Limited Edition, Signed, in slipcase, 500 copies.

d   New York: Random House, 1982, 624 pages.
Special leather bound autographed edition with signature page tipped in.

e   London: Secker & Warburg, 1982, 624 pages.

f   New York: [Book-of-the-Month Club], [1982/Fall], 622 pages.
Selection. BOMC edition has a small square indentation at bottom of back cover.

g   London: Corgi Books, 1983, 816 pages. ISBN 0-552-12283-1. Paperback.

h   New York: Ballantine Books, 1983/08, 808 pages. Paperback.
International Edition.

i   New York: Ballantine Books, 1983/11, 808 pages. Paperback. American Edition.
The sixth printing cover is a tie-in to the TV mini-series "Space."

j   Norwalk: Easton Press, 1990, 624 pages. With a special introduction by Michener.
Illustrated by Bob Eggleton. Collector's Edition. 2 volumes, leather bound.

k   London: Mandarin Paperbacks, 1992, 816 pages. Paperback.

A.044   COLLECTORS, FORGERS —AND A WRITER: A MEMOIR.

New York: Targ Editions, 1983, 64 pages.   *First Edition.*
Limited Edition, Signed, in slipcase.
May also be listed as "Book Collecting, Forgeries and Other Amenities."

A.045   POLAND.

a   New York: Random House, 1983. Uncorrected proof, in red printed wraps.

b   New York: Random House, 1983, 556 pages.   *First Edition.*
ISBN 0-394-53189-2; LC 83-4477.

c   New York: Random House, 1983, 556 pages. ISBN 0-394-53388.
Limited Edition, Signed, in slipcase, 500 copies.

Section A.II - First Printings and Subsequent Publications

d   New York: Random House, 1983, 556 pages. It is believed that a special autographed edition was prepared for The First Edition Circle, with signature page tipped in. See note at A.018.d.

e   Garden City: International Collectors Library, [1983?], 620 pages. Leather bound.

f   London: Secker & Warburg, 1983, 556 pages.

g   New York: [Literary Guild], [1983], 620 pages.
"Book Club Edition" noted at bottom of front dust jacket flap.

h   New York: [Literary Guild], [1983], 1330 pages. Large Print Edition. 2 volumes.
"Book Club Edition" noted at bottom of front dust jacket flap.

i   London: Corgi Books, 1984, 849 pages. ISBN 0-552-12461-3. Paperback.

j   Boston: G.K. Hall, 1984, 1016 pages. ISBN 0-8161-3689-0. Large Print Edition.

k   Boston: G.K. Hall, 1984, 1016 pages. ISBN 0-81-61-3728-5.
Paperback. Large Print edition.

l   New York: Ballantine Books, 1984/11, 617 pages. Paperback.

m   London: Mandarin Paperbacks, 1993, 849 pages. Paperback.

A.046   TESTIMONY.

Honolulu: White Knight Press, 1983, 19 pages.   *First Edition.*
Paperback. Limited Edition, 200 copies. The White Knight Press was the private press of A. Grove Day begun in 1940 at Stanford.

A.047   TEXAS.

a   New York: Random House, 1985. Uncorrected proof, in yellow printed wraps.

b   New York: Random House, 1985, 1096 pages.   *First Edition.*
ISBN 0-394-54154-5; LC 85-8248.

c   New York: Random House, 1985, 1096 pages.
ISBN 0-394-54154-5. Limited Edition, Signed, in slipcase, 1000 copies.

d   New York: Random House, 1985, 1096 pages. It is believed that a special autographed edition was prepared for The First Edition Circle, with signature page tipped in. See note at A.018.d.

e   London: Secker & Warburg, 1985, 1001 pages.

f   New York: [Literary Guild], [1985/10], 1096 pages. Bound in rust colored cordoba kid leather, title embossed in black, with Random House imprint. A special promotional edition offered to attract new members and also available to current members of the Literary Guild Book Club. Approximately 5,000 were printed.

g   New York: [Literary Guild], [1985], 1185 pages.
2 volumes. "Book Club Edition" noted at bottom of front dust jacket flap.

h   Austin: University of Texas Press, 1986. Illustrated by Charles Shaw.
ISBN 0-292-78071-0; LC 85-20383.
Sesquicentennial Edition produced specifically for presentation to those who make contributions of $2000 or more to the University of Texas Press Endowment. A two volume set in large quarto format bound in polished quarter half buffalo leather with gold stamping in publisher's full cloth slipcase. Accompanied by "Impressions of Texas" by Charles Shaw, (signed by the author on the title page), a bound volume of fourteen scenic color paintings illustrating regions of the state featured in "**Texas**." Limited Edition, Signed by Michener and Shaw, leather bound, 400 copies.

i   Austin: University of Texas Press, 1986, 943 pages. Illustrated by Charles Shaw.
ISBN 0-292-78071-0; LC 85-20383. Commemorative issue, 2 volumes,
9200 copies. Published on the occasion of the Texas Sesquicentennial.

j   London: Corgi Books, 1986, 1520 pages. ISBN 0-552-13089-3. Paperback.

k   New York: Ballantine Books, 1986/07, 1322 pages. Paperback.
International Edition.

l   New York: Ballantine Books, 1987/08, 1322 pages. ISBN 0-449-21092-8.
Paperback. American Edition.

m   Norwalk: Easton Press, 1992, 1096 pages. With a special introduction by Michener. Illustrated by Richard Sparks. Collector's Edition. 2 volumes, leather bound.

A.048   **LEGACY**.

a   New York: Random House, 1987. Uncorrected proof, in yellow printed wraps.

b   New York: Random House, 1987, 176 pages.   *First Edition.*
ISBN 0-394-56432-4; LC 87-42644.

c   New York: Random House, 1988, 176 pages. ISBN 0-394-56526-6.
Limited Edition, Signed, in slipcase, 500 copies.

d   London: Secker & Warburg, 1987, 181 pages.

e   New York: [Literary Guild], [1987], 176 pages.
"Book Club Edition" noted at bottom of front dust jacket flap.

f   New York: [Doubleday Large Print], [1987], 176 pages. Large Print Edition.

g   New York: Ballantine Books, 1988/04, 214 pages. Paperback. International Edition.

h   New York: Ballantine Books, 1988/09, 264 pages. ISBN 0-449-21641-1.
Paperback. American Edition. An addendum was added commemorating The Year of the Reader titled, *"The Book That Made a Difference."*

i   London: Corgi Books, 1988, 175 pages. ISBN 0-552-13391-4. Paperback.

j   Thorndike, Maine: Thorndike Press, n.d., 253 pages.
ISBN 0-89621-143-6; LC 88-2227. Large Print Edition.

k   Thorndike, Maine: Thorndike Press, n.d., 253 pages.
ISBN 0-89621-203-3; LC 88-2227. Paperback. Large Print Edition.

A.049   ALASKA.

a   New York: Random House, 1988. Uncorrected proof, in yellow printed wraps.

b   New York: Random House, 1988, 868 pages.   *First Edition.*
ISBN 0-394-55154-0; LC 87-43232.

c   New York: Random House, 1988, 868 pages. ISBN 0-394-56981-4.
Limited Edition, Signed, in slipcase, 1000 copies.

d   London: Secker & Warburg, 1988, 915 pages.

e   New York: [Book-of-the-Month Club], [1988/07], 868 pages. Selection.

f   London: Corgi Books, 1989, 1280 pages. ISBN 0-552-13394-9. Paperback.

g   New York: Ballantine Books, 1989/04, 1088 pages. Paperback.
International Edition.

h   New York: Ballantine Books, 1989/07, 1088 pages. ISBN 0-449-21726-4.
Paperback. American Edition.

i   Norwalk: Easton Press, 1992, 868 pages. With a special introduction by Michener.
Illustrated by Alan Phillips. Collector's Edition. 2 volumes, leather bound.

A.050   JOURNEY.

a   Toronto, Canada: McClelland and Stewart, 1988, 240 pages.   *First Edition.*
Illustrated by Mark Summers. ISBN 0-7710-5866-7. No additional printings noted.
The Canadian publication preceded the First American Edition by one year.

b   New York: Random House, 1989. Uncorrected proof, in yellow printed wraps.

c   New York: Random House, 1989, 244 pages.   *First American Edition.*
ISBN 0-394-57826-0; LC 88-43224.

d   London: Secker & Warburg, 1989, 240 pages.

e   London: Secker & Warburg/Mandarin, 1989, 304 pages. Paperback. Export Edition.

f   New York: [Literary Guild], [1989], 244 pages.
"Book Club Edition" noted at bottom of front dust jacket flap.

g   New York: [Doubleday Large Print], [1989], 244 pages.
ISBN 0-89621-635-6; LC 89-48690. Large Print Edition. Copyright page notes
"This Large Print Edition prepared especially for Doubleday Book & Music Clubs."

h   New York: [Book-of-the-Month Club], [1989/01], 176 pages.

i   Toronto, Canada: M & S Paperback, 1989/09, 240 pages.
ISBN 0-7710-5866-7. Paperback.

j   New York: Ballantine Books, 1989/11, 239 pages. ISBN 0-449-21893-7.
Paperback. International Edition.

k   London: Mandarin Paperbacks, 1990, 304 pages. Paperback.

l   Thorndike, Maine: Thorndike Press, 1990, 353 pages.
ISBN 0-89621-976-3; LC 89-48690. Paperback. Large Print Edition.

m   Thorndike, Maine: Thorndike Press, n.d., 353 pages. ISBN 0-89621-935-6;
LC 89-48690. Large Print Edition. Issued without dust jacket.

n   New York: Ballantine Books, 1994/11, 323 pages. ISBN 0-449-21847-3.
Paperback. American Edition.

A.051   **CARIBBEAN.**

a   New York: Random House, 1989, 669 pages.
Unrevised proof in yellow printed wraps.

b   New York: Random House, 1989, 673 pages.   *First Edition.*
ISBN 0-394-56561-4; LC 89-42785.

c   New York: Random House, 1989, 673 pages. ISBN 0-394-57655-1.
Limited Edition, Signed, in slipcase, 1000 Copies.

d   London: Secker & Warburg, 1989, 673 pages.

e   New York: [Book-of-the-Month Club], [1989/11-12], 673 pages. Split Selection.

f   New York: Ballantine Books, 1990/08, 811 pages. ISBN 0-449-21921-6
Paperback. International Edition.

g   New York: Ballantine Books, 1991/02, 811 pages. ISBN 0-449-21749-3.
Paperback. American Edition.

h   London: Mandarin Paperbacks, 1990, 944 pages. Paperback.

A.052   **SIX DAYS IN HAVANA.**

a   Austin: University of Texas Press, 1989, 144 pages.   *First Edition.*
ISBN 0-292-77629-2; LC 89-31091. Written with John Kings.

b   New York: [Literary Guild], [1989], 144 pages.

c   London: Souvenir Press, 1990, 144 pages.

Section A.II - First Printings and Subsequent Publications

A.053   **THE EAGLE AND THE RAVEN.**

    a   Austin: State House Press, 1990, 167 pages.
          Uncorrected proof, in blue printed wraps. 100 copies.

    b   Austin: State House Press, 1990, 214 pages.   *First Edition.*
          Illustrated by Charles Shaw. ISBN 0-938349-57-0; LC 90-9684.
          The first 5,000 copies, missing an accent mark over the word "Yucatán."

    c   Austin: State House Press, 1990, 214 pages. Limited Edition, Signed, in slipcase,
          350 copies.

    d   New York: [Literary Guild], [1990], 214 pages.
          Printing and binding by Edwards Brothers, Inc., Ann Arbor, Michigan.

    e   New York: [Doubleday Large Print], [1990], 212 pages. Large Print Edition.
          Copyright page notes "This Large Print Edition prepared especially for Doubleday
          Book & Music Clubs."

    f   London: Secker & Warburg, 1991, 196 pages.

    g   London: Mandarin Paperbacks, 1991, 196 pages. Paperback.

    h   New York: Tor Books, 1991/04, 230 pages. ISBN 0-812-51301-0. Paperback.

A.054   **PILGRIMAGE, A MEMOIR OF POLAND & ROME.**

    a   Emmaus, Pa.: Rodale Press, 1990, 119 pages. Paperback. Galley proof.

    b   Emmaus, Pa.: Rodale Press, 1990, 119 pages.   *First Edition.*
          ISBN 0-87857-910-9; LC 90-43039.

A.055   **JAMES A. MICHENER ON THE SOCIAL STUDIES.**

    Washington, D. C.: National Council for the Social Studies, 1991, 119 pages.
    ISBN 0-87986-060-X. Bulletin No. 85. A collection of Michener's education in
    publications of National Council for the Social Studies from 1938 to 1987, spanning
    almost fifty years in a single volume.   *Special Collection.*

A.056   **THE NOVEL.**

    a   New York: Random House, 1991. Uncorrected proof, in stiff glossy red,
          black, and white wraps.

    b   New York: Random House, 1991, 446 pages.   *First Edition.*
          ISBN 0-679-40133-4; LC 90-53489.

    c   New York: Random House Large Print, 1991, 704 pages. ISBN 0-679-40348-5.
          Large Print Edition.

    d   London: Secker & Warburg, 1991, 464 pages.

    e   New York: Ballantine Books, 1991/09, 435 pages. Paperback. International Edition.

f   New York: Ballantine Books, 1992/09, 435 pages. ISBN 0-449-22143-1.
Paperback. American Edition.

g   London: Mandarin Paperbacks, 1991, 464 pages. Paperback.

A.057   **THE WORLD IS MY HOME: A MEMOIR.**

a   New York: Random House, 1992. Advance uncorrected proof, in blue and white
glossy printed wraps.

b   New York: Random House, 1992, 520 pages.   *First Edition.*
ISBN 0-679-40134-2; LC 91-18447.

c   New York: Random House, 1992, 520 pages. ISBN 0-679-41118-6.
Limited Edition, Signed, in slipcase, 500 copies.

d   New York: Random House, 1992, 520 pages. Special Edition, commemorating
Michener's 85th birthday. Issued without dust jacket. Special maroon cloth binding.
On front cover, in gold print:. "J A M: Eighty-fifth birthday edition." On the special
dedication page, tipped in: "Presented in celebration of the eighty-fifth birthday of
James A. Michener February 3, 1992"

e   New York: Random House Large Print, 1992, 1062 pages.
ISBN 0-679-73981-5; LC 91-53203. Paperback. Large Print Edition.

f   London: Secker & Warburg, 1992.

g   New York: [Book-of-the-Month Club], [1992/01], 520 pages.
No price stated on dust jacket. No BOMC marking on rear cover.
No statement on copyright page of edition number.

h   London: Mandarin Paperbacks, 1992/12, 618 pages. SBN 0-7493-1303-X. Paperback.

i   London: Mandarin Paperbacks, n.d., 618 pages. SBN 0-7493-1493-1. Paperback.

A.058   **JAMES A. MICHENER'S WRITER'S HANDBOOK:
EXPLORATIONS IN WRITING AND PUBLISHING.**

a   New York: Random House, 1992, 182 pages.   *First Edition.*
ISBN 0-679-74126-7; LC 92-22120. Paperback. A guide for writers, editors, and
booklovers, Michener describes the many steps in creating a book.

b   New York: [Literary Guild], [1992], 182 pages. Literary Guild Edition is hard cover.

A.059   **SOUTH PACIFIC, as told by James Michener.**

a   San Diego, New York, London: Harcourt Brace Jovanovich,   *First Edition.*
1992, 64 pages. Illustrated by Michael Hague. ISBN 0-15-200618-4; LC 91-28934.
Based on Rodgers and Hammerstein's "South Pacific" as told by Michener.

b   San Diego, New York, London: Harcourt Brace Jovanovich, 1992, 64 pages.
ISBN 0-15-200615-X. Limited Edition, Signed, in slipcase, 250 copies.
Also signed by Hague.

Section A.II - First Printings and Subsequent Publications

A.060 **MEXICO.**

    a   New York: Random House, 1992. Advance uncorrected proof, in blue and white glossy printed wraps.

    b   New York: Random House, 1992, 626 pages.   *First Edition.*
        ISBN 0-679-41649-8; LC 92-50151.

    c   New York: Random House, 1992, 626 pages. ISBN 0-679-41844-X.
        Limited Edition, Signed, in slipcase, 400 copies.

    d   New York: Random House Large Print, 1992, 626 pages. ISBN 0-679-74329-4;
        LC 92-50238. Paperback. Large Print Edition.

    e   New York: Random House, 1992, [22 pages]. Paperback. A free sampler from
        Random House distributed through bookstores. Excerpt titled "American Ancestors:
        In Virginia."

    f   London: Secker & Warburg, 1992, 629 pages.

    g   London: Mandarin Paperbacks, 1993, 629 pages. Paperback.

    h   New York: Ballantine Books, 1993/06, 580 pages. ISBN 0-449-22237-3
        Paperback. International Edition.

    i   New York: Ballantine Books, 1994/04, 646 pages. ISBN 0-449-22187-3
        Paperback. American Edition.

A.061 **MY LOST MEXICO.**

    a   Austin: State House Press, 1992, 165 pages.
        Uncorrected proof, in white glossy wraps. 100 copies.

    b   Austin: State House Press, 1992, 165 pages.   *First Edition.*
        ISBN 0-938349-93-7; LC 92-26953.

    c   Austin: State House Press, 1992, 165 pages. ISBN 0-938349-94-5.
        Limited Edition, Signed, in slipcase, 350 copies.

    d   New York: Tor Books, 1993/12, 278 pages. ISBN 0-812-53437-9. Paperback.

A.062 **JAMES A. MICHENER, TWO COMPLETE NOVELS: ALASKA, HAWAII.**

        New York: Wings Books, 1993, 1539 pages.   *Special Collection.*
        ISBN 0-517-09151-8; LC 92-42529.

A.063 **CREATURES OF THE KINGDOM: STORIES OF ANIMALS AND NATURE**

    a   New York: Random House, 1993, 278 pages. Advance uncorrected proof, in blue
        and white glossy printed wraps.
        Originally sub-titled, "**Stories About Animals and Nature.**"

b New York: Random House, 1993, 283 pages.   *First Edition.*
Illustrated by Karen Jacobsen. ISBN 0-679-41367-7; LC 92-46075.
Sixteen tales of geological forces and man's relationship to the earth's creatures
excerpted from Michener's novels.

c London: Secker & Warburg, 1993, 282 pages.

d New York: [Book-of-the-Month Club], [1993/01], 283 pages. Selection.

e New York: Ballentine Books, 1995/09, 314 pages. ISBN 0-449-22092-3. Paperback.

A.064 **LITERARY REFLECTIONS: MICHENER ON MICHENER, HEMINGWAY, CAPOTE & OTHERS.**

a Austin: State House Press, 1993, 207 pages. Advance uncorrected proof.
Printed in black on a glossy white cover. 100 copies.

b Austin: State House Press, 1993, 213 pages.   *First Edition*
ISBN 1-880510-06-5; LC 93-32356. Includes reprints of rare earlier limited
printings, along with insightful commentaries on other authors.

c Austin: State House Press, 1993, 213 pages. ISBN 1-880510-07-3.
Limited Edition, Signed, in slipcase, 200 copies.

d New York: Forge Books, 1994/11, 290 pages. ISBN 0-812-55052-8. Paperback.

A.065 **JAMES A. MICHENER'S AMERICANA.**

New York: Fawcett Crest, [1993/11]. Paperback.   *Special Collection.*
Collectors' Edition boxed set of three paperback works: **"Texas," "Alaska,"**
and **"Chesapeake."**

A.066 **RECESSIONAL: A NOVEL.**

a New York: Random House, 1994, 482 pages. Advance uncorrected proof, in blue
and white glossy printed wraps.

b Franklin Center, Pa.: Franklin Library, 1994, 487 pages.   *First Edition.*
With a special message by Michener for the members of THE SIGNED FIRST
EDITION SOCIETY.
Illustrated by Franca Nucci Haynes with special frontis piece by Rafal Olbinski.
Limited Edition, Signed, leather bound, 2300 copies.

c New York: Random House, 1994, 486 pages.   *First Trade Edition.*
ISBN 0-679-43612-X; LC 94-17414.
A story about aging in a Florida retirement community.

d New York: Random House, 1994, 486 pages.
ISBN 0-679-43828-9. Limited Edition, Signed, in slipcase, 500 copies.

e New York: [Book-of-the-Month Club], 1994, 486 pages.

Section A.II - First Printings and Subsequent Publications

f   New York: Random House Large Print, 1994, 792 pages.
ISBN 0-679-75691-4; 94-3780. Paperback. Large Print Edition.

g   New York: Ballantine Books, 1995/04. Paperback. International edition.

h   New York: Ballantine Books, 1995/12, 522 pages. ISBN 0-449-22345-0. Paperback.
First Domestic Edition.

A.067   **WILLIAM PENN.**

    [Morrisville, Penn.]: The Pennsbury Society, 1994, 20 pages.   ***First Edition.***
Illustrated by Violet Oakley. Paperback. 2500 copies.
Tract donated to the Pennsbury Society to commemorate the 350th birthday
of the first governor and proprietor of Pennsylvania.

A.068   **MIRACLE IN SEVILLE.**

a   New York: Random House, 1995, 88 pages. Advance uncorrected proof,
in blue and white glossy printed wraps.

b   New York: Random House. 1995, 118 pages.   ***First Edition.***
Illustrated by John Fulton. ISBN 0-679-41822-9; LC 94-10187. An American
journalist covers a rancher's efforts to revive his once proud line of bulls, the
tribulations of the bullfighter, and a miracle in Seville.

c   New York: Random House. 1995, 118 pages.
Limited edition, Signed, in slipcase, 500 copies. ISBN 0-679-44385-1.

d   Seville: Ultra deluxe edition of 100 numbered and 26 lettered copies will be
privately published for distribution.

e   New York: Random House Large Print, 1995, 183 pages.
ISBN 0-679-76510-7.

A.069   **VENTURES IN EDITING.**

a   Huntington Beach, Cal.: James Cahill Publishing, 1995, 95 pages.
Proof. 50 copies

b   Huntington Beach, Cal.: James Cahill Publishing, 1995, 95 pages.   ***First Edition.***
Limited Edition, Signed, in slipcase. 26 lettered copies, 148 numbered
copies. The signature page indicates that 274 numbered copies were
published. In fact, Michener only signed 148 numbered copies.

Through a

Quaker Archway

A Treasury of *

Contemporary Quaker Writings

Among the Contributors

Fritz Eichenberg	Christopher Morley
Herbert Hoover	Richard M. Nixon
James A. Michener	Nora Waln
Jessamyn West	

Edited by

HORACE MATHER LIPPINCOTT

B.
Contributions to Anthologies, Collections, and Books

"I never ask if a meal is well cooked. I'm interested in only one thing: is there enough of it?"

–James A. Michener
BUCKS (THE ARTISTS' COUNTY) COOKS, 1950

FIVE BRILLIANT ESSAYS ON THE ARTS IN RENEWAL

- **LEWIS MUMFORD**

  From Revolt to Renewal

- **PETER VIERECK**

  Beyond Revolt: The Education of a Poet

- **WILLIAM SCHUMAN**

  On Freedom in Music

- **JAMES A. MICHENER**

  The Conscience of the Contemporary Novel

- **MARC CONNELLY**

  The Old Theatre and the New Challenge

THE ARTS
IN RENEWAL

Edited by
SCULLEY BRADLEY

The Arts in Renewal. B.007.

Section B - Contributions to Anthologies, Collections, and Books

B.001   **THE NEW HIGH SCHOOL IN THE MAKING.**
Wrinkle, William L.; Contribution by James A. Michener. New York: American
Book Company, 1938, pp. 49-76. The acknowledgments state that James Michener
assisted in the preparations of the materials in the chapter on social studies.

B.002   **THE UTILIZATION OF COMMUNITY RESOURCES IN THE SOCIAL
STUDIES.**
(*"PARTICIPATION IN COMMUNITY SURVEYS AS SOCIAL EDUCATION"*).
West, Ruth, ed.; Contribution by James A. Michener. Cambridge: National Council
for Social Studies, 1938, pp. 144-63. 9th Yearbook. American education should
train for citizenship in a democracy. Student surveys of local problems can teach it.

B.003   **THE IN-SERVICE GROWTH OF SOCIAL STUDIES TEACHERS.**
(*"THE BEGINNING TEACHER"*).
Phillips, Burr W., ed.; Contribution by James A. Michener. Cambridge: National
Council for Social Studies, 1939, pp. 1-37. 10th Yearbook. Michener analyzes the
criteria that identify the potentially successful beginning teachers.

B.004   **A TREASURY OF SEA STORIES.** (*"THE LANDING ON KURALEI"*).
Aymar, Gordon C., comp.; Contribution by James A. Michener. Illustrated by
Rockwell Kent. New York: A. S. Barnes, 1948, pp. 1-17.
Excerpt from "**Tales of the South Pacific.**"

B.005   **BUCKS (THE ARTIST'S COUNTY) COOKS; A GOURMET'S
GUIDE TO ESTIMABLE COMESTIBLES WITH PICTURES.**
Solebury: Trinity Chapel, 1950, p. 60.
Paperback. Prepared by the Women's Auxiliary of Trinity Chapel, Solebury,
Pennsylvania. Michener is quoted and his signature is reproduced.

B.006   **THE WRITER'S BOOK.**
(*"THE CHANCES AGAINST THE BEGINNING WRITER"*).
Hull, Helen, ed.; Contribution by James A. Michener. Michener illustrates the
mathematical odds against getting a first novel published.

    a   New York: Harper & Brothers, 1950, pp. 102-10. Presented by the Authors Guild.

    b   New York: Barnes & Noble, 1956, pp. 102-10. Paperback. Everyday Handbooks,
presented by the Author's Guild.

B.007   **THE ARTS IN RENEWAL.**
(*"THE CONSCIENCE OF THE CONTEMPORARY NOVEL"*).
Bradley, Sculley, ed.; Contribution by James A. Michener.
Essays on renewal in the Arts. Includes essays by Michener, Lewis Mumford,
Peter Viereck, William Schuman, and Marc Connelly.

    a   Philadelphia: University of Pennsylvania Press, 1951, pp. 107-40.

    b   New York: A. S. Barnes and Company, 1961, pp. 107-40. Paperback.

B.008   **THE FIRESIDE BOOK OF FLYING STORIES.** (*"THE MILK RUN"*).
Jensen, Paul, ed.; Contribution by James A. Michener. New York: Simon
& Schuster, 1951, pp. 305-12. Excerpt from "**Tales of the South Pacific.**"

Section B - Contributions to Anthologies, Collections, and Books

B.009   **READER'S DIGEST CONDENSED BOOKS**. (*"RETURN TO PARADISE"*).
Contribution by James A. Michener. Pleasantville: Reader's Digest
Association, 1951, pp. 72-219. Condensed from "**Return to Paradise**."

B.010   **AN AMERICAN RHETORIC**.
Watt, William W.; Contribution by James A. Michener.
Illustrates Michener's use of punctuation in "**Tales of the South Pacific**."

   a   New York, Toronto: Rinehart & Company, 1952, pp. 129, 175, 193.

   b   **Revised Ed.** New York: Rinehart & Company, 1957, pp. 201, 220.

   c   **3RD ED.** New York: Holt, Rinehart and Winston, 1964.

   d   **4TH ED**. New York: Holt, Rinehart and Winston, 1970, pp. 105, 397-98.

   e   **5TH ED**. Fort Worth: Holt, Rinehart and Winston, 1980, p. 81. Paperback.

B.011   **THE BEDSIDE CORONET**. (*"THE PERFECT TEACHER"*).
Contribution by James A. Michener. New York: Doubleday, 1952, pp. 191-95.
The best of *Coronet* in a single volume, selected by the editors of Coronet.
Also in *Coronet*, 30:2 (1951/06) 21-24.

B.012   **OUTSIDE READINGS IN AMERICAN GOVERNMENT**.
(*"BLUNT TRUTHS ABOUT ASIA"*).
MacDonald, H. Malcolm, ed.; Contribution by James A. Michener. New York:
Crowell, 1952, pp. 845-60. Also in *Reader's Digest*, 59:353 (1951/09) 73-78; and
Life, 30:23 (1951/06/04) 96-100. Michener recognized that "Never in our national
history have we been so feared and despised as we are in Asia." Failure to develop a
knowledgeable and working relationship with this overly populated gargantua could
spell doom for Americans in the future.

B.013   **READINGS FOR OPINION**. (*"IDEALISM TODAY"*).
Davis, Earle, and William C. Hummer, eds.; Contribution by James A. Michener.
Michener concludes that the future decency of the world rests largely in the hands of
English teachers. "Literature must keep alive the sparks of idealism, human decency,
hope, belief in a better world, and dedication to the goodness of mankind." Also in
High Points, 31 (1949/05) 13-21; and *Education Digest*, 15:4 (1949/12) 44-47.

   a   New York: Prentice-Hall, 1952, pp. 34-39.

   b   **2D ED.** New York: Prentice-Hall, 1960, pp. 252-59.

B.014   **THE ESQUIRE TREASURY.** (*"THE PRECIOUS DROP"*).
Gingrich, Arnold, ed.; Contribution by James A. Michener.
New York: Simon & Schuster, 1953, pp. 228-41.

B.015   **READER'S DIGEST CONDENSED BOOKS**. (*"THE BRIDGES AT TOKO-RI"*).
Contribution by James A. Michener. Pleasantville: Reader's Digest Association,
1953, pp. 6-83. From "**The Bridges at Toko-ri**."

Section B - Contributions to Anthologies, Collections, and Books

B.016   **A RHETORIC CASE BOOK**. (*"A JAPANESE HOME"*).
Connolly, Francis, ed.; Contribution by James A. Michener.

    a   New York: Harcourt, Brace, 1953, pp. 556-62.

    b   **2D ED.** New York: Harcourt, Brace, 1959, pp. 594-600.

B.017   **SATURDAY REVIEW READER 2.** (*"PORTRAITS FOR THE FUTURE"*).
Contribution by James A. Michener. New York: Bantam Books, 1953, pp. 122-33.
Paperback. Reprinted from *Saturday Review of Literature*, 34:31 (1951/08/04) 19-21.

B.018   **BEST-IN-BOOKS**. (*"THE BRIDGES AT TOKO-RI"*).
Contribution by James A. Michener. Garden City: Nelson Doubleday, 1954,
pp. 5-95. Includes works by Mary Roberts Rinehart, Daphne du Maurier, A. J.
Cronin, J. Y. Cousteau, George Sixta, and de Maupassant.

B.019   **BOOKS ABRIDGED**. (*"SAYONARA"*).
Contribution by James A. Michener. New York: Books Abridged, 1954, pp. 5-142.
Includes works by Theodore H. White, Jule Mannix, and Jessamyn West.

B.020   **SIDEWALKS OF AMERICA**. (*"HOSPITALITY AT WHITEMARSH HALL"* AND
"CHANGES ALONG PHILADELPHIA'S MAIN LINE").
Botkin, B. A., ed.; Contribution by James A. Michener. Indianapolis:
Bobbs-Merrill, 1954, pp. 414-15, 548-52.

B.021   **THIS I BELIEVE: 2**. (*"A SHAMELESS OLD WOMAN"*).
Swing, Raymond, ed.; Contribution by James A. Michener.
Book written for, and with a foreword by, Edward R. Murrow.
Retitled "This I Believe," *Reader's Digest*, 65:387 (1954/07) 143.

    a   New York: Simon & Schuster, 1954, pp. 96-97.

    b   New York: Simon & Schuster, 1954, pp. 96-97. Paperback.

B.022   **GREAT STORIES OF THE SOUTH SEA ISLANDS**. (*"A BOAR'S TOOTH"*).
Stead, Christina, ed.; Contribution by James A. Michener.
Excerpt from **"Tales of the South Pacific."**

    a   London: F. Muller, 1955, pp. 163-85.

    b   New York: Saunders, Otley, 1956.

B.023   **ADVENTURES IN MODERN LITERATURE.** (*"WHAT I LEARNED"*).
Freier, Robert, Arnold Leslie Lazarus, and Herbert Potell, eds.;
Contribution by James A. Michener. Excerpt from **"Return to Paradise."**

    a   **4TH ED.** New York, Chicago: Harcourt, Brace, 1956, pp. 476-81.

    b   **5TH ED**. New York: Harcourt, Brace & World, 1962, pp. 502-7.

B.024   **THE LADIES' HOME JOURNAL TREASURY.** (*"MR. MORGAN"*).
Contribution by James A. Michener. New York: Simon & Schuster, 1956, pp. 381-92.
Excerpt from **"Return to Paradise."**

Section B - Contributions to Anthologies, Collections, and Books

B.025 **THE MARYKNOLL GOLDEN BOOK: AN ANTHOLOGY OF MISSION LITERATURE.** (*"PORTRAITS FOR THE FUTURE," "THE NEW MEM-SAHIBS"*). Nevins, Albert J., ed.; Contributions by James A. Michener. New York: Book Treasures, 1956, pp. 244-54, 315-21. Slipcase. LC 56-6277. Excerpt from **"The Voice of Asia."** Also in *Saturday Review of Literature*, 34:31 (1951/08/04) 19-21.

B.026 **THE BEST SHORT STORIES OF WORLD WAR II.** (*"THE AIRSTRIP AT KONORA"*). Fenton, Charles A., ed.; Contribution by James A. Michener. New York: Viking Press, 1957, pp. 189-214. Excerpt from **"Tales of the South Pacific."** A collection of wartime experiences by twenty authors.

B.027 **BEST-IN-BOOKS.** (*"RASCALS IN PARADISE"*). Contribution by James A. Michener and A. Grove Day. Garden City: Nelson Doubleday, 1957, pp. 421-74. Includes works by Ernest Gann, Helen and Frank Schreider, Roske and Van Doren, and Richard Joseph.

B.028 **BEST-IN-BOOKS.** (*"THIS GREAT BIG WONDERFUL WORLD"*). Contribution by James A. Michener. Garden City: Doubleday, 1957, pp. 449-59. Originally appeared in *Holiday*, 19:3 (1956/03) 40-51. Excerpt appears in *Travel Holiday*, 174:2 (1991/02) 118, retitled "Home at Last."

B.029 **READING FOR PLEASURE.** (*"MR. MORGAN"*). Cerf, Bennett, ed.; Contribution by James A. Michener. New York: Harper, 1957, pp. 287-306. Excerpt from **"Return to Paradise."**

B.030 **COLLEGE READING. 2D ED.** (*"THE BRIDGES AT TOKO-RI"*). Sanderlin, George, ed.; Contribution by James A. Michener. Boston: D. C. Heath, 1958, pp. 1024-42. A collection of prose, plays, and poetry. From **"The Bridges at Toko-ri."**

B.031 **MID-CENTURY, AN ANTHOLOGY OF DISTINGUISHED CONTEMPORARY AMERICAN SHORT STORIES.** (*"THE CAVE"*). Prescott, Orville, ed.; Contribution by James A. Michener. New York: Pocket Books, 1958, pp. 289-320. LC 57-11177. Paperback. Excerpt from **"Tales of the South Pacific."**

B.032 **READING FOR UNDERSTANDING.** (*"A VISIT TO A JAPANESE HOME"*). MacNamee, Maurice B.; Contribution by James A. Michener. New York: Rinehart, 1958, pp. 352-56.

B.033 **READING-FOR-MEN.** (*"THE GLOBE MUTINEERS"*). Contribution by James A. Michener and A. Grove Day. Garden City: Nelson Doubleday, 1958, pp. 81-115. The story of 'Heaven Forsaken' Samuel Comstock. Excerpt from **"Rascals in Paradise."**

B.034 **ROUND THE WORLD WITH FAMOUS AUTHORS.** (*"KYOTO, THE BOSTON OF JAPAN," "PAGEANT OF HISTORY," AND "FIJIAN STAGE SETTING."*) Contribution by James A. Michener. Garden City: Doubleday, 1958, pp. 129, 141, 152. Introduction by Lowell Thomas. Reprinted from *Holiday*. "Japan," 12:2 (1952/08) 26-41; "New Zealand," 9:1 (1951/01) 44-47; and "Fiji," 7:6 (1950/06) 60-63.

Section B - Contributions to Anthologies, Collections, and Books

B.035 **THE AIR FORCE BLUE BOOK.** (*"WHILE OTHERS SLEEP"*).
Compere, Tom, ed.; Contribution by James A. Michener. A condensed version
of the article in *Reader's Digest*, 71:426 (1957/10) 68-75. Michener relates his first-
hand review of SAC bases, SAC airplanes and SAC pilots. He concludes that Soviet
knowledge of SAC capabilities is desirable as a deterrent to Soviet aggression.

  a New York: Military Publishing Institute, 1959, pp. 50-64. LC 59-10069. Paperback.

  b New York: Bobbs-Merrill, 1959, pp. 50-64. LC 59-10069.
Deluxe edition. Printed subsequent to the paperback edition.

B.036 **A NEW TREASURY OF WORDS TO LIVE BY.** (*"BOLDNESS"*).
Nichols, William, ed.; Contribution by James A. Michener. New York:
Simon & Schuster, 1959, pp. 96-97. Michener examines successful people and
concludes they are like the turtle which never progresses unless he sticks out his neck.

B.037 **READER'S DIGEST CONDENSED BOOKS.** (*"WEST WIND TO HAWAII"*).
Contribution by James A. Michener. Pleasantville: Reader's Digest Association,
1959, pp. 6-79. Excerpt from **"Hawaii."**

B.038 **THROUGH A QUAKER ARCHWAY.** (*"SOME PRACTICAL APPLICATIONS"*).
Lippincott, Horace Mather, ed.; Contribution by James A. Michener.
New York: T. Yoseloff, 1959, pp. 61-75. "...the truth is that works and faith are
interacting elements in the religious experience." Lack of either dooms a religion.

B.039 **A BEST-IN-BOOKS SPECIAL - OUTSTANDING BOOKS OF 'THE
FASCINATING FIFTIES.'** (*"UNTIL THEY SAIL"*).
Contribution by James A. Michener. Garden City: Nelson Doubleday,
1960, pp. 653-701. Excerpt from **"Return to Paradise."**

B.040 **FIFTY MODERN STORIES.** (*"DRY ROT"*).
Blair, Thomas M. H., ed.; Contribution by James A. Michener.
Excerpt from **"Tales of the South Pacific."**

  a Evanston, Elmsford: Row, Peterson, 1960, pp. 418-29.

  b New York: Harper & Row, n.d., pp. 418-29. Paperback.

B.041 **READER'S DIGEST CONDENSED BOOKS.**
(*"FROM THE FARM OF BITTERNESS TO THE PAGAN ISLES"*).
Contribution by James A. Michener. Pleasantville: Reader's Digest Assoc., 1960,
pp. 82-224. Excerpt from **"Hawaii."** Illustration and sketch of the author at page 225.

B.042 **OFFICIAL INAUGURAL PROGRAM.** (*"SALUTE TO THE NEW STATES"*).
Contribution by James A. Michener. Washington, D.C.: Kennedy-Johnson Inaugural
Committee, 1961. A 64 page program with contributions by John F. Kennedy, Robert
Frost, Michener, et al. Publication and sale of the Inaugural program for $1.25 was
reported in the *New York Times*, (1960/12/26) 14. This was also included in a special
hardcover limited edition prepared for VIPs, with the inaugural address and photos.

Section B - Contributions to Anthologies, Collections, and Books

B.043 **BEST SELLERS FROM READER'S DIGEST CONDENSED BOOKS.**
(*"WEST WIND TO HAWAII" AND "FROM THE FARM OF BITTERNESS"*).
Contributions by James A. Michener. Pleasantville: Reader's Digest Association,
1961, pp. 4-75, 76-207. Excerpts from "**Hawaii.**"

B.044 **THE READER'S DIGEST 40TH ANNIVERSARY TREASURY.**
(*"WHY I LIKE JAPAN"*).
Contribution by James A. Michener. Pleasantville: Reader's Digest Association,
1961, pp. 380-86.

B.045 **PULITZER PRIZE READER.** (*"THE MILK RUN"*).
Hamalian, Leo, and L. Volve Edmond, eds.; Contribution by James A. Michener.
New York: Popular Library, 1961/05, pp. 206-12. LC 61-9791.
Paperback. Excerpt from "**Tales of The South Pacific.**"

B.046 **THE RHETORIC READER.** (*"SOHAN LAL"*).
Talmadge, John Erwin; Contribution by James A. Michener. Chicago: Scott,
Foresman, 1962, pp. 253-54. Reprinted from *Saturday Review of Literature*, 34:31
(1951/08/04) 19-22, titled "Portraits for the Future."

B.047 **ADVENTURES IN READING.** (*"HAWAII"*).
Lodge, Evan, and Marjorie Braymer, eds.; Contribution by James A. Michener.
New York: Harcourt, Brace and World, 1963, pp. 173-79.
Abridged from a magazine article in *Holiday*, 13:5 (1953/05) 34-45, 88-95.
Also in *Reader's Digest*, 63:376 (1953/08) 102-7.

B.048 **BEST-IN-BOOKS.** (*"TALES OF THE SOUTH PACIFIC"*).
Contribution by James A. Michener. Garden City: Nelson Doubleday,
1963, pp. 649-97. Includes works by Robert Penn Warren, John Hersey,
Charles A. Lindbergh, Edward William Bok, and Robert Lewis Taylor.

B.049 **BEST SOUTH SEA STORIES.** (*"MUTINY"*).
Day, A. Grove, and Carl Stroven, eds.; Contribution by James A. Michener.
Excerpt from "**Tales of the South Pacific.**"

    a   New York: Appleton-Century, 1964, pp. 107-33.

    b   New York: Popular Library, 1964/02, pp. 111-36. Paperback.

    c   Honolulu: Mutual Publishing, n.d., pp. 107-33. Paperback.

B.050 **READING, WRITING, AND REWRITING: A RHETORIC READER.**
Moynihan, William T., Donald W. Lee, and Herbert Weil, Jr., eds.; Contribution by
James A. Michener. Philadelphia, New York: J. B. Lippincott, 1964, p. 181. Illustrates
Michener's use of figurative language in "**Tales of the South Pacific.**"

B.051 **SWARTHMORE REMEMBERED.** (*"SWAT'MORE COLLITCH"*).
Gillespie, Maralyn Orbison, ed.; Contribution by James A. Michener.
Swarthmore: Swarthmore College, 1964, pp. 79-85. Paperback. Thirty-nine alumni
recollect college experiences in this centennial year publication by the college.

Section B - Contributions to Anthologies, Collections, and Books

B.052   **THE BEST OF BEST-IN-BOOKS.** (*"THE BRIDGES AT TOKO-RI"*).
Contribution by James A. Michener. Garden City: Nelson Doubleday, 1965,
pp. 81-148. Includes works by Jim Bishop, Graham Greene, W. S. Maugham,
Ernest Hemingway, Jean Kerr, Irving Stone, and Bruce Catton.

B.053   **HOW TO LIVE WITH LIFE.**
("NEVER STOP LEARNING" and "ALL MEN ARE MY BROTHERS").
Contribution by James A. Michener. Pleasantville: Reader's Digest Association,
1965, pp. 179-82, 566-67. "Never Stop Learning" is condensed from Michener's
address delivered to Macalester College. "All Men Are My Brothers" is condensed
from a statement for Edward R. Murrow's series of radio broadcasts.

B.054   **MODERN COMPOSITION 6.**
Stegner, Dr. Wallace E., Dr. Edwin H. Sauer, Clarence W. Hatch, and Dr. Raven
McDavid, eds.; Contribution by James A. Michener. Chicago: Holt, Rinehart and
Winston, 1965, p. 392. Quotes **"Tales of the South Pacific,"** and illustrates the use
of incomplete sentences in literary description.

B.055   **READER'S DIGEST CONDENSED BOOKS.** (*"THE SOURCE"*).
Contribution by James A. Michener. Pleasantville: Reader's Digest
Association, 1965, pp. 239-389. Excerpt from **"The Source."**

B.056   **BEST SELLERS FROM READER'S DIGEST CONDENSED BOOKS.**
("THE SOURCE").
Contribution by James A. Michener. Pleasantville: Reader's Digest
Association, 1966, pp. 4-147. Includes major episodes from **"The Source."**

B.057   **FOUR COMPLETE TRUE ADVENTURES.** (*"THE BRIDGE AT ANDAU"*).
Nunn, Jesse Alford, comp.; Contribution by James A. Michener. New
York: Globe Book Company, 1966, pp. 477-756.
Also includes works by R. J. Donovan, E. Rickenbacker, and L. Stowe.

B.058   **TRUE TALES OF THE SOUTH SEAS.** (*"THE GLOBE MUTINEERS"*).
Day, A. Grove, and Carl Stroven, eds.; Contribution by James A. Michener
and A. Grove Day.

    a   New York: Appleton-Century, 1966, pp. 193-236.

    b   London: Souvenir Press, 1967, pp. 193-236.

    c   Retitled **"TRUE TALES OF HAWAII AND THE SOUTH SEAS."** Honolulu:
Mutual Publishing, 1993, pp. 193-236. Paperback.

B.059   **24 GREAT BOOKS FROM READER'S DIGEST.**
(*"SOME AMERICANS FROM HAWAII"*).
Contribution by James A. Michener. Pleasantville: Reader's Digest Association,
1966, pp. 29-64. Condensation from **"Hawaii."** Also in *Reader's Digest*,
75:452 (1959/06) 82-89.

B.060   **AMERICAN MEN AT ARMS.** (*"ALLIGATOR," "THE LANDING AT KURALEI,"*
"THE TRIPLE TWO," AND "MAYDAY").
Mason, F. van Wyck, Selected and Introduced by; Contributions by

Section B - Contributions to Anthologies, Collections, and Books

James A. Michener. Excerpts from "**Tales of the South Pacific,**"
"**The Bridges at Toko-ri,**" and "**Hawaii.**"

a   Boston, Toronto: Little, Brown and Company, 1964, pp. 171-79, 190-208, 243-58, 569-76.

b   New York: Pocket Books, 1966/01, pp. 209-18, 232-48, 295-313, 690-99. Paperback.

B.061   **AUTHORS TAKE SIDES ON VIET NAM.** (*"JAMES A. MICHENER"*).
Woolf, Cecil, and John Bagguley, eds.; Contribution by James A. Michener.
Two questions on the war in Viet Nam answered by the authors of several nations.

a   London: Owen, 1967, pp. 176-78.

b   New York: Simon & Schuster, 1967, pp. 51-52. LC 67-28040.
Paperback. U.S. printing comes only in paperback.

B.062   **BEST STORIES OF THE SOUTH SEAS.**
(*"CHARLES I, EMPEROR OF OCEANIA [NEW IRELAND]"*).
Snow, Philip, ed.; Contribution by James A. Michener and A. Grove Day. London:
Faber and Faber, 1967, pp. 121-52. Paperback. Excerpt from "**Rascals in Paradise.**"

B.063   **COMPOSITION OF THE ESSAY.** (*"4100 MILES ON A RAFT"*).
Hyde, Simeon, and William H. Brown, eds.; Contribution by James A. Michener.
Reading, Mass.: Addison-Wesley, 1967, pp. 166-70. Reprinted from *Saturday Review of Literature*, 33:38 (1950/09/23) 12-13. A review by Michener of Thor Hayerdahl's "Kon Tiki."

B.064   **HAWAII, A LITERARY CHRONICLE.** (*"FROM THE SUN-SWEPT LAGOON"*).
Lee, W. Storrs, ed.; Contribution by James A. Michener. New York:
Funk & Wagnalls, 1967, pp. 1-18. Excerpt from "**Hawaii.**"

B.065   **READINGS TO ENJOY.** (*"THE BRIDGE AT ANDAU"*).
Naas, H. Norman, and Morton H. Lewittes, eds.; Contribution by James A. Michener.
New York: Macmillan, 1967, pp. 100-17. Paperback. Literary Heritage Series.
A collection of nonfiction stories with biographical information about the authors.

B.066   **ADVANCED COMPOSITION.** (*"THE JAPANESE HOUSE"*).
Warriner, John E., Richard M. Ludwig, and Francis X. Connolly, eds.;
Contribution by James A. Michener. New York: Harcourt, Brace, and World,
1968, pp. 89-99.

B.067   **AN EDITOR'S TREASURY. 2 VOLS.** (*"BOY-SAN"*).
Mayes, Herbert R., ed.; Contribution by James A. Michener. New York:
Atheneum, 1968, pp. 437-39. Excerpt from "**The Voice of Asia.**"

B.068   **DEMOCRATIC FACT BOOK - 1968.**
(*"HUBERT H. HUMPHREY: PORTRAIT OF A PRESIDENT -"*).
Contribution by James A. Michener. Washington: Democratic National Committee,
1968, pp. v-xii. Michener writes a thumb-nail sketch of Democratic candidate Hubert
Humphrey for the 1968 convention fact book.

Section B - Contributions to Anthologies, Collections, and Books

B.069 **ISRAEL: A READER.** (*"ISRAEL: A NATION TOO YOUNG TO DIE"*).
Adler, Bill, ed.; Contribution by James A. Michener. Philadelphia:
Chilton Book Company, 1968, pp. 146-66. LC 68-58350.
A portrait of Israel and its people. Anthology of the keenest writers of
the day. Reprinted from *Look*, 31:16 (1967/08/08) 64-74.

B.070 **POINT OF VIEW 2, SELECTED READINGS.** (*"THE CAVE"*).
Lighthall, Nancy, ed.; Contribution by James A. Michener. Chicago: Follett
Educational Corp., 1968, pp. 61-93. Excerpt from **"Tales of the South Pacific."**

B..071 **THE SPELL OF HAWAII.**
(*"FROM THE BOUNDLESS DEEP"* AND *"GIBSON, THE KING'S EVIL ANGEL"*).
Day, A. Grove, and Carl Stroven, eds.; Contributions by James A. Michener and
A. Grove Day. Excerpts from **"Hawaii"** and **"Rascals in Paradise."**

    a New York: Meredith Press, 1968, pp. 3-20, 180-216.

    b Honolulu: Mutual Publishing, n.d., pp. 3-20, 180-216. Paperback.

B.072 **SUCCESS IN WRITING 2.** (*"A FAMOUS SEA AUTHOR'S CHOICE -
ADVENTURES OF MEN AND THEIR SHIPS"*).
Steward, Joyce S., and Marion C. McKinney, eds.;
Contribution by James A. Michener. Menlo Park: Addison-Wesley, 1968, pp. 1-2.
Reprinted from *Life*, 53:25 (1962/12/21) 96.

B.073 **PAGE 2 - THE BEST OF "SPEAKING OF BOOKS" FROM THE NEW YORK
TIMES BOOK REVIEW.** (*"AN HONEST ACCOUNT OF WHAT TRANSPIRED"*).
Brown, Francis, ed.; Contribution by James A. Michener. New York:
Holt, Rinehart and Winston, 1969, pp. 180-86.

B.074 **READER AND WRITER.** (*"WHAT TRANSPIRED"*).
Hayford, Harrison, and Howard P. Vincent, eds.; Contribution by James A.
Michener. Boston: Houghton, Mifflin, 1969, pp. 376-81.

B.075 **AMERICA'S 85 GREATEST LIVING AUTHORS PRESENT THIS IS MY
BEST IN THE THIRD QUARTER OF THE CENTURY.**
(*"FROM THE BOUNDLESS DEEP"*).
Burnett, Whit, ed.; Contribution by James A. Michener.
Garden City: Doubleday, 1970, pp. 806-23.
Excerpt from **"Hawaii."** Includes a short biography of Michener at page 1005.

B.076 **THE DOODLE BOOK.**
Uris, Norman Burton, comp.; Contribution by James A. Michener.
London: Collier-Macmillan, Collier Books, 1970, p. 82. LC 75-119128. Paperback.
Doodles of famous people are collected. Michener's doodle demonstrates
a mathematical propensity.

B.077 **A THOUSAND AFTERNOONS.** (*"THE AFICIONADOS"*).
Haining, Peter, ed.; Contribution by James A. Michener.
Compendium of bullfighting. Includes works by eighteen authors, including
Hemingway, Steinbeck, Mailer, Lawrence, Ruark, et al. Excerpt from **"Iberia."**

    a New York: Cowles Book Company, 1970, pp. 92-98.

b   London: Peter Owen, 1970, pp. 109-14.

B.078   ATTACKS OF TASTE. (*"JAMES A. MICHENER"*).
Byrne, Evelyn B., and Otto M. Penzler, eds.; Contribution by James A. Michener.
Various authors describe the books that influenced their lives and writings. A project
of E. B. Browning Junior High School in New York City. 271 prominent people were
asked to list the literature which had most influenced them and the book is a
compilation of 70 responses. The correspondence is located at the J. S. Copley Library
in La Jolla, California.

a   New York: Gotham Book Mart, 1971, pp. 29-30.

b   New York: Gotham Book Mart, 1971, pp. 29-30. Limited Edition,
Signed, 500 copies of which the first 100 were special presentation copies.

B.079   AMERICAN GOVERNMENT: THE CLASH OF ISSUES.
Burkhart, James A., Samuel Krislov, and Raymond L. Lee, eds.; Contribution by
James A. Michener. Paperback. Excerpt from **"The Quality of Life."**

a   4TH ED. (*"CAN WE PRESERVE THE AMERICAN SPIRIT?"*).
Englewood Cliffs, N.J.: Prentice-Hall, 1972, pp. 445-47. ISBN 0-13-026955-7.

b   5TH ED. Hereafter retitled **THE CLASH OF ISSUES: READINGS AND
PROBLEMS IN AMERICAN GOVERNMENT.**
(*"CAN WE PRESERVE THE AMERICAN SPIRIT?"*).
Englewood Cliffs, N.J.: Prentice-Hall, 1976, pp. 537-40.
ISBN 0-13-135095-1; LC 75-44260.

c   6TH ED. (*"AN IMPERFECT SOCIETY WITH GREAT POTENTIAL"*).
Englewood Cliffs, N.J.: Prentice-Hall, 1978, pp. 12-14.
ISBN 0-13-135061-7; LC 77-27012.

d   7TH ED. (*"AN IMPERFECT SOCIETY WITH GREAT POTENTIAL"*).
Englewood Cliffs, N.J.: Prentice-Hall, 1981, pp. 8-10.
ISBN 0-13-135087-0; LC 80-21907.

e   8TH ED. ("THE *AMERICAN FUTURE"*).
Englewood Cliffs, N.J.: Prentice-Hall, 1984, pp. 19-21.
ISBN 0-13-135146-X; LC 83-19108.

f   9TH ED. (*"THE AMERICAN FUTURE"*).
Krislov, Samuel, and Raymond L. Lee, eds.; Englewood Cliffs, N.J.:
Prentice-Hall, 1989, pp. 7-9. ISBN 0-13-135278-4; LC 88-2538.

B.080   PATTERNS OF EXPOSITION. 2D ED.
(*"THE ASSUMPTION OF THE MIDDLE CLASS"*).
Decker, Randall E., ed.; Contribution by James A. Michener.
Boston: Little, Brown and Company, 1972, pp. 60-68. Excerpt from
"America vs. America: the Revolution in Middle-Class Values."

Section B - Contributions to Anthologies, Collections, and Books

B.081   **READER'S DIGEST 50TH ANNIVERSARY TREASURY.**
(*"YOU NEVER STOP LEARNING"*).
Contribution by James A. Michener. Pleasantville: Reader's Digest Association,
1972, pp. 461-63. Reprinted from *Reader's Digest*, 81:488 (1962/12) 153-56, where it
was titled "When Does Education Stop?"

B.082   **READINGS IN POPULATION.**
(*"WHAT TO DO ABOUT THE PALESTINIAN REFUGEES"*).
Petersen, William, ed.; Contribution by James A. Michener. New York: Macmillan,
1972, pp. 165-75. Paperback. Reprinted from *New York Times Magazine*,
120:41,154 (1970/09/27) VI, 22-25+.

B.083   **OUR ENVIRONMENT: PATHWAYS TO SOLUTION.**
Van Dyke, Henry Thomas. Lexington, Mass.: Ginn and Co., 1972. Material from
"**The Quality of Life**" is included in a collection about environmental problems.

B.084   **UNDERSTANDING AMERICAN POLITICS THROUGH FICTION.**
(*"THE DRIFTERS"*).
Clowers, Myles L., comp.; Contribution by James A. Michener.
New York: McGraw-Hill, 1973, pp. 35-38.

B.085   **CLARENCE CARTER:**
A JOINT EXHIBITION 30 APRIL THROUGH 1 JUNE.
Contribution by James A. Michener. New York: Gimpel & Weitzenhiffer,
1974, p. 8. Art exhibit catalog. Text by James A. Michener.

B.086   **THE HUMAN EXPERIENCE.** (*"THE SOURCE"*).
Weitzman, David L., and Richard E. Gross, eds.; Contribution by James
A. Michener. Boston: Houghton, Mifflin, 1974, pp. 89-94.

B.087   **VIOLENCE IN THE FAMILY.** (*"THE KENT STATE FOUR / SHOULD HAVE
STUDIED MORE"*).
Steinmetz, Suzanne K., and Murray A. Straus, eds.; Contribution by
James A. Michener. New York: Dodd, Mead, 1974, pp. 180-87.
ISBN 0-396-06864-2; LC 73-11991. Paperback. Reprinted from "**Kent State:
What Happened and Why**," as condensed in the *Reader's Digest* 98:588
(1971/04) 218, 263-76.

B.088   **READER'S DIGEST CONDENSED BOOKS.** (*"CENTENNIAL"*).
Contribution by James A. Michener. Pleasantville: Reader's Digest
Association, 1975, pp. 94-309. Condensed from "**Centennial**." Also includes an
afterword by Michener titled "About Centennial."

B.089   **WORDS AND IDEAS: A HANDBOOK FOR COLLEGE WRITING.**
Guth, Hans P.; Contribution by James A. Michener. Quotes Michener's
"Portraits for the Future," *Saturday Review*, 34:31 (1951/08/04) 19-21.

    a   **3RD ED.** Belmont, Calif.: Wadsworth Publishing, 1969, p. 477. LC 69-18083.

    b   **4TH ED.** Belmont, Calif.: Wadsworth Publishing, 1975, p. 344.
ISBN 0-534-00371-0; LC 74-82554.

Section B - Contributions to Anthologies, Collections, and Books

B.090   **CREATIVE RHETORIC.**
Hardaway, Francine; Contribution by James A. Michener. Englewood Cliffs, N.J.:
Prentice-Hall, 1976, pp. 60, 68. Paperback. Excerpts from **"Iberia"**
and **"The Drifters."**

B.091   **THE GAME AND THE GLORY.** (*"THE GAME"*).
Reichler, Joe, ed.; Contribution by James A. Michener. Englewood Cliffs, N.J.:
Prentice-Hall, 1976, pp. 1-15. Michener's analysis of the history of baseball
provides a backdrop for contemporary articles on the game today.

B.092   **NOTHING IS LONG AGO, A DOCUMENTARY HISTORY OF COLORADO,
1776/1976.** (*"THE LAND AND THE PEOPLE"*).
Contribution by James A. Michener. Catalogue of exhibit in Denver Public Library
commemorating the centennial of statehood and bicentennial of the Republic.

   a   Denver: Denver Public Library, 1976, pp. 1-7. Paperback.

   b   Denver: Denver Public Library, 1976, pp. 1-7. Limited Edition, 100 copies.
Signed by Thomas Hornsby Ferril, James Michener, Richard Lamb, and W. H.
McNichols.

B.093   **MAYBE YOU SHOULD WRITE A BOOK.**
(*"THE HARDEST-WORKING OF THEM ALL"*).
Daigh, Ralph, ed.; Contribution by James A. Michener.
From "Unusually Close Working Relationship: James A. Michener and
Albert Erskine," *Publishers Weekly*, 201:15 (1972/04/10) 12.

   a   Englewood Cliffs, N.J.: Prentice-Hall, 1977, pp. 145-52.

   b   Englewood Cliffs, N.J.: Prentice-Hall, n.d., pp. 145-52. Paperback.

B.094   **TV GUIDE, THE FIRST 25 YEARS.** (*"A HIT IN ANY LANGUAGE"*).
Harris, Jay S., ed. and comp.; Contribution by James A. Michener.
Reprinted from *TV Guide*, 18:22 (1970/05/30) 4-9.

   a   New York: Simon & Schuster, 1978, pp. 169-71.

   b   New York: Plume, 1980, pp. 169-71. Paperback.

B.095   **ANIMALS TAME & WILD.** (*"A BEAVER'S HOME"*).
Phelps, Gilbert, and John Phelps, comps.; Contribution by James A. Michener.
Illustrated by Sheila Wright. Excerpt from **"Centennial."**

   a   New York: Sterling Publishing, 1979, pp. 59-63. ISBN 0-8069-3098-5; LC 78-57781.

   b   Retitled **"ANIMAL STORIES: TAME & WILD"** New York: Sterling Publishing,
1985, pp. 59-63. ISBN 0-8069-4722-5; LC 85-12575.

B.096   **THE BOOK OF QUOTES.**
Rowes, Barbara. Michener lauds this book as the modern day Bartlett's.
He is quoted about noisy modern music and getting published.

Section B - Contributions to Anthologies, Collections, and Books

a   New York: E. P. Dutton, 1979, pp. 184, 302.

b   New York: Ballantine Books, 1980/09, pp. 174, 287. Paperback.

B.097   **HOW GEORGE WASHINGTON GOT HIS GUNPOWDER.**
Morris, Charles V., ed.; Contribution by James A. Michener. Engraving by John
De Pol. New York: Private, 1980, pp. v-xv. The foreword includes excerpts from
"**Chesapeake.**" Commemorates the birthday of Ben Franklin. Michener
received the medal of the Franklin Society in 1980, which was reported in the *New
York Times*, January 25, 1980, at page III, 19, and January 28, 1980, at page II, 4.

B.098   **TREASURY OF GREAT BOOKS.** (*"THE WATERMEN"*).
Contribution by James A. Michener. Pleasantville: Reader's Digest Association,
1980, pp. 546-75. Excerpt from "**Chesapeake.**" A collection of stories
previously appearing in *Reader's Digest.*

B.099   **REFLECTIONS OF AMERICA.**
(*"THE QUALITY OF AMERICAN LIFE AND THE STATISTICAL ABSTRACT"*).
Cousins, Norman, Honorary Editor; Contribution by James A. Michener.
Washington, D.C.: Bureau of the Census, 1980/12, pp. 157-66. LC 80-607843.
Michener relies on the *"Statistical Abstract"* for demographic information
such as education, ethnic facts, families, etc.

B.100   **READER'S DIGEST CONDENSED BOOKS.** (*"THE COVENANT"*).
Contribution by James A. Michener. Pleasantville: Reader's Digest Association,
1981, pp. 114-315.
Condensed from "**The Covenant.**" Also includes a new afterword by Michener.

B.101   **BUCKS COOKS VOL. II; A GOURMET'S GUIDE TO ESTIMABLE
COMESTIBLES WITH PICTURES.**
Solebury: Trinity Episcopal Church, 1983, p. 62.
Paperback. Prepared by the Cookbook Committee of Trinity Chapel, Solebury,
Pennsylvania. Michener contributed *"Boeuf Bourguignon #1."*

B.102   **THE OMNI BOOK OF SPACE.** (*"LOOKING TOWARD SPACE"*).
Davies, Owen, ed.; Contribution by James A. Michener. New York:
Kensington Publishing, [1983?], pp. 367-75. ISBN 0-8217-1275-6.
Paperback. Reprinted from magazine article in *Omni*, 2:8 (1980/05) 56-59, 121.

B.103   **SPORTS CLASSICS: AMERICAN WRITERS CHOOSE THEIR BEST.**
Siner, Howard, ed.; Contribution by James A. Michener. New York: Coward-Mc-
Cann, 1983, pp. 77-85. ISBN 0-698-11248-2; LC 83-7487. Three articles from the
New York Times; "Life and Death Through the Years with the Phillies,"
November 19, 1978; "Ode to Robin Roberts, a Pitcher with Good Qualities,"
November 24, 1974; "Poetic Celebration in Midair," November 9, 1980.

B.104   **THE ARMCHAIR BOOK OF BASEBALL.** (*"ODE TO THE PHILLIES"*).
Thorn, John, ed.; Contribution by James A. Michener. Illustrated by James Stevenson.
Michener was invited to throw out the ball for the opening of the second playoff game.

a   New York: Charles Scribner's Sons, 1985, p. 217.

b   New York: Collier-Macmillan, 1992, p. 217. Paperback.

Section B - Contributions to Anthologies, Collections, and Books

B.105   **THE BEST WAR STORIES.** (*"THE CAVE"* AND *"FO' DOLLA' "*).
Contributions by James A. Michener. Excerpts from **"Tales of the South Pacific."**
A collection of thirty short stories.

    a   Twickenham, Middlesex: Hamlyn Publishing, 1985, pp. 530-607.

    b   New York: Mallard Press, 1990, pp. 358-82.

B.106   **HOW TO USE THE POWER OF THE PRINTED WORD.**
(*"HOW TO USE A LIBRARY"*).
Fuess, Billings S., Jr., ed.; Contribution by James A. Michener.
Garden City: Doubleday, Anchor Press, 1985, pp. 40-48.
One of a collection of articles by different authors, used for
an advertising campaign by The International Paper Company.

B.107   **A TREASURY OF WORLD WAR II STORIES.** (*"CORAL SEA"*).
Pronzini, Bill, and Martin H. Greenberg, eds.; Contribution by James A. Michener.
Excerpt from **"Tales of the South Pacific."**
Stories from pulp magazines of the forties.

    a   New York: Bonanza, 1985, pp. 485-500.

    b   New York: Bonanza, 1991, pp. 485-500. Reprint.

B.108   **THE BOOK OF THE MONTH:**
SIXTY YEARS OF BOOKS IN AMERICAN LIFE.
(*"BEHIND THE BOOK: A SEARCH FOR JIMMIE FOXX IN SUDLERSVILLE"*).
Silverman, Al, ed.; Contribution by James A. Michener. Boston: Little, Brown and
Company, 1986, pp. 270-72. ISBN 0-316-10119-2; LC 86-7511. Notes on
"Chesapeake" and how Michener came to write it; also a biographical sketch about
Michener by Joseph Barbato.

B.109   **DOUBLY GIFTED: THE AUTHOR AS VISUAL ARTIST.**
    a   Hjerter, Kathleen; Contribution by James A. Michener. New York: Harry N. Abrams,
1986, pp. 132-33. ISBN 0-8109-1842-0; LC 85-23024. Foreword by John Updike.
Includes three works of art by Michener.
1. BIOGRAPHY. 1966. Collage, acrylic on board, 36 x 47".
The composition consists of 137 squares, many of which contain symbols indicative of
special events in Michener's life.
2. DESIGNS. 1965. Five panels, acrylic on hardboard, overall 48x120". Four moving
vertical panels which can be shifted to produce contrasting results. The final panel is a
kind of self portrait set amid the alphabet with the sequential words IDEA, WORD,
PAGE, BOOK emerging, pretty much as they do in reality.
3. INFURIATING SIMPLICITY. 1964. Three panels, acrylic on board, overall
24x72". Michener's description: "Take five square blocks and arrange them in every
conceivable way, contiguously. You get twelve completely different forms for a total
of sixty individual squares. If you arrange a tray of 10 spaces by 6 spaces, you have an
area into which the twelve pieces can be fitted. There are hundreds of possible
solutions. Solving the problem, painting it, and reflecting upon it in tranquility, have
given me much satisfaction."

    b   New York: Harry Abrams, 1986, pp. 132-33. ISBN 0-8109-2333-5. Trade paperback.

Section B - Contributions to Anthologies, Collections, and Books

B.110   **THE LURE OF TAHITI.** (*"POVENAAA'S DAUGHTER"*).
Day, A. Grove, ed.; Contribution by James A. Michener. Honolulu:
Mutual Publishing, 1986, pp. 21-78. Paperback. Fifteen stories from the literature
of the most romantic island in the world. Excerpt from **"Return to Paradise."**

B.111   **PEOPLE AS ANIMALS.**
Cowles, Fleur, comp.; Contribution by James A. Michener.
Illustrated by Fleur Cowles. Michener indicates his preference to be an "armadillo."

   a   London: Robin Clark, 1986, pp. 92-93. First British edition.

   b   First American Edition retitled **"If I Were An Animal."**
New York: William Morrow, [1987], p. 119. ISBN 0-688-06150-8; LC 86-18035.

B.112   **READER'S DIGEST CONDENSED BOOKS.** (*"TEXAS"*).
Contribution by James A. Michener. Pleasantville: Reader's Digest
Association, 1986, pp. 122-487. Condensed from **"Texas."**

B.113   **EQUUS REINED.**
Vavra, Robert; Contribution by James A. Michener. Photos by Robert Vavra.
New York: William Morrow, 1987, pp. 22-23, 131-42. ISBN 0-688-05089-1;
LC 87-13911. Excerpts from **"Centennial,"** and note by Vavra acknowledging
his debt to Michener that can never be repaid.

B.114   **THE FIRESIDE BOOK OF BASEBALL. 4TH ED.**
(*"LINES COMPOSED IN EXULTATION OVER THE NORTH ATLANTIC"*).
Einstein, Charles, ed.; Contribution by James A. Michener. New York:
Simon & Schuster, 1987, p. 262. Paperback. Michener's ode to the Phillies'
first-ever world championship. Also in the *New York Times*, (1980/11/09) V, 2.

B.115   **EXCELLENCE: AN AMERICAN TREASURY.**
("MAKE THE MOST OF YOUR TALENTS").
Contribution by James A. Michener. Luke, Md: Westvaco, 1988, pp. 223-24.
Slipcase. Privately published as the 31st annual Christmas edition by Westvaco,
a manufacturer of fine paper, commemorating Westvaco's centennial year.

B.116   **GREAT WORLD WAR II STORIES.** (*"THE LANDING AT KURALEI"*).
Contribution by James A. Michener. London: Chartwell Books, 1989, pp. 178-94.
50th Anniversary Collection. Published in Great Britain by The Octopus
Group Limited for Chartwell Books, Secaucus, New Jersey.

B.117   **READER'S DIGEST CONDENSED BOOKS.** (*"ALASKA"*).
Contribution by James A. Michener. Pleasantville: Reader's Digest Association, 1989,
pp. 130-485. Condensed from **"Alaska."**

B.118   **ANIMAL FAMILIES OF THE WILD.** (*"BEAVER LODGE"*).
Russell, William F., ed.; Contribution by James A. Michener. Illustrated
by John Butler. Anthology of nature writing and animal stories for gradeschoolers.
Excerpt from **"Centennial."**

   a   New York: Crown Publishers, 1990, pp. 49-64.
ISBN 0-517-57358-X; LC 89-22226. Trade edition.

Section B - Contributions to Anthologies, Collections, and Books

b   New York: Crown Publishers, 1990, pp. 49-64. ISBN 0-517-57359-8. Library binding.

B.119   **MEN IN THE AIR.** (*"THE MILK RUN"*).
Aymar, Brandt, ed.; Contribution by James A. Michener. New York:
Crown Publishers, 1990, pp. 330-35. ISBN 0-517-58115-9; LC 89-10012.
The best flight stories of all time from Greek Mythology to the Space Age.

B.120   **READER'S DIGEST CONDENSED BOOKS.** (*"JOURNEY"*).
Contribution by James A. Michener. Montreal, Quebec: Reader's Digest
Association (Canada), 1990, pp. 7-133. From **"Journey,"**
Toronto, Canada: McClelland and Stewart, 1988.

B.121   **ADVICE FROM THE MASTERS: A COMPENDIUM FOR WRITERS.**
Conrad, Barnaby; Contribution by James A. Michener. Summerland, Calif.:
Charters West Publications, 1991, pp. 4, 60. The philosophies of writing ranging from
Samuel Johnson to Joseph Wambaugh.

B.122   **BASEBALL'S GREATEST QUOTATIONS.**
Dickson, Paul, comp.; Contribution by James A. Michener. New York: Harper
Collins, 1991, p. 292. ISBN 0-06-270001-4; LC 90-55531.
Quote from the *Los Angeles Times Book Review*, (1975/07/25), regarding the insanity
of getting caught up in sports.

B.123   **THE FABER BOOK OF TALES OF THE SEA.**
(*"POLYNESIANS FROM BORA BORA TO HAWAII"*).
Coote, John, ed.; Contribution by James A. Michener.
London: Faber and Faber, 1991, pp. 275-83. ISBN 0-571-16137-5.
Excerpt from **"Hawaii."**

B.124   **HEAVEN IS UNDER OUR FEET.** (*"OF LIVING CREATURES"*).
Henley, Don, and Dave Marsh, eds.; Contribution by James A. Michener.
The Walden Woods project is to acquire and preserve the woods.
Michener was a member of the Walden Woods Project Advisory Board.

a   Stamford: Long Meadows Press, 1991, pp. 94-97. ISBN 0-681-41129-5.

b   New York: Berkley Books, 1992/12, pp. 94-97. Paperback.

B.125   **THE NEW BASEBALL READER: MORE FAVORITES FROM THE
FIRESIDE BOOKS OF BASEBALL.**
(*"LINES COMPOSED IN EXULTATION OVER THE NORTH ATLANTIC"*).
Einstein, Charles, ed.; Contribution by James A. Michener.
New York: Viking Penguin, 1991, pp. 264-65.
Michener's ode to the Phillies' first-ever world championship.

B.126   **THE NEW BASEBALL READER: AN ALL-STAR LINEUP FROM THE
FIRESIDE BOOK OF BASEBALL.**
(*"LINES COMPOSED IN EXULTATION OVER THE NORTH ATLANTIC"*).
Einstein, Charles, ed.; Contribution by James A. Michener.
New York: Viking Penguin, 1991, p. 264. Paperback.

Section B - Contributions to Anthologies, Collections, and Books

B.127 **WRITERS ON WORLD WAR II: AN ANTHOLOGY.** (*"CORAL SEA"*).
Mordecai, Richler, ed.; Contribution by James A. Michener.
Excerpt from "**Tales of the South Pacific.**"

  a New York: Knopf, 1991, pp. 285-94. ISBN 0-394-57258-0; LC 91-52723.

  b New York: Vintage, 1993, pp. 285-94. ISBN 0-679-74234-4; LC 95-50620.
Paperback.

B.128 **GOOD ADVICE ON WRITING: WRITER'S PAST AND PRESENT ON HOW TO WRITE WELL.**
Safire, William, and Leonard Safir, eds.; Contribution by James A. Michener.
New York: Simon & Schuster, 1992, pp. 122-23, 241. ISBN 0-671-77995-5;
LC 92-19222. Quotes Michener.

B.129 **THE NORTON BOOK OF SPORTS.**
Plimpton, George, ed.; Contribution by James A. Michener. New York, London:
Norton, 1992, p. 473. ISBN 0-393-03040-7. Quotes Michener's observation that
most pro athletes end their careers at an age before Michener started his.

B.130 **TODAY'S BEST NONFICTION.** (*"THE WORLD IS MY HOME"*).
Contribution by James A. Michener. Pleasantville: Reader's Digest Association, 1992,
pp. 7-157. Condensed. Special comments about the authors at page 574.

B.131 **THE WRITER'S QUOTATION BOOK.**
Charlton, James, ed.; Contribution by James A. Michener.

  a New York: Penguin, 1992, pp. 16, 54. Paperback. Quotes Michener.

  b Wainscott, N.Y.: Pushcart Press, n.d., pp. 16, 54. ISBN 0-916366-66-9.
Quotes Michener.

B.132 **COMBAT: GREAT TALES OF WORLD WAR II.** (*"CORAL SEA"*).
Pronzini, Bill, and Martin H. Greenberg, eds.; Contribution by James A.
Michener. New York: Signet, 1992/05, pp. 9-24. ISBN 0-451-16571-3.
Paperback. Fourteen stories of the pathos and glory of World War II.
Excerpt from "**Tales of the South Pacific.**"

B.133 **THE COLORADO BOOK.** (*"ABOUT CENTENNIAL"*).
Gehres, Eleanor M., Sandra Dallas, Maxine Benson, and Stanley Cuba,
eds.; Contribution by James A. Michener. Golden, Colo.: Fulcrum Publishing,
1993, pp. 18-20. ISBN 1-55591-116-1; LC 92-53034.
Excerpt from "**About Centennial.**"

B.134 **THE MAMMOTH BOOK OF MODERN WAR STORIES.**
(*"WINE FOR THE MESS AT SEGI"*).
Lewis, Jon E.; Contribution by James A. Michener. New York: Carroll & Graf
Publishers, 1993, pp. 346-64. ISBN 0-88184-958-8.
Excerpt from "**Tales of the South Pacific.**"

Section B - Contributions to Anthologies, Collections, and Books

B.135   **WHO'S WRITING THIS?** (*"MICHENER AND I"*).
Halpern, Daniel, ed.; Contribution by James A. Michener. Hopewell, N.J.: Ecco Press, [1994], pp. 125-28. ISBN 0-88001-377-X; LC 94-17421
55 essays by various authors about fictional persona that are the authors' spokesmen to the public.

C.
Forewords,
Introductions, and
Miscellaneous Commentary

"I am invited to write forewords to many books; those doing the inviting spell it 'forward', as does my secretary. She handed me a note the other day: 'Latest count, foreword 7, forward 13. The good guys are winning.'"

—James A. Michener
TESTIMONY
Honolulu: White Knight Press, 1983

Mustard Plasters and Printer's Ink

A KALEIDOSCOPE OF A COUNTRY DOCTOR'S OBSERVATIONS ABOUT PEOPLE, PLACES AND THINGS

ALLEN H. MOORE, M.D.

With a Foreword by JAMES A. MICHENER
and an Introduction by LINDSAY C. WARREN,
Former Comptroller General of the United States

Mustard Plasters and Printer's Ink. C.009.

Section C - Forewords, Introductions, & Miscellaneous Commentary

C.001   **THE CHRISTMAS BOOK.**
Foreword by James A. Michener. Pottstown, Pa.: The Hill School, 1929, p. [7].

C.002   **THE SPELL OF THE PACIFIC, AN ANTHOLOGY OF ITS LITERATURE.**
Stroven, Carl, and A. Grove Day, eds.; Introduction by James A. Michener.
New York: Macmillan, 1949, pp. vii-xi. 100 selections from 86 authors covering
400 years. Includes brief descriptions of each offering and notes about each author.

C.003   **TOKYO AND POINTS EAST.**
Beech, Keyes; Introduction by James A. Michener. Garden City: Doubleday, 1954,
pp. 7-15. LC 54-11159. The personal world of a veteran overseas press man
following the wars and covering the more difficult peace in the Far East.

C.004   **MASTERPIECES OF JAPANESE PRINTS.**
Foreword by James A. Michener. Chicago: Art Institute of Chicago, 1955,
pp. 11-14. A catalogue of the exhibition March 10-April 17.

C.005   **SOMETHING IS MISSING.**
Goodfriend, Arthur; Postscript by James A. Michener.
To build democracy, Americans and Asians from Pakistan to Japan must build
a bridge of understanding, respect, and cooperation.

    a   New York: Farrar, Straus & Young, 1955, pp. 108-11. LC 54-12229.

    b   New York: Farrar, Straus & Young, n.d., pp. 108-11. Paperback.

C.006   **MODERN JAPANESE PRINTS: AN ART REBORN.**
Statler, Oliver; Introduction by James A. Michener.
A new art form synthesis of East and West, the Hanga, or block print,
evolved from ukiyoe techniques, is shown in 102 prints.

    a   Tokyo: Charles E. Tuttle, 1956, pp. xv-xvii. LC 56-6810.

    b   Rutland, Tokyo: Charles E. Tuttle, 1959, pp. xv-xvii.
ISBN 0-8048-0406-0; LC 59-8180. Paperback.

C.007   **THE TALE OF RODGERS AND HAMMERSTEIN'S SOUTH PACIFIC
[THE MOVIE SOUVENIR PROGRAM].**
Introduction by James A. Michener. New York: A Lehmann Book, 1958, pp. 4-5.
Issued without dust jacket. Michener gives historical notes to illustrate how the truth of
the war exceeded fiction.

C.008   **A HAWAIIAN READER.**
Day, A. Grove, and Carl Stroven, eds.; Introduction by James A. Michener.
Thirty-seven selections by thirty authors who have written about Hawaii.

    a   New York: Appleton-Century-Crofts, 1959, pp. xi-xvii. LC 59-14048.

    b   New York: Popular Library, 1961, pp. 9-14. Paperback.

    c   Honolulu: Mutual Publishing, 1984, pp. xi-xvii. ISBN 0-935180-07-9. Paperback.

Section C - Forewords, Introductions, & Miscellaneous Commentary

C.009   **MUSTARD PLASTERS AND PRINTER'S INK.**
Moore, Allen H., M.D.; Foreword by James A. Michener. New York:
Exposition Press, 1959, p. 7. A kaleidoscope of a country doctor's observations.
Moore was Michener's personal physician in Doylestown, Pennsylvania.

C.010   **HERE'S HAWAII.**
.   Krauss, Bob; Foreword by James A. Michener. This material first appeared in some-
what different form in the *Honolulu Advertiser*. Observations of life in the islands.

    a   New York: Coward-McCann, 1960, pp. 7-9. LC 60-9501.

    b   New York: Pocket Books, 1961/11, pp. vii-ix. Paperback.

C.011   **KISHI AND JAPAN. THE SEARCH FOR THE SUN.**
Kurzman, Dan; Foreword by James A. Michener. New York: Ivan Obolensky,
1960, pp. xi-xiii. LC 60-9041. Kishi was Prime Minister of Japan in 1955.

C.012   **FODOR'S HAWAII 1961.**
Davenport, William W.; Foreword by James A. Michener. New York: David
McKay, 1961, pp. 5-8. Revised, republished and dated annually, Michener's
foreword appeared from 1961 through 1978 in this practical travel guide.

C.013   **THE LOST EDEN.**
Rizal, Jose; Foreword by James A. Michener. Translated by Leon Maria Guerrero.
Originally titled "Noli Me Tangere," this novel is a source of Phillippine
nationalism. Rizal was a Phillippine patriot (1861-1896).

    a   Bloomington: Indiana University Press, 1961, pp. vi-viii.
LC 60-53368. 2500 copies, 1500 first printings.

    b   London: Longmans, Green and Company, 1961.

    c   New York: Greenwood Press, 1968, pp. vi-viii. LC 68-9712.
567 copies, issued without dust jacket.

    d   New York: Norton Press, 1968, pp. vi-viii. Paperback.

C.014   **THE JAMES A. MICHENER FOUNDATION COLLECTION: EXHIBITION,
FEBRUARY 2-MARCH 20, 1963.**
Foreword by James A. Michener.
Allentown, Pa.: Allentown Art Museum, 1963, pp. iii-vi.

C.015   **THE WESTWARD TILT.**
Morgan, Neil; Foreword by James A. Michener. New York: Random House,
1963, pp. vii-x. LC 63-7644. A survey of American westward migration and the
evolving political, social, and economic forces it is producing.

C.016   **THE GRAPHIC WORK OF PHILLIP EVERGOOD: SELECTED DRAWINGS
AND COMPLETE PRINTS.**
Lippard, Lucy R.; Proem by James A. Michener.
Michener's Proem introduces this first extended study of Evergood's graphic work.
121 Drawings and 56 prints.

Section C - Forewords, Introductions, & Miscellaneous Commentary

a New York: Crown Publishers, 1966, p. 8. LC 65-17022.

b New York: Crown Publishers, 1966, p. 8. Limited Edition. Signed.
Colophon
THIS SPECIAL EDITION IS LIMITED TO 150 COPIES EACH CONTAINING AN
ORIGINAL ETCHING Girl With Sunflowers MADE ESPECIALLY FOR THIS BOOK AND
SIGNED BY THE ARTIST. FIFTEEN COPIES ARE FOR PRIVATE PRESENTATION AND ARE
NUMBERED 1 TO 15. ONE HUNDRED AND THIRTY-FIVE ARE FOR SALE AND ARE
NUMBERED 16 TO 150. THIS IS COPY ___.

C.017 **HAWAII: COOKBOOK AND BACKYARD LUAU.**
Toupin, Elizabeth Ahn; Introduction by James A. Michener.

a Norwalk: Silvermine Publishers, 1967, pp. 9-10. LC 67-16149.
Cookbook Guild Edition published June, 1967. A condensation appeared in
Ladies' Home Journal, 83:11 (1966/11) 122, 139-42.

b New York: Bantam Books, 1967/06, pp. 9-10. Paperback.

c New York: Bantam Books, 1967/06, pp. 9-10. Paperback.
Special "Singer Edition," noted at top of front cover.
On back cover, "What's new for tomorrow is at Singer today."

C.018 **ADVENTURERS OF THE PACIFIC.**
(*"TO ALL THOSE WHO SEEK PACIFIC ADVENTURE"*).
Day, A. Grove; Foreword by James A. Michener.
Eight true episodes from the history of the Pacific.

a New York: Meredith Press, 1969, pp. vii-xiii. LC 69-14770.

b Retitled **Rogues of the South Seas**. Honolulu: Mutual Publishing, 1986,
pp. vii-xiii. ISBN 0-935180-24-9. Paperback.

C.019 **SELECTED PAINTINGS FROM THE MICHENER COLLECTION**
(*"A FOREWORD: WHY TEXAS?"*).
Foreword by James A. Michener. Austin: University of Texas, 1969, pp. 7-10.
Paperback. Catalog of exhibition November 2, 1969 - January 5, 1970.

C.020 **BEGINNING OF THE BEGINNING.**
Akston, Joseph James; Introduction by James A. Michener. New York:
Harry N. Abrams, 1971, pp. 8-9. LC 70-135656. Paintings and text depict an
unfolding story of how nature and life evolved on our planet.

C.021 **AMERICAN IN DISGUISE.**
Okimoto, Daniel Iwao; Foreword by James A. Michener. New York:
Walker/Weatherhill, 1971, pp. ix-xiv. ISBN 0-8027-2438-8; LC 70-121065.
A second generation American, interned in World War II, searches for
identity in America and Japan.

C.022 **BULLS OF IBERIA, LIFE AND DEATH OF THE FIGHTING BULL.**
Vavra, Robert; Foreword by James A. Michener.
A pictorial survey of of the life of the fighting bull, from conception to
weaning, and finally to the afternoon of the fight.

a   Seville, Spain: Imprenta Sevillana, 1972, pp. 1-3.
Limited Edition. In slipcase, Signed by Vavra, 1000 copies.
A trade edition of 5000 copies in Spanish was published by Editorial Olivo of Sevilla.
A deluxe edition of 1000 copies in Spanish was published by Osborne Winery.

b   Seville, Spain: Imprenta Sevillana, 1972, pp. 1-3.
Limited Subscribers Edition. In slipcase, Signed by Vavra. 230 copies.
The following is noted on the copyright page: "Of a limited signed and numbered
Subscribers' Edition of two hundred and thirty copies printed, this is number ___"

c   King Ranch Edition. 1972, pp. 1-3. In slipcase, Signed by Vavra, 1000 copies. The
verso preceding the half-title page contains a printed inscription by Vavra. He
discusses the ancient Concha y Sierra breed of fighting bull introduced to Iberia from
Africa and the Santa Gertrudis breed, reknowned for its beef production, introduced to
Iberia from America. He states that "If the fighting bull should disappear, it is my
hope that this book would be a lasting document of the life of this unique and ancient
cattle."

C.023   **GONE WITH THE WIND.**
Mitchell, Margaret; Introduction by James A. Michener. New York: Macmillan, 1975,
pp. v-xii. ISBN 0-02-585350-3; LC 76-355793. Special Anniversary Edition.
Slipcase.

C.024   **YEARS OF INFAMY:**
THE UNTOLD STORY OF AMERICA'S CONCENTRATION CAMPS.

Weglyn, Michi; Introduction by James A. Michener.
Michener's six page introduction highlights this history of the evacuation and
relocation of Japanese-Americans in World War II.

a   New York: Morrow, 1976, pp. 27-31. ISBN 0-688-02996-5; LC 75-34397.

b   New York: Morrow, Quill, 1976, pp. 27-31. ISBN 0-688-07996-2; LC 80-16643.
Paperback.

C.025   **BEDNARIK, LAST OF THE SIXTY-MINUTE MEN.**
McCallum, Jack, with Chuck Bednarik; Foreword by James A. Michener.
Englewood Cliffs, N.J.: Prentice-Hall, 1977, pp. ix-x. ISBN 0-13-066753-6;
LC 77-7800. Voted one of the greatest professional football linemen, Bednarik
was one of the last men to play both ways, offense and defense, in the NFL.

C.026   **THE JAMES A. MICHENER COLLECTION: TWENTIETH CENTURY**
AMERICAN PAINTING. (*"THE COLLECTOR AN INFORMAL MEMOIR"*).
Powell, Earl A., III; Introduction by James A. Michener.
Michener examines the mental aberrations of the collector which lead to bizarre
activities which can be beneficial to him.

a   Austin: University of Texas Art Museum, 1977, pp. ix-xviii. LC 77-89177.

b   Austin: University of Texas Art Museum, 1977, pp. ix-xviii. Paperback.

Section C - Forewords, Introductions, & Miscellaneous Commentary

C.027   **EQUUS: THE CREATION OF A HORSE.**
Vavra, Robert; Foreword by James A. Michener.
Originally published in Spanish titled *"El Noble Bruto."* Vavra photographs the action, poetry and color of horses.

     a   New York: William Morrow, 1977, pp. 5-6. ISBN 0-688-03239-7; LC 77-78061.

     b   London: William Collins and Sons, 1977, pp. 5-6.

     c   New York: Morrow, Quill, 1984/10, pp. 5-6. ISBN 0-688-03958-8; LC 84-61114.
Paperback.

C.028   **IN SEARCH OF CENTENNIAL, A JOURNEY WITH JAMES A. MICHENER.**
Kings, John; Introduction by James A. Michener. New York: Random
House, 1978, p. 7. ISBN 0-394-50292-2; LC 78-14389.
With photographs by Tessa Dalton, James A. Michener and the author, Kings, traces
the writing of **"Centennial"** and then its filming.

C.029   **DELILAH, A NOVEL.**
Goodrich, Marcus; Afterword by James A. Michener.
The severe trials faced by the men of a ship on the brink of World War I and the tests
that all but the hardiest must fail.

     a   Carbondale: Southern Illinois University Press, 1978, pp. 497-512.
ISBN 0-8093-0739-1; LC 77-26042.

     b   New York: Popular Library, n.d., pp. 553-573. ISBN 0-445-04433-0. Paperback.

C.030   **YOUNG FREDERICK DOUGLASS, THE MARYLAND YEARS.**
Preston, Dickson J.; Foreword by James A. Michener. Douglass's life from birth,
slavery, flight to freedom, and role as black American spokesman.

     a   Baltimore: Johns Hopkins University Press, 1980, pp. ix-xii.
ISBN 0-8018-2439-7; LC 80-7992.

     b   Baltimore: Johns Hopkins University Press, 1985, pp. ix-xii.
ISBN 0-8018-2739-6; LC 80-7992. Paperback.

C.031   **PRIMITIVE UKIYO-E FROM THE JAMES A. MICHENER COLLECTION
IN THE HONOLULU ACADEMY OF ARTS.**
Link, Howard A.; Foreword by James A. Michener. Honolulu: Honolulu
Academy of Arts, 1980, p. ix. ISBN 0-8248-0483-X; LC 79-6397.
Assisted by Juzo Suzuki and Roger S. Keyes. Published for the Honolulu
Academy of Arts by The University Press of Hawaii.

C.032   **THE TROUBLE WITH NOWADAYS: A CURMUDGEON STRIKES BACK.**
Amory, Cleveland. New York: Ballantine Books, 1981/06, p. 1.
ISBN 0-345-29720-2; LC 79-52255. Paperback. Note to Amory that Michener could
not give the book to friends because 9/10ths would sue Amory for invasion of privacy.

C.033   **JAMES A. MICHENER'S USA.**
Chaitin, Peter; Foreword by James A. Michener. New York: Crown Publishers, 1981,
pp. vii-viii. Based on the TV series titled "James Michener's USA."

Section C - Forewords, Introductions, & Miscellaneous Commentary

C.034   MARYLAND'S FLAVOR. FROM THE ALLEGHENY MOUNTAINS TO THE
SANDS OF THE EASTERN SHORE.
Preface by James A. Michener. Maryland: Amer. Cancer Society, Md. Div.,
1981, p. 3. Cookbook. Michener was Honorary Cookbook Chairman, and resident of
St. Michael's, Maryland. The book may also come in hardcover.

C.035   E.L. THE BREAD BOX PAPERS.
Gemmill, Helen H.; Introduction by James A. Michener.
Biography of Mrs. T. Bigelow Lawrence, a Victorian "Auntie Mame."

a   Bryn Mawr: Dorrance & Company, 1983, pp. 1-2. ISBN 0-8059-2870-7;
LC 83-90063. Co-published by The Bucks County Historical Society.

b   Doylestown, Pa.: Tower Hill Press, 1989, pp. 1-2.
ISBN 0-941668-02-9; LC 89-55330.

C.036   THE UNDISCOVERED ZANE GREY FISHING STORIES.
Grey, Zane; George Reiger, ed.; Foreword by James A. Michener.
Illustrated by Frank Stick, et al. Eight stories and essays that had
previously appeared only in *Outdoor America* magazine.

a   Piscataway, N.J.: Winchester Press, 1983, pp. ix-xi.
ISBN 0-8329-0316-7; LC 83-17082.

b   Piscataway, N.J.: Winchester Press, 1983, pp. ix-xi. ISBN 0-8329-0342-6.
Deluxe Edition, in slipcase.

C.037   WHITE WALL OF SPAIN: THE MYSTERIES OF ANDALUSIAN CULTURE.
Josephs, Allen; Foreword by James A. Michener. A focus on its oriental origins,
its ancient commerce and industry, its religious practices, artistry, music, and dance.

a   Ames: Iowa State University Press, 1983, p. ix. ISBN 0-8138-1921-0; LC 90-37933.

b   Pensacola: University of West Florida Press, 1990/11, p. ix.
ISBN 0-08130-1013-6; LC 90-37933. Paperback. 1200 to 1300 copies.

C.038   DALLAS COWBOYS: THE FIRST TWENTY-FIVE YEARS.
Stowers, Carlton; Foreword by James A. Michener. Dallas: Taylor Publishing,
1984, pp. vii-ix.

C.039   GOLDEN MOMENTS, A COLLECTION OF 1984 COMMEMORATIVE
OLYMPIC ISSUES.
Introduction by James A. Michener. Washington: U.S. Postal Service, 1984,
pp. 8-11. To commemorate the U.S. Olympic Postage Stamps issued in 1984.
Paintings and 1984 Olympic Postage designs by Robert Peak.

C.040   THE 1984 OLYMPIC GAMES.
Schaap, Dick; Introduction by James A. Michener. Michener philosophizes on the
effects of commercialization, nationalism, racism, politics, and drugs on the Olympics.

a   New York: Random House, 1984, pp. 8-9. ISBN 0-394-53678-9; LC 84-42909.

b   New York: Random House, 1984, pp. 8-9. ISBN 0-394-72162-4. Paperback.

Section C - Forewords, Introductions, & Miscellaneous Commentary

C.041 **THE CONSTITUTION.**
Fink, Sam; Foreword by James A. Michener.
68 pages, unpaginated. Inscribed and illustrated by Sam Fink to honor the two-hundredth anniversary, September 17, 1987.

    a   New York: Random House, 1985, p. [11]. ISBN 0-394-54304-1; LC 85-2438.

    b   New York: Random House, 1985, p. [11]. ISBN 0-394-75273-2. Paperback.

C.042 **THE DANGEROUS SUMMER.**
Hemingway, Ernest; Introduction by James A. Michener. Commissioned by *Life* magazine as a short article on bullfighting, this was Hemingway's last major work.

    a   New York: Charles Scribner's Sons, 1985, pp. 3-40.
ISBN 0-684-18355-2; LC 84-27578.

    b   New York: Charles Scribner's Sons, 1985. LC 85-17349. Large Print Edition.

    c   New York: Charles Scribner's Sons, 1986, pp. 3-40. SBN 0-684-18720-5.
Paperback.

    d   New York: Macmillan. ISBN 0-685-09991-1. Paperback.

    e   Thorndike, Maine. Thorndike Press, n.d., pp. 11-65.
ISBN 0-89621-666-7; LC 85-17349. Large Print Edition.

C.043 **ALL WE DID WAS FLY TO THE MOON.**
Lattimer, Dick, ed.; Foreword by James A. Michener. Alachua, Fla.: Whispering Eagle Press, 1985/07, p. vii. ISBN 0-9611228-0-3; LC TXU 116-653.
Paperback. By the Astronauts as told to Dick Lattimer. Volume I of the History-Alive Series: A mini-history of the manned space program.

C.044 **THE SEVILLA OF CARMEN.**
Vavra, Robert; Foreword by James A. Michener.
Photographs by Robert Vavra.
New York: William Morrow, 1985, pp. 6-8. ISBN 0-688-05880-9; LC 85-60714.
Part one is 130 photographs revealing the living history of Sevilla.
Part two introduces the opera "Carmen" by Bizet.

C.045 **CONVERSATIONS WITH CAPOTE.**
Grobel, Lawrence; Foreword by James A. Michener. A series of interviews between July 16, 1982, and Capote's death on August 24, 1984, reflecting Capote's artistic genius.

    a   New York: New American Library, 1985/02, pp. 1-12. ISBN 0-453-00494-6;
LC 84-27324.

    b   New York: New American Library, Plume, 1986/03, pp. 1-12. ISBN 0-452-25802-2;
Paperback.

    c   New York: Signet, 1988/07, pp. 1-12. ISBN 0-451-15796-6. Paperback.

Section C - Forewords, Introductions, & Miscellaneous Commentary

C.046 **SWARTHMORE COLLEGE: AN INFORMAL HISTORY.**
Walton, Richard J.; Introduction by James A. Michener.
Swarthmore: Swarthmore College, 1986, pp. IX-XI.
The first complete history of the institution in modern times.

C.047 **AMERICA THROUGH AMERICAN EYES.**
Introduction by James A. Michener. Association of American Publishers, 1987.
Prepared for 1987 Moscow International Book Fair. Catalog includes 200 titles
from past two years by American authors.

C.048 **INDIAN LIFE IN TEXAS.**
Shaw, Charles: Foreword by James A. Michener. Photographs by Reagan Bradshaw.
Illustrated by the author with more than 100 pages of pen and ink drawings
and narrative of the history of the Texas Indian.

   a. Austin: State House Press, 1987, pp. ix-x. ISBN 0-938349-20-1; LC 87-17950.

   b Austin: State House Press, 1987, pp. ix-x. ISBN 0-938349-22-8.
Limited edition, signed, in slipcase, 100 copies.

   c Austin: State House Press, 1987, pp. ix-x. ISBN 0-938349-21-X. Paperback.

C.049 **TEXAS COLLECTOR: GAINES DE GRAFFENRIED.**
Conger, Roger N.; Introduction by James A. Michener. Graffenried was a gun
collector who advised Michener on the "great guns of the West" while writing
"**Texas**."

   a Waco, Tex.: Texian Press, 1987, iii-iv. ISBN 0-87244-080-X; LC 87-51532.

   b Waco, Tex.: Texian Press, 1987, iii-iv. ISBN 0-87244-080-X; LC 87-51532.
Limited Edition, leather bound. 50 copies, signed by Conger, Graffenried,
Michener, and R. L. Wilson.

C.050 **PLATTE RIVER ROAD NARRATIVES.**
Mattes, Merrill J.; Foreword by James A. Michener. Urbana: University of
Illinois Press, 1988, pp. ix-x. Two thousand personal accounts of travel over
the Great Central Overland Route (1812-1866). Published without dust jacket.

C.051 **TEXAS COLLECTS: FINE ART, FURNITURE, WINDMILLS & WHIMSEYS.**
Nathan, Paul; Foreword by James A. Michener.
Dallas: Taylor Publishing, 1988, pp. 8-9. ISBN 0-87833-554-4; LC 88-10182.
Profiles of a wide assortment of Texas collectors, their motivations, and their
whimsical collections.

C.052 **THE EDWIN POPE COLLECTION.**
Pope, Edwin; Introduction by James Michener. Dallas: Taylor Publishing, 1988,
pp. vii-x. ISBN 0-87833-609-5. A collection of the personal favorite sports
columns written by the author. The Sportswriter's Eye Series.

Section C - Forewords, Introductions, & Miscellaneous Commentary

C.053   **SOUTHEAST ALASKA.**
Simmerman, Nancy, photographer; Foreword by James A. Michener.
Text by Sarah Eppenbach. The book is a captivating photographic panorama
of the bountiful southern extremity of Alaska.

   a   Portland: Graphic Arts Center, 1988, pp. 9-10. ISBN 0-932575-65-X; LC 88-80473.

   b   Portland: Graphic Arts Center, 1988, pp. 9-10. ISBN 0-932575-73-0. Paperback.

C.054   **AGGIE GRAY: A SAMOAN SAGA.**
Alailima, Fay; Foreword by James A. Michener. Honolulu: Mutual Publishing,
1989, pp. vii-ix. ISBN 0-935180-79-6; LC 88-061418. Paperback. The life story
of a cross-cultural woman whose ninety year biography reviews Samoa's modern
history.

C.055   **KENNETH ROBERTS: THE MAN AND HIS WORKS.**
Bales, Jack; Afterword notes by James A. Michener. Metuchen, N.J.:
Scarecrow Press, 1989, p. 68. Scarecrow Author Bibliographies, No. 85.

C.056   **SHAPING EDUCATIONAL CHANGE: THE FIRST CENTURY OF THE
UNIVERSITY OF NORTHERN COLORADO AT GREELEY.**
Larson, Robert W.; Foreword by James A. Michener. Boulder: Colorado
Associated University Press, 1989, pp. xi-xv. ISBN 87081-172-X; LC 88-35288.
A chronicle of the first 100 years of the University. Michener was a member of the
faculty from 1936 to 1941.

C.057   **THUNDER GODS: THE KAMIKAZE PILOTS TELL THEIR STORY.**
Naito, Hatsuho; Foreword by James A. Michener. Translated by Mayumi Ichikawa
Originally published in 1982 by Bungei Shunju titled "Ohka hijo no tokko heiki."

   a   Tokyo, New York: Kodansha International, 1989, p. 7.
ISBN 0-87011-909-5; Japan ISBN 4-7700-1409-0; LC 88-81848.

   b   New York, Tokyo: Dell Publishing, 1990/07, p. v. ISBN 0-440-20498-4. Paperback.

C.058   **CLARENCE HOLBROOK CARTER.**
Trapp, Frank, Douglas Dreishpoon and Ricardo Pau-Llosa; Foreword by
James A. Michener. New York: Rizzoli, 1989, p. 7.
The foreword was originally published in *Arts Magazine*, 45:7 (1971/05) 43-44.

C.059   **THE HACIENDAS OF MEXICO: AN ARTIST'S RECORD.**
Bartlett, Paul Alexander; Foreword by James A. Michener. Niwot, Colo.:
University Press of Colorado, 1990, p. xv. Pen-and-ink and photographic illustrations
of the hacienda system which played such a formative role in Mexico's history.

C.060   **CHESAPEAKE BAY.**
Grieser, Robert; Introduction by James A. Michener. Photographs by Robert
Grieser. New York: Harry N. Abrams, 1990, pp. 6-7. ISBN 0-8109-3159-1.
A book of photographs. Michener says "This would be the Bay that I had
been trying to describe, and a great deal more."

Section C - Forewords, Introductions, & Miscellaneous Commentary

C.061 **THE FRAGILE SOUTH PACIFIC: AN ECOLOGICAL ODYSSEY.**
(*"HOME TO MY ISLANDS"*).
Mitchell, Andrew; Introduction by James A. Michener.
Austin: University of Texas Press, 1990, pp. 7-11. ISBN 0-292-72466-7.
Corrie Herring Hooks Series, No. 16. 2500 copies.

C.062 **AMERICA.**
Rajs, Jake; Foreword by James A. Michener. Photographs by Jake Rajs.
New York: Rizzoli, 1990, pp. 17-21. ISBN 0-8478-1244-8; LC 90-8169.
A book of photographs capturing in poetic visions America's untouched
ranges, wild forests, bustling cities and quiet towns.

C.063 **WORLD WAR II REMEMBERED - 1941: A WORLD AT WAR.**
Findley, Rowe; Introduction by James A. Michener. Washington: U.S. Postal
Service, 1991, p. 3. ISBN 0-15645-88842-5. The first of a series of five
books commemorating World War II. A sheet of 8 stamps is included,
designed by William H. Bond.

C.064 **OVER HAWAI'I.**
Goldsberry, Steven; Foreword by James A. Michener. Photographs by Reg Morrison.
New York: Mallard Press, 1991, pp. 14-15. "How elegantly 'Over Hawai'i' presents
an aerial view of Hawai'i's islands." ...from the foreword.

C.065 **WITH FIRE AND SWORD.**
("HENRY SIENKIEWICZ").
Sienkiewicz, Henryk; Foreword by James A. Michener. Translated by W. S.
Kuniczak. Published by the Society, Edward J. Piszek, president, to inaugurate
translations of Polish literary classics.

    a New York: Copernicus Society of America, 1991, pp. vii-x.
ISBN 0-87052-974-9; LC 91-161.

    b New York: Collier Books, 1993, pp. vii-x. ISBN 0-02-082044-5; LC 93-6524.
Paperback.

C.066 **THE ANDALUSIAN.**
Vavra, Robert; Foreword by James A. Michener. Photographs by Robert Vavra.
San Antonio: International Andalusian Horse Association, 1991, pp. 5-6.
ISBN 0-9629943-0-8; LC 91-91056. An anthology of Vavra's pictorial images of
Andalusian horses which evokes the glorious physique and inner nature of the breed.

C.067 **THE CHILD WHO NEVER GREW. 2ND ED.**
Buck, Pearl S.; Foreword by James A. Michener. Rockville: Woodbine House,
1992, pp. i-xi. ISBN 0-933149-49-2; LC 92-34844. Paperback.
Buck's inspiring account of her struggle to help and understand her daughter.
A discussion of the history of mental retardation.

C.068 **HAWAII AND POINTS SOUTH: TRUE TALES FROM THE PACIFIC.**
Day, A. Grove; Foreword by James A. Michener. Honolulu: Mutual Publishing,
1992, pp. vi-x. Paperback. A collection of many of Day's shorter writings from
forty years. It includes "The Globe Mutineers," written with Michener.

Section C - Forewords, Introductions, & Miscellaneous Commentary

C.069 **AMERICA: A HISTORY OF THE FIRST 500 YEARS.**
Grafton, John W.; Preface by James A. Michener. New York: Crescent Books,
1992, p. iii. ISBN 0-517-06681-5; LC 91-35553. A historical portrait of America.
350 photographs, engravings, paintings, lithographs and drawings. A mosaic.

C.070 **FACES OF THE EASTERN SHORE.** (*"MY FORWARD"*).
Van Riper, Frank; Forward by James A. Michener. Washington, D.C.:
Quesada House, 1992, pp. 6-7. ISBN 1-56566-012-9; LC 92-80364.
Paperback. Michener responds to a solicitation for a "forward" and in the
process, alters the meaning and spelling of the word "foreword."

C.071 **ROBERT VAVRA'S CLASSIC BOOK OF HORSES.**
Vavra, Robert; Introduction by James A. Michener. Photographs by Robert
Vavra. New York: William Morrow, 1992, pp. 5-6. ISBN 0-688-12019-9.
A celebration of Vavra's finest equine photographs followed by the stories
of the horses and the men who love them.

C.072 **BREAKING FREE FROM CORPORATE BONDAGE.**
Dainard, Michael; Foreword by James A. Michener. Chicago: Enterprise
Dearborn, 1993, pp. xi-xii. ISBN 0-79310-575-7; LC 92-45058.
Paperback. A roadmap for those wanting to change careers, and help in
eliminating the fear of striking out on your own.

C.073 **BARTON SPRINGS ETERNAL: THE SOUL OF A CITY.**
Pipkin, Turk, and Marshall Frech, eds.; Introduction by James A. Michener.
Austin: Softshoe, 1993, p. vii. ISBN 1-881484-05-X; LC 93-83037.
A fund raiser to preserve a cold water spring from pollution and ruin.
2500 copies, the first 500 are specially numbered.

C.074 **THE GREATEST ADVENTURE: STORIES AND PHOTOGRAPHS
BY MEN AND WOMEN WHO HAVE FLOWN IN SPACE.**
Foreword by James A. Michener. Sidney, Australia: C. Pierson, 1994,
ISBN 0-947068-19-8.

C.075 **MOUNTAINS IN THE MIST.**
Bansemer, Roger; Foreword James A. Michener. Dallas: Taylor Publishing, 1994,
pp. v-ix. ISBN 0-87833-839-x; LC 93-19261. Award winning artist takes you through
the Smokey region, explores a vanishing way of life, and captures remnants of its
people and habitats.

C.076 **PHILADELPHIA & ITS COUNTRYSIDE.**
Seitz, Ruth Hoover; Foreword by James A. Michener. Photographs by Blair Seitz.
Harrisburg: RB Books, 1994, p. 4. ISBN 1-879441-94-2; LC 94-092129.

C.077 **MEXICO.**
Hollenbeck, Cliff, and Nancy Hollenbeck, photographers;
Foreword by James A. Michener; essay by Richard J. Pietschmann. Portland, Ore.:
Graphics Arts Center, 1994, pp. 11-12. ISBN 1-55868-200-7; LC 94-77263.
A photographic display of Mexico.

Section C - Forewords, Introductions, & Miscellaneous Commentary

C.078   **JAMES A. MICHENER: THE BEGINNING TEACHER AND HIS TEXTBOOKS.**
Dybwad, G. L., and Joy V. Bliss; Foreword, notes and reminiscences by James A. Michener; Albuquerque: The Book Stops Here, 1995, pp. 9+.
ISBN 0-9631612-1-0; LC 95-79641. 12 signed and limited, 800 first editions.
The discovery of 18 of Michener's old teaching textbooks, with Michener's handwritten notes and original poetry. Comments on the seven books that most influenced him. A biography of his student and teaching years.

D.
Magazine Articles
by
James A. Michener

"When a recent publication asked me for six sharp pages
on a pressing topic, I warned them:
'In six pages I can't even say hello. But I'll invite you to cut.' "

—James A. Michener
LITERARY REFLECTIONS
State House Press, 1993

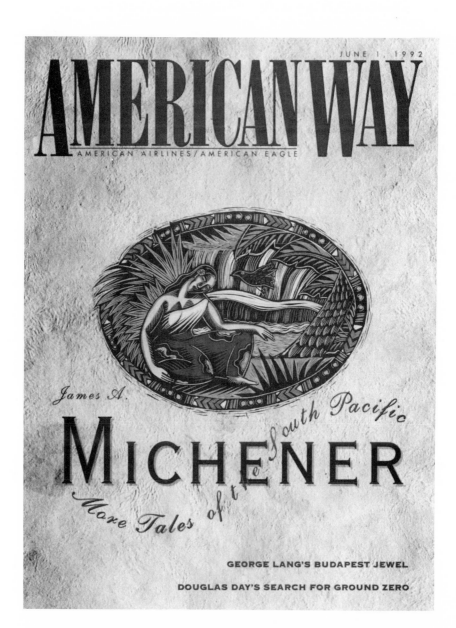

JUNE 1, 1992

AMERICANWAY

AMERICAN AIRLINES/AMERICAN EAGLE

James A.

MICHENER

More Tales of the South Pacific

GEORGE LANG'S BUDAPEST JEWEL

DOUGLAS DAY'S SEARCH FOR GROUND ZERO

American Way. D.254.

Section D - Magazine Articles by JAMES A. MICHENER

D.001 "**Diversions in the Student's Life.**" *Doylestown High School*, (1925/06/23). Commencement Program. Michener's address as class president presenting the class gift, a $500 scholarship endowment.

D.002 "**Dos Sabios.**" *The Portfolio*, (1926/11) 30. A poem about a Spanish legend from the Spanish of Calderon. *The Portfolio* is a literary quarterly publication of the students of Swarthmore College.

D.003 "**Gold.**" *The Portfolio*. A one act play about the impoverishment of an English nobleman. Noted as winning second prize in the Curtain Theater competition. (Not seen by bibliographer. Noted in "James A. Michener: A Bibliography" by John P. Hayes. New York: Bobbs-Merrill Company, 1984, p. 39.)

D.004 "**Pirate Gold.**" *The Portfolio*, 3:1 (1927/03) 18.

D.005 "**The Wizardry of Dis.**" *The Portfolio*, 3:3 (1927/10) 15-17.

D.006 "**Spring Virtue.**" *The Portfolio*, 4:1 (1928/03) 10-12. A poignant, melancholy poem about love, lost love, and lovers in search of love.

D.007 "**The Dramatists - in three acts.**" *The Portfolio*, 4:3 (1928/10) 8-10.

D.008 "**The Perils of Endowment.**" *Manuscript*, 2:2 (1931/01) 2-5, 20-29. A periodical published by Swarthmore College students.

D.009 "**Music and the Social Studies.**" *Social Studies*, 28:1 (1937/01) 28-30.

D.010 "**A Functional Social Studies Program.**" *Curriculum Journal*, 9 (1938/04) 163-64.

D.011 "**Sex Education: A success in Our Social Studies Classes.**" *Clearing House*, 12:8 (1938/04) 461-65.

D.012 "**Bach and Sugar Beets.**" *Music Educators Journal*, 25:1 (1938/09) 29, 43. Michener was the Director of Social Studies at Colorado State College of Education.

D.013 "**Discussion in the Schools.**" *Social Education*, 4 (1940/01) 4-5.

D.014 "**An Improved Unit Method.**" *Harvard Educational Review*, 10:2 (1940/03) 211-24.

D.015 "**P.E.A. Report.**" *Social Education*, 4:8 (1940/12) 530-31.

D.016 "**Teachers See New England.**" *Progressive Education*, 17:8 (1940/12) 546-47. Teachers in the community (Summary), from the article in *Social Studies*, 33:5 (1941/05) 219-21.

D.017 "**Democratic Education.**" *Social Education*, 5 (1941/04) 247-49.

D.018 "**Teachers in the Community.**" *Social Studies*, 32:5 (1941/05) 219-21. Summary in *Progressive Education*, 17 (1940/12) 546-47. Teachers visit three New England communities in an experiment in democracy.

Section D - Magazine Articles by JAMES A. MICHENER

D.019   **"Who is Virgil T. Fry?"**
Reprinted in **"Literary Reflections: Michener on Michener, Hemingway, Capote & Others."** (See A.064.)

    a   *Clearing House,* 16:2 (1941/10) 67-70.

    b   *Education Digest,* 7:3 (1941/11) 4-6.

    c   *Clearing House,* 19 (1944/10) 69-72.

    d   *Clearing House,* 23 (1948/09) 12-16.

    e   *Education Digest,* 20:9 (1955/05) 530-31.

    f   *Scholastic, 67* (1955/09/22) 97.

    g   *NEA Journal,* 50:6 (1961/09) 23-24.

    h   *Education Digest,* 51:3 (1985/11) 26-28.
Fiftieth Anniversary Commemorative Edition of *Education Digest.*

D.020   **"What are We Fighting For?"** *Progressive Education,* 18:7 (1941/11) 342-48.
Michener lists reasons why America should intervene in the war against
Nazi Germany.

D.021   **"Steps in Unit Learning and Teaching."**
Eastern Community Teachers Association, (1942) 58-68. 15th Yearbook.

D.022   **"Remittance Man."** *Saturday Evening Post,* 219:24 (1946/12/14) 16-17, 108-34.
Excerpt from **"Tales of the South Pacific."** Michener's first story sold to
a recognized magazine.

D.023   **"Best Man in de Navy."** *Saturday Evening Post,* 219:29 (1947/01/18) 18-19, 95-107.
Excerpt from **"Tales of the South Pacific."** Published in the *Post* prior to
the book.

D.024   **"The Empty Room."** *Ladies' Home Journal,* 64:9 (1947/09) 72-73, 139-53.

D.025   **"Yancy and the Blue Fish."**
Ladies' Home Journal, 64:11 (1947/11) 48-49, 149-59.

D.026   **"Out to Pasture."** *Nation's Business,* 37:4 (1949/04) 32-33, 70-74.

D.027   **"Reading Before Writing."**
Saturday Review of Literature, 32:18 (1949/04/30) 7-8+.

D.028   **"Idealism Today."**
Reprinted in "Readings for Opinion," New York: Prentice-Hall, 1952, pp. 34-39.

    a   *High Points,* 31 (1949/05) 13-21.

    b   *Education Digest,* 15:4 (1949/12) 44-47.

Section D - Magazine Articles by JAMES A. MICHENER

D.029   **"Main Line."** *Holiday,* 7:4 (1950/04) 34-57, 134.
Abridged in "Sidewalks of America." B. A. Botkin, ed. Indianapolis:
Bobbs-Merrill, 1954, pp. 414-15, 548-52.

D.030   **"Circles in the Sea."** *Holiday,* 7:5 (1950/05) 68-71. Excerpt, in part, from
"Return to Paradise," where the chapter is titled "The Atoll."

D.031   **"Fiji."** *Holiday,* 7:6 (1950/06) 60-63.
Excerpt from **"Return to Paradise."** Also in "Round the World with Famous
Authors." Garden City: Doubleday, 1958, p. 152.

D.032   **"Milk Run."** *Reader's Digest,* 56:338 (1950/06) 57-60.
Excerpt from **"Tales of the South Pacific."**

D.033   **"Myna Birds."** *Holiday,* 8:1 (1950/07) 26-29.
Excerpt from **"Return to Paradise,"** where it is titled "Mynah Birds."

D.034   **"Guadalcanal."** Chapter from **"Return to Paradise."**

    a   *Holiday,* 8:2 (1950/08) 66-72.

    b   Retitled **"Guadalcanal Today."** *Reader's Digest,* 58:350 (1951/06) 105-8.

D.035   **"The Ultimate Swine."** *Collier's,* 126:9 (1950/08/26) 18-19, 74-76.

D.036   **"4,100 Miles on a Raft."** *Saturday Review of Literature,* 33:38 (1950/09/23) 12-13.
Michener's review of "Kon-Tiki." Excerpt in "Composition of the Essay."
Reading, Mass.: Addison-Wesley, 1967, pp. 166-70.

D.037   **"Australia."** *Holiday,* 8:5 (1950/11) 98-109, 133-44.
Excerpt from **"Return to Paradise."**

D.038   **"Hawaii."** *Flair,* 1:11 (1950/12) 28-30. A precursor to the major themes in the novel
"Hawaii." Includes paintings by Edward John Stevens.

D.039   **"New Guinea."** *Holiday,* 8:6 (1950/12) 73. Excerpt from **"Return to Paradise."**

D.040   **"New Zealand."** Holiday, 9:1 (1951/01) 44-47.
Excerpt from **"Return to Paradise."** Also in "Round the World with Famous
Authors." Garden City: Doubleday, 1958, p. 141.

D.041   **"The Jungle."** *Today's Woman,* 23:136 (1951/02) 27-28, 132-51.
Excerpt from **"Return to Paradise."**

D.042   **"Polynesia."** *Holiday,* 9:3 (1951/03) 52-57, 94-97, 127+.
Excerpt from **"Return to Paradise."**

D.043   **"Siva Tonight!"** *Esquire,* 35:3 (1951/03) 40-41, 99.
Describes a native party for U. S. servicemen hosted by the famed Aggie
Grey. Native girls want babies by Americans.

Section D - Magazine Articles by JAMES A. MICHENER

D.044 "Proud Queen." *Esquire,* 35:4 (1951/04) 76, 141.
The Queen of Rivatabu writes a letter to a married serviceman who had crash landed on her island.

D.045 "Mr. Morgan." *Ladies' Home Journal,* 68:5 (1951/05) 58-59, 211-53.
Excerpt from "Return to Paradise."

D.046 "The Perfect Teacher." *Coronet,* 30:2 (1951/06) 21-24.
Also in "The Bedside Coronet." Garden City: Doubleday, 1952, pp. 191-95.
The story of Mother Margaret, island teacher.

D.047 "Blunt Truths About Asia."
Also in "Outside Readings in American Government."
New York: Crowell, 1952, p. 845.

   a *Life,* 30:23 (1951/06/04) 96, 100-21.

   b *Reader's Digest,* 59:353 (1951/09) 73-78. Condensed.

D.048 "Portraits for the Future."
Saturday Review of Literature, 34:31 (1951/08/04) 19-21.
Discusses leaders of and relations with India. Also appears in "Saturday Review Reader No. 2." New York: Bantam Books, 1953/02, pp. 122-33; and in "The Rhetoric Reader." Chicago: Scott-Foresman, 1962, pp. 253-54, titled "Sohan Lal."

D.049 "The Precious Drop." *Esquire,* 36:6 (1951/12) 121, 193-99. Reprinted in "Esquire Treasury." New York: Simon and Schuster, 1953, pp. 228-41.

D.050 "Chinese Success Story." *Life,* 31:27 (1951/12/31) 76-81.

D.051 "On the Sendai Train." *Esquire,* 37:4 (1952/04) 48-49.
A Japanese train carrying Korean combat casualties.

D.052 "Forgotten Heroes of Korea." *Saturday Evening Post,* 224:45 (1952/05/10) 19-21, 124-28. This story was the basis for the 1954 movie, "Men of the Fighting Lady," originally to have been titled "Panther Squadron."

D.053 "Tough Man for a Tough Job."
Lt. Gen. Matt Ridgway headed the peace negotiations in Korea.

   a *Life,* 32:19 (1952/05/12) 103-14.

   b *Reader's Digest,* 62:364 (1952/08) 15-20. Condensed.

D.054 "All for One: A Story from Korea." *Reader's Digest,* 61:363 (1952/07) 1-2.
This was Michener's inspiration for "The Bridges at Toko-ri."

D.055 "Japan." *Holiday,* 12:2 (1952/08) 26-41, 76-78. Also in "Round the World with Famous Authors." Garden City: Doubleday, 1958, p. 120.

D.056 "Mystery of Angkor." *Holiday,* 12:5 (1952/11) 44-47.

Section D - Magazine Articles by JAMES A. MICHENER

D.057   **"American in Tahiti."** *Paradise of the Pacific,* 65 (1953/01) 28-29.
Michener reviews the autobiography of James Norman Hall.

D.058   **"The Way it is in Korea."** *Reader's Digest,* 62:369 (1953/01) 15-20.
The stalemate between democracy and communism.

D.059   **"Hawaii."**

   a   *Holiday,* 13:5 (1953/05) 34-45, 88-95.

   b   Retitled **"Hawaii: A State of Happiness."** *Reader's Digest,* 63:376
(1953/08) 102-7. Condensed.

D.060   **"The Bridges at Toko-ri."** *Life,* 35:19 (1953/07/06) 58-87.
First published in *Life* prior to book publication.

D.061   **"Sayonara Means Goodbye."** *McCall's,* 81:1 (1953/10) 30-31, 121-28.
Part I of a three part series.

D.062   **"Sayonara Means Goodbye."** *McCall's,* 81:2 (1953/11) 30-31, 113-53.
Part II of a three part series.

D.063   **"Sayonara Means Goodbye."** *McCall's,* 81:3 (1953/12) 38-39, 89-119.
Part III of a three part series.

D.064   **"Facts About the GI Babies."** *Reader's Digest,* 64:383 (1954/03) 5-10.

D.065   **"Kabuki Is a Must for America."** *Theater Arts,* 38 (1954/03) 74-75.

D.066   **"One Must Respect Korean Culture."** *Reader's Digest,* 64:384 (1954/04) 15-19.

D.067   **"This I Believe."** *Reader's Digest,* 65:387 (1954/07) 143-44.
Reprint of "A Shameless Old Woman," in "This I Believe:2."
Raymond Swing, ed. New York: Simon & Schuster, 1954, pp. 96-97.

D.068   **"Sea of the Talented Traveler."** *Saturday Review,* 37:43 (1954/10/23) 47-48.

D.069   **"Pakistan: Divided It Stands."** *Reader's Digest,* 65:391 (1954/11) 136-46.

D.070   **"Thailand, Jewel of Asia."** *Reader's Digest,* 65:392 (1954/12) 57-66.

D.071   **"Islam: The Misunderstood Religion."**
The West should learn the facts about Muslims (not "Mohammedans").

   a   *Reader's Digest,* 66:397 (1955/05) 67-75.

   b   *Muslim Sunrise,* 27:3 (1955) 11.

   c   *The Ahmadiyya Movement in Islam,* (1955?) 2-12.

D.072   **"Japanese Comes Home."** *Saturday Review,* 38:4 (1955/01/22) 26.
Michener reviews "Homecoming," by Jiro Osaragi.

Section D - Magazine Articles by JAMES A. MICHENER

D.073   **"Writer's Wars."** *Saturday Review*, 38:4 (1955/01/22) 44.
Michener expresses appreciation for Hollywood's treatment of
"The Bridges at Toko-ri."

D.074   **"Pursuit of Happiness by a GI and a Japanese."** *Life*, 38:8 (1955/02/21) 124-41.

D.075   **"Historic Meeting in Indonesia."**
Reader's Digest, 67:400 (1955/08) 75-79.

D.076   **"Indonesia: Islands of Beauty and Turmoil."**
Reader's Digest, 67:401 (1955/09) 30-38.

D.077   **"Afghanistan: Domain of the Fierce and the Free."**
Reader's Digest, 67:403 (1955/11) 161-72.

D.078   **"International Maturity: A Report on Asia."**
Vital Speeches, 22 (1955/12/15) 147-51.
Speech as president of Fund for Asia, Inc. New York, October 5, 1955.

D.079   **"Legacy: The Australian Way."** *Reader's Digest*, 68:407 (1956/03) 57-60.

D.080   **"This Great Big Wonderful World."**
Also in "Best-In-Books." Garden City; Doubleday, 1957, pp. 449-59.

     a   *Holiday*, 19:3 (1956/03) 40-51.

     b   Condensed and retitled "**Home at Last.**" *Travel Holiday*, 174:2 (1991/02) 118.

D.081   **"Today's Wild West: The Great Australian North."**
Reader's Digest, 68:408 (1956/04) 63-70.

D.082   **"The Riddle of Pandit Nehru."** *Reader's Digest*, 69:411 (1956/07) 96-102.

D.083   **"Why I Like Japan."** *Reader's Digest*, 69:412 (1956/08) 182-91.
Collected in "Reader's Digest 40th Anniversary Treasury." Pleasantville:
Reader's Digest Association, 1961, pp. 380-86.

D.084   **"The Gift of Phan Tat Thanh."** *Reader's Digest*, 69:413 (1956/09) 163-64.
A pot-bellied porcelain Buddhist god, the good luck charm of an
Indo-Chinese baker, is given to General Eisenhower.

D.085   **"Madame Butterfly in Bobby Sox."** *Reader's Digest*, 69:414 (1956/10) 21-27.

D.086   **"The Bridge at Andau."** *Reader's Digest*, 70:419 (1957/03) 23-30.
Condensed from "**The Bridge at Andau.**" Michener received the Overseas Press
Club Award for this article, April 30, 1958.

D.087   **"The Prison at Recsk."** *Reader's Digest*, 70:421 (1957/05) 93-98.
Condensed from "**The Bridge at Andau.**"

D.088   **"Rascals in Paradise-Chapter I, Abridged ("The Globe Mutineers")." Part 1.**
This Week, (1957/05/05). Written with A. Grove Day.

Section D - Magazine Articles by JAMES A. MICHENER

D.089   **"Rascals in Paradise-Chapter I, Abridged ("The Globe Mutineers")." Part 2.**
This Week, (1957/05/12). Written with A. Grove Day.

D.090   **"Rascals in Paradise-Chapter I, Abridged ("The Globe Mutineers")." Part 3.**
This Week, (1957/05/19). Written with A. Grove Day.

D.091   **"Rascals in Paradise-Chapter I, Abridged ("The Globe Mutineers")." Part 4.**
This Week, (1957/05/26). Written with A. Grove Day.

D.092   **"Rascals in Paradise-Chapter I, Abridged ("The Globe Mutineers")." Part 5.**
This Week, (1957/06/02). Written with A. Grove Day.

D.093   **"While Others Sleep."** *Reader's Digest,* 71:426 (1957/10) 68-75.
Collected in "The Air Force Blue Book." Tom Compere, ed. New York:
Military Publishing Institute, 1961, pp. 50-64.

D.094   **"The Wonderful Art of Leeteg the Legend."** *True,* (1958/02) 36-39, 115-19.
Written with A. Grove Day. Abridged version of "**Rascals in Paradise**," Chapter 10.

D.095   **"A Present for Aunt Bessie."** *Vogue,* 131:6 (1958/03/15) 107.

D.096   **"Battle for Burma."** *Reader's Digest,* 72:432 (1958/04) 107-13.

D.097   **"Magic Malaya."** *Reader's Digest,* 73:437 (1958/09) 228-40.

D.098   **"Hawaii: The Case for Our Fiftieth State."**
Reader's Digest, 73:440 (1958/12) 158-60.

D.099   **"The Hardest-Working Women in the World."**
Reader's Digest, 74:443 (1959/03) 42-46.
American mothers, not having the housekeeping and baby sitting assistance
of mothers throughout the world, have to do it all.

D.100   **"The Magic Hand of Hokusai."** *Reader's Digest,* 74:446 (1959/06) 236-40.
Condensed from "**The Floating World**."

D.101   **"A View of 'Adventures in Paradise.' "** *TV Guide,* 7:40 (1959/10/03-10) 6-8.

D.102   **"South Pacific."** *Saturday Review,* 42:42 (1959/10/17) 41, 51-52.

D.103   **"Birth of Hawaii."** *Life,* 47:17 (1959/10/26) 154-70.
The opening chapter of "**Hawaii**." Published one month prior to hard cover.

D.104   **"Writing a Book in Hawaii."** *Paradise of the Pacific,* 71:11 (1959/11) 154-56.

D.105   **"Some Americans from Hawaii."** *Reader's Digest,* 75:452 (1959/12) 82-89.
Condensed from "**Hawaii**."

D.106   **"A Special Report to the Stockholders."** *Hawaiian Airlines, Ltd.* (1960) 11-18.
Testimony of James A. Michener on October 28, 1959, regarding the Trans-
Pacific Route Case.

Section D - Magazine Articles by JAMES A. MICHENER

D.107 "An Eastern Art Goes Western." *Horizon,* 2:5 (1960/05) 102-14.

D.108 "The Red Brute."
Man's Magazine, 8:9 (1960/09) 24-27, 44-48.
Excerpt from "The Bridge at Andau."

D.109 "People of the Pacific." *Saturday Review,* 43:46 (1960/11/12) 41-43.
Includes sightseer's map of the Pacific by Michener and Doug Anderson.

D.110 "Hawaiian Holidays." *Look,* 24:26 (1960/12/20) 31-32.
Christmas in Hawaii, in full color, with text by Michener.

D.111 "My Other Books." *Harper's Magazine,* 222:1328 (1961/01) 42-44.
Michener appreciates fans' erroneous impressions that he wrote such famous
books as "From Here to Eternity," "Kon Tiki," etc.

D.112 "Frances Sabin Gets People to Buy Books They Didn't Know They Wanted."
Publishers Weekly, 179:2 (1961/01/09) 31-34.
Frances Sabin was a good friend of Michener's who worked an all-night
shift at the Waikiki Branch of The Honolulu Bookstore.

D.113 "I Would Not Minimize That Apprenticeship."
A tape-recorded interview before writing classes of Sylvan Karchmer and
Ralph J. Salisbury at the University of Oregon.

    a   *Northwest Review,* 4:2 (1961/Spring) 5-27.

    b   Excerpt titled "Two-Finger Exercise." *Beacon,* 1 (1961/05) 8-9.

    c   Excerpt titled "Thoughts on Writing." *Writer,* 75:5 (1962/05) 12-13, 46.

D.114 "Inside Kennedy's Election." *Look,* 25:10 (1961/05/09) 56-81.
Excerpt from "Report of the County Chairman."

D.115 "Golden People." *Coronet,* 50:3 (1961/07) 49-65. Excerpt from "Hawaii."

D.116 "Mexico's Mild-Mannered Matador." *Reader's Digest,* 79:471 (1961/07) 202-6.
(See A.020.) Reprinted as "The Matador Who Conquered Mexico."
A student project of A. C. Townsend. Oxford: College of Technology, 1965-66.

D.117 "Should Artists Boycott New York?" *Saturday Review,* 44:34 (1961/08/26) 12.

D.118 "Speaking Out - Why I Am Running for Congress." *Saturday Evening Post,*
235:18 (1962/05/05) 8, 12.

D.119 "Confessions of a Political Candidate." *Reader's Digest,* 81:487 (1962/11) 199-204.
Reprint of "What Every New Candidate Should Know,"
New York Times Magazine, 112:38,228 (1962/09/23) VI, 23.

D.120 "James A. Michener writes 'Elect me to Congress.' "
Panorama, 4:9 (1962/11) 16-18.

D.121 "Michener on Reichenburg." *Art Voices,* (1962/11) 22.

Section D - Magazine Articles by JAMES A. MICHENER

D.122   **"When Does Education Stop?"** *Reader's Digest,* 81:488 (1962/12) 153-56.
Condensed from address at MacAlester College. Also in "Reader's Digest
50th Anniversary Treasury." Pleasantville: Reader's Digest Association, 1972,
pp. 461-63, titled "You Never Stop Learning."

D.123   **"Adventures of Men and Their Ships."** *Life,* 53:25 (1962/12/21) 96-98, 111-14.
Collected in "Success in Writing 2." Menlo Park: Addison-Wesley, 1968, pp. 1- 2.

D.124   **"Caravans."** *Ladies' Home Journal,* 80:6 (1963/07-08) 79-86, 112-44. Excerpt.

D.125   **"The Hermitage - Russia's Fabulous Art Palace."**
Reader's Digest, 86:515 (1965/03) 133-41. Located on the Neva River,
Leningrad. 2500 rooms containing 2,300,000 art objects with 14,000 paintings.
A 15 mile tour.

D.126   **"Miracles of Santiago."** *Reader's Digest,* 87:519 (1965/07) 228-34.
A story of an annual religious pilgrimage by hundreds of thousands to Spain's
sacred city of Santiago de Campostela.

D.127   **"The Writer's Public Image."** *Esquire,* 64:6 (1965/12) 150, 264-74. Letter.

D.128   **"James Michener's Tribute to 'Unknown Friend.' "** *Horizons,* 7:1 (1965/Fall) 20.
Haverford College. Granville Toogood's book, "Huntsman in the Sky," played
an important role in Michener's literary career.

D.129   **"Don't Knock the Rock."** *Reader's Digest,* 88:526 (1966/02) 157-60.
Condensed from the *New York Times Magazine,* 115 (1965/10/31) 56-57, titled
"One Near Square Who Doesn't Knock the Rock."

D.130   **"J. Michener on THE Desire To Explore."**
Pennsylvania State University Collegian, (1966/03/04) 1.
Regarding the need to develop a new American spirit for the developing
social revolution in this country.

D.131   **"Four Miracles - And a Masterpiece."** *Reader's Digest,* 89:535 (1966/11) 158-65.
Andrew Mellon, the Widener family, Samuel H. Kress, and Chester Dale,
endow the National Gallery of Art with art treasures.

D.132   **"Lee Gatch."** *Art International,* 11:2 (1967/02/20) 20-21.
Gatch, a contemporary American artist, was Michener's neighbor. Michener examines
the use of stone in his art.

D.133   **"Israel: Nation Too Young to Die."** *Look,* 31:16 (1967/08/08) 64-74. Collected in
"Israel: A Reader." Philadelphia: Chilton Book Company, 1968, pp. 146-66.

D.134   **"A Christmas Present."**
Reader's Digest, 91:548 (1967/12) 60-63. An elderly lady's gift of carbon paper
disappointed a young Michener, who expected skates, but opened new worlds of ideas.

D.135   **"Iberia: Spanish Travels and Reflections."**
Saturday Evening Post, 241:4 (1968/02/24) 34-56. Excerpt from "**Iberia**."

Section D - Magazine Articles by JAMES A. MICHENER

D.136   **"Spain's Secret Wilderness."** *Holiday,* 43:4 (1968/04) 40-45, 110-22.
Excerpt from "**Iberia**."

D.137   **"Publishing on a Sub-Tropical Island."**
Publishers Weekly, 194:1 (1968/07/01) 26-27.

D.138   **"The Weapons We Need to Fight Pornography."**
Reader's Digest, 93:560 (1968/12) 125-30. Though opposed to censorship,
Michener believes that obscene materials should not be available to young people.

D.139   **"GMRX: An Alternative to Movie Censorship."**
Reader's Digest, 94:561 (1969/01) 87-93.
The motion picture industry creates a code system to restrict children viewers in order
to avoid government censorship.

D.140   **"Presidential Lottery: The Reckless Gamble in Our Electoral System."**
Reader's Digest, 94:565 (1969/05) 247-76. Condensed.

D.141   **"Madrid's Fabulous Prado."** *Reader's Digest,* 94:566 (1969/06) 145-51.
Spain's royal collection (13th to the 19th centuries), includes works by
Titian, Rubens, Goya, El Greco, and Velazquez.

D.142   **"Those Fabulous Italian Designers."** *Reader's Digest,* 95:569 (1969/09) 157-66.
The "Italian line," including everything from cars to high fashion, becomes Italy's
prime export.

D.143   **"A hit - in any language."** *TV Guide,* 18:22 (1970/03/30) 4-9.
The glowing account of how Michener became involved with "The Forsyte Saga,"
which has captivated audiences in 55 nations. Reprinted in "TV Guide, the First 25
Years." New York: Simon & Schuster, 1978, pp. 169-71.

D.144   **"Why I Collect Art."** *Reader's Digest,* 96:577 (1970/05) 147-52.
Art exhibition in Venice leads Michener to a decision to invest his
savings each year in American art created in his lifetime.

D.145   **"Soccer's Wild World Cup Scramble."** *Reader's Digest,* 96:578 (1970/06) 173-82.
16 international teams compete for the Jules Rimet Cup (World Cup) named
after the French official who originated the event.

D.146   **"The Social Critic and 'Somber Witness on an Enchanted Holiday.' "**
Orientations, 1 (1970/10) 24ff.

D.147   **"The Drifters."** *Ladies' Home Journal,* 87:11 (1970/11) 161-68. Excerpt.

D.148   **"The Mature Social Studies Teacher."** *Social Education,* 34 (1970/11) 760-67.
Anniversary Edition. Michener's experiences as a social studies teacher.

D.149   **"Can a Sixty-two-year-old with a History of Heart Trouble Find Fulfillment
Running with the Bulls in the Streets of Pamplona?"**
Esquire, 74:6 (1970/12) 177-83. Pages 182 and 183 set forth seven theories why
a sixty-two-year old would seek such fulfillment.

Section D - Magazine Articles by JAMES A. MICHENER

D.150   *"The Collector: An Informal Memoir." Texas Quarterly,* 13 (1970/Spring) 6-25.
The entire issue is devoted to the Michener Collection at the University of Texas.
An 18 page insight into Michener's psyche.

D.151   **"Novelist Reviews Kent Tragedy."** *Kent State University FYI,*
3:13 (1971/01/04) 2-3. Complete text of Michener's commencement address
regarding the Kent State University riot of May 4, 1970.

D.152   **"Kent State - Campus Under Fire.** *Reader's Digest,* 98:587 (1971/03) 57-63.
Part I of two parts. Condensed from **"Kent State; What Happened and Why."**

D.153   **"Kent State; What Happened and Why."**
Reader's Digest, 98:588 (1971/04) 217-20.
Part II of two parts. Condensed from **"Kent State; What Happened and Why."**

D.154   **"Clarence Carter."** *Arts Magazine,* 45:7 (1971/05) 43-44.
Used as a foreword in "Clarence Holbrook Carter." New York: Rizzoli, 1989.

D.155   **"Peace of Mind."** *Look,* 35:15 (1971/07/27) 22.

D.156   **"What the F.B.I. Has on Me."** *Esquire,* 76:6 (1971/12) 134-35, 224.
Michener's tongue-in-cheek description of a hypothetical file on himself.

D.157   **"One-and-a-Half Cheers for Change.** *Reader's Digest,* 99:596 (1971/12) 209.
Abridged from *New York Times Magazine,* 120:41,497 (1971/09/05) VI, 9, 35-39.
Not all change is progress. Lack of change spells doom for a society.

D.158   **"How to Think About Race."** *Sepia,* 20:4 (1971/04) 44-50.
"A guide for white Americans... and blacks, too..."
Excerpt from **"The Quality of Life."**

D.159   **"Unusually Close Working Relationship: James A. Michener and
Albert Erskine."**
Publishers Weekly, 201:15 (1972/04/10) 12, 104-5.

D.160   **"Homesick for Hawaii."** *Ladies' Home Journal,* 89:5 (1972/05) 58-60.

D.161   **"China Diary."** *Reader's Digest,* 100:601 (1972/05) 241-44.
Michener accompanies President Nixon on a precedent-breaking visit to
Peking to re-establish communications with China.

D.162   **"The Arts. (James A. Michener)."**
Swarthmore College Bulletin, 76:7 (1972/07) 4-12.
Alumni issue. Michener joins in a symposium on "A Life in the Arts," in
the 50th anniversary of his graduation.

D.163   **"To Moscow: A Mission for Peace."** *Reader's Digest,* 101:605 (1972/09) 111-17.
Michener reports on an historic Soviet-American summit meeting. A vivid
personal impression of the country and its people.

D.164   **"Background: 'Hawaii.' "** *TV Guide,* 22:1 (1974/01/05-12) 27-28.

Section D - Magazine Articles by JAMES A. MICHENER

D.165   **"More Than an Enlightened Rabbi."** *Jewish Exponent,* 155:4 (1974/01/25) 31. Michener reviews the biography of Joseph Krauskopf, founder of Farm School (a Jewish agricultural school) west of Doylestown.

D.166   **"Lame Beaver; The Life of a Plains Indian."** *Reader's Digest,* 104:624 (1974/04) 205-56. Excerpt from **"Centennial."**

D.167   **"The Wagon and the Elephant."** *Ladies' Home Journal,* 91:9 (1974/09) 100-1. Excerpt from **"Centennial."**

D.168   **"Go Waste, Young Man."** Wasting time is not always wasted time. Experiences that many people consider wasted time can lead to productivity and insight.

    a   *Campus Colloquy,* 1:1 (1974/Winter) 6-7.

    b   Retitled **"On Wasting Time."** *Reader's Digest,* 105:630 (1974/10) 193-96.

D.169   **"Life and Death of the Dinosaur."** *Reader's Digest,* 105:631 (1974/11) 219-23. Excerpt from **"Centennial."**

D.170   **"The Crime."** *Ladies' Home Journal,* 92:3 (1975/03) 78-79. Excerpt from **"Centennial."**

D.171   **"Michener off the cuff."** *Swarthmore College Bulletin,* (1975/04) 1-7. Alumni issue. Also, at page 28, a brief note on the publication of **"Centennial."**

D.172   **"Our 200th Birthday."** *TV Guide,* 23:26 (1975/06/28) 2-11. Television's approach to the Bicentennial will be "...without the soul-lifting celebration we might have hoped for."

D.173   **"The Jungle World of Juvenile Sports."** *Reader's Digest,* 107:644 (1975/12) 109-12. Excerpt from **"Sports in America."**

D.174   **"Pilgrimage for Peace."** *Saturday Evening Post,* 248:1 (1976/01-02) 66-67. Michener reflects on Cardinal John Joseph Krol's journey to the Holy Land.

D.175   **"What America Means to Me."** *Reader's Digest,* 108:646 (1976/02) 171-72. An opportunity for upward mobility where everyone has a chance to win an education, land a good job, and contribute to society.

D.176   **"Women Who Win."** *Ladies' Home Journal,* 93:3 (1976/03) 70-71, 82-85. Excerpt from **"Sports in America."**

D.177   **"Where Did the Animals Go?"** *Reader's Digest,* 108:650 (1976/06) 123-27. Contrasting theories for extinct species: that nomadic hunters from Asia killed them, or, climatic changes destroyed them.

D.178   **"Work to make the world work better."** An autobiographical statement about his Puritan work ethic.

    a   *Think,* 42:3 (1976/07) 70-71. The IBM magazine. Bicentennial issue.

Section D - Magazine Articles by JAMES A. MICHENER

b   Condensed and retitled "**The Path to Achievement**." *Reader's Digest,* 110:657 (1977/01) 149-50.

D.179   "**South Pacific - Returning to Paradise**." *Clipper,* 16:11 (1976/11) 12-19. Excerpt from "**Return to Paradise**." Published by Pan Am/Inter-Continental Hotels for passengers.

D.180   "**He Painted the West**." *Reader's Digest,* 110:661 (1977/05) 60-61. Frederic Remington captured the salient characteristics of the American West in art, sculpture, and writing.

D.181   "**James Michener Comments on Worlds and Exploration**." *Social Education,* 41 (1977/05) 377. Comments excerpted from a transcript of a panel discussion June 2, 1976, sponsored by NASA. [This could be July 2, 1976.] (See F.073.)

D.182   "**Sights and Sounds Of Far-off Lands**." *TV Guide,* 25:25 (1977/06/18-25) 24-26. The first installment of "James Michener's World" seeks to bring alive the sights and sounds of the Holy Land.

D.183   "**Author James Michener on the Future of this Country**." *U.S. News & World Report,* 83:11 (1977/09/12) 60-61.

D.184   "**The American Family**." *Ladies' Home Journal,* 94:12 (1977/12) 87-89, 158-66.

D.185   "**Islands**."

a   *Travel and Leisure,* 8:1 (1978/01) 37-39.

b   Condensed and retitled "**Reflections of a Nesomaniac**." *Reader's Digest,* 112:674 (1978/06) 189-90.

c   "**Reflections of a Nesomaniac**." *Mutual Publishing Catalog,* (1990/Fall) 3-6.

D.186   "**Rosalind's Revenge**." *Ladies' Home Journal,* 95:6 (1978/06) 94-95. Part I of two parts. Excerpt from "**Chesapeake**."

D.187   "**Rosalind's Revenge**." *Ladies' Home Journal,* 95:7 (1978/07) 115-22. Part II of two parts. Excerpt from "**Chesapeake**."

D.188   "**The Watermen**." *Reader's Digest,* 113:678 (1978/10) 164-73. Condensed from "**Chesapeake**."

D.189   "**Chesapeake**." *Book Digest,* 6:1 (1979/01) 177-206. Excerpt from "**Chesapeake**." Development in the area beginning with Jamestown and continuing through independence in 1637.

D.190   "**Space Exploration: Military and Non-military Advantages**." *Vital Speeches,* 45:19 (1979/07/15) 578-81. Testimony before the U.S. Senate Subcommittee on Science, Technology, and Space, February 1, 1979.

Section D - Magazine Articles by JAMES A. MICHENER

D.191   "How to Use a Library." *International Paper Co.* (1980) 2.
An advertisement used in newspapers and magazines for International Paper
Company's series "The Power of the Printed Word." Collected in "How To Use The
Power of The Printed Word." New York: Anchor Press, Doubleday, 1985, pp. 40-48.

D.192   "Looking Toward Space." *Omni*, 2:8 (1980/05) 56-58, 121.
"....if a nation misses the great movements of its time, it misses the foundations on
which it can build the future."

D.193   "James A. Michener Comments on 'The Anti-Science Epidemic.' "
Social Education, 44 (1980/05) 376-80. A speech delivered at the Washington
conference of the National Space Institute on June 15, 1979.

D.194   "Memoirs of a Pacific Traveler." *Saturday Review*, 7:10 (1980/06) 40-56.

D.195   "Keepers of the Covenant." *Reader's Digest*, 117:700 (1980/08) 126-36, 185-220.
Part I of two parts. Condensed from "**The Covenant**."

D.196   "Star of Freedom." *Reader's Digest*, 117:701 (1980/09) 200-35.
Part II of two parts. Condensed from "**The Covenant**."

D.197   "Covenant." *Ladies' Home Journal*, 97:11 (1980/11) 94-95.
Excerpt from "**The Covenant**." A sixteen year old Dutch girl is rejected by
boy and rebounds to marry older schoolmaster.

D.198   "Watermen." *Country Gentleman*, (1980/Fall) 38.
Excerpt from "**The Watermen**."

D.199   "The Little Wanderers." *Families*, 1:1 (1980/Fall) 134-52.
Premier Issue. A Reader's Digest publication. Condensed from
"**The Covenant**." Family characteristics in the African Bushmen.

D.200   "Covenant, Part I." *People Weekly*, 15:1 (1981/01/12) 57-60.
Excerpt from "**The Covenant**." Frenchman flees religious persecution for a
new frontier, South Africa.

D.201   "Covenant, Part II." *People Weekly*, 15:2 (1981/01/19) 49-52.
Excerpt from "**The Covenant**." Frenchman Paul de Pre covets his neighbor's
house and daughter.

D.202   "Covenant, Part III." *People Weekly*, 15:3 (1981/01/26) 41-44. Excerpt from
"**The Covenant**." Two women struggle to save a vineyard and a dynasty.

D.203   "The Covenant." *Family Circle*, 94:2 (1981/03/03) 32, 34-36.
Excerpt from "**The Covenant**." Oxford graduate, Frank Saltwood, decides to
leave employment with Cecil Rhodes to marry Maud Turner.

D.204   "The Covenant." *Book Digest*, 8:4 (1981/04) 185-215.
Excerpt from "**The Covenant**." Growing hostility to English rule by the
Dutch erupts into the Boer War.

D.205   "Manifest Destiny." *Omni*, 3:7 (1981/04) 48-50, 102-4.
Michener visits the world's first spaceship.

Section D - Magazine Articles by JAMES A. MICHENER

D.206 **"James A. Michener on Integrity in Journalism."**
U.S. News & World Report, 90:17 (1981/05/04) 80.

D.207 **"Straight from the Source. Michener Talks Back."** *Philadelphia,* (1981/08) 21.
An edited version of Michener's response to Bruce Bean's article
"The Source," *Philadelphia,* (1986/06) 126.

D.208 **"Michener Remembers."** *The Hill School,* (1981/09) 12-13. Hill School Bulletin.

D.209 **"How America Lives."** *Ladies' Home Journal,* 98:10 (1981/10) 87, 121-24.

D.210 **"Why We'll Never Elect a Bald President."** *TV Guide,* 29:40 (1981/10/03-10) 4-6.
Michener discusses the potential for the future of television, its effect
on politics, education, etc.

D.211 **"Why Man Explores."** *Omni,* 4:2 (1981/11) 60-62, 116-18.
Reprint. With Carl Sagan, Arthur C. Clarke, Ray Bradbury, Philip Morrison
and Norman Cousins, Michener reflects on Space. (See F.073.)

D.212 **"Michener Looks at Today and Tomorrow."**
Nation's Business, 70:2 (1982/02) 70-72.
Excerpts from "James A. Michener's USA."New York: Crown Publishers, 1981.

D.213 **"Six Against the Heavens."** *People Weekly,* 18 (1982/09/20) 66-68.
Excerpt from "**Space**," appearing prior to book publication. The astronaut
candidates are examined and tested. Six are chosen.

D.214 **"Death and Daring on the Moon."** *People Weekly,* 18:13 (1982/09/27) 62-64.
Astronauts are supposed to lead exemplary lives but struggle to resist
seductive temptations.

D.215 **"Space."** *Ladies' Home Journal,* 99:10 (1982/10) 88-89, 154-62.
Excerpt from "**Space**." Astronaut hopeful, John Pope, and high school
sweetheart, Penny Hardesty, discover the universe.

D.216 **"Space."** *Playboy,* 29:10 (1982/10) 88-92+. Excerpt from "**Space**." The final Apollo
mission. Three men on their way to the far side of the moon.

D.217 **"James A. Michener: My First 75 Years."** *Family Weekly,* (1982/10/10) 4-9.
Michener discusses his Dickensian boyhood, his late-in-life success as a
novelist and the pleasures and pressures of fame.

D.218 **"Historical Fiction."** *American Heritage,* 33:3 (1982/4-5) 44-48.

D.219 **"The Courtship."** *McCall's,* 110:11 (1983/08) 110-18. Excerpt from "**Poland**."

D.220 **"Poland: 1939."** *Penthouse,* 15:2 (1983/10) 74-78, 160-67. Excerpt from "**Poland**."

D.221 **"Why I Am For Walter Mondale."** *New Republic,* 190:22 (1984/06/04) 16-18.

D.222 **"A Bizarre, Extraordinary Convention."**
U.S. News & World Report, 97:5 (1984/07/30) 30-32.

Section D - Magazine Articles by JAMES A. MICHENER

D.223   **"A Buoyant, Optimistic Convention."**
U.S. News & World Report, 97:10 (1984/09/03) 30-32.

D.224   **"James Michener's Recipe for a Longer, Better Life."**
Reader's Digest, 125:752 (1984/12) 87-90.
Discipline, diet and reasonable exercise. Condensed from *New York Times Magazine,* (1984/08/19), titled "Living With an Ailing Heart."

D.225   **"Introducing Hemingway."** *Publishers Weekly,* 227:2 (1985/01/11) 40-41.
Excerpt from "The Dangerous Summer." New York: Charles Scribner's Sons, 1985.

D.226   **"Hemingway, Bullfighting, and Me."** *Signature,* 20:5 (1985/05) 46-51.
Published by Diner's Club.

D.227   **"Texas."** *McCall's,* 112:10 (1985/07) 94-102. Excerpt from "**Texas**."

D.228   **"Taxing Charitable Giving Would Undermine Our Worthiest Institutions."**
Swarthmore College Bulletin, (1985/08) 8. Alumni issue.

D.229   **"Liberal Arts Decline is Not Gain For Technology."**
Swarthmore College Bulletin, (1985/08) 9-10. Alumni issue.

D.230   **"The Secret of America."** *Parade,* (1985/09/15) 6.
Michener marvels at the genius of the Founding Fathers. Excerpt from
Michener's introduction to "The Constitution," by Sam Fink.

D.231   **"Comment."** *Discovery,* 10:2 (1986) 2-3.
Michener comments on the Texas Sesquicentennial in this quarterly publication of the
University of Texas.

D.232   **"James A. Michener's USA."** *Popular Mechanics,* 163:7 (1986/07) 108-9.
Excerpt from "James A. Michener's USA." New York: Crown Publishers, 1981.

D.233   **"Legacy."** *Ladies' Home Journal,* 104:9 (1987/09) 104. Excerpt from "**Legacy**."

D.234   **"Together for Life."** *Reader's Digest,* 131:785 (1987/09) 106-9.
Excerpt from "**Chesapeake**."

D.235   **"Saving the Nation."** *Art & Antiques,* (1987/10) 92-97.
Henry Mercer's mad dash to capture living history.

D.236   **"A Do-it-yourself Novel."** *Sports Illustrated,* 68:10 (1988/03/07) 111-13. Plot for
a story about the NCAA basketball championships, with fictitious teams involved.

D.237   **"What Should We Tell Our Children About Viet Nam."** *American Heritage,*
39:4 (1988/05-06) 70. Numerous persons answer the question, including Michener.

D.238   **"Alaska."** *Cosmopolitan,* 205:1 (1988/07) 200-7. Excerpt from "**Alaska**."

D.239   **"The Great American Bathroom Conspiracy."**
Reader's Digest, 133:796 (1988/08) 58-60. "...the American water closet has become
so complicated that no mere mortal can make it function."

Section D - Magazine Articles by JAMES A. MICHENER

D.240   **"Patriotism and the Olympics: There Can Be Too Much of a Good Thing."**
TV Guide, 36:38 (1988/09/17-23) 16-18.

D.241   **"Inflated Reputations."** *American Heritage*, 39:5 (1988/7-8) 59.
Comments on General Custer and James N. Polk.

D.242   **"Giving it Away."**
Art & Antiques, 6 ((1989/03) 137-8. Michener discovers the collector's last resort.

D.243   **"The Unlikely Paradise of Presidio. (My Favorite Place)."**
Texas Monthly, 17 (1989/05) 100.

D.244   **"Caribbean."** *American Way*, 22:20 (1989/10/15) 63-64, 114-21.
Published by American Airlines. Excerpt from **"Caribbean."**

D.245   **"Caribbean."** *Islands*, 9:6 (1989/11/01) 90.
Excerpt from **"Caribbean."** A zombie returns to her Haitian village and is
rescued from the living dead.

D.246   **"Once in a Lifetime. (Series of short related articles)."**
American Heritage, 40:8 (1989/12) 51-65.
A Brush With History. Michener's TV interview with Karol Cardinal Wojtyla
(Voy-tee-ya), later to become Pope John Paul II.

D.247   **"Rings of Deceit: The Olympic Hypocrisy."**

    a   *SportsTravel*, 2:1 (1990/01) 49-51.
Magazine provides travel information for the sports world.

    b   Retitled **"The Olympic Hypocrisy: Rings of Deceit."**
Track & Field Quarterly Review, 91:4 (1991/Winter) 4-6.

D.248   **"Michener on the Movies."**
Endless Vacation, (1990/May-June), 30-32, 111. A fictional tongue in cheek
recommendation to take a cruise as a way of seeing current movies.

D.249   **"Are There Limits To Free Speech?"** *Parade*, (1990/11/18) 4-6.
An essay on censorship.

D.250   **" 'And Then I Wrote.' "** 238:4 (1991/01/24) 10-17.
A collection of authors. Some of spring's top authors give an inside look at their new
books. Spring Announcements Issue.

D.251   **"What is the Secret of Teaching Values?"**
"1492-Rediscover America-1992." Part of advertising program by Chrysler
Corporation titled "How to Make Our Nation Better."

    a   *People Weekly*, 35:10 (1991/03/18) 68-69.

    b   *Fortune*, 123:6 (1991/03/25) 78-79.

    c   *Life*, 14:4 (1991/04) 52-53.

Section D - Magazine Articles by JAMES A. MICHENER

d   *Money,* 20:4 (1991/04) S14-15.

e   Retitled '**Early Echoes.**' In "Personal Glimpses,"
Reader's Digest, 140:842 (1992/06) 163.

D.252   **"We Can Create a Decent Society."** *Parade,* (1991/11/24) 4-7.
Full cover photo of Michener. Excerpt from "**The World is My Home.**"

D.253   **"The Honest Merchant of Herat."** *Reader's Digest,* 140:841 (1992/05) 131-33.
Condensed from "**The World is My Home.**" Story first appeared in "A Present
for Aunt Bessie," *Vogue,* 131:6 (1958/03/15) 107.

D.254   **"Return to Paradise."** *American Way,* 25:11 (1992/06/01) 62-68, 108-10.
An American Airlines complementary magazine.
The cover headnotes "James A. Michener: More Tales of the South Pacific."

D.255   **"Foreword" [Bulls of Iberia].** *La Busca,* 28: 11-12 (1992/11-12) 52-53.

D.256   **"Who's Patriotic?"** *Town & Country,* 146:5146 (1992/12) 47-51.
Michener and 30 other prominent Americans answer the question.
Compiled by Jennifer Ash and Stephanie H. O'Brien.

D.257   **"The Road to Worlds Unknown."** *Current Books,* 1:1 (1992/Summer) 22-26.
Excerpt from "**The World is My Home: A Memoir.**"

D.258   **"Space and the Human Quest. (America at 500: Pioneering the Space Frontier)."**
National Forum, 72 (1992/Summer) 3.

D.259   **"In Appreciation of a Hesitant Bull."** *At Random,* 1:1 (1992/Winter) 50-51.
Excerpt from "**The World is My Home.**" Also includes a photograph of Michener
titled "Portrait of the artist as an old man sucking in his gut."

D.260   **"A Debt of Honor."** *At Random,* 1:1 (1992/Winter) 47-49.
Excerpt from "**The World is My Home.**" Anecdote first appeared in "A Present
for Aunt Bessie," *Vogue,* 131:6 (1958/03/15) 107.

D.261   **"After the War: The Victories at Home."** *Newsweek,* 121:3 (1993/01/11) 26-27.
How World War II changed America. Seven noted authors reflect on the
legacy of the World War II generation.

D.262   **"A Novel Approach: Mr. Megabook's Dream Machine."**
Forbes ASAP, 151 (1993/06/07) 25-27.
Michener expresses his enthusiastic support for word processors and
describes the computer accessories for future writers.

D.263   **"My Advice to Young America."**
New Choices For Retirement Living, 33:7 (1993/09) 22-25.
Michener's advice: Develop rules for your profession; extend productivity
for many decades; develop morality. Also includes note titled "Some Wisdom
for the Elders, Too," at p. 25.

Section D - Magazine Articles by JAMES A. MICHENER

D.264   **"Whose Turf is it Anyway - The Colonels or the Squirrels?"**
New Choices For Retirement Living, 33 (1993/11) 46-50.
Excerpt from **"Creatures of the Kingdom."**

D.265   **"Earth and Flame."** *La Busca,* 29 (1993/11-12) 36-41.
This essay is interspersed between ongoing dialogue and narrative in **"Mexico."**
It is uninterrupted in *La Busca.*

D.266   **"Pointed Reminder."** In "Personal Glimpses,"
Reader's Digest, 143:859 (1993/12) 25-26.
Michener's formula for stimulating new productivity from old apple trees and authors.

D.267   **"Life Outside Academe."** *The Key Reporter,* (1994/Spring) 4-5.
Michener describes the role that education played in his career success.
A Phi Beta Kappa publication.

D.268   **"Reminiscences of a Grand Game."** *Soccer Watch '94,* (1994/06) 2-3.
An official publication of World Cup USA 94.

D.269   **"What I Learned About Our Health-Care System—and Myself."**
New Choices for Retirement Living, 34:9 (1994/11) 50-53.
His illness and recovery led him to self-understanding.

D.270   **"How Have We Changed?"** *American Heritage,* 45:8 (1994/12) 75-76.
In this 40th Anniversary issue, writers and other public figures state their
impressions of how America has changed since 1954, and why.

D.271   **"Michener ON PAIN?"** *Vim & Vigor,* 10:4 (1994/Winter) 32-36.
Excerpt from **"The World is My Home."** This periodical is published in 26
regional versions.

SWARTHMORE

August 1985

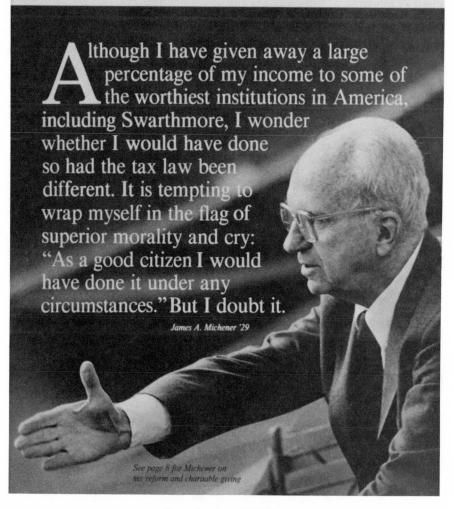

Although I have given away a large percentage of my income to some of the worthiest institutions in America, including Swarthmore, I wonder whether I would have done so had the tax law been different. It is tempting to wrap myself in the flag of superior morality and cry: "As a good citizen I would have done it under any circumstances." But I doubt it.

James A. Michener '29

See page 8 for Michener on tax reform and charitable giving

Swarthmore. D.228.

E.
Newspaper Articles
by
James A. Michener

*"I wrote an ill-advised article . . . .. But in the ensuing years
several writers confided in me that my article
had been unusually relevant."*

—James A. Michener
THE WORLD IS MY HOME
New York, Random House,1992

A SIGNET SPECIAL BROADSIDE #6 • P3819 • 60¢

James A. Michener

Author of
Iberia, The Source, Hawaii

AMERICA VS. AMERICA

THE REVOLUTION IN MIDDLE-CLASS VALUES

66 I am heartened by our young people, black and white. What some of their elders see as rebellion, I see as the proper assumption of responsibility and a long-overdue attention to problems requiring change. **99**

America vs. America. A.024.

Section E - Newspaper Articles by JAMES A. MICHENER

E.001 **"THE NIGHT AFTER CHRISTMAS."**
Torch, 8:2 (1923/12) 3-4.
The cure for the children's candy overindulgence.
The *Torch* was the Doylestown High School student newspaper.

E.002 **"THE PLAYER'S SOLILOQUY."**
Torch, 8:3 (1924/01) 7.
This work shows the eternal conflict between academics and sports.

E.003 **"SILLY SENTIMENTALITIES."**
Torch, 8:3 (1924/01) 2.
Michener's satirical essay regarding lovesick sentimentalities on campus
and inviting membership in association to abolish it.

E.004 **"MI PROPIO AMO."**
Torch, 8:4 (1924/02-03) 10-11.
A poem about Michener's friends raving about their girls.

E.005 **"THE CASTLE OF MY DREAMS."**
Torch, 8:5 (1924/05-06) 10. Written with Lindsay Johnson. A poem about
the writers' imaginary retreat from the pain and sadness of reality.

E.006 **"AN ALL BUX-MONT TEAM."**
Torch, 9:4 (1925/05) 13-15. Michener comments on the successful
basketball season and selects a first team and second team all-star roster.

E.007 **"AN OLD, OLD THEME [EDITORIAL]."**
Torch, 9:4 (1925/05) 10-11. Regarding school spirit which Michener defined
as a combination of respect and love.

E.008 **"PERSONAL OPINION."**
Swarthmore Phoenix, (1929/03/12) 4. Letter expressing opinion that most sports
should be styled after intramural play, not varsity.

E.009 **"LITERARY AND DRAMATIC CRITICISM."**
Swarthmore Phoenix, (1929/03/19) 4.
A review of five one-act plays presented by students.

E.010 **"IVY ORATOR EXPRESSES NEW VALUATION OF COLLEGE LIFE."**
Swarthmore Phoenix, (1929/06/03) 7. Baccalaureate address, Swarthmore College.

E.011 **"FACULTY REVIEWER LAUDS FORMAT AND PRECISE STYLE OF
CHRISTMAS RECORD, BUT CRITICIZES GENERAL THEME OF
STORIES."**
Hill School News, (1930/01/23) 1-3. Michener reviews prose and poetry of
five short pieces by students and comments on the common theme of
hopelessness and defeat that each displayed.

E.012 **"MR. MICHENER IS FACULTY MEMBER TO REVIEW FEBRUARY
ISSUE OF RECORD; LATEST NUMBER HAS MUCH NOTEWORTHY
PROSE."**
Hill School News, (1931/03/12) 2+. Michener extolls the virtures of prose over
poetry as a medium that may be readily and fairly evaluated.

Section E - Newspaper Articles by JAMES A. MICHENER

E.013 "MR. MICHENER REVIEWS APRIL RECORD; PRAISES 'CHAOS' AND
'THE QUEST OF SIR BELAINE'; SAYS THEMES ARE TOO FORCED."
Hill School News, (1931/05/01) 3+.
Early comments by Michener on writing style.

E.014 "CORRESPONDENCE."
George School News, (1934/10/24) 2. Michener lists the ten best books that
he considered preeminent in the George School Library.

E.015 "THE PROMPTER."
George School News, (1935/06/10) 2. Michener recommends having students
give oral presentations of poetry and essays.

E.016 "[LETTER TO THE EDITOR]."
New York Times, 95:32,327 (1946/04/29) 20. Letter opposing the unification
of the armed forces. Michener's first appearance in the *Times*.

E.017 "OUT OF THE WIDE BLUE YONDER."
New York Times Book Review, (1947/07/20) VII, 1, 22.
Michener reviews "Air Force Diary," by Col. James H. Straubel.

E.018 "SIX CHILDREN AND A TREE."
Philadelphia Inquirer Book Review, (1948/12/05) 1.

E.019 "THIS SAVAGE WATER."
New York Times Book Review, (1949/05/08) VII, 1, 25.
Michener reviews "The Coral Sea," by Alan Villiers.

E.020 "HAPPY TALK: TRIBUTE TO THE WRITERS OF SOUTH PACIFIC."
New York Times, 98:33,398 (1949/07/03) II, 1.
Michener lauds the musical adaptation of his novel by
Messrs. Oscar Hammerstein, 2d, Richard Rodgers, and Josh Logan.

E.021 "THE CAPACITY TO LOVE."
New York Times Book Review, (1949/08/21) VII, 5.
Michener reviews "The Question of Gregory," by Elizabeth Janeway.

E.022 "A WORM OF A MAN."
New York Times Book Review, (1950/10/22) VII, 4.
Michener reviews "The Choice," by Marc Brandel.

E.023 "SAMOA IS DIFFERENT."
New York Times Book Review, (1951/01/07) VII, 6.
Michener reviews "The Samoan Dance of Life," by John Dixon Copp.

E.024 "OUR FRIENDS DOWN UNDER."
New York Times Books Review, (1951/04/16) VII, 14, 16.
Michener reviews "The United States and the Southwest Pacific," by
C. Hartley Gratten.

Section E - Newspaper Articles by JAMES A. MICHENER

E.025   **"TALES OF SOUTH ASIA."**
New York Herald Tribune, 111:38,153 (1951/05/02) 1, 21.
Part 1 of 15 - Excerpts from **"The Voice of Asia."** Strange case of
Moslem-adopted Dutch girl whose annulment set off riots.

E.026   **"TALES OF SOUTH ASIA."**
New York Herald Tribune, 111:38,154 (1951/05/03) 1, 19.
Part 2 of 15 - Excerpts from **"The Voice of Asia."** The marginal man: Half
Asian, half European, he straddles two societies.

E.027   **"TALES OF SOUTH ASIA."**
New York Herald Tribune, 111:38,155 (1951/05/04) 1, 21.
Part 3 of 15 - Excerpts from **"The Voice of Asia."** Indonesia's first
premier relates why young men rule the young nation.

E.028   **"TALES OF SOUTH ASIA."**
New York Herald Tribune, 111:38,157 (1951/05/06) 1, 6.
Part 4 of 15 - Excerpts from **"The Voice of Asia."** Comments from Indonesian
editors about Indonesia's claim to New Guinea (Irian).

E.029   **"TALES OF SOUTH ASIA."**
New York Herald Tribune, 111:38,158 (1951/05/07) 1, 20.
Part 5 of 15 - Excerpts from **"The Voice of Asia."** Comments from a Dutchman
who was kicked out of Java.

E.030   **"TALES OF SOUTH ASIA."**
New York Herald Tribune, 111:38,159 (1951/05/08) 1, 8.
Part 6 of 15 - Excerpts from **"The Voice of Asia."** Life of Buddhist Monk: 2
more years before he may again talk to wife.

E.031   **"TALES OF SOUTH ASIA."**
New York Herald Tribune, 111:38,160 (1951/05/09) 1, 22.
Part 7 of 15 - Excerpts from **"The Voice of Asia."** Enterprising Samlor boy
is Bangkok 'capitalist.'

E.032   **"TALES OF SOUTH ASIA."**
New York Herald Tribune, 111:38,161 (1951/05/10) 1, 10.
Part 8 of 15 - Excerpts from **"The Voice of Asia."** Liberal Burmese patriot
tells why he is afraid of Reds' anger.

E.033   **"TALES OF SOUTH ASIA."**
New York Herald Tribune, 111:38,162 (1951/05/11) 1, 21.
Part 9 of 15 - Excerpts from **"The Voice of Asia."** American couple teach
Burmese the revolutionary idea of canning food.

E.034   **"TALES OF SOUTH ASIA."**
New York Herald Tribune, 111:38,164 (1951/05/13) 1, 30.
Part 10 of 15 - Excerpts from **"The Voice of Asia."** Great debate rages in
India over banning polygamy and legalizing divorce.

Section E - Newspaper Articles by JAMES A. MICHENER

E.035   **"TALES OF SOUTH ASIA."**
New York Herald Tribune, 111:38,165 (1951/05/14) 1, 6.
Part 11 of 15 - Excerpts from **"The Voice of Asia."** Opponent of Hindu Code
bill says it would wreck families, farms, and India.

E.036   **"TALES OF SOUTH ASIA."**
New York Herald Tribune, 111:38,166 (1951/05/15) 1, 18.
Part 12 of 15 - Excerpts from **"The Voice of Asia."** Wed young, a Hindu wife
never speaks her husband's name. Arvna marries for love.

E.037   **"TALES OF SOUTH ASIA."**
New York Herald Tribune, 111:38,167 (1951/05/16) 1, 19.
Part 13 of 15 - Excerpts from **"The Voice of Asia."** An old Indian describes
the horrors of famine and the plight of his nation.

E.038   **"TALES OF SOUTH ASIA."**
New York Herald Tribune, 111:38,168 (1951/05/17) 1, 23.
Part 14 of 15 - Excerpts from **"The Voice of Asia."** Ali Jinnah's ideas
still rule Pakistan. Sister Fatima still wields influence.

E.039   **"TALES OF SOUTH ASIA."**
New York Herald Tribune, 111:38,169 (1951/05/18) 1, 11.
Part 15 of 15 - Excerpts from **"The Voice of Asia."** Bad attitudes of Mem
Sahib's toward natives blamed for hatred of British.

E.040   **"ADMIRAL'S NERVES CAN'T TAKE IT - BRAVEST PILOT TO PUSH
A PENCIL NOW."**
New York World-Telegram and Sun, (1952/02/05) 10.

E.041   **"NIGHT RIDERS BLAST THE DAYLIGHTS OUT OF FOE - AUTHOR
TAKES A DARE, HITCHES RIDE WITH A BOMBING MISSION."**
New York World-Telegram and Sun, (1952/02/26) 10.

E.042   **"FAIRY TALE AT PANMUNJOM."**
Sunday Mirror, (1952/05/25) 3, 36.
A six part series about United Nations negotiations seeking armistice in
Korea. "The Real Story of Korea - Panmunjom Setting Weird as 'The Talks.' "

E.043   **"THEY CHOSE FREEDOM. "**
Daily Mirror, (1952/05/26) 3, 24.
Part two of a six part series about United Nations negotiations seeking armistice
in Korea. "The Real Story of Korea - How Red Troops Risk Death to Surrender."

E.044   **"THE FRONT LINES."**
Daily Mirror, (1952/05/27) 3, 26.
Part three of a six part series about United Nations negotiations seeking armistice
in Korea. "The Real Story of Korea - Red Guns '3-to-1' Bar Allied March to North."

E.045   **"CHAPTER FOUR."**
Daily Mirror, (1952/05/28) 2, 30.
Part four of a six part series about United Nations negotiations seeking armistice
in Korea. "The Real Story of Korea - 'Old Men' in Antique Planes Fighting Reds."

Section E - Newspaper Articles by JAMES A. MICHENER

E.046   **"CHAPTER FIVE."**
Daily Mirror, (1952/05/29) 2, 18.
Part five of a six part series about United Nations negotiations seeking armistice
in Korea. "The Real Story of Korea - Future Dim for Babies Left in Japan by GIs."

E.047   **"CHAPTER SIX."**
Daily Mirror, (1952/05/30) ?
Part six of a six part series about United Nations negotiations seeking armistice in
Korea. "The Real Story of Korea - Swing Left (and Right) Due If U.S. Quits Japan."

E.048   **"AUSTRALIA'S BRISBANE LINE; RUMOR RELATIVE TO**
ABANDONMENT OF QUEENSLAND SET AT REST."
New York Times, 101:34,471 (1952/06/10) 26. Letter. Michener discounts rumor
that Australia in '42 decided to abandon northern Australia to the Japanese.

E.049   **"KANDY BAR KID'S A SWEET MACHINE; HE FIGHTS BEHIND ENEMY**
LINES."
New York Times, 101:34,520 (1952/07/29) 3. Michener dispatch on the exploits of
the U.S. Marines in Korea, and the extraordinary bravery of Lyle Lewis.

E.050   **"A GENTLEMAN LOST IN A MODERN WORLD."**
New York Times Book Review, (1952/10/19) VII, 1, 42.
Michener reviews "My Island Home," by James Norman Hall.

E.051   **"ONE MORE VOTE FOR KABUKI THEATRE."**
New York Times, 102:34,658 (1952/12/14) II, 2. Michener lauds Kabuki in
Japanese theatre. He concludes that Kabuki is too long and tedious but Americans
should see it.

E.052   **"WHAT HAWAII MEANS TO ME."**
Honolulu Star-Bulletin, (1954/07/10) 5. Saturday Section.

E.053   **"WIDE, BLUE YONDER."**
New York Times Book Review, (1954/12/05) VII, 3, 48.
Michener reviews "Song of the Sky," by Guy Murchie.

E.054   **"MICHENER ON VISIT TO MATSU ISLE, FINDS TROOPS PREPARING**
TO FIGHT."
New York Times, 104:35,473 (1955/03/09) 4. Matsu, a tiny island five miles from
Red China, is an important morale factor to Nationalist China, and is being defended.

E.055   **"A PRIMITIVE TREASURY."**
New York Times Book Review, (1955/04/03) VII, 3, 37. Michener reviews
"The Clarence Buckingham Collection of Japanese Prints," catalogue by Helen
C. Gunsaulus.

E.056   **"MEDICAL CARE IN FOREIGN POSTS."**
New York Times, 104:35,610 (1955/07/24) IV, 8.
Letter to the *Times.* Michener deplores the lack of a U.S. physician
to take care of employees in Afghanistan.

Section E - Newspaper Articles by JAMES A. MICHENER

E.057   *Journal-American,* (1955/09/22) 28. Michener returned from 16,000 miles to write this article about the Archie Moore-Rocky Marciano fight. Also in "The Press." New York: Ballantine Books, 1961.

E.058   **"HOW TOLERANCE GREW IN HAWAII: A REVIEW OF THE NEW LIND BOOK."**
Honolulu Star-Bulletin, (1956/06/12) B1. Written with Mari Michener.
A review of "Race Relations in World Perspective." Honolulu: University of Hawaii Press, 1968, by Andrew W. Lind.

E.059   **" 'SOUTH PACIFIC' VS. 'MY FAIR LADY.' "**
New York Times, 106:36,037 (1956/09/23) II, 1, 3. Michener thinks that "My Fair Lady" is delightful but believes that "South Pacific" compares well.

E.060   **"AT 8 IN THE MORNING OF DECEMBER 7."**
New York Times Book Review, (1957/03/24) VII, 1, 30.

E.061   **"A SLOPING SEA BEYOND ISLAND PALMS."**
New York Times Book Review, (1957/10/13) VII, 6. Michener reviews "Return to the Islands: Life and Legend in the Gilberts," by Sir Arthur Grimble.

E.062   **"HAWAII'S STATEHOOD URGED."**
New York Times, 108:36,867 (1959/01/01) 30. Letter dated from Honolulu, December 14, 1958, declares that Hawaiian population is loyal, statehood is the right thing.

E.063   **"HAWAII STILL WAITS."** *Long Island Star-Journal,* (1959/01/24) 4.

E.064   **"HAWAII DESERVES STATEHOOD NOW."**
San Diego Union, (1959/02/10) B2.

E.065   **" 'ALOHA' FOR THE FIFTIETH STATE."**
New York Times Magazine, 61 (1959/04/19) VI, 14-15, 90-94.
See also, editorial note, (1959/05/10) VI, 4.

E.066   **"STATEHOOD IS CONCRETE ANSWER TO REDS."**
Honolulu Advertiser, (1959/06/23) 12-A8. Statehood Edition.

E.067   **"MICHENER TELLS WHY HE TURNED PEN TO TV EFFORTS."**
Los Angeles Times, (1959/10/06) B1.

E.068   **"QUINN'S POLITICAL INSTINCT CALLED MAJOR STATE ASSET: GOVERNOR QUINN'S GREAT START."**
Honolulu Star-Bulletin, (1959/11/01) II-2. Hawaii politics. Part I of a five part series.

E.069   **"BEN DILLINGHAM CALLED HERO OF ELECTION."**
Honolulu Star-Bulletin, (1959/11/08) II-2.
Hawaii politics. Part II of a five part series.

E.070   **"MICHENER TELLS 'HOW TO LOSE AN ELECTION.' "**
Honolulu Star-Bulletin, (1959/11/15) II-2.
Hawaii politics. Part III of a five part series.

Section E - Newspaper Articles by JAMES A. MICHENER

E.071 **"FOUR SMART GIRLS OF THE FIRST STATE ELECTION."**
Honolulu Star-Bulletin, (1959/11/22) II-2.
Hawaii politics. Part IV of a five part series.

E.072 **"HOW THINGS NOW LOOK TO MICHENER."**
Honolulu Star-Bulletin, (1959/11/29) II-2.
Hawaii politics. Part V of a five part series.

E.073 **"ELECTORAL COLLEGE UPHELD."**
New York Times, 10:37,620 (1961/01/23) 22. Letter. Michener defends the
electoral college system against arguments for a popular vote.

E.074 **"LETTER TO CLARICE B. TAYLOR."**
Honolulu Star-Bulletin, (1961/07/28) 18.
Concerns reception in Honolulu of New York interview of previous April.

E.075 **"REPORT FROM THE FRENZIED FIFTIES."**
New York Times Magazine, 110:37,822 (1961/08/13) VI, 15, 94.

E.076 **"WHAT EVERY NEW CANDIDATE SHOULD KNOW."**
New York Times Magazine, 112:38,228 (1962/09/23) VI, 23, 92-93. Reprinted as
"Confessions of a Political Candidate," *Reader's Digest,* 81:487 (1962/11)
199-204.

E.077 **"ONE NEAR-SQUARE WHO DOESN'T KNOCK THE ROCK."**
New York Times Magazine, (1965/10/31) VI, 56-57, 92-96. Michener, Cousin Brucey,
and Phil Specter judge the World Rock 'n' Roll Championship, won by the Galaxies
IV of Trenton, N.J. Condensed in *Reader's Digest,* 88:526 (1966/02) 157-62, titled
"Don't Knock the Rock."

E.078 **"THE BOY WHO FOUND CHRISTMAS."**
Chicago Tribune, 119:346 (1965/12/12) 8A. Illustrated by B. Wiseman.
A supplement to the Sunday Edition. A children's story which can be cut
out and folded together. A make-it-yourself book.

E.079 **"JERUSALEM'S FUTURE."**
New York Times, 116:39,957 (1967/06/18) IV, 15.
Letter to the editor by Michener hails the reunion of Jerusalem, lauds
Kolleck dealings with Christians and Moslems.

E.080 **"NOBLE JERUSALEM."**
Jerusalem Post (Israel), (1967/08/01) 7, 11.
Written for a special supplement called "Jerusalem the Golden," to mark
the reuniting of the city and breaking down of barriers.

E.081 **"SPEAKING OF BOOKS: WHAT TRANSPIRED."**
New York Times Book Review, 72:51 (1967/12/17) VII, 2.
Michener on the etymology of 'transpire' and 'amuse.'

E.082 **"REVOLUTION IN MIDDLE-CLASS VALUES."**
New York Times Magazine, (1968/08/18) VI, 20-21.

Section E - Newspaper Articles by JAMES A. MICHENER

E.083   **"WHAT TO DO ABOUT THE PALESTINIAN REFUGEES?"**
New York Times Magazine, 120:41,154 (1970/09/27) VI, 22-25, 114,
116-21, 123, 130.

E.084   **"JAMES MICHENER'S RETURN TO BALI HA'I."**
Philadelphia, (1970/11/22) B1, 6. Michener's assignment to find out why
servicemen refused to return home from Bora-Bora. The Sunday Bulletin.

E.085   **"[LETTER TO THE EDITOR]."**
New York Times, 120:41,424 (1971/06/24) 38. Letter to the editor. Michener's
views on the publication of the Pentagon Papers by the *Times.*

E.086   **"ONE AND A HALF CHEERS FOR PROGRESS."**
New York Times Magazine, 120:41,497 (1971/09/05) VI, 9, 35-39.
Discusses major social changes confronting Americans. Abridged in *Reader's
Digest,* 99:596 (1971/12) 209.

E.087   **"LAMENT FOR PAKISTAN."**
New York Times Magazine, (1972/01/09) VI, 11-13.

E.088   **"FIVE WARRING TRIBES OF SOUTH AFRICA."**
New York Times Magazine, (1972/01/23) VI, 6-7.

E.089   **"SOUTH AFRICA: BEAUTIFUL... AND INHUMAN."**
Plain Dealer, (1972/01/24) A10. Appeared in the *New York Times Magazine*
as "Five Warring Tribes of South Africa," (1972/01/23).

E.090   **"SOUTH AFRICA: A LAND OF FIVE WARRING TRIBES."**
Arizona Daily Star, (1972/01/30) D3.

E.091   **"ONE MAN'S PRIMARY AND HOW HE LOST."**
New York Times Magazine, 121:41,756 (1972/05/21) VI, 28-29, 98-104.

E.092   **"SOVIET JEWRY: WE WANT MORAL OUTCRY."**
New York Times, 122:41,904 (1972/09/16) 29.

E.093   **"THE RED KIMONO."**
New York Times Magazine, 122:41,945 (1972/11/26) VI, 35, 116. Japanese
men, at 60, attain statesman status, exemplified by wearing a red kimono.

E.094   **"IS AMERICA BURNING?"**
New York Times Magazine, 122:42,162 (1973/07/01) VI, 10-11, 22-28.
Michener's article on America's reaction to the Watergate affair. He notes
the social repercussions of Kent State.

E.095   **"WHEN THE 'MANDATE OF HEAVEN' HAS BEEN LOST."**
New York Times, 123:42,295 (1973/11/11) IV, 13.
Michener calls for President Nixon's resignation following Watergate.

E.096   **"ODE TO ROBIN ROBERTS, A PITCHER WITH GOOD QUALITIES."**
New York Times, 124:42,673 (1974/11/24) V, 2.
Michener promotes Robin Roberts for baseball hall of fame.

Section E - Newspaper Articles by JAMES A. MICHENER

E.097 **"A SLICE OF CAKE IN EVERY HAMLET."**
New York Times, 124:42,805 (1975/04/05) 29.
Michener is asked to draft the final report of the Bicentennial Advisory
Committee to celebrate America's 'rite of passage.'

E.098 *New York Times,* 124:42,869 (1975/06/08) IV, 16.
Letter. Michener, et al, hail April 27 article by William Korey warning
that politicization of UNESCO will be self-destructive.

E.099 **"ANTI-ZIONISM RESOLUTION: AN ATTACK ON THE U. N."**
New York Times, 125:43,046 (1975/12/02) 38.
Letter. Michener and others condemn U. N. resolution equating Zionism
with racism, as aimed at liquidation of the state of Israel.

E.100 **"U. N. AGENCIES: TO STOP THE MANIPULATORS."**
New York Times, 125:43,231 (1976/06/04) 24.
Letter from Michener, et al; Writers and Artists for Peace in the Middle
East criticize unfounded accusations against Israel.

E.101 **"WOES OF SPORTS IN U.S."**
New York Times, 125:43,331 (1976/09/12) V, 2.
Excerpt from "**Sports in America**." Michener condemns the failure of
sports programs to promote lifetime athletics for all citizens.

E.102 **" 'ROOTS,' UNIQUE IN ITS TIME."**
New York Times Book Review, 82:9 (1977/02/27) VII, 39.
Michener reviews Alex Haley's "Roots" and concludes that it is the black
man's answer to "Gone With the Wind."

E.103 **"A PLAN FOR COLLEGE FOOTBALL AND A SUPER LEAGUE."**
New York Times, 127:43,933 (1978/05/07) V, 2.
Michener offers plan for a super league of major college teams, with playoffs to
determine national football champions.

E.104 **"LIFE AND DEATH THROUGH THE YEARS WITH THE PHILLIES."**
New York Times, 128:44,041 (1978/11/19) V, 2.
Michener article on the frustrations of being a baseball fan.

E.105 **"POETIC CELEBRATION IN MIDAIR."**
New York Times, 130:44,762 (1980/11/09) V, 2.
Michener poem hailing Phillies' baseball team victory. Michener portrait. Also in "The
New Fireside Book of Baseball. 4th ed." New York: Simon & Schuster, 1987, p. 262.

E.106 **"I WOULD LIKE TO HAVE WRITTEN."**
New York Times Book Review, (1981/12/06) VII, 7, 68, 70.
Various authors comment on what book they would have liked to have written.

E.107 **"DENVER TO NEW DELHI: A WRITER'S MOVES."**
New York Times, 131:45,255 (1982/03/17) III, 1, 9. Michener article on the pleasures and pitfalls of running two homes and the need to live where he is writing about.

E.108   **"KOSINSKI IS WORTHY OF OUR SUPPORT."**
New York Times, 132:45,511 (1982/11/28) II, 23. Michener, et al, write letters
responding to ideological attacks against Jerzy Kosinski.

E.109   **"THE BOOK THAT I'M WRITING."**
New York Times Book Review, 88:24 (1983/06/12) VII, 12.
Michener's report on the progress of "**Poland**."

E.110   **"LIVING WITH AN AILING HEART."**
New York Times Magazine, (1984/08/19) VI, 26.
Research by heart specialist, Paul Dudley White, on the heart attacks to runner
Jim F. Fixx. Condensed in *Reader's Digest,* 125:752 (1984/12) 87-90, titled
"James Michener's Recipe for a Longer, Better Life."

E.111   **"BEST SELLER ON LITTLE DIOMEDE."**
New York Times Magazine, 135:46,715 (1986/03/16) VI, 8. Michener describes
a visit to a lonely arctic outpost such as Little Diomede which is only two miles
from Soviet territory.

E.112   **"YOU CAN CALL THE 1980'S 'THE UGLY DECADE.' "**
New York Times, 136:47,006 (1987/01/01) 27.
Op-Ed article that 1980's are "The Ugly Decade" characterized by "know
nothingness" where problems are evaded, not dealt with.

E.113   **"KEEP THE RADIOS BROADCASTING TO THE EAST."**
New York Times, 136:47,191 (1987/07/05) IV, 15.
Op-Ed article calling for renewed national commitment to broadcasts of
Radio Liberty and Radio Free Europe.

E.114   **"WHY GLASNOST CAME TO THE SOVIET AIRWAVES."**
Christian Science Monitor, 81 (1989/01/18) 19.
Soviet Government stops jamming Radio Free Europe.

E.115   **"HILARY AND HEATHER."** *Chicago Tribune Magazine,* (1990/11/18) 20-23.
The tribulations faced by a college professor's wife who has to compete with
attractive college coeds.

E.116   **"IMAGES OF ASIANS. ('BLOODY MARY IS THE GIRL WE LOVE')."**
New York Times, 140:48,710 (1991/09/01) II, 2. Michener disputes article
"Challenging the Asian Illusion." Bloody Mary is not the docile Asian that
Gish Jen criticizes.

E.117   **"CLOSE CALL CHANGES AUTHOR'S LIFE."**
Los Angeles Times, (1992/01/26) L9, 11. Travel Section.

E.118   **"MICHENER'S WORLD. (PART I - MICHENER: RUG MERCHANT)."**
Los Angeles Times, (1992/01/26) L1, 8, 10.
Travel Section. Series of three excerpts from "**The World is My Home**." Full
page caricature of Michener sitting on globe.

E.119   **"MICHENER'S WORLD. (PART II- MAD ABOUT THE MATADORS)."**
Los Angeles Times, (1992/02/02) L9, 13, 22. Travel Section.
Series of three excerpts from "**The World is My Home**."

Section E - Newspaper Articles by JAMES A. MICHENER

E.120   "MICHENER'S WORLD.
(PART III- A NEW FORTUNE-TELLING SENSATION)."
Los Angeles Times, (1992/02/09) L7, 8. Travel Section. Series of three excerpts
from "**The World is My Home**."

E.121   "THE OLD MAN AND THE SOUTHERN SEA."
Los Angeles Times Magazine, 111 (1992/05/17) 13, 44, 46, 48.
Michener's 85th birthday present to himself, a cruise to Antarctica.
Includes Michener's travel guide.

E.122   "AN EYE FOR FACES."
New York Times Book Review, (1992/12/06) 14.
Michener reviews "Cornell Capa: Photographs," a book by Cornell Capa and
Richard Whelan.

E.123   "A BIBLICAL PARABLE FOR OUR TIMES."
Los Angeles Times, 112 (1993/01/15) B7.   Bill Clinton is like King David.

E.124   "GOD IS NOT A HOMOPHOBE."
New York Times, 142 (1993/03/30) A15.   Debate over gays in the military.

E.125   "BIBLICAL EDICTS ON SIN A RESULT OF ANCIENT TIMES."
Austin American-Statesman, (1993/04/08) A17.
Regarding Western society's biblical reactions to homosexuality.

E.126   "HOLOCAUST HORRORS WERE NOT IMAGINED."
Austin American-Statesman, (1993/05/04) A9.
Michener refuses to rewrite history of the holocaust to accommodate modern
revisionists.

E.127   "THE WRITING LIFE - LESSONS OF A LIFETIME."
Washington Post, 23:40 (1993/10/03) 1, 6.
Advice to fledgling writers and some observations on how the field of writing has
changed in the last 70 years.

TWAYNE'S UNITED STATES AUTHORS SERIES

JAMES A.
MICHENER

A. GROVE DAY

James A. Michener. F.024.

F.
Books About
or Related to
James A. Michener

"He has cast a wide net and touched men and women
confronting practical problems and [who] are looking to
the written word for clues to life. He has made the word
'popular' respectable, and that's a solid accomplishment
in this slippery era."

—Arthur Miller
JAMES A. MICHENER:
FIRST CITIZEN OF THE REPUBLIC OF LETTERS
A TRIBUTE BY HIS WRITING COLLEAGUES
The Authors League Fund, 1990.

South Pacific. F.004.

Section F - Books About or Related to JAMES A. MICHENER

F.001   **HISTORY OF THE UNITED STATES NAVAL STATION BORA BORA, SOCIETY ISLANDS OF FRENCH OCEANIA.**
Allen, John J. Bora Bora: 1945/07/09. Quotes Lieut. J. A. Michener's Navy field report (80 pages) of the military occupation. He was ComSoPac Historical Officer.

F.002   **HISTORY OF THE UNITED STATES NAVAL ADVANCED BASE TOGATABU.**
Burke, John, Lieut. Cmdr. Noumea: [1946?]. Not attributed to him, but based largely upon Michener's 80 page field report of an aborted court marshal proceeding on Tonga.

F.003   **CURRENT BIOGRAPHY.**
Rothe, Anna, ed. New York: H. W. Wilson, 1948, pp. 448-50.
An early source of information derived from Michener himself.

    a   New York: H. W. Wilson, 1948, pp. 448-50.

    b   New York: H. W. Wilson, 1975, pp. 270-75.

F.004   **SOUTH PACIFIC, A MUSICAL PLAY.**
Hammerstein, Oscar II, and Joshua Logan. New York: Random House, 1949.
First produced in association with Leland Hayward and Joshua Logan. Music by Richard Rodgers, lyrics by Oscar Hammerstein II. The true first printing states as follows on the copyright page: "Copyright, 1949, by Richard Rodgers, Oscar Hammerstein, 2d, and Joshua Logan." "Copyright, 1949, by Williamson Music Corporation." A letter to Random House from attorneys for Rodgers and Hammerstein, dated October 7, 1949, stated that "Any reference to Joshua Logan or Williamson Music in the copyright notice or any other form of copyright notice is completely unauthorized..." "We, therefore, ask that you immediately correct copyright notice in all copies to be published or offered for sale..." The first printing, second state, omits Joshua Logan and Williamson Music Company from the copyright.

F.005   **50 YEARS OF THE AMERICAN NOVEL.**
Gardiner, Harold C., ed. New York, London: Charles Scribner's Sons, 1951.

F.006   **AMERICAN NOVELISTS OF TODAY.**
Warfel, Harry R. New York: American Book Company, 1951, pp. 299-300.

F.007   **IN MY OPINION: AN INQUIRY INTO THE CONTEMPORARY NOVEL.**
Prescott, Orville. Indianapolis: Bobbs-Merrill, 1952, pp. 146-64. LC 52-5807.
Prescott discusses World War II authors including Hersey, Wouk, Michener, Jones, Mailer. Reviews Michener's first four works.

F.008   **SOME ENCHANTED EVENINGS.**
Taylor, Deems. New York: Harper & Brothers, 1953, pp. 185-86.
LC 53-7750. The story of Rodgers and Hammerstein.

F.009   **SAYONARA.**
Osborn, Paul. [Burbank]: [Warner Bros. Pictures], [1956], 1 Vol.
Var. pp. Screenplay based on the novel by James A. Michener.

F.010   **TWENTIETH CENTURY AUTHORS: FIRST SUPPLEMENT.**
Kunitz, Stanley J. New York: H. W. Wilson, 1955, pp. 665-66. Biographical.

Section F - Books About or Related to JAMES A. MICHENER

F.011   **SOUTH PACIFIC.**
Rodgers, Richard, and Oscar Hammerstein II. New York: Williamson Music, c1956.
Libretto. Music by Richard Rodgers; lyrics by Oscar Hammerstein II;
book by Oscar Hammerstein II and Joshua Logan.

F.012   **ADVENTURES IN AMERICAN LITERATURE.**
Gehlmann, John, and Mary Rives Bowman. New York: Harcourt, Brace &
World, 1958, p. 294. Discusses the effects of war on novelists such as Michener.

F.013   **MASTERPLOTS: 1958 ANNUAL.**
Magill, Frank N., ed. New York: Salem Press, 1958, pp. 42-44.
Review of **"The Bridge at Andau."** The Magill Masterplots is an annual
series of essay-reviews of 100 books published that year.

F.014   **THE MICHENERS IN AMERICA.**

    a   Shaddinger, Anna E. Tokyo: Charles E. Tuttle, 1958, p. 341.
LC 58-9312. A prime source for data on Michener's parentage.

    b   Updated and retitled **MORE MICHENERS IN AMERICA.**
Shaddinger, Anna E. Hatfield, Pa.: Bone Kemper Typesetting, 1970, pp. 608-9.
LC 72-141858. An annual update is maintained in the Buck's County Historical
Library in Doylestown, Pennsylvania.

F.015   **6 PLAYS BY RODGERS AND HAMMERSTEIN. ("SOUTH PACIFIC").**
Rodgers, Richard and Oscar Hammerstein. New York: Random House,
Modern Library, 1959, pp. 267-366.

F.016   **THE MAGIC MIRROR. ("SOUTH PACIFIC AND ITS CRITICISM").**
Nathan, George Jean. New York: Knopf, 1960, pp. 250-57.
Selections from the author's many literary criticisms. About "South Pacific,"
"Infinitely more intellectual musical than most."

F.017   **MASTERPLOTS: 1960 ANNUAL.**
Magill, Frank N., ed. New York: Salem Press, 1960, pp. 85-88.
Review of **"Hawaii."** The Magill Masterplots is an annual series of
essay-reviews of 100 books published that year.

F.018   **NO! IN THUNDER: ESSAYS ON MYTH AND LITERATURE.**
Fiedler, Leslie A. Boston: Beacon Press, 1960, pp. 13-14. LC 60-14676.
Michener is "sentimental protester," racing to write about latest indignity.

F.019   **THE ARTIST'S AND WRITER'S COOKBOOK. ("BEEF BURGUNDY").**
Barr, Beryl, and Barbara Turner Sachs, eds. Sausalito: Contact Editions, 1961, p. 134.

F.020   **AMERICAN AUTHORS AND BOOKS: 1640 TO THE PRESENT DAY. REV.**
Burke, W. J., and Will D. Howe. New York: Crown Publishers, 1962.
An encyclopedia of American books, authors, personalities, periodicals,
organizations and other pertinent information.

Section F - Books About or Related to JAMES A. MICHENER

F.021   **DR. BARNES OF MERION.**
Hart, Henry. New York: Farrar, Straus, 1963, pp. 232-33.
An account of the feud between Michener and Dr. Barnes, regarding a subterfuge by Michener to see the Barnes art collection.

F.022   **THE JAMES A. MICHENER COLLECTION OF TWENTIETH CENTURY AMERICAN PAINTINGS.**
Little Rock: Arkansas Art Center, 1962. Catalog of Exhibition May 3 - June 3, 1962.

F.023   **THE RODGERS AND HAMMERSTEIN STORY.**
Green, Stanley. New York: John Day, 1963, pp. 129-36.
LC 63-10221. Background to the development of the musical, "South Pacific."

F.024   **JAMES A. MICHENER.**
Day, A. Grove.

   a   New York: Twayne Publishers, 1964. Contains an excellent bibliography to date.

   b   New Haven: College and University Press, 1964.
Paperback. Twayne's United States Authors Series.

   c   **2D ED.** Boston: Twayne Publishers, 1977.

F.025   **THE READER'S ADVISER.**

   a   Hoffman, Hester R. New York: R. R. Bowker, 1964. Short biography with notations of original prices at issue for books through "**Caravans**."

   b   **THE READER'S ADVISER: A GUIDE TO THE BEST IN LITERATURE. 11TH ED., REV. AND ENLARGED. 2 VOLS.** Courtney, Winifred F. New York, London: R. R. Bowker, 1968. LC 57-13277. Bibliography, poetry, essays, fiction, drama, and foreign literature, biography, reference, bibles, religion, etc.

F.026   **HAWAII.**
Trumbo, Dalton. Hollywood: Mirisch Corporation, 1965, 145 leaves.
Screenplay based on the novel by James A. Michener.

F.027   **HAWAII.**
Hill, George Roy. Hollywood: Mirisch Corporation, n.d.
Pre-production screenplay adapted from Michener's novel.

F.028   **JAMES A. MICHENER'S PLEA FOR SOCIAL HARMONY.**
Rose, Don D. Huntsville, Tex.: Private, 1966/05. A Masters Thesis presented to the Faculty of Sam Houston State College for the Degree of Master of Arts.

F.029   **MY LIFE IN PUBLISHING. ("JAMES MICHENER").**
Latham, Harold S. New York: E. P. Dutton, 1965, pp. 86-89.
Explains how Macmillan lost Michener as a client.

F.030   **THE SUBJECT IS ISRAEL: CONVERSATION BETWEEN JAMES MICHENER & DORE SCHARY.**
Schary, Dore. New York: Anti-Defamation League of B'nai B'rith, 1968?
Anti-defamation League of B'nai B'rith. Audio and video tapes were also produced.

Section F - Books About or Related to JAMES A. MICHENER

F.031   **THE OXFORD COMPANION TO AMERICAN LITERATURE.**
Hart, James D. Biographical comments.

    a   **3D ED.** New York: Oxford University Press, 1956, p. 480.

    b   **4TH ED.** New York: Oxford University Press, 1965, p. 546.

F.032   **THE DICTIONARY OF BIOGRAPHY.**
Robinson, Herbert Spenser, ed. Garden City: Doubleday, Dolphin Books,
1966, p. 288. Paperback. A brief capsule biography.

F.033   **THE MIRISCH CORPORATION PRESENTS JAMES A. MICHENER'S
HAWAII.**
New York: National Publishers, c1966. Movie souvenir book. Movie produced by the
Mirisch Corporation based upon the novel **"Hawaii."** Issued without dust jacket.

F.034   **THE PULITZER PRIZE NOVELS; A CRITICAL BACKWARD LOOK.**
Stuckey, W. J.
Author says awards criteria was changed to accommodate poorly written sketches.

    a   Norman: University of Oklahoma Press, 1966, pp. 13, 138-64.

    b   **2ND ED.** Norman: University of Oklahoma Press, 1981, pp. 11, 138ff.
ISBN 0-8061-0688-3; LC 66-10295.

F.035   **"HAWAII": FACT AND FICTION.**
Honolulu: Hawaiian Missionary Children's Society, 1967.
Criticism of the motion picture **"Hawaii,"** based on the novel by James A. Michener.

F.036   **70 YEARS OF BEST SELLERS: 1895-1965.**
Hackett, Alice Payne. New York: R. R. Bowker, 1967.
**"Hawaii," "Tales of the South Pacific," "Sayonara," "Fires of Spring,"
"Return to Paradise," "Caravans,"** and **"The Source."**

F.037   **CENTRAL CITY FESTIVAL CELEBRITY COOK BOOK.
("BEEF BOURGUIGNONNE").**
Barrett, Marjorie, ed.; Contribution by James A. Michener. Denver:
Monitor Publications, 1967, p. 106. Proceeds were used to support the Central
City Festival Museum. Michener was a member of the 1949 Central City Critique.

F.038   **CONVERSATIONS.**
Newquist, Roy, ed. N.p.: Rand McNally & Company, 1967, pp. 245-56.
LC 67-14953. Forty-three prominent figures give opinions on writing, politics,
religion, censorship, what's wrong and right in the world.

F.039   **THE PEACE CORP READER. ("ON HOW TO AVOID BEING A HICK,
AN INTERVIEW WITH JAMES A. MICHENER").**
Interview by Robert Hatch and Jack Keyser on the eve of the Peace Corps' announced
entry into the South Pacific.

    a   Washington: Quadrangle Books, 1967/09, pp. 64-74. LC 66-62201. Paperback.

    b   N.p. 1968/09, pp. 33-39. Paperback.

Section F - Books About or Related to JAMES A. MICHENER

c   N.p. 1969/09, pp. 9-15. Paperback.

F.040   SOURCES FOR TOMORROW: 50 AMERICAN PAINTINGS, 1946-1966.
Allentown, Pa.: Allentown Art Museum, 1967? Circulated by Smithsonian Institute.
Traveling Exhibition Service, 1967-68.
From the James A. Michener Foundation collection.

**F.041   PROCEEDINGS OF THE COLLEGE OF ELECTORS OF THE
COMMONWEALTH OF PENNSYLVANIA.**
Pennsylvania Electoral College. Harrisburg, Pa.: 1968. Election of
Michener as President, his speech and further remarks.

**F.042   HERE'S HOW BY WHO'S WHO: HOW TO SUCCEED BY 101 MEN
WHO DID. REV. ED.**
Bell, Jessie Grover. Lakewood, Ohio: Private, 1968.

F.043   200 CONTEMPORARY AUTHORS.
Harte, Barbara, and Carolyn Riley, eds. Bio-bibliographies of selected leading
writers of the day with critical and personal sidelights.

a   Detroit: Gale Research, 1969, pp. 188-89. LC 75-94113.

b   Detroit: Gale Research, 1969, pp. 188-89. LC 75-94113. Paperback.

F.044   CONTEMPORARY AUTHORS - VOLS. 5-8. 1ST REV.
Detroit: Gale Research, 1969, pp. 279-80.

F.045   FAMOUS WRITERS ANNUAL: BOOK ONE.
Carroll, Gordon. Westport, Conn.: Famous Writers School, 1970, p. 183.
Michener is pictured campaigning for a Congressional seat in a photograph
section titled "The Author's World."

F.046   MASTERPLOTS: 1970 ANNUAL.
Magill, Frank N., ed. New York: Salem Press, 1970, pp. 246-50. LC 55-41212.
Review of **"Presidential Lottery**." The Magill Masterplots is an annual
series of essay-reviews of 100 books published that year.

F.047   LITERATURE STUDY IN THE HIGH SCHOOLS.
Burton, Dwight L. Brief references about **"The Bridges at Toko-ri**."

a   New York: Holt, Rinehart and Winston, 1961, pp. 8, 37 +. LC 59-5888.

b   **REV. ED.** New York: Holt, Rinehart and Winston, c1964, pp. 9, 41+.
LC 64-12917.

c   **3RD ED.** New York: Holt, Rinehart and Winston, n.d. pp. 9, 73, 312.
ISBN 03-081119-8; LC 74-94346.

Section F - Books About or Related to JAMES A. MICHENER

F.048 **AMERICAN PAINTINGS OF THE SIXTIES FROM THE JAMES A. MICHENER COLLECTION ON LOAN FROM THE UNIVERSITY ART MUSEUM, UNIVERSITY OF TEXAS.**
Tyler, Tex.: Tyler Museum of Art, 1971.
Paperback. Exhibition Catalogue, August 8 - September 16, 1971.

F.049 **ART AND THE CREATIVE TEACHER. ("ILLUSTRATIONS FROM THE MICHENER COLLECTION").**
Fearing, Kelly, et al; Regarding art collection contributed by James A. Michener. Austin: W. S. Benton, 1971. Illustrations on pages 14, 15, 17, 20, 21, 36, 37, 81, 144, 167. A textbook.

F.050 **THE COLLECTED ESSAYS OF LESLIE FIEDLER. 2 VOLS.**
Fiedler, Leslie A. New York: Stein and Day, 1971, pp. 233-34, 407-14.
SBN 8128-1333-2; LC 76-122420. Michener is "sentimental protester," racing to write about latest indignity. Writer appreciates "**The Floating World.**"

F.051 **THE FILMS OF PAUL NEWMAN.**
Quirk, Lawrence J. New York: Citadel Press, 1971, pp. 53-56. ISBN 0-8065-0223-9; LC 74-147830. Contains details of the movie "Until They Sail" filmed in 1957, which was based upon a chapter from "**Return to Paradise.**"

F.052 **MASTERPLOTS: EIGHTEEN VOLUME EDITION [VOL. XVII].**
Magill, Frank N., ed. New York: Salem Press, 1971, pp. 4674-77.
Review of "**Hawaii.**" This Magill Masterplots set contains 1810 plot stories and essay reviews from the world's fine literature.

F.053 **NOMINATIONS TO THE U.S. ADVISORY COMMISSION ON INFORMATION.**
U.S. Congress. Senate. Committee on Foreign Relations. Washington: U.S. Gov. Printing Office, 1971. Hearings, 92nd Congress, First Session, on nominations of F. Stanton, H. Lewis, J. A. Michener, and F. Shaheen.

F.054 **PACIFIC ISLANDS LITERATURE: ONE HUNDRED BASIC BOOKS. ("JAMES A. MICHENER, TALES OF THE SOUTH PACIFIC").**
Day, A. Grove. Honolulu: University Press of Hawaii, 1971, pp. 144-45.

F.055 **THE PENGUIN COMPANION TO AMERICAN LITERATURE.**
Bradbury, Malcolm, Eric Mottram, and Jean Franco, eds. New York: McGraw-Hill Book Company, 1971, p. 175. Short biography by A. Grove Day.

F.056 **THE SIXTIES: A COLLECTION OF PAINTINGS FROM THE JAMES A. MICHENER COLLECTION.**
Springfield, Mo.: Springfield Art Museum, 1971. Paperback. Exhibition Catalogue, Sept. 19 - Oct. 18, 1971. Reproduces 12 paintings. Foreword by Marian B. Davis.

F.057 **THE LATE JOHN MARQUAND.**
Birmingham, Stephen. Philadelphia: L. P. Lippincott, 1972, p. 322.
Comments on Marquand's low opinion of Michener.
He opposed the selection of "**Hawaii**" by Book-of-the-Month Club.

F.058 **CONTEMPORARY LITERARY CRITICISM. VOL. 1.**
Detroit: Gale Research, 1973, pp. 214-15.

Section F - Books About or Related to JAMES A. MICHENER

F.059   **ON STAGE - SELECTED THEATER REVIEWS FROM THE NEW YORK TIMES 1920-1970.**
Beckerman, Bernard, and Howard Siegman, eds. Arno Press, [1973].
ISBN 0-8129-0363-3; LC 73-3053. Review of "South Pacific," by Brooks Atkinson, in the *New York Times*.

F.060   **THE TRUTH ABOUT KENT STATE.**
Davies, Peter. Author's rebuttal of Michener's conclusions in "**Kent State**."

   a   New York: Farrar Straus Giroux, 1973, pp. 9-10+. LC 72-94722.

   b   New York: Farrar Straus Giroux, 1973, pp. 9-10+. ISBN 0-374-51041-5. Paperback.

F.061   **PAUL NEWMAN: A PYRAMID ILLUSTRATED HISTORY OF THE MOVIES.**
Kerbel, Michael. New York: Pyramid Publications, 1974, pp. 36-38.
ISBN 0-515-03418-5; LC 73-21126. Contains details of the movie "Until They Sail" filmed in 1957, which was based upon a chapter from "**Return to Paradise**."

F.062   **WHAT DID I DO RIGHT? AN AUTO-BIBLIOGRAPHY.**
Day, A. Grove. Honolulu: White Knight Press, 1974, p. 22.
Comments by James A. Michener, dated 11/20/75, are typed and tipped in following page 22 in the copy at Swarthmore College Library.
Some copies have been noted to include a tipped-in four page addenda.

F.063   **MASTERPLOTS: 1975 ANNUAL.**
Magill, Frank N., ed. Englewood Cliffs, N.J.: Salem Press, 1975, pp. 50-53.
ISBN 0-89356-075-8; LC 55-41212. Review of "**Centennial**." The Magill Masterplots is an annual series of essay-reviews of 100 books published that year.

F.064   **MUSICAL STAGES.**
Rodgers, Richard. New York: Random House, 1975.
Comments about the musical "South Pacific."

F.065   **WRITING WITH STYLE.**
Timble, John R. Quotes Michener.

   a   Prentice-Hall, 1975, p. 21. ISBN 0-13-970376-4.

   b   Prentice-Hall, 1975, p. 21. ISBN 0-13-970368-3. Paperback.

F.066   **HOW I LEARNED TO LIKE MYSELF.**
Bryant, Gay, and Bockris-Wylie. New York: Warner Paperback Library, 1975/05.
Paperback. James Michener and nine other celebrities give advice on how they make their own lives work and the guidelines they follow.

F.067   **A CRITICAL STUDY OF THE SOCIAL STUDIES PROSPECTIVE OF JAMES ALBERT MICHENER.**
Maxey, Frances Burns. Ann Arbor: University Microfilms International, 1975/08.
Doctoral thesis submitted to the Faculty of the University of Mississippi.

Section F - Books About or Related to JAMES A. MICHENER

F.068   **THE PRESS.**
Liebling, A. J. Analyzes an account by Michener about the Moore-Marciano fight from *The Journal-American*, (1965/09/22) p. 28.

    a   New York: Ballantine Books, 1961, pp. 276-78. Paperback.

    b   **REV. ED.** New York: Ballantine Books, 1964, pp. 276-77. Paperback.

    c   **2D REV. ED.** New York: Ballantine Books, 1975/08, pp. 388-91. Paperback.

    d   New York: Pantheon Books, 1981, pp. 388-91. Paperback.

F.069   **AUTHORS IN THE NEWS. VOL. 1.**
Nykoruk, Barbara, ed. Detroit: Gale Research, 1976, pp. 338-40.
ISBN 0-8103-0043-5; LC 75-13541. A compilation of news stories and feature articles covering writers and members of the communications media.

F.070   **CONTEMPORARY LITERARY CRITICISM. VOL. 5.**
Detroit: Gale Research, 1976, pp. 288-91.

F.071   **JOSH.**
Logan, Joshua. Background in the creation and development of "South Pacific."

    a   New York: Delacorte Press, 1976.

    b   New York: Dell, 1977/06. Paperback.

F.072   **MY HEART BELONGS.**
Martin, Mary. Chapter on how "South Pacific," the musical, came to be.

    a   New York: William Morrow, 1976, pp. 157-80.
ISBN 0-688-03009-2; LC 75-31857.

    b   Warner Books, 1977/07, pp. 157-80. ISBN 0-446-89355-2. Paperback.

F.073   **WHY MAN EXPLORES. ("JAMES MICHENER").**
Washington, D.C.: U.S. Government Printing Office, 1976, pp. 29-42.
NASA Educational Publication (EP 125). Also in *Omni*, 4:2 (1981/11) 60-62, 116-18. Prepared from a transcript of a panel discussion held on July 2, 1976, in conjunction with the Viking missions to Mars. Panel members were selected as authorities in classical disciplines relating to exploration. The discussions were unrehearsed. The report transcript was presented in conversational style to convey the impromptu atmosphere and thoughts developed. Norman Cousins moderated the panel consisting of Michener, Philip Morrison, Jacques Cousteau, and Ray Bradbury.

F.074   **80 YEARS OF BEST SELLERS: 1895-1975.**
Hackett, Alice Payne, and James Henry Burke. New York: R. R. Bowker, 1977.

F.075   **AT RANDOM: THE REMINISCENCES OF BENNET CERF.**
Cerf, Bennett. New York: Random House, 1977, pp. 184, 220, 228, 239-41, 248, 278.

Section F - Books About or Related to JAMES A. MICHENER

F.076 **THE BOOK OF LISTS.**
Wallechinsky, David, Irving Wallace, and Amy Wallace.
Twelve writers who ran (unsuccessfully) for public office.

    a New York: William Morrow, 1977, p. 245. ISBN 0-688-03183-9; LC 77-1521.

    b New York: Bantam Books, 1978/02, p. 245. ISBN 0-553-11150-7. Paperback.

F.077 **BOOKS ABOUT HAWAII, 50 BASIC AUTHORS.**
("JAMES A. MICHENER: HAWAII").
Day, A. Grove. Honolulu: University Press of Hawaii, 1977, pp. 31-32.

F.078 **CARAVANS.**
Crawford, Nancy Voyles, and Thomas A. McMahon. Los Angeles: Ibex
Films, 1977?, 116 leaves. Screenplay based on the novel by Michener.

F.079 **THE THEATRICAL PRINTS OF THE TORII MASTERS, A SELECTION OF**
SEVENTEENTH AND EIGHTEENTH CENTURY UKIYO-E.
Link, Howard A. Rutland, Vt.: Charles E. Tuttle, 1977.
Also published by Honolulu Academy of Arts, Honolulu, Hawaii.

F.080 **UTAMARO AND HIROSHIGE; IN A SURVEY OF JAPANESE PRINTS**
FROM THE JAMES A. MICHENER COLLECTION OF THE HONOLULU
ACADEMY OF ARTS.
Link, Howard A.; Introductory essays by Seiichiro Takahashi, et al.
Honolulu: Honolulu Academy of Arts, 1977. Catalog by Howard A. Link.

F.081 **CONVERSATIONS WITH WRITERS II. ("JAMES A. MICHENER").**
Ellin, Stanley. Detroit: Gale Research, 1978, pp. 142-80.

F.082 **IN CONVERSATION WITH WRITERS II.**
Wilson, Richard F. Detroit: Gale Research, 1978.

F.083 **KENT STATE AND MAY 4TH: A SOCIAL SCIENCE PERSPECTIVE.**
Hensley, Thomas R., and Jerry M. Lewis. Dubuque, Iowa: Kendall/Hunt
Publishing, 1978, pp. 3, 5, 8,+. ISBN 0-8403-1856-1; LC 77-95547.
Paperback. Kent State departments of political science and sociology
analyze May 4th, citing Michener's **"Kent State."**

F.084 **MOVIE STARS, REAL PEOPLE, AND ME.**
Logan, Joshua. New York: Delacort Press, 1978.

F.085 **THE SOUND OF THEIR MUSIC.**
Nolan, Frederick. New York: Walker and Company, 1978, pp. 143-45 +.
Background material about the creation and development of the musical play
"South Pacific." Photo of Michener at p. 147.

F.086 **CONTEMPORARY LITERARY CRITICISM. VOL. 11.**
Detroit: Gale Research, 1979, pp. 374-76.

Section F - Books About or Related to JAMES A. MICHENER

F.087 **DIRECT POPULAR ELECTION OF THE PRESIDENT AND VICE-PRESIDENT OF THE U.S.**
U.S. Congress. Committee on the Judiciary; Comments by Michener. Washington: U.S. Gov. Printing Office, 1979, pp. 74-82. Hearings before the subcommittee, U.S. Senate, 96th Congress, First Session.

F.088 **GROLIER'S MASTERPLOTS: 1979 ANNUAL.**
Danbury: Grolier Enterprises, 1979, p. 41. Review of "**Chesapeake**." Grolier's Masterplots is an annual series of essay-reviews of 100 books published that year.

F.089 **STATEMENTS OF JAMES A. MICHENER.**
U.S. Congress. Committee of Commerce, Science and Transportation; Comments by James A. Michener. Washington: U.S. Gov. Printing Office, 1979, pp. 220-24. Hearings before the subcommittee on Science, Technology and Space, U.S. Senate, 96th Congress, First Session.

F.090 **A TALENT FOR LUCK.**
Strauss, Helen M. New York: Random House, 1979. ISBN 0-394-50428-3; LC 78-21804. Strauss was Michener's longtime literary agent.

F.091 **CONSTITUTIONAL CONVENTION PROCEDURES: STATEMENT OF JAMES A. MICHENER.**
U.S. Congress. Senate. Committee on the Judiciary. Subcommittee on the Constitution. Washington: U.S. Government Printing Office, 1980, pp. 360-63. Hearings before the subcommittee, U.S. Senate, 96th Congress, First Session.

F.092 **DICTIONARY OF LITERARY BIOGRAPHY. VOL. 6.**
Kibler, James E., Jr., ed. Detroit: Gale Research, 1980, pp. 232-36. American novelists since World War II, Second Series. The section about Michener was authored by A. Grove Day.

F.093 **THE KENT STATE COVERUP.**
Kelner, Joseph, and James Munves. Includes several quotations from Michener's "**Kent State, What Happened and Why**."

    a   New York: Harper & Row, 1980.

    b   New York: Kayem Books, 1980. ISBN 0-06-012282-X; LC 77-11813. Paperback.

F.094 **THE WRITER'S IMAGE: LITERARY PORTRAITS BY JILL KREMENTZ.**
Krementz, Jill. Boston: David R. Godine, 1980, [p.71].
ISBN 0-87923-349-4; LC 80-66461. 1974 photograph of Michener at Bucks County, Pennsylvania, in casual attire sitting in the woods.

F.095 **AMERICAN IMAGES: SELECTIONS FROM THE JAMES AND MARI MICHENER COLLECTION OF 20TH CENTURY AMERICAN ART.**
Mayer, Susan M., and Becky Duval Reese. Austin: University of Texas, 1981. Paperback. A special publication for children by the Archer M. Huntington Art Gallery, College of Fine Arts. 15 loose prints.

Section F - Books About or Related to JAMES A. MICHENER

F.096   **GROLIER'S MASTERPLOTS: 1981 ANNUAL.**
Danbury: Grolier Enterprises, 1981, p. 62. Review of "**The Covenant**." Grolier's
Masterplots is an annual series of essay-reviews of 100 books published that year.

F.097   **JAMES A. MICHENER: A REGISTER OF HIS PAPERS IN THE
SWARTHMORE COLLEGE LIBRARY.**
Nicholas, Lisa, comp. Swarthmore: Swarthmore College Library, 1981. Paperback.
Catalogued by Swarthmore students initially; organized by Cheryl Leibold. Martha
Swain arranged and classified correspondence. Papers for "**The Covenant**" are housed
at the Swarthmore College Library and include manuscripts, correspondence,
speeches, essays, committee reports, newspaper articles, photographs, notebooks,
certificates and awards, television and radio specials, report from the censorship board
of the South African government, galleys, and page proofs. The papers are stored in 13
archival containers, occupying approximately 12 linear feet of shelf space. The register
includes 2 1/2 pages of biographical notes, books by Michener, contributions to books,
translations, books about Michener, and video cassettes and recordings.

F.098   **THE LITERARY GUIDE TO THE UNITED STATES.**
Benedict, Stewart, ed. New York: Facts On File, 1981, pp. 190-92.
ISBN 0-87196-304-3; LC 80-25823. Michener and "**Centennial**" illustrate the
mountain states and southwest in a collection of portrayals of America.

F.099   **PROFILES IN EXCELLENCE 1981.**
Hershey, Pa.: Pennsylvania Public T.V. Net. Comm., 1981. The Governor's Haslett
Memorial Awards for Excellence in the Arts. Pennsylvania Council on the Arts.

F.100   **WRITERS AND FRIENDS.**
Weeks, Edward. Boston: Little, Brown and Company, 1981, p. 30.
ISBN 0-316-92791-0; LC 81-19383. Quotes Michener in "**Return to Paradise**,"
regarding James Norman Hall's popularity in Tahiti.

F.101   **KENT STATE / MAY 4: ECHOES THROUGH A DECADE.**
Bills, Scott L., ed. Kent State, Ohio: Kent State University Press, 1982, pp. 4, 72, 89.
ISBN 0-87338-278-1; LC 82-10102. A collection of essays and interviews
representing a broad spectrum of viewpoints regarding May 4 and its aftermath.

F.102   **THE OXFORD ILLUSTRATED LITERARY GUIDE TO THE UNITED
STATES.**
Ehrlich, Eugene, and Gorton Carruth. New York, Oxford: Oxford
University Press, 1982, pp. 197, 212+. ISBN 0-19-503186-5; LC 82-8034.
Geographical areas where Michener lived in Hawaii, Doylestown, Pottstown,
and Swarthmore.

F.103   **A COMPARATIVE STUDY OF THE VALUE OF SPORT BASED UPON
THE PHILOSOPHIES OF EARLE F. ZEIGLER AND JAMES A. MICHENER.**
Mock, Mary S. Ann Arbor: University Microfilms International,1982/05. Doctoral
thesis submitted to the School of Education at the University of South Dakota.

F.104   **OUR WHOLE VOICE: THE PASTORAL AND THE HEROIC IN HAWAII'S
LITERATURE.**
Sumida, Stephen Hiro. Ann Arbor: University Microfilms International,1982/12/01.
Doctoral thesis submitted to the University of Washington.

Section F - Books About or Related to JAMES A. MICHENER

F.105   **THE AMERICAN SHORT STORY: 1945-1980.**
Weaver, Gordon, ed. Boston: Twayne Publishers, 1983, pp. 2, 31.

F.106   **THE BOOK OF LISTS #3.**
Wallace, Amy, David Wallechinsky, and Irving Wallace. Interracial marriages, famous people who were adopted.

    a   New York: William Morrow, 1983, pp. 285, 289. ISBN 0-688-01647-2; LC 82-20373.

    b   New York: Bantam Books, 1983/12, pp. 285, 289. ISBN 0-553-72868-1. Paperback.

F.107   **GROLIER'S MASTERPLOTS: 1983 ANNUAL.**
Danbury: Grolier Enterprises, 1983, p. 328. Review of "**Space**." Grolier's Masterplots is an annual series of essay-reviews of 100 books published that year.

F.108   **CONTEMPORARY LITERARY CRITICISM. VOL. 29.**
Detroit: Gale Research, 1984, pp. 309-17.

F.109   **GROLIER'S MASTERPLOTS: 1984 ANNUAL.**
Danbury: Grolier Enterprises, 1984, p. 287. Review of "**Poland**." Grolier's Masterplots is a series of essay-reviews of 100 books published that year.

F.110   **JAMES A. MICHENER, A BIOGRAPHY.**
Hayes, John P.

    a   Indianapolis: Bobbs-Merrill, 1984. ISBN 0-672-52782-0; LC 83-15575.

    b   London: W. H. Allen, n.d. ISBN 0-86379-024-0. Paperback. Comet Books.

F.111   **JAMES A. MICHENER.**
Becker, George J.

    a   New York: Frederick Unger, 1984. ISBN 0-8044-2044-0; LC 82-40279.

    b   New York: Frederick Unger, 1984. ISBN 0-8044-6031-0. Paperback.

F.112   **NEW AMERICAN PAINTING: A TRIBUTE TO JAMES AND MARI MICHENER.**
McCready, Eric. Austin: Archer M. Huntington Gallery, 1984. Paperback. Exhibition Catalog: January 12 - March 5, 1983. This exhibition was dedicated to and inspired by the Micheners.

F.113   **THE ROLE OF PLACE IN LITERATURE.**
Lutwack, Leonard. Syracuse: Syracuse University Press, 1984, pp. 57, 233. ISBN 0-8156-2305-4; LC 83-24264.

F.114   **JAMES A. MICHENER: AN AMERICAN WRITER.**
Hayes, John P. Ann Arbor: University Microfilms International, 1984/05. Submitted to the Temple University Graduate Board in partial fulfillment of the requirements for his Ph.D. degree.

Section F - Books About or Related to JAMES A. MICHENER

F.115   **JAMES A. MICHENER: EDUCATOR.**
Galvez-Hjornevik, Cleta Maria. Ann Arbor: University Microfilms International,
1984/08. Doctoral thesis submitted to the Faculty of the Graduate School
of the University of Texas.

F.116   **THE BOOK BOOK: A COMPENDIUM OF LISTS, QUIZZES, & TRIVIA
ABOUT BOOKS.**
Gilbar, Steven. New York: Bell Publishing, 1985, pp. 19, 93, 116+.
ISBN 0-517-467836; LC 84-24304. A compilation of lists, quizzes, and trivia
about books. Contains nine references to Michener's writings.

F.117   **CONTEMPORARY AUTHORS - NEW REVISION SERIES. VOL. 21.**
Straub, Deborah A., ed. Detroit: Gale Research, 1985, pp. 292-99.

F.118   **HAWAII, TRUTH STRANGER THAN FICTION: THE TRUE TALES
OF MISSIONARY TROUBLES AND TRIUMPHS FICTIONALIZED BY
MICHENER.**
Piercy, LaRue W. Kailua-Kona, Hawaii: L.W. Piercy, 1985.
3000 copies of the first printing were issued.

F.119   **SPORTS AND SOCIAL VALUES.**
Simon, Robert L. Englewood Cliffs, N.J.: Prentice-Hall, 1985,
pp. 62n, 78-80, 98n, 118, 125n. ISBN 0-13-837881-9; LC 84-16924.

F.120   **GROLIER'S MASTERPLOTS: 1986 ANNUAL.**
Danbury: Grolier Enterprises, 1986, pp. 358-61. Review of "**Texas.**" Grolier's
Masterplots is a series of essay-reviews of 100 books published that year.

F.121   **IMPRESSIONS OF TEXAS.**
Shaw, Charles. Illustrated by Charles Shaw. Austin: University of Texas Press,
1986. A portfolio of fourteen scenic paintings. 400 signed copies printed
to accompany the Sesquicentennial Edition of "**Texas.**"

F.122   **WEBSTER'S 3RD NEW INTERNATIONAL DICTIONARY.**
Springfield, Mass.: Merriam-Webster, 1986, p. 2430. A new definition of
"transpire" is attributed to Michener. "...to come to pass, happen, occur."
(See B.073.)

F.123   **W. O. W.: Writers on Writing.**
Winokur, Jon, selected and compiled by.

    a   Philadelphia: Running Press Book Publishers, 1986,
pp. 7,13, 80, 83, 87, 121, 325, 334, 344. ISBN 0-89471-877-0.

    b   Philadelphia: Running Press Book Publishers, 1986,
pp. 7,13, 80, 83, 87, 121, 325, 334, 344. ISBN 0-89471-877-0. Paperback.

    c   London: Headline Book Publishing, 1988,
pp. 5, 11, 92, 95, 150, 167, 202, 216, 218. ISBN 0-7472-0099-8. Paperback.

Section F - Books About or Related to JAMES A. MICHENER

F.124   **THE DEVIL AND DR. BARNES: PORTRAIT OF AN AMERICAN ART COLLECTOR.**

    a   Greenfeld, Howard. New York: Viking Penguin, 1987, pp. 130-31.
        ISBN 0-670-80650-1; LC 88-21846.

    b   Greenfeld, Howard. New York: Penguin Books, 1989, pp. 130-31. Paperback.
        ISBN 0-14-011735-0.

F.125   **MAD ABOUT ISLANDS - NOVELISTS OF A VANISHED PACIFIC.**
Day, A. Grove. Literary adventures and profiles of major writers who found allurement among the far islands of the South Seas.

    a   Honolulu: Mutual Publishing, 1987, pp. 236-55. ISBN 0-935180-46-x; LC 87-61309.

    b   Honolulu: Mutual Publishing, 1987, pp. 236-55. ISBN 0-935180-47-8. Paperback.

F.126   **SAYONARA, A MUSICAL PLAY;**
BASED ON THE NOVEL BY JAMES A. MICHENER.
Luce, William. Milburn, N.J.: Peppermill Playhouse, 1987.
Produced by the Peppermill Playhouse. Music by George Fischoff, lyrics by Hy Gilbert. Directed by Robert Johanson.

F.127   **WRITING CREATIVE NONFICTION.**
Cheney, Theodore A. Rees. Cincinatti: Writer's Digest Books, 1987, pp. 95-96.
Uses excerpt from "**Iberia**" to illustrate bureaucratic absurdity.

F.128   **EXPLORING THE SIXTIES; SELECTED AMERICAN PAINTINGS FROM THE MICHENER COLLECTION.**
McCready, Eric S.(Foreword); John R. Clarke (Essay). Austin:
University of Texas, 1988. Paperback. Archer M. Huntington Art Gallery,
College of Fine Arts. Exhibition Catalogue, June 10 to July 31, 1988.

F.129   **POLITICAL MYTHOLOGY AND POPULAR FICTION.**
Yanarella, Ernest J., and Lee Sigelman, eds. Westport: Greenwood
Press, 1988, pp. 81-99. ISBN 0-313-15976-3; LC 87-17802.
Essay "Political Change in America: Perspectives from the Popular
Historical Novels of Michener and Vidal."

F.130   **GROLIER'S MASTERPLOTS: 1989 ANNUAL.**
Danbury: Grolier Enterprises, 1989, pp. 1-4. Review of "**Alaska**." Grolier's
Masterplots is a series of essay-reviews of 100 books published that year.

F.131   **ON BEING A WRITER.**
Strickland, Bill, ed. In this April, 1972, interview by John Hayes, Michener
talks about the art of making a living as a full-time writer.

    a   Cincinnati: Writer's Digest Books, 1989, pp. 86-91.

    b   Cincinnati: Writer's Digest Books, 1992, pp. 86-91. Paperback.

Section F - Books About or Related to JAMES A. MICHENER

F.132 **RANGE WARS: HEATED DEBATES, SOBER REFLECTIONS, AND OTHER ASSESSMENTS OF TEXAS WRITING.**
Clifford, Craig, and Tom Pilkington, eds. Authors Clay Reynolds and Celia Morris conclude that Michener's **"Texas"** is "flagrantly overwritten," and short on female roles.

   a Dallas: Southern Methodist University Press, 1989, pp. 69, 73, 79-81+.

   b Dallas: Southern Methodist University Press, 1989, pp. 69, 73, 79-81+. Paperback.

F.133 **THE COMPLETE GUIDE TO WRITING FICTION.**
Conrad, Barnaby. Cincinnati: Writer's Digest Books, 1990, pp. 12-14, 24. ISBN 0-89879-395-5; LC 90-12287.

F.134 **CONTEMPORARY LITERARY CRITICISM. VOL. 60.**
Detroit: Gale Research, 1990, pp. 254-63.

F.135 **JAMES A. MICHENER. FIRST CITIZEN OF THE REPUBLIC OF LETTERS. A TRIBUTE BY HIS WRITING COLLEAGUES.**
New York: The Authors League Fund, 1990. 28 of his colleagues offer brief tributes to the greatness of his writing and his benevolence to his colleagues. 500 copies.

F.136 **KABUKI THROUGH THEATRE PRINTS: COLLECTION OF THE HONOLULU ACADEMY OF ARTS JAMES A. MICHENER COLLECTION.**
Link, Howard A., Juzo Suzuki, and Masakatsu Gunji. Honolulu: Honolulu Academy of Arts, 1990. Paperback. Exhibition catalogue co-sponsored by Azuba Museum of Arts and Crafts. Text in Japanese and English. 227 color, 44 black-and-white prints.

F.137 **WHO'S WHO IN AMERICA. 46TH ED. 2 VOLS.**
Wilmette, Ill.: Marquis Who's Who, 1990, p. 2267. ISBN 0-8379-0146-4; LC 4-16934. Michener's selection was based upon one or both of two factors; position of responsibility held, or significant achievement. Michener has been noted in editions at least as early as 1954-1955.

F.138 **BIBLIOGRAPHY OF BOOKS, ARTICLES AND OTHER WORKS BY, ABOUT, OR CONTRIBUTED TO BY JAMES A. MICHENER.**
Roberts, James W., comp. St. Petersburg: Oriental Bookshelf, 1991. Paperback. A loosely organized, ongoing bibliography. A compilation of sales catalogs of the Oriental Bookshelf.

F.139 **BIBLIOHOLISM: THE LITERARY ADDICTION.**
Raabe, Tom. Illustrated by Craig M. Brown. Golden, Colo.: Fulcrum Publishing, 1991, pp. 97-98. ISBN 1-55591-080-7; LC 91-7260. Paperback. A two page analysis of the affliction known as "Micheneritis."

F.140 **PRINTS BY UTAGAWA HIROSHIGE IN THE JAMES A. MICHENER COLLECTION. 2 VOLS.**
Link, Howard A. Honolulu: Honolulu Academy of Arts, 1991. ISBN 0-937426-13-X; LC 91-071377. Paperback. Exhibition June 4 - July 12, 1992. Text in Japanese and English. Volume 1 includes a catalog and essay covering eight series of prints. Volume 2 consists of essays and catalog commentaries by Howard A. Link. Volume 1 was sold individually or with Volume 2 as a boxed set.

Section F - Books About or Related to JAMES A. MICHENER

F.141   **BATTLE HYMNS: THE RHETORICAL STRATEGIES OF TWENTIETH CENTURY AMERICAN WAR NOVELS.**
Brown, Brenda Gabioud. Ann Arbor: University Microfilms International,1991/05. Doctoral thesis submitted to the Texas Christian University Graduate Faculty of AddRan College of Arts and Sciences.

F.142   **GOOD ADVICE ON WRITING: WRITERS PAST AND PRESENT AND HOW TO WRITE WELL.**
Safire, William, and James Safir, eds. New York: Simon & Schuster, 1992, pp. 122-23. ISBN 0-671-77005-5; LC 92-19222.

F.143   **THE BOOK OF LISTS: THE '90s EDITION.**
Wallechinsky, David, and Amy Wallace. New York: Little, Brown and Company, 1993, pp. 211, 339-40, 346. ISBN 0-316-92079-7; LC 93-17197.
Includes Michener under famous orphans. Lists Michener's 10 favorite novels. Lists "**Hawaii**" as James Stewart's favorite novel.

F.144   **AUTHOR PRICE GUIDES ("JAMES MICHENER").**
Ahearn, Allen, and Pat Ahearn. Rockville, Md.: Quill & Brush, 1993/12. An ongoing, loose-leaf compilation of 56 (to date) Author Price Guides prepared and based upon available information in bibliographies, dealer catalogs, auction records and personal experience of the preparers.

F.145   **JAMES A. MICHENER: A CHECKLIST OF HIS WORKS WITH A SELECTED, ANNOTATED BIBLIOGRAPHY.**
Roberts, F.X., and C.D. Rhine, comps.; Westport, Conn.: Greenwood Press, 1995.

F.146   **JAMES A. MICHENER: THE BEGINNING TEACHER AND HIS TEXTBOOKS.**
Dybwad, G.L., and Joy V. Bliss; Foreword, notes and reminiscences by James A. Michener; Albuquerque: The Book Stops Here, 1995.

G.
Video
Materials

"Artists in other fields who must work with one of my books earn their pay, and my gratitude . . . ."

—James A. Michener
THE WORLD IS MY HOME
New York, Random House, 1992

Return to Paradise. G.001.

Section G- Video Materials

G.001   **RETURN TO PARADISE.**
Metro Goldwyn Mayer, 1953. Screenwriter - Charles Kaufman.
Director - Mark Robson. Producer - Theron Warth. Based on "Mr. Morgan," a
chapter from **"Return to Paradise."** Starring - Gary Cooper, Barry Jones,
Roberta Haynes, and Moira MacDonald. Cooper portrays a vagabond desiring to
be left alone and is confronted by a puritanical minister who harshly disciplines
local natives on a remote Polynesian island.

G.002   **THE BRIDGES AT TOKO-RI.**
Paramount Pictures, 1954. Screenwriter - Valentine Davies. Director - Mark Robson.
Producers - William Perlberg and George Seaton. A fictional account of a naval
pilot recalled to duty in the politically unpopular Korean War. Based on Michener's
novel. Starring - William Holden, Grace Kelly, Fredric March, Mickey Rooney,
Robert Strauss, and Earl Holliman.

G.003   **MEN OF THE FIGHTING LADY.**
Metro Goldwyn Mayer, 1954. Screenwriter - Art Cohn. Director - Andrew Marton.
Producer - Henry Berman.
Based on two factual articles appearing in *The Saturday Evening Post*, "The
Forgotten Heroes of Korea," by James A. Michener, and "The Case of the Blind
Pilot" by Commander Harry A. Burns, USN. The technical advisor for the movie
was Comdr. Paul N. Gray, USN, who was celebrated by Michener as "The Bald
Eagle of the Essex," a story written by Michener and donated to the Navy to be
distributed free to servicemen. Starring - Van Johnson, Walter Pidgeon, Dewey
Martin, Keenan Wynn, Frank Lovejoy, and with Louis Calhern portraying
James Michener in the movie.

G.004   **SAYONARA.**
Samuel Goldwyn, 1957. Screenwriter - Paul Osborn. Director - Joshua Logan.
Producer - William Goetz. A fictional account of an American pilot who falls in
love with a Japanese entertainer, and is torn between a desire to buck the system
and marry for love, or yield to conventional forces and marry a more socially and
politically acceptable American girl that he does not love. Based on Michener's novel.
Starring - Marlon Brando, Red Buttons, James Garner, Patricia Owens, Martha Scott,
Ricardo Montalban, Miiko Taka, and Miyoshi Umeki.

G.005   **UNTIL THEY SAIL.**
Metro Goldwyn Mayer, 1957. Screenwriter - Robert Anderson. Director - Robert
Wise. Producer - Charles Schnee. Based on the chapter of the same name from
"Return to Paradise" by James A. Michener, this is the story of the defense of New
Zealand by American forces during World War II, while New Zealand men were
fighting elsewhere. The vagaries of war create antagonistic emotions and needs in its
participants. Starring - Jean Simmons, Joan Fontaine, Paul Newman, Piper Laurie,
Charles Drake, and Sandra Dee.

G.006   **ASSIGNMENT: SOUTHEAST ASIA.**
NBC-TV, 1957/10? A 90-minute "telementary" scheduled for showing on NBC in
April or May, 1957. Mentioned in *Good Housekeeping*, 144:4 (1957/04) 276.

Section G- Video Materials

G.007 **SOUTH PACIFIC.**
Rodgers and Hammerstein, 1958. Screenwriter - Paul Osborn.
Director - Joshua Logan. Producer - Buddy Adler.
Based on the play "South Pacific" by Richard Rodgers, Oscar Hammerstein II,
and Joshua Logan, which was based on **"Tales of the South Pacific"**
by James A. Michener, this is the story of the tedious monotony and escapades of
American sailors occupying South Pacific Islands during World War II. Starring -
Rossano Brazzi, Mitzi Gaynor, John Kerr, Ray Walston, Juanita Hall, France Nuyen,
and Russ Brown.

G.008 **ADVENTURES IN PARADISE.**
ABC-TV, 1959/10/05. A weekly 60-minute series based on stories by
Michener, starring Gardner McKay as skipper of the "South Seas."
It ran until April, 1962.

G.009 **HAWAII.**
1966. Producer-Director-George Roy Hill. C-171. Based on James Michener's
novel. Starring Julie Andrews, Max von Sydow, Richard Harris, Torin Thatcher,
Gene Hackman, Carroll O'Connor.

G.010 **HAWAII.**
Mirisch Corporation, 1966. Screenwriter - Dalton Trumbo. Director - George Roy
Hill. Producer - Walter Mirisch. Based on the novel **"Hawaii."** An account of the
geological formation of the islands, and a fictional story of the missionary
proselytization of the natives, and the coalescing of cultures to produce Hawaii's
"Golden People." Starring - Julie Andrews, Max von Sydow, Richard Harris, Torin
Thatcher, Gene Hackman, and Carroll O'Connor.

G.011 **POINT OF VIEW - JAMES MICHENER ON THE MIDDLE EAST, WITH
DORE SCHARY.**
Anti-Defamation League, 1967. 28:30m. 16mm, film, black-and-white, with sound.
An interview with Michener following the six days war in June, 1962.

G.012 **THE HAWAIIANS.**
Mirisch Productions, 1970. Screenwriter - James R. Webb. Director - Tom Gries.
Producer - Walter Mirisch. Based on the novel **"Hawaii"** by James A. Michener, this
is the sequel to the movie **"Hawaii."** This sequel follows several decades of restless
changes in Hawaii's more recent economic, political, and social development.
Starring - Charlton Heston, Geraldine Chaplin, John Phillip Law, Tina Chen,
Alec McCowen, and Mako.

G.013 **THE TODAY SHOW.**
NBC-TV, 1971/04/28. A televised debate by Michener, Joe Eszterhas, I. F. Stone
and others regarding the Kent State tragedy.

G.014 **JAMES A. MICHENER.**
University of Northern Colorado, Greeley, Colo.: p1973/05/01. ISN 0394560566.
1 cassette (? hours) black-and-white 3/4 in. An interview with James A. Michener
produced by the Department of Radio and Instructional Television at the University
of Northern Colorado.

Section G- Video Materials

G.015 **WRITER TO WRITER.**
NETCHE, 1974. Michener talks about his first novel. Prepared by the Nebraska
ETV Council for Higher Education for use in College-Adult Education in American
Literature. 30 minutes.

G.016 **WRITER TO CRITIC.**
NETCHE, 1974. Michener talks about his first novel.
Prepared by the Nebraska ETV Council for Higher Education for use in
College-Adult Education in American Literature. 30 minutes.

G.017 **JAMES MICHENER'S DYNASTY.**
NBC-TV, 1976. Screenwriter - Sidney Carroll. C-100m.
A story of two brothers establishing homes and businesses in Ohio in the 1820's.
A review in the *New York Times* (1976/03/13), attributes the actual script to
Sidney Carroll, who has 'adapted Michener's story for television.'

G.018 **HAWAII: REVISITED.**
Krainin Productions, 1977. 52m. Produced, written and directed by Julian Krainin.
Highlights - Volcanic origins, Polynesian myths and legends, Chinese, Japanese,
Philippine and Portuguese immigration, unification under King Kamehameha,
leper colonies, and statehood in 1959.

G.019 **ISRAEL: A SEARCH FOR FAITH.**
Reader's Digest Association, 1977. 52m.
Produced, written and directed by Albert Waller. Co-produced by Ken Golden.
Highlights - Jerusalem, a square mile of real estate which has become a focal point in
the religious disputes between Christian, Muslim and Jew. The Dome of the Rock
is an important nexus of the three religions; it was there that Abraham almost
slew his son, Isaac; Solomon built his Temple there; Jesus came there to purify his
religion; and Mohammed ascended from there to Heaven. The Arabic word "tell" is
described as an artificial mound created by successive layers of civilization imposed
one upon the other. The "tell" was the central theme for the action in "The Source."

G.020 **CARAVANS.**
Universal, 1978. Screenwriters - Nancy Voyles Crawford, Thomas A. McMahon
and Lorraine Williams. Director - James Fargo. Producer - Elmo Williams.
Based on the novel, this is a fictional story about a rebellious, free spirited
Senator's daughter who marries a mid-easterner and then disappears in the wilds
of Afghanistan. Starring - Anthony Quinn, Jennifer O'Neill, Michael Sarrazin,
Behrooz Vosoughi, Christopher Lee, Barry Sullivan, and Joseph Cotten.

G.021 **CENTENNIAL.**
Universal Studios, 1978. A 12-part, 26 hour, miniseries.
Written for television by John Wilder. Producer - George E. Crosby.
Executive Producer - John Wilder. Supervising Producer-Richard Caffey.
Director -Virgil W. Vogel. Director of Photography - Duke Callaghan.
The series premiered beginning October 1, 1978, on NBC television.
Based on the novel **"Centennial"** by James A. Michener, this is the story of the U.S.
expansion into the American West. The State of Colorado celebrated its centennial
concurrently with the U.S. Bicentennial, thus the title. Starring - Raymond Burr,
Barbara Carrera, Richard Chamberlain, Robert Conrad, Richard Crenna, Chad Everett,
David Janssen, Alex Karras, Brian Keith, Sally Kellerman, Donald Pleasence, Lynn
Redgrave, Dennis Weaver, William Atherton, Timothy Dalton, Cliff De Young,

Section G- Video Materials

Sharon Gless, Andy Griffith, Gregory Harrison, Stephen McHattie, Lois Nettleton, Cristina Raines, Robert Vaughn, Anthony Zerbe, Stephanie Zimbalist, Michael Ansara, Merle Haggard, and Mark Harmon. Special cameo appearances by Mari Michener and John Kings.   (See Study Guide, Appendix IV)

G.022   **POLAND: THE WILL TO BE.**
Emlen House Productions, 1978. 52m. Produced, written and directed by Albert Waller. The central geographical and political fact of Poland - it has borders that cannot be defended. "Over and over again the Polish Plain has been a vast highway for the ambitions of neighboring powers." Highlights include tours of Warsaw and Krakow, and Michener's interview of Cardinal Wojtyla (pronounced Voy-tee-ya) who was later to become the first Polish Pope.

G.023   **THE SOUTH PACIFIC: END OF EDEN?**
Krainin Productions, 1978. 52m. Produced, written and directed by Julian Krainin. A thumbnail sketch of culture shock imposed on island life by intruders. Highlights include Pitcairn Island, The Easter Islands, Bora Bora, Eniwetok, Solomon Islands, Fiji, New Zealand, and Tahiti.

G.024   **SPAIN: THE LAND AND THE LEGEND.**
Emlen House Productions, 1978.   52m. Produced, written and directed by Albert Waller. Highlights - The 2,000 year old Roman aqueduct symbolizes Spain's Roman heritage. The Great Mosque of Cordoba symbolizes the religious conflicts between Muslims, Christians and Jews.

G.025   **JAMES MICHENER'S WORLD - THE BLACK ATHLETE.**
Cappy Productions, 1980. Produced, directed and written by Bud Greenspan.

G.026   **JAMES MICHENER'S WORLD - WOMEN IN SPORTS.**
Cappy Productions, 1980.
Produced, directed and written by Bud Greenspan.

G.027   **JAMES MICHENER'S WORLD - CHILDREN IN SPORTS.**
Cappy Productions, 1980.
Produced, directed and written by Bud Greenspan.

G.028   **POPE JOHN PAUL II - THE POPE FROM POLAND.**
Emlen House Productions, 1980. Produced by Albert Waller. Directed by Stanis-law Moszuk, Andrew de Ruttie, and Albert Waller. Written by Andrew de Ruttie.

G.029   **THE ENDURING TRADITION - ART IN POLAND.**
Emlen House Productions, [1980]. 22m. Produced by Albert Waller. Directed by Stanislaw Moszuk. Written by Andrew de Ruttie.

G.030   **THE ENDURING TRADITION - MUSIC IN POLAND.**
Emlen House Productions, [1980]. 22m. Produced by Albert Waller. Directed by Stanislaw Moszuk. Written by Andrew de Ruttie.

G.031   **THE ENDURING TRADITION - FILM IN POLAND.**
Emlen House Productions, [1980]. 22m. Produced by Albert Waller. Directed by Stanislaw Moszuk. Written by Andrew de Ruttie.

Section G- Video Materials

G.032   THE ENDURING TRADITION - THEATER IN POLAND.
Emlen House Productions, [1980]. 22m. Produced by Albert Waller.
Directed by Stanislaw Moszuk and Roman Zoluski. Written by Andrew de Ruttie.

G.033   THE ENDURING TRADITION - DANCE IN POLAND.
Emlen House Productions, [1980]. 22m. Produced by Albert Waller.
Directed by Stanislaw Moszuk. Written by Andrew de Ruttie.

G.034   JAMES MICHENER'S U.S.A. - THE SOUTHWEST.
Emlen House Productions, 1981. 52m. Executive Producer and Director,
Albert Waller. Produced by John Mernet. Written by Patty Conroy.

G.035   JAMES MICHENER'S U.S.A. - THE FAR WEST.
Emlen House Productions, 1981. 52m. Executive Producer and Director,
Albert Waller. Produced and written by John Mernet.

G.036   JAMES MICHENER'S U.S.A. - THE NORTHEAST.
Emlen House Productions, 1981. 52m. Executive Producer and Director,
Albert Waller. Co-produced by John Mernet. Written by Albert Waller.

G.037   JAMES MICHENER'S U.S.A. - THE NEW SOUTH.
Emlen House Productions, 1981. 52m. Executive Producer and Director,
Albert Waller. Produced by John Mernet. Written by Patty Conroy.

G.038   JAMES MICHENER'S U.S.A. - THE MIDWEST.
Emlen House Productions, 1981. 52m. Produced and Directed by Albert Waller.
Co-produced by John Mernet. Written by Stuart Hersh.

G.039   LOWELL THOMAS - JAMES MICHENER: A DIALOGUE.
Emlen House Productions, 1981. Produced and directed by Albert Waller.
Co-produced by Patricia Millman and Larry Klein.

G.040   CONESTOGA I - DAWN OF A NEW SPACE ERA?
ABC-TV, 1982. Nightline. Aired September 9, 1982.

G.041   [MICHENER INTERVIEW].
ABC-TV, 1983. Good Morning America, September 8, 1983.

G.042   OUTER SPACE: THE DREAM AND THE REALITY.
ABC-TV, 1983. Nightline. Aired May 20, 1983.

G.043   [MICHENER IN AN INTERVIEW WITH HEYWOOD HALE BROUN].
CBS-TV, 1984. One sound tape reel (18 min.) 3 3/4 ips, mono.; 7 in. 1/4 in.
tape. Aired on "Sunday Morning," November 11, 1984.

G.044   QUESTIONS AND ANSWERS BY JAMES A. MICHENER.
1984/04/28. Michener was guest speaker for the Permian Historical Society at the
University of Texas Permian Basin, Odessa, Texas. The videotape was prepared by
the Instructional Media Division, Martha Edwards, Director, and was transcribed by
Betsy L. Seidel, Senior Secretary of the Division of Humanities and Fine Arts.

Section G- Video Materials

G.045   **RODGERS AND HAMMERSTEIN: THE SOUND OF AMERICAN MUSIC.**
Camera Three, 1985. Written and produced by JoAnn G. Young. Directed by
John Musilli. Executive producer Stephan Chodorov and John Musilli. Michener
appears twice in the segment dealing with "**South Pacific**." He opposed taking out
the song "You've Got to Be Taught."

G.046   **SPACE.**
Columbia Broadcasting System, 1985. Screenwriters - Dick Berg and Stirling
Silliphant. Directors - Lee Phillips and Joseph Sargent. Based on the novel. The lives
of five characters are drawn together in this story of the U.S. on the "final Frontier."
A 5-part, 13 hour, miniseries premiered beginning April 13, 1985, on CBS Television.
Starring - James Garner, Blair Brown, Susan Anspach, Bruce Dern, Beau Bridges,
Harry Hamlin, and Michael York. (See Study Guide, Appendix IV)

G.047   **[JAMES MICHENER RETURNS TO THE SOUTH PACIFIC ISLAND WHICH
INSPIRED HIM TO BECOME A WRITER].**
CBS-TV, c[1986]. 1 Sound tape reel, (25 min.), 3 3/4 ips, mono.; 7 in. 1/4 in.
tape. Broadcast on "Sixty Minutes," with Diane Sawyer, March 9, 1986.

G.048   **SLOW FIRES: ON THE PRESERVATION OF THE HUMAN RECORD.**
American Film Foundation, 1987. Film on methods to preserve and restore
intellectual documents such as pamphlets, photographs, films, drawings and maps.
Sponsored by The Council on Library Resources, Library of Congress, National
Endowment for the Humanities. Written by Ben Maddow and Terry Sanders;
narrated by Robert MacNeil. James Michener, Barbara Tuchman, and Vartan
Gregorian express spirited and studied concern for preserving the records of our
civilization.

G.049   **UKIYO-E: PRINTS OF JAPAN.**
Art Institute of Chicago, [198-?] Writer - Oliver Statler. Director - Francis Haar.
1 video cassette (30 min.): sound, color; 1/2 in.VHS format.
A survey of Ukiyo-e prints of Japan from the collection of the Institute.
Presented with the aid of the Japan Society, New York.

G.050   **HAWAII, THE MOTION PICTURE.**
Mirisch Corp. of Delaware, Culver City, Ca.: 1990.
Two video cassettes (190 minutes) VHS format.
Film Version of James Michener's novel, starring Julie Andrews, Max Von
Sydow, Richard Harris.

G.051   **THE LEGEND OF STAN THE MAN MUSIAL.**
TMM, Inc. 1990. Narrated by Jack Buck. Written and directed by Mark Durand.
Produced by Thomas Ashley. Introduction and some commentary by Michener.

G.052   **[MICHENER INTERVIEW WITH CHARLES GIBSON].**
ABC-TV. 1990. Interview regarding Michener's "**Pilgrimage: A Memoir of
Poland and Rome**." Aired October 18, 1990, on Good Morning America.

G.053   **MANDELA: THE MAN AND HIS COUNTRY.**
MPI, 1990/07.
A comprehensive video biography of the anti-apartheid movement. Included
are interviews with Jesse Jackson and Michener.

Section G- Video Materials

G.054   **[MICHENER INTERVIEW WITH ROBIN LEACH].**
CBS-TV, 1991. Survey of art donated by the Micheners to the University of Texas.
Aired on "Life Styles of the Rich and Famous," January 11, 1991.

G.055   **[MICHENER INTERVIEW WITH CHARLES GIBSON].**
ABC-TV, 1991. Interview regarding Michener's new book "**The Novel**."
Aired on "Good Morning America," April 2, 1991.

G.056   **[MICHENER INTERVIEW WITH CHARLES GIBSON].**
ABC-TV, 1991. A review of his auto-biography "**The World is My Home**."
Aired on "Good Morning America," December 2, 1991.

G.057   **JAMES MICHENER AT WORK.**
Films for Humanities & Sciences. Princeton: 1992. Michener explains the craft
of writing. (48 min.) Color. Produced by Carl Hersh and Kathy Hersh.

G.058   **[MICHENER AND COUSIN, VIRGINIA TRUMBULL,**
INTERVIEW WITH CHARLES GIBSON].
ABC-TV, 1992. The search for the lost manuscript of "**Mexico**," discovered
by Trumbull. Aired on "Good Morning America." November 6, 1992.

G.059   **[12 MINUTE VIDEO BY MICHENER ART MUSEUM AT DOYLESTOWN].**
James A. Michener Art Museum, Doylestown, Pa. (1993). Written by Brian
Peterson, Curator. Narrated by Linda Lanesi. Michener's life and work with
special emphasis on race relations and the brotherhood of man.

G.060   **TEXAS.**
Republic Entertainment, Inc., Los Angeles, 1994.
Color. Two video cassettes (180 minutes) VHS 9724. Teleplay by Sean Meredith.
Director - Richard Lang. Executive Producers - Aaron Spelling, E. Duke Vincent, and
John Wilder. Produced by Howard Alston. Based on the novel.
Starring - Stacy Keach, Patrick Duffy, John Schneider, David Keith, Maria Conchita
Alonso, Benjamin Bratt, Chelsea Field, Randy Travis, and Rick Schroder. Narrated
by Charlton Heston. Aired on ABC-TV on April 16-17, 1995.

James Michener's Favorite Music of the South Sea Islands. H.007.

H.
Audio
Materials

"I owe the world a debt of grace,
Some rental on the precious space
I am allowed to occupy,
From whence I publish forth my cry
That magnifies the human race."

James A. Michener
From "Rondeau Of A Writer On
Attaining Age Seventy-Five"
TESTIMONY
Honolulu, White Knight Press, 1983

AUDIO RENAISSANCE TAPES

The Eagle And The Raven

*Sam Houston, Santa Anna and the epic struggle
over the independence of Texas*

James A. Michener

The Eagle and the Raven. H.034.

Section H- Audio Materials

H.001 **SOUTH PACIFIC.** [**The Stage Play**]
Richard Rodgers and Oscar Hammerstein II in association with Leland Hayward
and Joshua Logan. Adapted from James A. Michener's "**Tales of the South
Pacific.**" Featuring Mary Martin, Ezio Pinza, members of the original Broadway
cast; musical direction by Salvatore Dell Isola.

a Columbia Masterworks, USA: c1949. MM-850. Boxed. 7 phonograph records.
14 sides, analog, 78 rpm.

b Columbia Masterworks, USA: c1949. A-850. Boxed. 4 phonograph records.
8 sides, analog, 45 rpm, high fidelity LP recording. Extended play.

c Columbia Masterworks, USA: 1949. ML 4180. 1 phonograph record.
2 sides, analog, 33 1/3 rpm, LP recording.

d Columbia Masterworks, USA: 1949. OL 4180. 1 phonograph record.
2 sides, analog, 33 1/3 rpm, high fidelity LP recording.

e CBS, [New York]: 1973. 1 cassette, analog recording. Sixteen songs.

f Columbia, New York: [1987?]. 1 Sound Disc: digital; 4 3/4 in. analog recording?

H.002 **JAMES MICHENER'S FAVORITE MUSIC OF HAWAII.**
Commentary by James A. Michener inside folding album.

a RCA Victor, New York: 1959. LPM-2150. Phonograph record.
2 sides, 33 1/3 rpm, living stereo recording.

b RCA Victor, New York: 1959. LPM LSP-2150. Phonograph record.
2 sides, 33 1/3 rpm, "new orthophonic" high fidelity recording.

c A Lehman Book, Camden: [1959]. LPM 2150. Phonograph record.
2 sides, 33 1/3 rpm.

H.003 **[JAMES MICHENER SAYS THAT ALL MEN ARE BROTHERS].**
CBS Radio, 1950, 1959. [With Edward R. Murrow]. 1 sound tape reel (5 min.)
7.5 ips, mono.; 7 in. 1/4 in. tape. Broadcast on CBS Radio ("This I Believe"), 1950s?

H.004 **WEBLEY EDWARDS PRESENTS ISLAND PARADISE.**

a Capitol Records, Middlesex England: [1950?]. ST-1229. Phonograph record.
2 sides, 33 1/3 rpm, full dimensional stereo recording.
Michener commentary on back of album jacket.

b Capitol Records, 1959. TAO-1229. Phonograph record. 2 sides, 33 1/3 rpm,
high fidelity recording. Michener commentary inside folding album.

c Capitol Records, 1959. STAO-1229. Phonograph record. 2 sides, 33 1/3 rpm,
full dimensional stereo recording. Michener commentary inside folding album.

Section H- Audio Materials

H.005   **SOUTH PACIFIC.** [Movie Sound Track]
Music by Richard Rodgers and lyrics by Oscar Hammerstein II in association
with Leland Hayward and Joshua Logan. Original soundtrack from the movie;
adapted from the stage play which was adapted from James A. Michener's "**Tales
of the South Pacific.**" Starring Rossano Brazzi, Mitzi Gaynor, Ray Walston and
John Kerr, with chorus and orchestra; conducted by Alred Newman.
The singing voice of Emile de Becque was Giorgio Tozzi.

    a   RCA, New York: 1958. LSO-1032. 1 Phonograph record, 2 sides.

    b   RCA Victor, p1959. LOC-1032.1 Phonograph record. 2 sides, analog, 33 1/3 rpm.
A "New Orthophonic" High Fidelity Recording.

    c   RCA, New York: [1970?]. AYKI-3681.1 Phonograph record, 2 sides, 33 1/3 rpm,
stereo, 12 inches.

H.006   **[CONCERTO, PIANO, NO. 1, OP. 15, D MINOR].**
RCA Victor, 1964. Brahms, Johannes. Commentary by James A. Michener
on album jacket. Phonograph record.

H.007   **JAMES MICHENER'S FAVORITE MUSIC OF THE SOUTH SEA ISLANDS.**
RCA Victor, New York: 1965. LSP-2995. Phonograph record. 2 sides, 33 1/3 rpm,
stereo dynagroove. Commentary by James A. Michener inside folding album.

H.008   **HAWAII.**
Original motion picture score from "Hawaii."

    a   United Artists Records, New York: 1966. UAL 4143.
Phonograph record. 2 sides, 33 1/3 rpm, high fidelity recording.

    b   United Artists Records, New York: 1966. UAS 5143.
Phonograph record. 2 sides, 33 1/3 rpm, stereo recording.

H.009   **POINT OF VIEW.**
Anti-Defamation League, 1967. (14:30m.)
A taped interview between Dore Schary and Michener following the six day war
of June, 1967. A discussion of the Middle-East.

H.010   **SCUTTLEBUTT.**
Adapted for radio dramatization for NBC University Theater. Radio plays.

    a   Nostalgia Broadcasting Corp. Davenport, Iowa: 1969, 1983.
1 sound cassette: 27 min. Distributed by Blackhawk Films.

    b   **S[C]UTTLEBUTT.**
Nostalgia Broadcasting Corp. Cedar Rapids, Iowa: 1977. 1 sound cassette:
(ca. 60 min.) 1/78 ips, 2 track, mono. Manufactured and distributed by DAK.

    c   Metacom, Minneapolis, Minn.: 1983. 1 sound cassette: (ca 60 min) 1 7/8 ips.

Section H- Audio Materials

H.011 **THE JAMES A. MICHENER WRITING SERIES.**
1970-1988. 3 sound cassettes (3 hrs.) analog, 1 7/8 ips, 2 track, mono.
A series of six half-hour interviews broadcast on a Buck's County radio station
between 1970 and 1979. Program 1 - How to Get Started. Program 2 - Development of
an Idea. Program 3 - Writing the Manuscript. Program 4 - Finding a Market Program.
5 - Working With An Editor. Program 6 -Financial Rewards & Pitfalls.

H.012 **BEING A WRITER.**
James A. Michener talks about his writing and about being a writer.

    a Learning Arts, Wichita: p1972. 1 cassette (87 min.) analog 2 track mono.

    b Writer's Voice, Cincinnati: p1972. 1 cassette (87 min.) analog 2 track mono.

H.013 **DISTINGUISHED CONTEMPORARY: JAMES MICHENER.**
Sound Perspectives, New York: 1974. 1 cassette tape; mono.

H.014 **A VISIT WITH JAMES A. MICHENER.**
Iona College, New Rochelle, N.Y.: 1975. Interview, conducted by Doug Cooper.
1 sound cassette (1 hour) analog. Michener discusses his work.

H.015 **[MICHENER IN AN INTERVIEW WITH GENE SHALIT].**
NBC-TV, 1976. 1 sound tape reel, 7.5 ips, mono.; 7 in. 1/4 in. tape. Aired on the
"Today Show," May 7, 1976. James Michener talks about his literary career, the
beauties of Bucks County, Pennsylvania, and its attraction for writers.

H.016 **JAMES MICHENER.**
Minnesota Public Radio, St. Paul: 1976. Radio interview, conducted by Bill
Siemering. 1 sound cassette (58 min.) analog. Recorded November 26, 1976.
In the first part, Michener talks about historic preservation on the Plains, from a
lecture he gave in Fargo, North Dakota.
In the second part, he discusses his novel, "**Centennial.**"

H.017 **INTERVIEW.**
James Michener interviewed by Steven Banker in San Michaels, Md.

    a American Audio Prose Library, Columbia, Mo.: 1978. 1 sound cassette.

    b Retitled **JAMES MICHENER.** Tapes for Readers, Washington: 1978.
1 sound cassette: 1 7/8 ips, 2-track, mono.

H.018 **PLA ALLIE BETH MARTIN AWARD LUNCH.**
American Library Association, [Chicago]: c1979. 1 sound cassette (ca. 60 min.)
analog, 1 7/8 ips. mono. A session recorded at the 98th Annual Conference of the
American Library Association, held in Dallas, Texas, June 23-28, 1979.

H.019 **JAMES MICHENER.**
National Public Radio, Washington, D.C.: p1979.1 sound cassette (1 hr.)
analog. Author James Michener discusses the state of the novel and contemporary
authors, including women writers, Oates, Plath, Didion, and Rossner. Concludes with
the question-and-answer session. Recorded at a National Press Club luncheon in
Washington, D.C., and broadcast August 24, 1979, on National Public Radio.

Section H- Audio Materials

H.020 **A CONVERSATION WITH AUTHOR JAMES MICHENER.**
CBS News Audio Resource Library, [New York]: c1980.
1 Cassette tape (21 min.). Vital history cassettes, No. 3,
recorded November 14, 1980, regarding "**The Covenant.**"

H.021 **OUR HEROINE.**
From the novel "**Tales of the South Pacific.**" Read by Michener.

    a Caedmon, New York: 1980. TC 1648.
Phonograph record. 2 sides (50 min. 11 sec.) 33 1/3 rpm, stereo.
Commentary by Michener on jacket cover.

    b Retitled **TALES OF THE SOUTH PACIFIC: OUR HEROINE.**
Caedmon, New York: c1986. A1648. ISN 0898455502.
1 sound cassette (58 min.) 1 7/8 ips, Dolby processed.
Caedmon Great Authors Soundbook Series.

H.022 **JAMES MICHENER'S SPACE.**
National Public Radio, Washington, D.C.: p1982. Interviewer, Noah Adams.
1 sound cassette (29 min.) analog. Originally broadcast October 19, 1982, on
National Public Radio. In the interview Michener discusses his novel "**Space**"
and the history of space flight, including Nazi Germany's rocket program, launching
of the Sputnik Satellite, use of space, and the possibility of life on other planets.

H.023 **[BILL KURTIS INTERVIEWS JAMES MICHENER].**
CBS-TV, 1984/09/26. 1 sound tape reel (10 min.) 3 3/4 ips, mono.; 7 in. 1/4 in. tape.
Michener, who recently gave 2 million dollars to Swarthmore College,
tells what a liberal arts education means.

H.024 **SPACE, ABRIDGED.**
Random House Audiobooks, p1985. Read by Darren McGavin.
ISBN 394-55041-2. RH 6. 2 sound cassettes (179 min.) 1 7/8 ips, Dolby processed.

H.025 **CHESAPEAKE, ABRIDGED.**
Random House Audiobooks, p1986. Read by George Grizzard.
ISBN 394-55695-X. RH 32. 2 sound cassettes (171 min.) analog, Dolby processed.

H.026 **SOUTH PACIFIC.**
Adapted from James A. Michener's "**Tales of the South Pacific.**"
Richard Rodgers & Oscar Hammerstein II in association with
Leland Hayward & Joshua Logan

    a CBS, New York: p1986. 1 Phonograph record (62 min.) 2 sides, analog,
33 1/3 rpm, stereo, 12 in. Featuring Kiri Te Kanawa, Jose Carreras, Sarah
Vaughan, Mindy Patinkin, and the Ambrosian Singers; London Symphony
Orchestra; Jonathan Tunick, conductor.

    b Craftsman, nd. C 8021.1 Phonograph record. 2 sides, analog, 33 1/3 rpm.
High fidelity recording. Featuring The Craftsmen with Marni Nixon,
Gene Merlino, Norma Zimmer, Bonnie Lou Williams, and Charles Peck;
Arranged and conducted by Gordon Fleming.

Section H- Audio Materials

H.027 **TEXAS, ABRIDGED.**
Random House Audiobooks, p1987. Read by Peter Graves.
ISBN 394-56056-6. RH 42. 2 sound cassettes (3 hours) analog, Dolby processed.

H.028 **ALASKA, ABRIDGED.**
Random House Audiobooks, p1988. Read by Peter Graves.
ISBN 394-57078-2. RH 60. 2 sound cassettes (3 hours) analog, Dolby processed.

H.029 **LEGACY, ABRIDGED.**
Random House Audiobooks, p1988. Read by Stephen Collins.
ISBN 394-57272-6. RH 61. 2 sound cassettes (2 hours) analog, Dolby processed.

H.030 **[MICHENER IN AN INTERVIEW WITH ROBERT PIERPOINT].**
CBS-TV, 1988. 1 sound tape reel (12 min.) 3 3/4 ips, mono. 7 in. 1/4 in. tape. Aired
on "Sunday Morning," September 25, 1988. A portrait interview of Michener in his
hometown of Doylestown, Pennsylvania, for the opening of the James A. Michener
Art Center, talking about his life as an art collector.

H.031 **JOURNEY, ABRIDGED.**
Random House Audiobooks, p1989. Read by David McCallum.
ISBN 394-57892-9. RH 79. 2 sound cassettes (2 hours) analog, Dolby processed.

H.032 **[EMINENT AUTHORS DISCUSS THE IMPACT OF THE APOLLO 11 MOON
LANDING ON AMERICAN SOCIETY IN THE 20 YEARS FOLLOWING].**
PBS (McNeil Lehrer Report), 1989/07/20. 1 sound tape reel (17 min) 3 3/4 ips;
7 in. 1/4 in. tape. With Maya Angelou, Isaac Asimov, James Michener, Daniel
Boorstin, and reporter Jim Lehrer.

H.033 **CARIBBEAN, ABRIDGED.**
Random House Audiobooks, p1989. Read by Roscoe Lee Brown.
ISBN 394-58046-X. RH 100. 2 sound cassettes (180 min) analog, dolby processed.

H.034 **THE EAGLE AND THE RAVEN.**
Audio Renaissance Tapes, Los Angeles: p1990. Read by Michael Rider.
2 sound cassettes (180 min.) analog, Dolby processed.

H.035 **HAWAII, ABRIDGED.**
Random House Audiobooks, p1990. Read by Philip Bosco.
ISBN 394-58282-9. RH 110. 2 sound cassettes (3 hours) analog, Dolby processed.

H.036 **PILGRIMAGE.**
Audio Renaissance Tapes, Los Angeles: p1990. Read by Michael McConnohie.
2 sound cassettes (180 min.) analog, Dolby processed.

H.037 **THE SOURCE, ABRIDGED.**
Random House Audiobooks, p1990. Read by Norman Lloyd.
Abridged by Joan Eades. ISBN 394-58281-0. RH 135.
2 sound cassettes (180 min.) analog, Dolby processed.

H.038 **HAWAII, UNABRIDGED.**
Books on Tape, p1991. Read by Larry McKeever.
Special library edition 2067 A, B & C. 36 sound cassettes (1 1/2 hr. each) analog.

Section H- Audio Materials

H.039 **THE NOVEL, ABRIDGED.**
Random House Audiobooks, p1991. Read by Len Cariou.
ISBN 679-40228-4. RH 166. 2 sound cassettes (3 hours) analog, Dolby processed.

H.040 **THE NOVEL, UNABRIDGED.**
Books on Tape, p1991. Read by Alexander Adams. 2835.
1 part. 10 sound cassettes (1 1/2 hr. each) analog.

H.041 **POLAND, ABRIDGED.**
Random House Audiobooks, p1991. Read by Robert Vaughn.
ISBN 394-58790-1. RH 181. 2 sound cassettes (3 hours) analog, Dolby processed.

H.042 **SAYONARA, UNABRIDGED.**
Sterling Audio Book, c1991. Read by Garrick Hagon.
ISN 1560549734. SAB 004.6 sound cassettes (480 min.) analog, Dolby processed.

H.043 **THE WORLD IS MY HOME, ABRIDGED.**
Random House Audiobooks, p1991. Read by George Grizzard.
ISBN 679-40814-2. RH 194. 2 sound cassettes (3 hours) analog, Dolby processed.

H.044 **IBERIA, ABRIDGED.**
Random House Audiobooks, p1992. Read by Philip Bosco. Abridged by Joan Eades.
ISBN 394-58792-8. RH 211. 2 sound cassettes (180 min.) analog, Dolby processed.

H.045 **MEXICO, ABRIDGED.**
Random House Audiobooks, p1992. Read by Tony Roberts.
Abridged by Liz Crawford.ISBN 679-41317-0. RH 233.
4 sound cassettes (4 hours) analog, Dolby processed.

H.046 **TEXAS, UNABRIDGED.**
Books on Tape, p1992. Read by Larry McKeever.
3095 A, B & C. 3 parts. 45 sound cassettes (1 1/2 hr. each) analog.

H.047 **THE WORLD IS MY HOME, UNABRIDGED.**
Books on Tape, p1992. Read by Alexander Adams. 2960.
1 part. 15 sound cassettes (1 1/2 hr. each) analog.

H.048 **CARIBBEAN, UNABRIDGED.**
Books on Tape, p1993. Read by Alexander Adams. 3147 A & B.
2 parts. 23 sound cassettes (1 1/2 hr. each) analog.

H.049 **CENTENNIAL, ABRIDGED.**
The Publishing Mills, p1993. Read by David Dukes.
4 sound cassettes (6 hours) ISBN 1-879371-46-4.

H.050 **CHESAPEAKE, UNABRIDGED.**
Books on Tape, p1993. Read by Larry McKeever.
3187 A, B & C. 3 parts. 36 sound cassettes (1 1/2 hr. each) analog.

H.051 **THE COVENANT, ABRIDGED.**
Random House Audiobooks, p1993. Read by Simon Jones.
ISBN 394-58791-X. RH 272. 2 sound cassettes (3 hours) analog, Dolby processed.

Section H- Audio Materials

H.052 **THE COVENANT, UNABRIDGED.**
Books on Tape, p1993. Read by Larry McKeever. 3315 A, B & C.
3 parts. 40 sound cassettes (1 1/2 hr. each) analog.

H.053 **CREATURES OF THE KINGDOM: STORIES OF ANIMALS AND NATURE, ABRIDGED.**
Random House Audiobooks, p1993. Read by John Cullum.
ISBN 679-42905-0. RH 308. 2 sound cassettes (120 min.) analog, Dolby processed.

H.054 **MEXICO, UNABRIDGED.**
Books on Tape, p1993. Read by Alexander Adams. 3164 A & B.
2 parts. 17 sound cassettes (1 1/2 hr. each) analog.

H.055 **POLAND, UNABRIDGED.**
Books on Tape, p1993. Read by Larry McKeever.
3127 A & B. 2 parts. 22 sound cassettes (1 1/2 hr. each) analog.

H.056 **THE SOURCE, UNABRIDGED.**
Books on Tape, p1993. Read by Larry McKeever.
3250 A, B & C. 3 parts. 38 sound cassettes (1 1/2 hr. each) analog.

H.057 **SPACE, UNABRIDGED.**
Books on Tape, p1993. Read by Larry McKeever.
3350 A & B. 2 parts. 27 sound cassettes (1 1/2 hr. each) analog.

H.058 **CARAVANS, UNABRIDGED.**
Books on Tape, p1994. Read by Larry McKeever. 3405.
1 part. 11 sound cassettes (1 1/2 hr. each) analog.

H.059 **RECESSIONAL: A NOVEL, ABRIDGED**
Random House Audiobooks, New York: Read by Len Carion, p1994.
ISBN 679-43717-7. RH 371. 2 sound cassettes (180 min.) analog,
Dolby processed.

H.060 **MIRACLE IN SEVILLE, ABRIDGED**
Random House Audiobooks, New York: Read by Robert Vaughn, p1995.
ISBN 679-43837-8. RH 430. 2 sound cassettes (120 min.) analog,
Dolby processed.

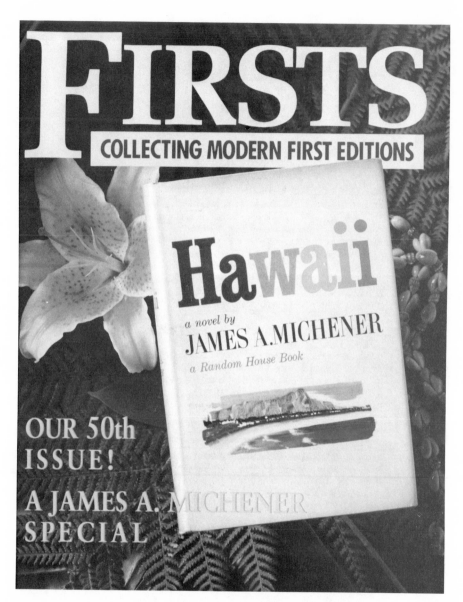

Firsts: Collecting Modern First Editions. Appendix I.

Appendixes

The Artist by David Adickes.
Portrait of James A. Michener, 1964

Appendix I - Magazine Articles About JAMES A. MICHENER

American Artist

"Clarence Holbrook Carter." Nelson, Mary Carroll.
American Artist, 53: 565 (1989/08) 33, 80. Book by Frank Anderson Trapp,
Douglas Dreishpoon, Ricardo Pau-Llosa, James A. Michener, and Clarence Holbrook Carter.

American Spectator

"Books For Christmas." *American Spectator*, (1989/12) 27-32. Lists and
reviews recommended tomes from eminent writers, including James A. Michener.

American Way

"Michener." Shahin, Jim. *American Way*, 22:20 (1989/10/15) 56-62, 112.
Published by American Airlines. Cover photo of Michener. Reprinted in
Saturday Evening Post, 262:2 (1990/03/01) 66-70, 106.

Americana

"America." *Americana*, 18:5 (1990/11-12) 61. Book review.
Photographic portrayal by Jake Rajs, with foreword by James A. Michener.

Art in America

"Windfall for Texas." Freed, Eleanor. *Art in America*, 57:6 (1969/11-12) 78-85.
An account of the reception of the Michener Collection by the University of Texas.

Arts   "Private Affinities and Public Uses: the Michener Collection." Hirsch, R.
Arts, 40 (1966/05) 14-24.

At Random

"Michener's Lost Manuscript." Karp, Jonathan. *At Random*, 1:1
(1992/Winter) 44-46. The search for a lost manuscript that Michener wrote
in 1961 about Mexico. "Mexico" was published in October, 1992.

Beacon (Honolulu)

"Is Michener a Skinflint?" Day, A. Grove. *Beacon* (Honolulu),
(1964/08) 14-15. Designed to controvert current comments that Michener was
too thrifty to buy drinks for news reporters.

Book Digest

"Conversation with an Author: James A. Michener." Gross, Martin L.
Book Digest, 6:3 (1979/03) 19-30. An excellent interview of Michener following
publication of "Chesapeake." Michener discusses progress of "The Covenant."

Book-of-the-Month Club News

"A Conversation with James A. Michener." Kuehl, Linda.
Book-of-the-Month Club News, (1974/09) 4-5.
"Centennial" was his contribution to the American Bicentennial celebration. He wrote of
men living on the land and the need for preserving harmony.

Booklist

"Poland." McCray, Nancy. *Booklist*, 88 (1992/05/15) 1708. Sound recording review.

"The Covenant." Spillman, Nancy. *Booklist*, 89 (1993/08) 2081. Audio-visual review.

Appendix I - Magazine Articles About JAMES A. MICHENER

Bucks County Life

"From footlights to political spotlight." Porter, James.
Bucks County Life, 2:2 (1961/08) 26-27.

"Michener Flexes His Political Muscles." Rodgers, Byron.
Bucks County Life, 3:4 (1962/04) 18-19.

"Michener." *Bucks County Life*, 4:1 (1962/10) 10-11.

"Mr. Michener Consents." Hoyle, Preston. *Bucks County Life*, (1963/03) 28.

"Bucks County Portraits, no. 12." Pogson, Joanna.
Bucks County Life, 9: 9 (1967/09) 16, 20-21, 32.

Canadian Geographic

"Fact and Fiction in the Land of the Midnight Sun." Fraser, J. Keith.
Canadian Geographic, 110:3 (1990/06-07) 8. Editorial about misinformation
in James A. Michener's "Alaska" and the role of bush pilot Weldy Phipps.

Carnival Currents

"Man of the World." Biondi, Joann. *Carnival Currents*, 5:1 (1992/Winter) 22-25.
Published for Carnival Line Passengers.

Chronicle of Higher Education

"Colleges that helped spawn Michener's career are the beneficiaries of his
philanthropy." Nicklin, Julie L.
Chronicle of Higher Education, 39 (1983/01/13) 28.

Church Herald

"My Dear Sunday School Teacher." Lotz, Louis. *Church Herald*, 44:5 (1987/03/06) 15.
The author states that Michener declined an invitation to meet President Eisenhower in order
to honor a teacher. An article in *the New York Times*, June 10, 1965, p. 22, indicates that
Lyndon Johnson, not Eisenhower, might have been the President in question.

College English

"Michener of the South Pacific." Havighurst, Walter. *College English*,(1952/10) 1-6.
Also in *English Journal*, 41 (1952/10) 397-402.

Colorado Country Life

"Michener's Colorado Centennial Country Revisited." Garner, Gerald W. *Colorado
Country Life*, 24:9 (1993/09) 6-8. Background on the novel and the TV miniseries.
The magazine is the official publication of the Colorado Rural Electric Association.

Colorado Heritage

"Colorado's People. (Through the Perceptive Pen of James A. Michener)." Gamble, Judith L.
Colorado Heritage, 1 (1982) 1-9. Journal of the Colorado Historical Society. Michener
dedicated "Centennial" to 3 men who enhanced his understanding of Colorado.

Contact

"The Artists' and Writers' Cookbook. *Contact*, 2:4 (1961/05) 63.
A preview of "The Artists' and Writers' Cookbook," to be published in October, 1961,
by Contact Editions. Includes Michener's recipe for "Beef Burgundy."

Appendix I - Magazine Articles About JAMES A. MICHENER

Coronet

"Broadway's Best." *Coronet*, 26:3 (1949/07) 10-1. Review of the play, "South Pacific,"
starring Mary Martin and Ezio Pinza. Two pages of photographs.

"Movies." Nichols, Mark. *Coronet*, 43:2 (1957/12) 10.
Review of the movie "Sayonara," starring Marlon Brando and Miiko Taka.

Dodge Adventurer

"James A. Michener on the American West: as told to John Kings." Kings, John.
Dodge Adventurer, 8:2 (1980/Spring) 4-7.

"James Michener, Master of the Epic." Clayton, Bill.
Dodge Adventurer, 18:4 (1988/Fall) 7-8. An interview with James A. Michener.

English Journal

"Michener of the South Pacific." Havighurst, Walter.
English Journal, 41 (1952/10) 397-402. Also in *College English*, 14 (1952/10) 1-6.

Entertainment Weekly

"Just Plain Jim." Lyons, Gene. *Entertainment Weekly*, (1992/01/10) 62.

Family Health

"How to Survive a Heart Attack." Olds, Sally Wendkos. *Family Health*, 9:1 (1977/01) 34-37.
Seven celebrities reveal how they survived their heart attacks.
Michener was treated by Dr. Paul Dudley White.

Firsts: Collecting Modern First Editions

"Points: Firsts Answers Your Questions." *Firsts: Collecting Modern First Editions*,
1:1 (1991/01) 27. True first printing of "The Bridges at Toko-ri" has no edition stated
on the copyright page. Subsequent printings are stated.

"Letters: More on Toko-ri." *Firsts: Collecting Modern First Editions*, 1:3 (1991/03) 3.
Notes two variants of endpapers on "The Bridges at Toko-ri."
One has blue endpapers, the other has white.

"Points: Firsts Answers Your Questions." *Firsts: Collecting Modern First Editions*
1:11 (1991/11) 33-34. Identification of first edition, first state of "The Eagle and The Raven."
There is no accent over "Yucatan" on front endpaper.

"Points: Firsts Answers Your Questions." *Firsts: Collecting Modern First Editions*,
2:1 (1992/01) 33-34. Number row "0 2 4 6 8 B 9 7 5 3 1" is Random House designation
of a tenth printing.

"A Collector's Guide to Publishers - Random House." *Firsts: Collecting Modern First
Editions*, 4:4 (1994/04) 42-43. The absence of "first printing" in "The Bridges at Toko-ri"
is an exception to the standard practice at Random House of identifying first editions on the
copyright page.

"Collecting James A. Michener." Groseclose, David A. *Firsts: Collecting Modern First
Editions*, 5:4 (1995/04) 18-31. Includes an informal checklist of collectibles and a list of
movies, miniseries and teleplays based upon works by James A. Michener. This 50th issue of
Firsts is designated "A James A. Michener Special."

Appendix I - Magazine Articles About JAMES A. MICHENER

Firsts: Collecting Modern First Editions (continued)
"Books Into Film. - Hawaii." Smiley, Robin. *Firsts: Collecting Modern First Editions*, 5:4 (1995/04) 45-46.

Forbes
"Gift List." *Forbes*, 144:9 (1989/10/23) 124-25. Discusses those who contributed $2 Million or more to charity in 1988, naming the recipient charities, and reasons they do so.

"Paging James Michener." Jaffe, Thomas. *Forbes*, 147:1 (1991/01/07) 328-29.

Frank Norris Studies
"Zelda Fitzgerald, Vladimer Nabokov and James A. Michener: Three Opinions on Frank Norris's McTeague." Davison, Richard Allan. *Frank Norris Studies*, 9 (1989/Spring) 11-12. A publication of the Norris Society, issued twice each year. This article includes a letter from Michener dated 12/19/81.

Frequent Flyer
"I Am Perpetually Grateful." Sutton, Horace. *Frequent Flyer*, (1990/09) 126. Anniversary Issue, Part 2, OAG (Official Airline Guides) Pocket Flight Guide.

Good Housekeeping
"The private life of James (Hawaii) Michener." Whitebread, Jane. *Good Housekeeping*, 150:2 (1960/02) 28. A brief interview with Michener at his home in Bucks County. Discusses personal views and Hawaii. Photo of the Micheners.

Harper's Bazaar
"The Best in Books: James Michener." Hurt, H.
Harper's Bazaar, 117: 3264 (1983/11) 194-95+.

Illustrated London News
"James Michener, Giving It All Away." Michener, James A.
Illustrated London News, 277 (1989/Summer) 87-90. The Micheners gave Japanese prints to Honolulu Institute of Fine Arts, and American art to University of Texas.

Inside Books
"James Michener. Need We Say More?" Rosenblatt, Leon. *Inside Books*,(1989/03) 28-31. Interview of Michener by the author. Includes photographs and an additional comment on page 9. Michener photo on cover.

Insight
"Chronicling a Billion Years of Alaska." Hagman, Harry. *Insight*, (1986/09/01) 54-55.

Islands
"James Michener, Nesomaniac." Maxwell, Jessica. *Islands*, 8:6 (1988/12) 41-49. Interview.

Japan Magazine
"A History Book in Roof Tiles." Hiratsuka, Un-ichi. *Japan Magazine*, 1: 3 (1958/Winter) 16-17. Photo of Michener and his friend, Un-ichi Hiratsuka, in Tokyo.

Appendix I - Magazine Articles About JAMES A. MICHENER

Journal of Geography

"The use of novels in geography classrooms." Lamme, A. J., III.
Journal of Geography, 76:2 (1977/02) 66-68. "Centennial" warrants consideration for use in courses on the geography of the United States.

"Caravans and Classrooms: the novel as a teaching aid." Davenport, David Paul.
Journal of Geography, 80:7 (1981/12) 259-63. "Caravans" used as a teaching aid in sophomore-level geography course at University High School in Urbana, Illinois.

"NCGE Special Award Presented to James A. Michener." Boehm, Richard G., and Anthony R. de Souza. *Journal of Geography*, 84:3 (1985/05-06) 135.
For his 'Outstanding Contributions to Geographic Education Through the American Novel.' Presented at South West Texas State University.

Journal of Popular Culture

"Michener's Space, the Novel and Miniseries: A Study in Popular Culture."
Osterholm, J. Roger. *Journal of Popular Culture*, 23:3 (1989/Winter) 51-64.

Journal of Reading

"Challenging Gifted Students with Michener's 'The Source' in a History Class."
Bathgate, Arlene J., and Lizabeth A. Connelly. *Journal of Reading*, 35:1 (1991/09) 48-49.

Kultura P

"Mila basn." Krzyzanowski, Jerzy R. *Kultura P*, (1984/01-02) 197-98.

La Busca

"From Joe Distler." Distler, Joe. *La Busca*, 29 (1993/11-12) 14-16.

"Iberia and Me." Conover, Don. *La Busca*, 29 (1993/11-12) 18-20. Official publication of the Taurine Bibliophiles of America. Michener is the theme of this special year-end edition.

"[Letter]." Fulton, John. *La Busca*, 29 (1993/11-12) 12-13. Fulton pays tribute to Michener and expresses appreciation for his encouragement and friendship.

Ladies' Home Journal

"Hawaii: Cookbook and Backyard Luau." Toupin, Elizabeth Ahn.
Ladies' Home Journal, 83:11 (1966/11) 122, 139-42. Condensation from the cookbook. Michener wrote the introduction for this cookbook.

Library Journal

"News: Interview with James Michener covers libraries and censorship."
Library Journal, 108:5 (1983/03/01) 433. Michener, censored in Hawaii, Burma, Texas and South Africa, believes communities should determine library books.

"Video Reviews - Michener at Work." Fryer, Philip.
Library Journal, 116:16 (1991/10/01) 152. Michener explains the craft of writing.

"The Novel." Leader, Jeanne P. *Library Journal*, 117 (1992/02/01) 144.
Sound recording review.

"Hawaii." Hilyard, Blaine. *Library Journal*, 117 (1992/02/15) 216.
Sound recording review.

217

Appendix I - Magazine Articles About JAMES A. MICHENER

Library Journal (continued)
"The World is My Home." Ridgeway, Trish. *Library Journal*, 117 (1992/06/15) 116.
Sound recording review.

"Iberia." Dudley, James. *Library Journal*, 117 (1992/10/01) 132. Sound recording review.

Life
"South Pacific - Theater Section." *Life*, 26:16 (1949/04/18) 93-96. Full cover photograph of
Mary Martin in sailor suit. Four pages of photos from the play. Also Ezio Pinza, Juanita Hall.

"How Would You Put a Glass of Ballantine Ale into Words?" *Life*, 31:8 (1951/08/20) 60-61.
Michener answers with a full page picture of Michener advertising Ballantine Ale.

"Author Enacts Own Plot." *Life*, 39:19 (1955/11/07) 55.
A brief, well illustrated account of Michener's third wedding.

"Editorial." *Life*, 7:12 (1984/11) 7. James Michener gave $2 million to Swarthmore striking
blow against wealth for its own sake.

Literary Digest
"Is the American Boy Quitting Baseball?" *Literary Digest*, 106:2 (1930/07/12).
Quotes a copyrighted article by Michener (a coach and teacher at the Hill School)
which appeared in the Philadelphia Ledger.

Maclean's
"Miner in the Bedrock of History. (Interview of James A. Michener)." Poulton, T.
Maclean's, 93 (1980/12/15) 8-9.

"A Northern Fondness." *Maclean's*, 101:47 (1988/11/14) 9. Michener visits Toronto to
promote "Journey" and announces that if George Bush wins presidency (1988), Michener
will move there.

Magill Book Reviews
"The Dangerous Summer." *Magill Book Reviews*, (1985?) Book Review.

Main Line
"Native Son: A Tribute to James A. Michener." Best, Hugh. *Main Line*, (1993/07) 9-13.
A magazine of Philadelphia's western suburbs. Full cover photo of Michener.

McCall's
"What Makes Love Last." Arnout, S. *McCall's*, 114:5 (1987/02) 166+.

Members Only
"Traveling with James Michener." *Members Only*, (1982/05) 1, 4. A newsletter for
American Express Members. Michener tells how card members can get more out of trips.

Modern Maturity
"James Michener: A spelunker in the caves of history." Ecenbarger, William.
Modern Maturity, 28:4 (1985/08-09) 24-27. Biographical. Michener claims he is never
recognized and even did an American Express commercial because of it.

Appendix I - Magazine Articles About JAMES A. MICHENER

Music News
    "New Use For Old Jail." Eike, C.M. *Music News*, 67 (1988) 10.
    The James A. Michener Arts Center of Bucks County, Doylestown, Pennsylvania.

National Motorist
    "The World is His Home." Dewey, Richard W. *National Motorist*, 70:4 (1994/Autumn) 8-9.
    An interview with writer/chronicler James A. Michener.

New Pacific
    "Aggie Grey Tells a Tale." Wesselhoeft, Conrad. *New Pacific*, (1979/03/01) 25.

New Republic
    "Spain Diarist." Kondracke, M. M. *New Republic*, 189:10 (1983/09/05) 42.
    Political update on Spain 15 years after "Iberia."

New York
    "The Last Author in America." Smith, Adam, II. *New York*, (1971/06/07) 95-96.
    Michener reacts to critics pans.

New York Magazine
    "A Piece of Cake." Fremont-Smith, Eliot. *New York Magazine*, (1974/09/02) 62.

New Yorker
    "The Air." Lardner, John. *New Yorker*, 35:36 (1959/10/24) 165-69.
    Reviews Michener's TV Series, "Adventures in Paradise."

Newsweek
    "Movies - Return to Paradise." *Newsweek*, 42:5 (1953/08/03) 76.
    Movie review. Return to Paradise.
    Starring Gary Cooper, Barry Jones, Roberta Haynes, Moira McDonald, and John Hudson.

    "Newsmakers: Return to Paradise." *Newsweek*, 46:18 (1955/10/31) 53.
    Michener's marriage to Mari Yoriko Sabusawa.

    "Author Explains: Why Michener Wrote 'The Bridge at Andau.'"
    Newsweek, 49:9 (1957/03/04) 104-5. Contains information on Michener's activities while
    covering the Hungarian Revolution.

    "Artists and Writers." *Newsweek*, 59 (1962/05/14) 102. Quotes Michener
    on the pleasures of collecting Japanese prints and modern American painters.

    "Newsmakers: This Is Whose Life?" *Newsweek*, 62:16 (1963/10/14) 58.
    Mentions Michener's article in *Paradise of the Pacific* magazine where Michener reveals
    he does not know who his parents are.

    "A Best Seller Big As Texas." Sawhill, R. *Newsweek*, 106:13 (1985/09/23) 73.

    "The Author is Game." *Newsweek*, 114:3 (1989/07/17) 57. Talks about new books
    "Journey" and "Caribbean" by Michener, and his newly created board game "Bestsell'r."

Appendix I - Magazine Articles About JAMES A. MICHENER

Openers

"Author! Author! Author!: James Michener." Cunniff, Ann. 5:2 (1985/Summer) 2.
Michener thinks "Madam Bovary" is about the best novel ever written, artistically,
but likes "Anna Karenina" better.

Paradise of the Pacific

"Michener and Names." Taylor, Clarice B. *Paradise of the Pacific*, 71:10 (1959/10) 54-55.
Mentions the search for some of the characters in "Hawaii."

"Success Story of a Story." Krauss, Bob. *Paradise of the Pacific*, 71:11 (1959/11) 157.
Reprint from column in *Honolulu Advertiser*, September 12, 1959.
Reports an interview concerning "Hawaii" before publication.

"James A. Michener Collection of Japanese Prints at the Academy of Arts."
Paradise of the Pacific, 72:1 (1960/11) 66-67.

"The Strange Case of James Michener." Sutton, Horace. *Paradise of the Pacific*,
75:9 (1963/09-10) 21-22. Michener's relationship with Hawaii.
Biographical information supplied by A. Grove Day.

People Weekly

"James A. Michener Puts His Birthday Gift in Writing."
People Weekly, 2 (1974/09/16) 54-57. Brief interview on the publishing of "Centennial".

"Biography." Rowes, B. *People Weekly*, 10:7 (1978/08/14) 84-86.

"After Space and Poland, James Michener Stalks Deep in the Heart of Texas."
Chambers, A. *People Weekly*, 19:2 (1983/03/28) 42-44.

Philadelphia

"Portrait of the Artist as an Elder Statesman." McCormick, Bernard.
Philadelphia, (1968/04) 74-77, 113-19. Regarding Michener's participation
in Pennsylvania's Constitutional Convention.

Philadelphia Magazine

"The Source." Beans, Bruce. *Philadelphia Magazine*, (1981/06) 118-35.

Philadelphia Bulletin Magazine

Philadelphia Bulletin Magazine, (1963/12/22) 6. Michener's comments on progress
of "The Source."

Playboy

"Playboy Interview: James A. Michener - Candid Conversation." Grobel, Lawrence.
Playboy, 28:9 (1981/09) 65-92. Michener discusses the millions he has made and given
away, close calls with death, wives, friends and writers.

"Mandela: The Man and his Country." *Playboy*, 37:7 (1990/07) 28. Review of video
recording. Includes interviews with Jesse Jackson and James Michener.

Progressive

"James Michener's Kent State; A Study in Distortion." Eszterhas, Joe, and Michael Roberts.
Progressive, 35:9 (1971/09) 35-40. Report of debate by Michener, I. F. Stone and others on
the "Today Show" (April 28, 1971) regarding the Kent State tragedy.

Appendix I - Magazine Articles About JAMES A. MICHENER

Publishers Weekly

"Biographical Note [James A. Michener]." *Publishers Weekly,* 163:1 (1953/01/03) 30.

"Rights and Permissions." Nathan, P., ed. *Publishers Weekly,* 193:26 (1968/06/24) 60. Miscellaneous comments on several of Michener's books.

"James A. Michener Speaks Out: excerpts from remarks at press conference on April, 27, 1971." *Publishers Weekly,* 199:19 (1971/05/10) 17-18. Remarks at time of publication of "Kent State: What Happened and Why."

"New Michener Novel Celebrates America." Neely, Mildred Sola. *Publishers Weekly,* 205:21 (1974/05/27) 38. Based on an interview with Michener with comments about "Centennial."

"Michener Triggers $500,000 Poetry Publishing Program." Reuter, Madalynne. *Publishers Weekly,* 214:25 (1978/12/25) 22-23.

"The Year's Best Selling Books." Maryles, Daisy. *Publishers Weekly,* 219:11 (1981/03/13) 31. Best seller statistics for "The Covenant."

"James Michener's USA is due from Crown." *Publishers Weekly,* 220:6 (1981/08/07) 36+. Based on a 5 part TV series. 100,000 first printing.

"Two Big Mass Market Titles to Hit Stores at Record Prices." Frank, Jerome P. *Publishers Weekly,* 220:25 (1981/12/18) 51, 54. Paperback publishing plans by Fawcett for "The Covenant."

"Ballantine's $350,000 Michener Space Launch." Turim, Gayle. *Publishers Weekly,* 224:11 (1983/09/09) 46. Paperback marketing plans for "Space."

"The Waiting Game." Nathan, Paul S. *Publishers Weekly,* 230:3 (1986/07/18) 52-56+. Discusses possible movie rights for "Alaska."

"The Edwin Pope Collection." Stuttaford, Genevieve. *Publishers Weekly,* 233:14 (1988/04/08) 84. Book review. Book by Edwin Pope (A newspaper sports writer) with foreword by James A. Michener.

"Southeast Alaska." Kaganoff, Penny. *Publishers Weekly,* 233:19 (1988/05/13) 268. Book review of book by Nancy Simmerman and Sarah Eppenbach.

"Texas Collects: Fine Art, Furniture, Windmills and Whimseys." Stuttaford, Genevieve. *Publishers Weekly,* 234:6 (1988/08/05) 79. Book review. Book by Paul Nathan with foreword by James A. Michener.

"Thunder Gods: The Kamikaze Pilots Tell Their Story." Stuttaford, Genevieve. *Publishers Weekly,* 235:15 (1989/04/14) 57. Book review. Book by Hatsuho Naito and Mayumi Ichikawa, with foreword by James A. Michener.

"Our Man in Havana." Levine, Beth. *Publishers Weekly,* 236:2 (1989/07/14) 50-51. James Michener explores the Cuban capital for a University of Texas book, "Six Days in Havana."

Appendix I - Magazine Articles About JAMES A. MICHENER

Publishers Weekly (continued)
"ABA, Michener Joins Others in Pantheon Reactions." Reuter, Madalynne.
Publishers Weekly, 237:13 (1990/03/30) 12-13.

"Publisher of Michener's Next Two Books Still Undecided." *Publishers Weekly,*
237:16 (1990/04/20) 19. "Novel" and "The World is My Home: A Memoir."

"Michener, Money and Random House." Feldman, G.
Publishers Weekly, 237:25 (1990/06/22) 34-35.

"Rodale Signals New Departure With Book From James Michener." Simson, Maria.
Publishers Weekly, 237:25 (1990/06/22) 34-35. Regarding "Pilgrimage."

"Pilgrimage." Stuttaford, Genevieve. *Publishers Weekly,* 237:31 (1990/08/03) 70.

"The World Is My Home." *Publishers Weekly,* 239 (1992/03/02) 30.
Sound recording review.

"Mexico: A Novel." *Publishers Weekly,* (1992/11/02) 32. Sound recording review. Mexico.

Reader's Digest
"Michener of the South Pacific." *Reader's Digest,* 64 (1954/04) 20.
Condensation of "James Michener: Again the Warm Voice of Asia,"
Newsweek, 43:4 (1954/01/25) 92-95.

"We Can Take It! - Say the 'Hardest-Working Women in the World.'" De Martini, P.,
J. M. Flaxman, J. Brown, E. I. Carman, D. J. Doherty, M. C. Tryon, R. Greer, J. Kane, and
E. Poteat. *Reader's Digest,* 74:446 (1959/06) 193-96.
Readers' responses to Michener's article "The Hardest-Working Women in the World,"
Reader's Digest, 74:443 (1959/03) 42-46.

"Personal Glimpses." *Reader's Digest,* 82:489 (1963/01) 134-35.
A brief version of the anecdote concerning Michener's masquerade that enabled him to view
the Barnes Art Collection.

"Straight Talk About Today's Youth." *Reader's Digest,* 104:623 (1974/03) 116-19.
Condensed from *U.S. News and World Report,* 75:24 (1973/09/10) 48-50.
An interview with James A. Michener.

Record Courier
"Michener Rejects Survey Results." *Record Courier,* (1972/01/27) 36.
A survey of students named or quoted in Kent State, in effort by two professors to show
inaccuracies and errors in the book.

Redbook
"Talking With James A. Michener." Crichton, Sarah. *Redbook,* 156:5 (1981/03) 14, 16.

RSVP
"Confetti: James Michener - Returning the Hero." Fuller, George.
RSVP, 6:3 (1989/03) 8-10. Interview of Michener by the author. Includes photographs, with
cover photo of Michener.

Appendix I - Magazine Articles About JAMES A. MICHENER

Saturday Evening Post
"Keeping Posted." *Saturday Evening Post,* 248:1 (1976/01-02) 12.
Photograph and background information about Michener.

"James Michener on South Africa." Northcott, Rosemary.
Saturday Evening Post, 250:8 (1978/11) 28+. Precursor to "The Covenant."

"At Home With James A. Michener." Harwell, Jenny Andrews.
Saturday Evening Post, 257:6 (1985/09) 30, 32, 34.

"The Continuing Sagas of James A. Michener." Shahin, Jim.
Saturday Evening Post, 262:2 (1990/03/01) 66-70, 106. Reprint from
American Way, 22: 2 (1989/10/15) 56-62, 112. Published by American Airlines.

Saturday Review
"On the Fringe." Frankel, Haskel, ed. *Saturday Review,* 48:30
(1965/07/24) 62. Comments on an interview after publication of "The Source."

"A Desire to Inform." Meras, Phyllis. *Saturday Review,* 51:18 (1968/05/04) 29.
An interview concerning "Iberia."

"Trade Winds." Amory, Cleveland. *Saturday Review,* 54:20 (1971/05/15) 12-13.
Discussion with Michener after "Kent State" and "The Drifters."

"Michener: Man of the Pacific, Man of Asia." Sutton, Horace.
Saturday Review, 7:10 (1980/06) 36-37.

"Why Michener Never Misses." Mitgang, Herbert. *Saturday Review,* 7:15 (1980/11) 20-24.

School Library Journal
"James Michener at Work." Ward, Barbara. *School Library Journal,* 37 (1991/12) 64.
Audio-visual review.

The Sewanee Review
"Creative Writing and American Publishing Now." Garrett, George.
TheSewanee Review, C:4 (1992/Fall) 669-75. Published by The University of the South,
Sewanee, Tennessee. Says "The Novel" is 'fairly accurate about how things go.'

Skeptical Inquirer
"James Michener's Tales of a Fortune-Teller." Frazier, Kendrick.
Skeptical Inquirer, 16:4 (1992/Summer) 351-53. A quarterly magazine published by the
Committee for the Scientific Investigation of Claims of the Paranormal (CSICOP).

Smithsonian
"Thinking Big and Better, too, at the University of Texas." Wernick, Robert.
Smithsonian, 14:8 (1983/11) 140-51. Mentions Michener's contribution of contemporary
American art to the University. Photograph of Michener writing "Texas."

Social Education
"James A. Michener: Reaffirmations of a Permanent Liberal." Galvez-Hjornevik, Cleta.
Social Education, 51:4 (1987/04-05) 250-55. A biographical sketch that was prepared as the
basis of a dissertation at the University of Texas. (See A.055).

Appendix I - Magazine Articles About JAMES A. MICHENER

Social Process in Hawaii
"Reactions to Michener's Hawaii." Lindley, Marion Wong. *Social Process in Hawaii*, 24 (1960) 41, 75, 83, 101. Comments by local readers on the novel "Hawaii."

South Bay
"James Michener." Grobel, Larry. *South Bay*, (1981/12) 33-38, 86.
An interview. Includes four photographs of Michener.

Southwest Art
"David Adickes, Archetypes of a Changing Scene." Stone, Nancy.
Southwest Art, (1980/07) 98-105. Mentions Michener's book
"Adickes, a Portfolio with Critique," Houston: Dubose Gallery, 1968.

Space World
"James A. Michener Visits Marshall Center." *Space World*, Q11-202 (1980/11) 15-16.

Spectrum
"James A. Michener, at U.N.C." *Spectrum*, 2:2 (1989/06) 18-21.
Alumni magazine for the University of Northern Colorado. Cover photo of Michener.

"Michener Endows Library." *Spectrum*, (1992/12) 4. University of Northern Colorado, official quarterly report for alumni, students, parents and friends.

"Letter on Michener." Jacobsen, James A. *Spectrum*, (1993/03) 7. A letter to the magazine asks if Michener was on the CSCE faculty while teaching social studies at College High. Yes.

"James A. Michener in the classroom." *Spectrum*, (1993/07) 6-9.
His students recall what happened - 50 years ago.

Sports Illustrated
"Wrong Man Behind the Mike." Jares, J. *Sports Illustrated*, 52:20 (1980/05/12) 45.
3 TV shows based on "Sports in America": The Black Athlete (March 17);
Women in Sports (April 21); Children in Sports (May 19).

Stars and Stripes
"Write On." Schmalz, Jeffrey. *Stars and Stripes*, (1989/11/25) 13.

Swarthmore College Bulletin
"Swarthmore Authors Write about Japanese Prints, Football and Banking."
Swarthmore College Bulletin, 60:6 (1963/05) 42. Alumni issue. A brief announcement of Michener's new book, "The Modern Japanese Print," a signed and limited edition.

"Michener Gives $100,000 to Explore Programs to Improve Racial Relations."
Swarthmore College Bulletin, 67:8 (1970/07) 6. Alumni issue.
The article quotes a letter from Michener on his reasons for the gift.

"Alumni Fete Terry and Joe: van de Kamp and Mautner Also Retire."
Swarthmore College Bulletin, 69:7 (1972/07) 2-3. Alumni issue. Michener addresses the alumni group and calls Joseph B. Shane "the best of the Swarthmore tradition."

"Stevens, Michener Receive First Shane Alumni Service Award."
Swarthmore College Bulletin, (1985/08) 16. Alumni issue.

Appendix I - Magazine Articles About JAMES A. MICHENER

Texas Monthly
"The 1986 Bum Steer Awards." *Texas Monthly*, (1986/02) 86-96. A composite of happenings and events that were claimed to be detrimental to Texas, including Michener's "Texas."

"Novel Approach." Thompson, Helen. *Texas Monthly*, 20 (1992/10) 90.
James Michener bequest for creative writing to the University of Texas, Austin.

Theater Arts
"Negative But Nice." *Theater Arts*, 37 (1953/11) 14.

Thomas Nelson
"What If Jesus Had Never Been Born." Kennedy, D. James, and Jerry Newcombe.
Thomas Nelson, (1994) pp. 228. Quotes Michener from *Parade Magazine*.

Time
"People." *Time*, 85:25 (1965/06/18) 36. Michener declines dinner with President
Johnson to speak at a dinner honoring high school teacher Hannah Kirk Mathews.

TV Guide
"The Making of 'Centennial.'" Russell, Dick. *TV Guide*, 26:39 (1978/09/30) 24-29.

"Space: Will This Colossus Fly?" Meisler, Andy. *TV Guide*, 33:15 (1985/04/13) 8-11.
CBS shot 13 hours of moonwalks and drama for $32 million.

U.S. News & World Report
"What's Good About Today's Youth?" *U.S. News & World Report*,
75:24 (1973/12/10) 48-50. Condensed as "Straight Talk About Today's Youth,"
Reader's Digest, 104:623 (1974/03) 116-19. An interview.

"The 80's - A Rocky, Exciting Time." *U.S. News & World Report*, 88:4 (1980/02/04) 39-42.
Interview with James A. Michener.

"The Man Who Loves Facts." Rosellini, Lynn.
U.S. News & World Report, 110:23 (1991/06/17) 58-59.

Vogue
"People Are Talking About." *Vogue*, 129:8 (1957/04/15) 85. A good portrait
of the Micheners not long after publication of "The Bridge at Andau."

"People Are Talking About." *Vogue*, 148:8 (1966/11/01) 180-81.
An interview with the Micheners.

Who, What, Where, When
"James A. Michener Tributes Day: May 8, 1985."
Who, What, Where, When, (1985/07-08) 6-8. A publication of the Central Bucks Chamber
of Commerce, this edition honored Michener, a Bucks County friend and patron.

World
"Thus Saith James Michener." Thomas, Cal. *World*, 8:5 (1993/04/24) 30.
Response to Michener's article "God is Not a Homophobe," which appeared in the
New York Times, 142 (1993/03/30) A15.

Appendix I - Magazine Articles About JAMES A. MICHENER

Writer's Digest

"An Interview with James A. Michener." Newquist, Roy.
Writer's Digest, 48 (1968/08) 38-42. Interview by literary editor of
Chicago American after publication of "The Source."

"James Michener: Exclusive Interview. (Part I)." Hayes, John P.
Writer's Digest, 52 (1972/04) 20-22, 41.
Part I of a two part interview. Hayes helped Michener research the Kent State story.

"James Michener: Exclusive Interview. (Part II)." Hayes, John P.
Writer's Digest, 52 (1972/05) 22-25, 52-54. Part II of a two part interview.

"MICHENER." Edmondson, Julee. *Writer's Digest*, 65:2 (1985/02) 28-32. An interview.

Appendix II - Newspaper Articles About JAMES A. MICHENER

Akron Beacon Journal
"Author Michener finds his own life chronicled." Lammerding, Betsy.
(1984/12/28) NewsBank, Names in the News, 1984, fiche 51, grid B2.
A review of John Hayes' biography of Michener. Hayes met Michener
while Michener was researching "Kent State."

"Opera Shaped Michener's Style." Mitgang, Herbert. (1992/01/12) D3.

Albuquerque Journal
"Michener's Travels, Talents Come to Life in Classroom." Mulligan, Hugh A.
(1993/04/04) C3.

Allentown Call-Chronicle
"Library Wants Michener Name for New Quakertown Branch." (1973/01/02)
Community objects to naming a library after Michener.

Anchorage Daily News
"Michener - What He Thinks." Warren, Elaine. (1973/05/27) D1, 10.
Sunday Punch Section.

"Sitka turns out for Michener." Lindback, John. (1988/07/06) NewsBank,
Names in the News, 1988, fiche 225, grid B1. Michener is honored by 500 at a $40-a-plate
dinner. Mayor John Dapcevich is saving "Alaska" to read on 'long winter night.'

Arizona Daily Star
"How does Michener do it? Routine, he says." Keever, Jack.
(1990/10/15) B3, 8. Interview.

Austin American-Statesman
"The Book on Michener." Szilagyl, Peter. (1991/04/07) NewsBank, Names in the News,
1991, fiche 105, grid G8. A brief discussion of Michener's routine on his annual return to
Austin to teach a writing workshop at the University of Texas.

"Micheners giving UT $15 million." Szilagyl, Pete. (1992/08/14) NewsBank,
Literature, 1992, fiche 75, grid E10. Single largest gift goes to graduate writing program.

"Missing text another twist in Michener epic novel." Szilagyl, Peter. (1992/11/01)
NewsBank, Literature, 1992, fiche 103, grid F13. Michener loses script for 31 years because
of discouraging comments from editor. He learned not to ask for opinions.

"Biblical Answers." Jackson, Carroll. (1993/05/03) A7.
Letter responding to Michener's article about homosexuals.

Baltimore Morning Sun
"Elder Author Shares Youth's Malaise." Bandler, Michael J. (1971/07-04).

"James Michener." (1982/10/17) NewsBank, Names in the News, 1982, fiche 26, grid D8.
Michener is between "Space" and "Texas" in this biographical interview.

Bangor Daily News
"MICHENER: Prolific writer could live anywhere, chooses Maine." Anstead, Alicia.
(1992/06/19) NewsBank, Literature, 1992, fiche 61, grid B3. Writer speculates that
Michener may be secretly writing a new novel about Maine and lobstering.

Appendix II - Newspaper Articles About JAMES A. MICHENER

Boston Sunday Globe
"James Michener, America's Storyteller." Claffey, Charles. (1987/12/06) 121-24.

Bucks County Intelligencer
"Local Brigade Teams Won One and Lost One." (1922/03/09) 3.
Michener was a substitute guard on the basketball team.

"Brigade Claims Junior Championship of Town." (1922/03/30) 1.
Michener was third in point standings on the basketball team.

"Junior Tennis Crown Being Fought For Now." (1922/09/28) 6.
Michener won his first match of the tournament.

"List of Grade Pupils in Doylestown Boro. Schools as Given by Dr. Carmon Ross."
(1924/09/11) 8. Michener was one of sixty member of the Senior Class.

"Swamp Sellersville in First Game Here." (1924/12/11) 1.
Michener plays basketball in the Doylestown High School league.

"Doylestown A Winner." (1925/02/05) 1+.
Michener was the unsung hero of the basketball game with thirteen points.

"Got Off to Poor Start." (1925/02/26) 1.
Michener's basketball team won, even with a poor start.

"Perkasie's Flying Start Won the Game." (1925/03/19) 1.
The basketball team suffered burnout from too long a season.

"County Seat Seniors Left for Washington." (1925/05/07) 1+. Michener and
forty-six other students take a three day Senior Class trip to Washington, D.C.

"Michener Won Prize." (1925/06/18) 4. Michener received a 4 year scholarship
valued at $2000 in competition with 155 candidates from 27 states.

"High School Students Give Boys' Week Talks." (1925/05/07) 7. Michener was one of
three to speak at Boys' Week sponsored by the Doylestown Legionnaires and Rotarians.

"Fifty-Six Graduated From the High School." (1925/06/25) 1. Michener was one of
fifty-six graduates from the Bucks County High School.

"Michener to Graduate." (1929/05/31) 6.

Chicago Tribune
"3 authors explore facets of America." Borcover, Alford. 135:17 (1982/01/17)
Sect. 11, 1. Book review. "James A. Michener's USA -- The People and the Land."

"Michener: King of the Blockbusters Soaks up the Caribbean for His 'Last Big Book.'"
Nieuwsma, Milton. 142:362 (1988/12/27) 1, 7.

"Antarctica." 146:257 (1992/09/13) 1, 10-11. Travel Section.

Christian Science Monitor
Taylor, Nora E. 62:171 (1970/06/17) 6. Movie review. "The Hawaiians."

Appendix II - Newspaper Articles About JAMES A. MICHENER

Colorado Springs Sun
"In the beginning, there was Colorado." Borden, Lark. (1974/08/22).

Congress Bi-Weekly
"Tales of Ancient Israel." Bellman, Samuel Irving. (1965/06/14) 18.

Congressional Record
"James A. Michener." Inouye, Honorable Daniel K. (1962/09/17) 1-2.
Proceedings and Debates of the 87th Congress. Speech in the House of
Representatives by the Congressman from Hawaii.

Courier Times (Bucks County)
"Michener's Views Reflect Novelist's Eye for Detail." Barnett, David, Jr. (1973/11/25) 3.
Michener's statements following Pennsylvania Constitutional Convention.

"County honors Michener with daylong events." Leffler, Peter J. (1985/05/09) A1, 3.
Highlights of a daylong celebration of Michener's homecoming.

"Halberstein's beat." Halberstein, Joe. (1985/05/09) A3.
"South Pacific came along at the right time. The world was tired of war.
People wanted to slow down again."

"It's standing room only on Michener's day." Kennedy, Morris. (1985/05/09) A3.
Arts center to be established in author's honor at former warden's residence of old
county prison in Doylestown.

"Faces in the news: Michener on art." (1989/10/22).
Government should leave the purchase of art to private individuals.
'Elected officials don't know what they are doing.'

"Texas-bound: With 'Caribbean' written, Michener sets new horizons."
Stuart, Kyle. (1989/11/17) ? Michener speaks to a small group at the
University of Miami following the completion of "Caribbean."

"At 85, he doesn't look back." Kennedy, Dana. (1992/11/30)

Daily Intelligencer (Doylestown, Pa.)
(1970/01/30).

"James Michener: Bucks Countian has rags to riches life story." Brunner, Richard Keppler.
(1978/01/07) 3, 7. An interview.

"A day for James A. Michener: On May 8 famous author will be given keys to his old
hometown." (1985/04/30) 1. Announces special James A. Michener edition of the Daily
Intelligencer to be published May 8, 1985.

"James Michener comes home to giant 'thank you' celebration."
Leffler, Peter J. (1985/05/08) 1. James A. Michener Tribute Day in Doylestown.

"Michener plays significant role in American literature." (1985/05/08) 2.
Letters by John P. Hayes, Pradyumna Chauhan, William Lynch, Sally Royal
Smith, Richard S. Kennedy and Dr. Louise E. Murphy.

Appendix II - Newspaper Articles About JAMES A. MICHENER

Daily Intelligencer (Doylestown, Pa.) (continued)

"The world is the source for Michener's prolific works." von Dobeneck, Monica. (1985/05/08) 2. Michener has traveled almost everywhere in the world except the South Pole.

"...a family celebration." Christensen, Mavis. (1985/06/09) 6. Michener comes home to Doylestown for an affirmation of townspeople's respect and love.

"A warm tribute to a favorite son." Leffler, Peter J. (1985/06/09) 1, 17. Doylestown honors Michener.

"Arts center named in honor of Michener." Kennedy, Morris. (1985/06/09) 1, 15. The James A. Michener Arts Center of Bucks County is built in the warden's residence of the old county prison in Doylestown.

"'Graduate' tells students: Be ready to profit from good luck." McBain, Roger L. (1985/06/09) 17. Michener is presented plaque and commemorative diploma honoring 60th anniversary of his own graduation.

"Michener earns Exemplar Award through lifetime of commitment." McFadden, James P. (1985/06/09) 6. This editorial is the text of the citation written for presentation of the Central Bucks Chamber of Commerce Award.

"Michener given key to Doylestown." Leffler, Peter J. (1985/06/09) 16.

"Michener: Homecoming 'joyous.'" Von Dobeneck, Monica. (1985/06/09) 1, 15. Doylestown honors Michener.

"Class Act: Michener teaches aspiring writers." Mulligan, Hugh A.(1993/04/04) C7.

"Michener's muses: The arts are related, problems the same." Benincasa, Robert. (1993/07/18) C1. Michener art collection is on exhibit at the James A. Michener Art Museum, July 18, 1993 - January 2, 1994.

Daily Oklahoman

"James Michener Working 'on the Last Big Book.'" Nieuwsma, Milton. (1989/01/01) NewsBank, Names in the News, 1989, fiche 50, grid F3. Interview of Michener following publication of "Alaska," and preparation for new book about the Caribbean.

Dallas Morning News

"Michener delves deep into the heart of Texas." Reeves, Monica. (1983/04/24) NewsBank, Names in the News, 1983, fiche 93, grid C5. Michener prepares to write his novel about Texas.

"Michener on Movies." Buchholz, Brad. (1990/04/01) NewsBank, Names in the News, 1990, fiche 139, grid G4. "Dangerous or not, it is the artist's responsibility to challenge the established thinking of the day" J. A. Michener.

"Micheners donate $15 million to UT." Kuempel, George. (1992/08/14) NewsBank, Names in the News, 1992, fiche 191, grid G13. For students attending the Texas Center for Writers, it focuses not only on books but also stage and film as well.

Appendix II - Newspaper Articles About JAMES A. MICHENER

Dallas Morning News (continued)

"James Michener." Harris, Joyce Saenz. (1992/08/16) NewsBank, Names in the News, 1992, fiche 197, grid F3. An interesting review of Michener's background. "He has run for Congress and run with the bulls at Pamplona."

"The latest word from Michener." Chism, Olin. (1992/11/30) NewsBank, Names in the News, 1992, fiche 266, grid A10. "Mexico" explores the ethnic tension between the Indian and the Spanish descended elite, a continuing cultural struggle.

Denver Post

"Michener's research assures more than travelogue." Biondi, Joanne. (1989/11/19) D10. Michener shows the Caribbean historically intermixed with our own American history.

"James Michener reveals secrets of creative vigor." Keever, Jack. (1990/09/08) E1, 4. Interview.

Evening Bulletin

"An Author Builds His Dream House." Polier, Rex. (1949/02/26). Designed by wife, Vange Nord, the rustic hilltop retreat gives panoramic view of wooded Bucks County country side.

Fairbanks Daily News-Miner

"Michener files, manuscript deposited in Rasmuson." (1988/07/14) NewsBank, Names in the News, 1988, fiche 225, grid A12. Material, research files and original manuscript of "Alaska" deposited with Rasmuson Library of University of Alaska, Fairbanks.

Florida Times-Union

"James A. Michener: Author hard at work writing latest tome." Nieuwsma, Milton. (1989/01/08) NewsBank, Names in the News, 1989, fiche 50, grid E14. Interview of Michener following publication of "Alaska," and preparation for new book about the Caribbean.

Gazette Telegraph (Colorado Springs)

"James Michener." (1992/02/08). A birthday party and presentation of a book commemorating him.

George School News

"Vitarelli Stars in Faculty Play `Phiz the Whiz'." (1933/10/11) 1. Play written by Michener.

"Coaches Attend Meeting." (1933/12/12) 3.

Training Tables Started." (1933/12/12) 4.

"Marionette Guild Begun." (1933/12/14) 4.

"Faculty Downs Varsity Quintet by Final Rally." (1934/02/28) 3.

"Scottish Trip Described." (1934/02/28) 3.

"Mr. Michener Possesses Collection of Old English, Scottish Ballads." (1934/03/16) 1+.

"Miccelli Marionettes in Shakespearean Scenes." (1934/04/12) 1.

Appendix II - Newspaper Articles About JAMES A. MICHENER

George School News (continued)
"Mr. Michener Speaks." (1934/05/23) 2.

Michener Chooses Cubs." (1934/05/02) 3.

"Mr. Michener Recovering." (1934/05/16) 1.

"Meijer Editor For Next Year; Eastburn, Swayne Associates." (1934/06/12) 1.

"Teachers Plan Summer to Include Travel, Study at Home and Abroad."
(1934/06/12) 1+.

"Faculty Travels Extended to All Parts of World." (1934/10/03) 4.

"Micelli Marionettes Fill Heavey *[sic]* Summer Schedule." (1934/10/03) 4.

"Faculty Quintet Trounce Varsity: Michener High Scorer for Teachers With 13 Points
Out of 45-16 Total." (1935/01/30) 3.

"Instructors at Meeting: Shane, Michener, Mohr, Mendenhall Attend Curriculum
Conference." (1935/05/15) 1.

"Instructors Will Paint, Play, Ponder, Plod --- at Home and All Over the Map."
(1935/06/10) 1+.

Greeley Tribune
"Michener Saw Hungarians Escape." (1957/02/16) 6.

"Michener dedicates library, gets degree." Craig, Jim. (1972/10/28) 1, 6.
Michener provides main address, announces start of work on "Centennial,"
receives honorary degree, doctor of humane letters.

"UNC Library named for James Michener." (1973/01/08) 10. Michener received his
masters of arts degree from UNC in 1936 and served on its faculty from 1936-41.

"The unveiling." (1973/05/02) Formal dedication of the James A. Michener Library
at the University of Northern Colorado. Photo.

"Michener office recreated." McConnellogue, Ken. (1990/07/30).
Office Michener used in writing "Centennial," is recreated at the James A. Michener
Library at the University of Northern Colorado.

"Novelist's Wife Visits Greeley: Mari Michener Tours Library, Sees Friends."
84:296 (1992/08/10) A3.

"Michener donates $600,000 to UNC library." (1992/10/24).
In 1937, Michener received a master's degree in secondary education from
UNC (then Colorado State College).

"The Story Teller. Literary legend James Michener, 85, looks back at the
story of his life." Kennedy, Dana. (1992/12/17) Preview 1, 3-4.
Preview section. A cover photo of the novel "Mexico," and one and one-half
pages of information about Michener.

Appendix II - Newspaper Articles About JAMES A. MICHENER

Greeley Tribune (continued)
"Readers Can Get High On 'South Pacific.'" Roberts, F. X. 85:149 (1993/03/18)
Preview, 29. Michener achieves oft-expressed wish to be remembered as both a
story teller and an educator.

"A Class Act: Michener Lends Hand To Budding Writers." Mulligan, Hugh A.
85:165 (1993/04/03) A10. Michener shares epitaph "Here lies a man who never
showed home movies or served vin rose."

"Michener's Biblical History is Flawed." Thomas, Cal. 85: 168 (1993/04/06) A10.
Thomas believes that Michener, as an agnostic, is ill-equipped to interpret Scripture in
which he does not believe.

The Guardian (Manchester)
"Fortunes in Men's Eyes." Hamilton, Alex. (1972/02/23) 10-15.

Hill School News
"Four New Members Added to the School Faculty." (1929/10/11) 2.

"Faculty Holds Novel Mauve Decade Party." (1929/11/14) 1-2.

"'A Christmas Carol' is Presented by Faculty." (1929/12/19) 2.

"Mr. Michener Stars as Squad Defeats Faculty." (1929/12/19) 2.

"'The Dover Road' is Presented by Faculty." (1930/03/13) 2-3.

"Much Enthusiasm Shown in Far Fields Baseball." (1931/05/01) 2.

Hill School Snooze
"Faculty Song Guide." (1929/11/28) 7. A parody issue of the Hill School News poking
fun at the faculty. Contemporary songs were assigned to faculty members. The song for
Michener was "Love Me or Leave Me." Also includes a photograph of Michener with
other faculty members titled "Why Girls Leave Home."

Honolulu Advertiser
"Portrait of an 'average' guy." Sones, Elizabeth. (1986/01/27) NewsBank,
Names in the News, 1986, fiche 73, grid B1. Biographical information
following the publication of "Texas."

"Life with Michener." Creamer, Beverly. (1987/07/15) NewsBank, Names in the News,
1987, fiche 333, grid F3. Mari talks about life with Michener. Art collection given to
Honolulu Academy of Arts because of the kindness of a Honolulu policeman.

Honolulu Star-Bulletin
(1954/04/14) 38. Michener's interview statement that a writer never qualifies for
public office.

"A Preface to a Novel." Taylor, Clarice B. (1959/06/06) 2-3.
Mrs. Taylor's humorous account of her personal role as technical advisor
to Michener in the writing of "Hawaii."

"The Lyons Den." Lyons, Leonard. (1960/02/18).

Appendix II - Newspaper Articles About JAMES A. MICHENER

Honolulu Star-Bulletin (continued)
"More on Michener's Hawaii." Taylor, Clarice B. (1960/06/05) 8.
Women's Section. Written by the author's research assistant on his giant novel.

"All About Hawaii." Akaka, The Reverend Abraham; Charles E. Frankel, ed.
Honolulu:(1967/?/?) 227.
Houston Post
"James A. Michener: THE MAN." Bennett, Elizabeth. (1991/04/21) NewsBank, Literature,
1991, fiche 36, grid C11. Reviews some of Michener's background and writing habits. He
had recently funded a creative writing program at the University of Houston.

Intelligencer
"Class of '25 knew Jimmy had future." Kennedy, Morris. (1985/05/08) 1, 17.
Special James A. Michener keepsake edition: Pages 1, 2, 17, 18. This article
is about Michener's 1925 high school yearbook.

"First published at 40, he won wealth, fame and Pulitzer Prize." Shultes, Anne.
(1985/05/08) 1, 17. Special James A. Michener keepsake edition: Pages 1, 2, 17, 18.

"Arts center to be named in honor of Bucks 'outstanding citizen.'"
Kennedy, Morris. (1985/05/10) C17.

"Michener is eager to move on to his next project." Stuart, Kyle. (1989/12/05) ?
Michener discusses his life, books and travels.

"The legend never looks back." Kennedy, Dana. (1992/12/27) 6.
Michener reflects on his life and writing.

"At Michener's work: Room gives inside look." Goldstein, Susan E. (1993/07/15) C1.
The James A. Michener Art Museum in Doylestown adds exhibit recreating room where
Michener wrote in his home.

Intelligencer-Record
"The lost Michener." Benincasa, Robert. (1991/10/27) NewsBank, Literature, 1991,
fiche 91, grid G6. Michener's manuscript for "Mexico" is found by his cousin, Virginia
Trumbull, after being lost for three decades.

"A conversation on now and then." Benincasa, Robert. (1992/02/02) NewsBank,
Names in the News, 1992, fiche 58, grid E14. Interview. Michener reflects on past eight
decades. Youth faces difficult problems. Prognosticates on life when he is 100.

Juneau Empire
"James Michener." Longenbaugh, Betsy. (1985/01/16) NewsBank, Names in the News,
1985, fiche 51, grid B1. Michener visits Alaska in preparation for a new novel.

"Micheners tour Capital City." Lund, Annabel. (1988/07/08) NewsBank, Names in the News,
1988, fiche 225, grid A13. Micheners visit Juneau and take horse and buggy tour.

Ketchikan Daily News
"81-year old American author promotes his book about Alaska." Williams, Lew M., Jr.
(1988/07/01) NewsBank, Names in the News, 1988, fiche 225, grid A10.
Michener says Bennett Cerf advised him to autograph as many books as possible.
"That way they can't return them for credit."

Appendix II - Newspaper Articles About JAMES A. MICHENER

Los Angeles Herald Examiner

(1983/10/16) NewsBank, Names in the News, 1983, fiche 26, grid A1.
Background to the novel "Poland." Michener quit leaving his papers with the
Library of Congress because of tax treatment.

"Travels with Michener." Boce, Martin. (1989/11/01) NewsBank, Names in the News,
1989, fiche 340, grid D12. "Caribbean" will be last big novel. He wants to visit the South
Pole. He will not write about Northern Ireland or South America.

Los Angeles Times

"Monitoring a Michener Blitz." Lochte, Dick. (1978/08/13). Comments about the 25 hour
mini-series "Centennial." Also, the release of John King's book "In Search of Centennial."

"Michener's New 192 - Page 'Legacy.'" Mehren, Elizabeth. (1987/04/09).
NewsBank, Names in the News, 1987, fiche 220, grid B5. Michener comments
on why he wrote "Legacy."

"Close to the Vest." Mehren, Elizabeth. 111 (1991/12/18) E1.
"The Fires of Spring"'may give more insight to Michener than his autobiography
"The World Is My Home" says agent Owen Laster.

Linn's Stamp News

"Sununu To Serve on Postal Museum Board." Griffith, Gary. 64:3295 (1991/12/30) 3.
Announcing Michener's appointment to fifteen member advisory Committee of the
Smithsonian's National Postal Museum.

Miami Herald

"Michener: Surprised At Success." Hutchinson, Bill. (1974/11/15)
Noted in "Authors in the News,"vol.1, Detroit: Gale Research, 1976, p. 340.

National Enquirer

"Hard Work Got Me Out of the Poorhouse, Says Millionaire Author James Michener."
Levy, Paul F. (1981/09/08) 13.

New Hope Gazette

"A visit with Michener." Shaw, Charles. (1981/07/30) 3. Michener talks about his childhood.

"Michener's next novel to be about value of Space." Shaw, Charles. (1981/08/06) 1-14.
An interview following publication of "The Covenant," which was No. 1, on the
New York Times best-seller list before it was published.

New York Daily Mirror

Fields, Sidney. (1957/02/17).

New York Herald Tribune

"Writer Resists Fame." Bromley, Dorothy Dunbar. (1949/05/29) 1.
Rodgers and Hammerstein's negotiations for dramatic rights to "Tales of the South Pacific."

"'South Pacific' Actor: Michener." Ross, Don. (1960/07/31) Section 4, 1.

New York Herald Tribune Book Review

"On an Author." Hutchins, J.K. (1951/05/20) 3.
Deals with the writing of "Return to Paradise."

Appendix II - Newspaper Articles About JAMES A. MICHENER

New York Herald Tribune Book Review (continued)
"Biographical Note." (1951/10/07) 6.
Contains useful information previous to the publication of "The Voice of Asia."

"Man Behind the Bridges." Hutchins, J.K. (1953/07/19) 2.
Deals with Michener's preparation of Korean War novel.

New York Post
"That Day at Kent." Soltis, Andy. (1971/04/30) 39. Biographical information
prior to publication of "Kent State," and "The Drifters."

New York Times
"Pulitzer Prizes." 97:32,973 (1948/05/04) 24. Announces fiction award to "Tales of the
South Pacific," the fine stories of James A. Michener.

"Pulitzer Prizes Go to 'Streetcar' and Michener's Stories of Pacific."
Adams, Frank S. 97:32,973 (1948/05/04) 1, 22. Announces Pulitzer Prize Winners.

"Sketches of those added by Columbia to the Roll of Pulitzer Prize winners.
(James A. Michener)." 97:32,973 (1948/05/04) 22. Short biography.

98:33,094 (1948/09/02) 18. Announces Michener's upcoming marriage.

98:33,162 (1948/11/09) 25. Speech by Michener at the NYC Forum.
He sees great American novels coming from writers under thirty-five.

"Confidence Held Nation's Top Need." 102:34,605 (1952/10/22) 25.
New York Herald Tribune Forum. Michener describes the role of youth in the
government and administration of "new democracies."

"New Heads Named for Asia Institute." 102:34,767 (1953/04/02) 29.
Michener is named president of the Asia Institute, the only graduate school
exclusively in Asian affairs in the U.S.

"Paramount Buys Michener's Novel." 102:34,869 (1953/07/13) 22.
Paramount Pictures buys screen rights to "The Bridges at Toko-ri," to be filmed by
William Perlberg and George Seaton.

"Ladejinsky Firing Protested." 104:35,398 (1954/12/24) 12. Letter. Michener protests the
ouster of W. Ladejinsky as Agricultural Attache at the U.S. Embassy, Tokyo.

"Wife Sues Michener." 104:35,409 (1955/01/04) 13.
Vange Nord seeks divorce from Michener.

"Charter Obtained for Fund for Asia." 104:35,443 (1955/02/07) 12. Michener, president of
the organization, reports on the incorporation of the Fund for Asia. Directors are named.

"Mobs Sack Hotels in Saigon, 60 Hurt." 104:35,607 (1955/07/21) 1,6. Michener escapes.

"Staffing Overseas Missions; Limitation on Size of Embassies in Remote Capitals
Suggested." Lang, William W. 104:35,616 (1955/07/30) 16. Reply to Michener's article of
July 24, 1955, deploring lack of a U.S. physician to take care of employees in Afghanistan.

Appendix II - Newspaper Articles About JAMES A. MICHENER

New York Times (continued)

"James Michener Divorced." 104:36,650 (1955/09/02) 37.
Announces Michener's divorce from Vange Nord.

"Medical Care in Kabul; Adequate Attention for Americans Is Said to Exist There."
Ackerman, Carl W. 104:35,651 (1955/09/03) 14. Letter. Rebuts Michener's letter, published
July 24, criticizing U.S. medical care for Americans in Afghanistan.

"Michener Will Marry a Japanese-American." 105:35,698 (1955/10/20) 9.
Announces Michener's plans to marry Mari Yoriko Sabusawa.

"James Michener Marries." 105:35,701 (1955/10/24) 48.
Announces Michener's marriage to Mari Yoriko Sabusawa.

"Fund for Asia Ending." 106:36,129 (1956/12/24) 4. Michener's comments as president of
Fund for Asia that recent events make continuance of the Fund inadvisable.

"Khruschev's Dare Cited by Gruenther." 106:36,301 (1957/06/14) 2.
Michener receives honorary Doctor of Laws degree from Temple University.
General Alfred Guenther was speaker.

"U.S. Gives Consent for 24 Newsmen to Go to Red China." Baker, Russell. 106:36,371
(1957/08/23) 1-2. *Reader's Digest* sends Michener to communist China with other newsmen.

"13 on Plane in Pacific Saved." 107:36,414 (1957/10/05) 35.
Michener unhurt when his plane ditches at sea.

"Arts Advisors Named." 107:36,426 (1957/10/17) 43.
Secretary of State John Dulles announces the appointment of 9 members,
including Michener, to Advisory Committee on the Arts.

"Matthews Named for Press Award." 107:36,597 (1958/04/06) 59.
Overseas Press Club Awards. Michener selected for best magazine of foreign
affairs for "The Bridge at Andau," in *Reader's Digest*.

107:36,621 (1958/04/30) 7. Presentation of Overseas Press Club Awards.

"Recreation Center Sold." 107:36,679 (1958/06/27) 8. Michener and associates sell
Fountainhead, a 14 acre resort type recreation center in Doylestown, Pennsylvania.

"Michener's Pacific on Television." Shanley, John P. 108:37,045 (1959/06/28) II, 15.
Michener supplies theme and stories for TV series "Adventures in Paradise,"
the adventures of Adam Troy in the South Pacific.

"New Michener Book is Bought for Film." 108:37,102 (1959/08/24) 15.
Michener sells movie rights to "Hawaii" for reported $600,000, or 10% of
gross. Fred Zinnemann will produce and direct.

(1959/10/06) 79. Premier of TV series "Adventures in Paradise."

"Author Joins Kennedy." 109:37,467 (1960/08/23) 19.
Announcement of Michener's appointment as chairman of a Citizens for
Kennedy and Johnson committee in Bucks County, Pa.

Appendix II - Newspaper Articles About JAMES A. MICHENER

New York Times (continued)

"Inaugural Book a Literary Event." 110:37,592 (1960/12/26) 14. Literary figures, including Michener, contribute to a 64 page Presidential inaugural program.

"Council to Advise on Food for Peace." 110:37,724 (1961/05/07) 50. Michener is named by Kennedy as co-chairman. The Council is to provide leadership for U.S. Food for Peace program.

"Cowell Laments Income on Music." Robertson, Nan. 111:37,972 (1962/01/10) 29. National Council of Women panel, including Michener, concludes that government subsidy is needed for America's musicians.

"In The Nation." Krock, Arthur. (1962/05/11) 30. Background information on Pulitzer Prize rules changes and the selection of "Tales of the South Pacific" in 1948.

"Michener Buoyed in Congress Race." Weart, William G. 111:38,187 (1962/08/13) 17. "Splendid receptions everywhere" convinced Michener that he might upset republican incumbent in race for seat in Congress.

"Curtin Defeats Michener in Bucks County House Race." 112:38,275 (1962/11/09) 38.

"Recapitulation of Congress and Governorship Races with Vote Percentages." 112:38,277 (1962/11/11) 68. Michener received 82,876 votes to Curtin's 100,313, or 45.2 percent of the vote to 54.8 percent.

"U.S. and Soviet Intellectuals Are Conferring in Leningrad." 113:38, 900 (1964/07/26) 2. Roundtable conference to promote understanding between the two countries.

"More Exchanges Urged in Soviet." Shabad, Theodore. 113:38, 909 (1964/08/04) 19. Unofficial Soviet-Americans Citizen's Conference agrees it would be "mutually beneficial" to exchange cultural material.

"For Michener, Teacher Comes Before Johnson." 114:39,219 (1965/06/10) 22. Michener declines invitation to dinner at White House to attend dinner honoring former Swarthmore teacher Hannah Kirk Mathews.

"Michener Has Heart Attack." 114:39,313 (1965/09/12) 57. Report of Michener's heart attack.

"Michener Resting Peacefully." 114:39,315 (1965/09/14) 20. Report of Michener's condition following heart attack.

"Bucks County Plans Annual Arts Fetes." 116:39,889 (1967/04/11) 52. Michener leads non-profit organization to open Bucks County Arts Festival in April, 1968, to provide repertory theater.

"Four Are Named Winners Of 1967 Einstein Awards." 16:39,902 (1967/04/24) 30. Michener to receive Einstein Commemorative Award for efforts in Americans for Peace in the Middle East.

"Einstein Awards Go To 4 World Figures." 116:39,916 (1967/05/08) 57. Announces presentation of Einstein Commemorative Award to Michener.

Appendix II - Newspaper Articles About JAMES A. MICHENER

New York Times (continued)
"A Group for Peace in the Mideast Formed." 116:40,010 (1967/08/10) 12.
Formation of Americans for Peace in the Middle East.

"80 Americans Urge U.S. to Seek Mideast Peace." 117:40,050 (1967/09/19) 2.
Prominent Americans sign statement urging the U.S. to work inside and
outside the U.N. for direct Arab-Israeli Peace Talks.

"U. of Texas Getting $3-Million Art Gift." 118:40,420 (1968/09/23) 35.
Gift of 250 modern American paintings valued at $3,000,000 by Michener
Foundation to University of Texas announced by Chancellor Ransom.

119:40,827 (1969/11/04) 52. Part of Michener's collection of twentieth century
American paintings are shown by the University of Texas Art Museum.

"Hungarian Fund To Give Awards to 5 at Dinner." 119:40,977 (1970/04/03) 49.
Michener to receive award for American-Hungarian studies.

"Michener Offers Aid to Racial Programs." 119:41,014 (1970/05/10) 56. Michener gave
Swarthmore College $100,000 over five years for Black studies and race relations programs.

120:41,181 (1970/10/24) 29.
Random House plans to publish art book with J. Levine and Michener.

120:41,226 (1970/12/08) 35.
Michener appointed to the U.S. Information Advisory Committee.

"Off to Bermuda - for a Bite of Lunch." Curtis, Charlotte. 121:41,628 (1972/01/14) 40.
David Frost takes a group of 60 celebrities, including Michener, to Bermuda for lunch.

"Kent State Study Scores Michener." 121:41,629 (1972/01/16) 76.
Kent State Professor Carl Moore conducts poll to show that "Kent State" is filled with errors
and misstatements.

"Nixon Hails Reader's Digest on Jubilee." 121:41,643 (1972/01/29) 26.
A 50th anniversary party for the *Reader's Digest* is staged at the White House for 100 guests,
including Michener.

"Michener Changes Kent State Theory." 121:41,735 (1972/04/30) 27.
Michener now believes that a conspiracy may have existed among National Guardsmen to
fire on antiwar demonstrators.

"A Moscow Parlay Ends in an Uproar." Shabad, Theodore. 121:41,761 (1972/05/26) 5.
Michener walks out of Soviet briefing to protest Soviet remarks which made light of Jewish
problems.

"Payments for Paperback Rights Soar." Raymont, Henry. 121:41,785 (1972/06/19) 38.
Paperback publishers are surpassing the film industry as the goose that lays the golden egg.
Fawcett deals with Michener.

"Student, 80, at Yeshiva U. Gets M.A. and Now Plans for Ph.D." 123:42, 503
(1974/06/07) 20. Michener receives honorary degree at Yeshiva University.

Appendix II - Newspaper Articles About JAMES A. MICHENER

New York Times (continued)

"Random House Is Raising Michener Novel to $12.50." Pace, Eric.
123:42, 595 (1974/09/07) 17. Random House raises the price for "Centennial" to
compensate for the higher cost of paper.

"'Centennial' Paperback Brings $1-Million." Pace, Eric. 123:42,599 (1974/09/11) 42.
Fawcett pays record price for a paperback novel.

"What was the Aim of the Aim?" Robinson, Ray. 124:42,694 (1974/12/15) V, 2.
Letter. Lauds Michener's promotion of Robin Roberts for baseball hall of fame.

"Poor Robin." Gottlieb, R.S. 124:42,715 (1975/01/05) V, 2. Letter.
Appreciates Michener's efforts to promote Robin Roberts for Baseball hall of fame.

"Writers and Actors Criticize UNESCO For Curb on Israel." 124:42, 748
(1975/02/07) 3. Letter of protest to UNESCO by Arthur Miller, Michener and
others to protest U.N. resolution denying cultural aid to Israel.

"Notables in Paris on UNESCO Issue." Kamm, Henry. 124:42, 785
(1975/03/16) 14. Cultural elite gather in Paris to pressure UNESCO into
lifting its ban on Israel's participation in its work.

"TV Is Again Looking to Books for New Specials." Brown, Les.
124:42,786 (1975/03/17) 59. Networks turn to books for new sources of material, including
Michener's "Hawaii," to be serialized to span 12 hours.

"Panel Aims to Strengthen Role of Arts in Education." Glueck, Grace.
124:42, 891 (1975/06/30) 1, 38. Panel to produce report aimed at influencing curricula
at all educational levels to enhance the role of the arts in education.

"Michener Fears Publishing Take-Overs May Ground Fledgling Novelists."
Buckley, Tom. 125:43,010 (1975/10/27) 31. Michener wonders if publishers that
have become corporate subsidiaries are still as hospitable to beginning writers.

"Notes on People." Johnston, Laurie. 125:43,125 (1976/02/19) 42.
Michener addresses the Colorado Legislature at their 100th anniversary session.

"After a Year, Governor of Colorado Is Under Fire From Environmentalists,
Businessmen and the Press." Lichtenstein, Grace. 125:43,130 (1976/02/24) 25.
Governor is criticized for paying Michener to write article for Business Week supplement
praising the virtues of Colorado.

"Notes on People." Johnston, Laurie. 125:43,137 (1976/03/02) 26.
Michener deplores tasteless commercialization of Bicentennial promotions.
Omaha zoo names bison 'Tennial.'

"TV: 'Dynasty' and 'Road.'" O'Connor, John J. 125:43,148 (1976/03/13) 50.
Michener story adapted for NBC-TV movie called "James Michener's Dynasty."
Actually written by Sidney Carroll.

"Michener Bids Pro Sports Repay Colleges for Talent." 125:43,334 (1976/09/15) 36.
In testimony before House special Committee, Michener says pro sports teams should pay
colleges for training athletes.

Appendix II - Newspaper Articles About JAMES A. MICHENER

New York Times (continued)

"21 Named by Ford to Receive Medal of Freedom." 126:43,443 (1977/01/02) 44.
Twenty-one Americans to receive Medal of Freedom from President Ford for
contributions to national, world and cultural endeavors.

"TV : 4-Part 'Michener's World' Goes to Holy Land." O'Connor, John J.
126:43,613 (1977/06/21) 67. Review of "Israel: A Search for Old Faith,"
part 1 of series "James Michener's World," produced for WNET-TV.

"Art: The Japan Of James Michener." Russell, John. 127:43,707 (1977/09/23) III, 14.
150 Japanese prints from Michener's collection are exhibited at the Japan House Gallery,
entitled 'Utamaro and Hiroshige.'

127:43,708 (1977/09/24) 23. Correction to article by J. Russell dated
September 23, 1977, about an art show review. The address was incorrect.

"Merger Fever in Publishing." Crittenden, Ann. 127:43, 737 (1977/10/23) III, 1, 9.
Publisher mergers worry authors.

"Hasidic Feat: Simple as Aleph, Beth, Gimel." Shenker, Israel. 127:43,748
(1977/11/03) 18. Michener praises the Polish Government for returning Jewish
historic writings believed to have been destroyed in W.W. II.

"Notes on People." Krebs, Albin. 127:43,753 (1977/11/08) 25. Michener to donate
"Chesapeake" materials to Talbot County Free Library on Maryland's Eastern Shore.

"Who's Who Of Santa's Stockings." Nemy, Enid. 127:43,788 (1977/12/13) 57.
Auction of celebrity stockings to benefit Trinity Missions which assists needy groups such as
mine workers and migrants.

"TV : Michener's Personal and Loving Look at Spain." O'Connor, John J.
127:43,886 (1978/03/21) 70. Review of Michener documentary "Spain:
The Land and the Legend." "James Michener's series."

"The Idea Is to Play." O'Dell, Robert H. 127:43,947 (1978/05/21) V, 2.
Letter from Williams College coach scores Michener article of plan for super league
of major college teams.

"Who Needs Super League?" Boni, Bill. 127:43,947 (1978/05/21) V, 2.
Letter. Criticizes Michener's plan for college football super league, as
overly emphasizing gate receipts and records.

"Publishing: A Trip Up the Chesapeake." Lask, Thomas. (1978/06/23) III, 22.
Michener says "I construct a little world that the reader can live in for a while."

(1978/10/17) 36. Michener's interview with Pope John Paul II to air Nov. 26
on KCET-TV. "James Michener's World."

"TV Weekend." O'Connor, John J. 128:44,046 (1978/11/24) III, 26.
Review of Michener documentary "Poland: The Will to Be." WNET series
"James Michener's World."

Appendix II - Newspaper Articles About JAMES A. MICHENER

New York Times (continued)
"WNET-TV Refuses to Use Michener Documentary." Shepard, Richard F. 128: 44,050 (1978/11/28) III, 22. WNET cancels Michener documentary "Poland: The Will to Be," because it was produced by commercial enterprise.

"Ex-Antiwar Figures Say Vietnam Abuses Rights." 128:44,234 (1979/05/31) 5. International Human Rights Commission publishes a letter to the Viet Nam Government.

Lask, Thomas. 128:44,256 (1979/06/22) III, 26. National Poetry Series, founded by Michener and others, names competition winners.

"Michener to Receive Printing's Franklin Award." 129:44,473 (1980/01/25) III, 19. Michener receives 1980 Franklin Award for Distinguished Service, sponsored by Printing Industries of Metropolitan NY.

"Printing Industries to Honor James Michener." Cummings, Judith. 129:44,476 (1980/01/28) II, 4. Harry Mallon, Chairman of Printing Industries of Metropolitan NewYork, pays tribute to Michener.

"Michener Aids Workshop." Herman, Robin. 129:44,519 (1980/03/11) II, 8. Michener announces endowment of $500,000 trust fund for young authors attending University of Iowa Writer's Workshop.

O'Connor, John J. 129:44,526 (1980/03/17) III, 18. Review of segment on Black athletes from "James Michener's World" TV series.

"TV : Sports Children, Immigrants and 'G.E. Theater.'" Shephard, Richard F. 129:44,588 (1980/05/19) III, 19. Review of segment on child athletes from "James Michener's World" TV series.

"Michener's 'Covenant' Bought by Literary Guild." Mitgang, Herbert. 129:44,612 (1980/06/12) III, 17. Michener sells "The Covenant" book club rights to Literary Guild for $1,750,000.

"Book Publishers Discern Hope in Fall Lists." Mitgang, Herbert. 129:44, 666 (1980/08/05) III, 9. Article on new books to be published in the fall. Portrait of Michener, Doctorow, Theroux and Gordimer.

"Michener's 'The Covenant' Banned by South Africa." 129:44,700 (1980/09/08) III, 15. Government of South Africa bans "The Covenant" as undesirable.

"South Africa Removes Ban On Michener's New Novel." 130:44,742 (1980/10/20) III,15. Government of South Africa lifts ban of "The Covenant."

"Coe to Direct 'Sayonara.'" Corry, John. 130:44,856 (1981/02/11) III, 20. Peter Coe will direct musical based on Michener's novel "Sayonara."

"To Recognize the Patrons." Clarity, James F., Warren Weaver, Jr. 132:45,661 (1983/04/27) 22. Announcement that the Whitehouse Arts Program is to recognize Michener for his financial assistance to artists.

"5 Named to Broadcast Board." 132:45,681 (1983/05/17) 23. Michener to join the Board for International Broadcasting, which administrates Radio Liberty and Radio Free Europe.

Appendix II - Newspaper Articles About JAMES A. MICHENER

New York Times (continued)

"Publishing: Michener and 'Poland.'" Mitgang, Herbert. 132:45,789 (1983/09/02) III, 20. Michener discusses travels in Poland and research for forthcoming book "Poland."

"Michener's 'Space' to be Mini-Series." Farber, Stephen. 133:45,960(1984/02/20) III, 17. Reviews plans by Dick Berg to adapt "Space" into a TV mini-series.

"Michener's Thanks to Swarthmore: $2 Million." Fiske, Edward B. 134:46,178 (1984/09/25) A1, 23. Michener repays $2,000 Scholarship with $1,998,000 interest to alma mater Swarthmore.

"Next Michener Novel Will Focus on Alaska." 134:46,235 (1984/11/21) III, 18. Michener reports that his next project will be a novel about Alaska. He holds a lifetime professorship at the University of Texas.

"The Space Program's Unsung Heroes Star in a Mini-Series." Farber, Stephen. 124:46,246 (1984/12/02) II, 25. Article about thirteen hour TV miniseries based on Michener's "Space," to be broadcast by CBS.

"Publishing: An Award In Honor of Hemingway." McDowell, Edwin. 124:46,286 (1985/01/11) III, 24. Scribner's plans a long Michener introduction for Hemingway's "The Dangerous Summer," New York: Charles Scribner's Sons, 1985.

"Donations by Authors and Publishers Grow." McDowell, Edwin. 135:46,579 (1985/10/31) III, 17. A limited edition of 400 copies of "Texas," bound in buffalo hide, is published by University of Texas to give to major donors.

"Michener, at 82, Says It's Time to Revert To the Smaller Novel." Schmalz, Jeffrey. 139:48,054 (1989/11/14) III, 19. At 82 Michener says it's time to tell tales a little less grand. Living Arts Section.

"Michener Threatens to Quit Random House in Protest." McDowell, Edwin. 139:48,180 (1990/03/20) IV, 21. Michener's threat to leave Random House for 'some small house obedient to the old traditions.'

"Michener on Publishing." McDowell, Edwin. 139:48,181 (1990/03/21) III, 20. It is unclear whether Michener will leave Random House as a result of criticism.

"Michener Talks." McDowell, Edwin. 139:48,188 (1990/03/28) III, 19. Michener discusses management problems with Random House book publishers, S. I. Newhouse and Alberto Vitale.

"Michener's Random Deal." 139:48,217 (1990/04/26) IV, 24. Michener to stay with Random House.

"Michener's Books." McDowell, Edwin. 139:48,244 (1990/05/23) III, 16. Michener signs a two book contract with Random House but will use two other publishers in the fall.

"Michener Writes to Three Young Men Convicted at Westchester." Anderson, Susan Heller. 139:48,260 (1990/06/08) II, 8. Young men convicted of writing anti-semitic graffitti on high school wall sentenced to study judaism and read parts of "Poland."

Appendix II - Newspaper Articles About JAMES A. MICHENER

New York Times (continued)

"Michener Gives Swarthmore $5 Million." Brozan, Nadine. 141:48,736 (1991/09/27) II, 10. Liberal arts colleges develop the value judgments of society, says Michener.

"Michener's 'Mexico.'" Fein, Esther B. 141:48,762 (1991/10/23) III, 22. Michener relocates manuscript of unfinished earlier work and finishes it; includes related book article.

141 (1992/08/16) 16. James Michener donates 15 million to the University of Texas.

"Michener Gives to University." (1992/08/17) A 14. Michener donates to University of Texas writers program.

New York Times Book Review

"Pulitzer Boy. (Interview)." 43:20 (1948/05/16) VII, 8. Michener said he hoped "Tales of the South Pacific" would sell a few hundred copies a year, six years after publication.

"Talk With Mr. Michener." Breit, Harvey. 44:21 (1949/05/22) VII, 26. Mentions "South Pacific" and the author's ideas on the novelist's function and the role of the Arts in society today.

"In and Out of Books." Breit, Harvey. 48:25 (1953/06/21) VII, 8. Comment on publication of "The Bridges at Toko-ri. " *Life* magazine ordered the magazine story published prior to the hardcover.

"Talk with Mr. Michener." Nichols, Lewis. 48:28 (1953/07/12) VII, 16. A discussion of the writing of "The Bridges at Toko-ri."

"Talk With Mr. Michener." Clurman, Robert. 52:9 (1957/03/03) VII, 18. Deals with Michener's experience in collecting material for "The Bridge at Andau."

"In and Out of Books." Nichols, Lewis. 71:29 (1966/07/17) VII, 8. Comments on Michener's success with "The Source," and his start on a new work in Spain.

"In and Out of Books." Nichols, Lewis. 71:30 (1966/07/24) VII, 8. Comments that "The Source" has been on the best seller list for 61 weeks and sales seem to be mysteriously increasing.

"What Transpired." Morris, William, Elizabeth R. Mertz, Walter Morse, Edith Schwager and Dolly Hecht. 73:3 (1968/01/21) VII, 30. Letters to the editor on James Michener's December 17, 1969, article regarding the etymology of 'transpire.'

"Paperback Talk." Walters, Ray. 83:31 (1978/07/30) VII, 31-32. Fawcett acquires paperback rights from Random House for "Chesapeake" and 14 older Michener works.

"Behind the Best Sellers; James A. Michener." Klemesrud, Judy. 83:48 (1978/11/26) VII, 106.

"Half a Million for the Muse." Lask, Thomas. 83:52 (1978/12/24) VII, 23. James A. Michener and others form consortium to underwrite five works of poetry a year.

"Works in Progress." Irving, John. 84:28 (1979/07/15) VII, 15. Michener's comments on the progress of "Chesapeake."

Appendix II - Newspaper Articles About JAMES A. MICHENER

New York Times Book Review (continued)
Katutani, Michiko. 85:47 (1980/11/23) VII, 3, 30. Interview with Michener.

"Zimbabwe Ruins." Fiedel, Stuart J. 85:51 (1980/12/21) VII, 22.
Letter responding to John F. Burns review of November 23, 1980, regarding
the building of Zimbabwe about 1200 A.D.

86:22 (1981/05/31) VII, 3. Interviews with authors on what they intend to read
and write about during the summer.

"Best-Selling Best Sellers." McDowell, Edwin. 87:41 (1982/10/10) VII, 34. Comment on
Michener's new novel "Space" and his phenomenal sales success since 1978.

New York Times Magazine
"Hawaii's Culture." Smart, Dick. 108:36,996 (1959/05/10) VI, 4. Letter.
Writer is disappointed in Michener's failure to expand on Hawaii's cultural interests
in "'Aloha' for the 50th State."

"Take Heart, Men." Hess, Harry. 110:37,836 (1961/08/27) VI, 16.
Letter. Comments on Michener's "Report from the Frenzied Fifties."

"Tennis, Unfrenzied." Shulman, David. 110:37,843 (1961/09/03) VI, 2.
Letter. Humorous response to "Report from the Frenzied Fifties." The toll of advancing
age on Michener's tennis game.

"Rock 'n' Roll." Stover, E. M. 115:39,362 (1965/11/14) VI, 60. Letter.
Disputes Michener's conclusion, in an article dated October 31, that rock 'n' roll is typically
a white phenomena.

"Rock 'n' Roll and Social Taboos." Conn, Stephen. 115:29,383 (1965/11/21) VI, 49. Letter.
Points out that Southern rock 'n' roll bands, based upon common love of music, helped break
down segregation.

"Caught in the Middle." Miner, Kenneth L., Winifred Scott, Frances
Tumerkan, John Meehan, and Sol D. Prensky. 117:40,398 (1968/09/01) VI, 12.
Letters responding to Michener's article of August 18, 1968, titled "The Revolution
in Middle Class Values."

"Changing Values." Maria Schiff. (1968/09/08) VI, 39-42. Letter. Disenchanted 16-year-old
is impressed by 61-year-old's awareness of confusion felt by young people.

Hovde, Carl F., and Robert C. Gilmore. 117:40,412 (1968/09/15) VI, 40.
Letters responding to Michener's article of August 18, 1968, titled "The
Revolution in Middle Class Values."

Mallinkoff, Dean. (1968/09/22) VI, 37. Letter to the editor in response to Michener's article,
August 18, 1968, titled "The Revolution in Middle Class Values."

Lewis, Flora. 120:41,175 (1970/10/18) VI, 64.
Letter lauds Michener's article of September 27, 1970.

Kurzman, Dan. 120:41,189 (1970/11/01) VI, 111.
Letter admiring objectivity of Michener's article of September 27, 1970.

Appendix II - Newspaper Articles About JAMES A. MICHENER

New York Times Magazine (continued)
"Michener's Progress Report." Toby, Sidney, and Mrs. Lyde H. Brenner.
120:41,518 (1971/09/26) VI, 98. Letters to the editor. Responses to Michener's article
of September 5, 1971, titled "One and a Half Cheers for Progress."

"Modest Proposal." Schindler, Saul. 122:42,190 (1973/07/29) VI, 2. Letter.
Reply to Michener's article "Is America Burning?" The writer believes Nixon should resign.

"The Michener Phenomenon." James, Caryn. 124:46,526 (1985/09/08) VI, 44-46+.
Discusses factors of Michener's success; notes latest and longest book, "Texas," will have
first printing of 750,000.

New York Tribune Book Review
"Royalties Aren't the Only Reward." (1963/12/01) VII, 5, 60.
Authors respond to The Book Review query about, besides money, what satisfaction do they
get from the popularity of their book.

"About Books and Authors: Introduction to Manhood." McDowell, Edwin.
(1982/10/03) VII, 34. Michener claims that of all the novels he had written to date
("Space" was latest), "The Fires of Spring" got most fan mail.

"Symposium: Books That Gave Me Pleasure." (1982/12/05) VII, 9, 63.
Michener says the best book on narrative is Erich Auerbach's "Mimesis:
The Representation of Reality in Western Literature."

The Oregonian
"Wife working partner in Michener writing." Wohler, Milly. (1986/12/07)
NewsBank, Names in the News, 1986, fiche 83, grid G3. Michener selected
as the first honorary member of Society of American Travel Writers.

Orlando Sentinel
"Bound for Florida." Trimarchia, Mickey. (1986/10/15) A2.
"Texas" completed, Michener is ready to start a novel about the Caribbean.

"Michener's Real Story: Ageless Quest For Learning." Thompson, Bailey. (1990/03/18) H3.
Michener is role model for retired octogenarians, dedicating efforts to programs for retired
professionals.

"Michener Threatens to Leave Random House." McDowell, Edwin. (1990/03/22) E4.

"Michener To Give School $1 Million." (1990/03/22) B4. Michener pledges $1 million to
the University of Miami, where he spent 3 years working on "Caribbean."

"Author Offers Advice, Help to 3 Convicted Men." (1990/06/07) A14.
Judge John Carey orders defendants, convicted of anti-Semitic vandalism,
to read "Poland" to learn about the holocaust.

"Michener Protection Plan - Great Wall of Wyoming." (1990/07/01) A2.
Michener, in Wyoming to celebrate the state's centennial, advises citizens
to preserve state as a national treasure.

"Michener Says His Secret is Sticking to a Routine." Keever, Jack.
(1990/10/12) A2. Interview.

Appendix II - Newspaper Articles About JAMES A. MICHENER

Orlando Sentinel (continued)
"James Michener." (1992/11/22) 4.
Drug traffic makes the Florida airports the most dangerous in the world.

Philadelphia Bulletin
"Michener to Critics: 'Someone Reads Me.'" Eisenberg, D. D. (1974/09/13)?
Noted in "Authors in the News. Vol. 1." Detroit: Gale Research, 1976, pp. 338-39.

Philadelphia Evening Bulletin
"Author Michener Reluctant On Bid To Run For Congress." (1962/01/24) B22.

Philadelphia Inquirer
"Michener, Dr. Barnes in Stormy Feud Over Art and Life on the Main Line."
(1950/04/05) 11. Michener's ruse to obtain a private viewing of Barnes' hidden
art collection.

"Barnes Wanted 'Plain People' Admitted To Art Gallery." Miller, Joseph. (1962/04/05).

"Interview with author James Michener." Goulden, Joseph C. (1965/11/21) 1.

"Michener Owes U. S. $390,103 in Taxes, IRS Officials Claim." Cahill,
Jerome S. (1967/12/26) 1, 37.

"James Michener Finds a New 'South Pacific' in a Jungle Village."
(1972/08/31) 23.

"Michener: Last Stand In Bucks." Neal, Steve. (1974/01/14) 1.

Javers, Ron. (1974/09/08) B10.
Reports Michener's summary of the Bicentennial Commissions' Bipartisanship.

"Tales of James Michener, From Bali Ha'i to Chesapeake Bay." Ecenbarger,
William. (1977/11/27) 33. Today Section.

"A Novel Job For Michener." DeWolf, Rose. (1977/12/26) C1.
Regarding Michener's participation in Pennsylvania's Constitutional Convention.

"A Michener review of his epic success." Herman, Jan. (1981/01/01) A9-12.
Interview following "Chesapeake." Michener reacts to critics' pans.

"James Michener in Space." Ecenbarger, William. (1982/10/10) 17-19, 35.
Today Section.

"A home-town tribute to Michener." Fine, Mary Jane. (1985/05/09) A1,14.
Doylestown rolls out red carpet for its favorite son.

"A writer at work with the eyes of Texas upon him." Leary, Mike.
(1985/06/04) E1, 10. Michener adopts Texas and Texans adopt Michener.

"Michener says his novel-in-progress is 'the last of the big books.'"
Nieuwsma, Milton. (1989/01/02) NewsBank, Names in the News, 1989, fiche 50,
grid F6. Interview of Michener following publication of "Alaska," and preparation for new
book about the Caribbean.

Appendix II - Newspaper Articles About JAMES A. MICHENER

Philadelphia Inquirer (continued)

"Author Michener to college: Merge." Beans, Kathleen Martin. (1991/03/08). NewsBank, Literature, 1991, fiche 28, grid B3. Delaware Valley College, founded by Rabbi Joseph Krauskopf in 1896, advised by Michener to merge with Pennsylvania State University.

"Tales of James Michener." Horner, Carol. (1992/03/03) NewsBank, Names in the News, 1992, fiche 58, grid F3. Discusses "The World is My Home," Michener's autobiography, and birthday parties in Manhatten.

Quakertown Free Press

"Michener Name Opposed by 750." (1972/10/10). Community objects to naming a library after Michener.

Rocky Mountain News

"Author would like to be in pictures." Sumners, Ruth. (1973/04/10) 44. A summary of Michener's three-hour workshop for young writers.

"Noted author claims role in state's growth." (1976/02/18) 6. Michener addresses Colorado Assembly and advises that the growth problem is more acute there than anywhere else.

"Pen, ink and paint." Dickenson, Carol. (1990/10/14) NewsBank, Names in the News, 1990, fiche 290, grid E11. 5,400 Japanese prints were donated to the Honolulu Academy of Arts, and 130 American works were donated to the University of Texas.

"A bold stance." Shiflett, Dave. (1993/04/03) A62. Editorial regarding Michener's article on homosexuals.

Rutland Herald

"Class Act: Michener Brings His Skills to the Classroom." Mulligan, Hugh A. (1993/04/09).

Sacramento Bee

"One for the books." (1992/03/26) NewsBank, Names in the News, 1992, fiche 85, grid G1. Michener advises aspiring writers to read Oates, Updike, Rice, Mailer, Cheever, Vidal and me, and then develop own visions.

San Diego Union

"Jim Michener at 87: A paragon of integrity." (1994/06/19) A2.

San Francisco Chronicle

(1952/05/06).

"Micheners Giving Away Art Collection." (1988/11/19) C6.

St. Petersburg Times

"Michener." Eliason, Niela. (1990/12/02) D1. Interview. Michener discusses education, the military buildup in the Middle East, growing old in America and retirement.

"Michener wraps up season in the sun." Miller, Betty Jean. (1991/02/02) NewsBank, Names in the News, 1991, fiche 56, grid A2. Michener joins Peter Meinke to teach a creative writing class under the Academy of Senior Professionals at Eckerd College.

Appendix II - Newspaper Articles About JAMES A. MICHENER

St. Petersburg Times (continued)
"Michener." Miller, Dave. (1993/02/07) D6. Reactions to a four week writing seminar conducted by Michener at Eckerd College.

Star-Ledger
"Tales of Michener." Sleed, Joel. (1988/06/19) NewsBank, Names in the News, 1988, fiche 193, grid E12. On the road to the 'Caribbean' with best-selling author.

Sun Sentinel (Miami)
"Michener: After Three Years in Miami a Long Goodbye from the Author Whose Home is Everywhere and Nowhere." Wilson, Amy. (1989/11/13) D1, 4.

Sunday Intelligencer
"Now, Michener sizes up Texas." Reeves, Monica. (1983/05/15) C7. Michener researches Texas.

"Abington man devoted 10 years to biography." Hill, David C. (1985/01/20) C1,12. Discusses "James A. Michener, A Biography," by John P. Hayes.

"Michener: the man, his roots....and the conflict." von Dobneck, Monica. (1985/01/20) C1,12. Discusses "James A. Michener, A Biography," by John P. Hayes.

"Michener returns to Bucks, a 'prophet' honored at home." Leffler, Peter J. (1985/05/05) A4.

Swarthmore Phoenix
"Two Out of Five Open Scholars Are Chosen From Pennsylvania." (1925/06/15) 1.

"Freshman Basketball Team Victors in First Two Games." (1926/01/19) 5.

"Collection Cuts." (1926/04/13) 6. "Collections" were daily convocations of students and faculty. Michener talked about his interest in traveling.

"Phi Delta Theta Wins Over Kappa Sigma in Interfraternity Finals." (1927/01/11) 5. Michener played basketball for Phi Delta Theta and his team won the Interfraternity basketball tournament.

"Lion and Kangaroo Produce Show With Twenty Lively Acts." (1927/11/22) 1-2. Michener performed in the student annual variety Hamburg Show.

"Five Interfraternity Basketball Contests Open Season This Year." (1927/12/06) 3.

"Little Theater Club Gives Unusual Drama as Spring Production." (1928/05/01) 1-3. Michener debuted as Henry in "Outward Bound."

"Michener Promotes Spirit By Speech At Mass Meeting." (1928/10/30) 5.

"Roaring Garnet Lion Prepares Snappy Acts for Hamburg Carnival." (1928/11/20) 3. Michener plays one part of a two-person pantomime, "The Hero."

"Swarthmore Celebrates As Talented Thespians Revel in Novel Roles." (1928/11/27) 1+. Michener's role was "superb" and the two-person pantomime "brought down the house."

Appendix II - Newspaper Articles About JAMES A. MICHENER

Swarthmore Phoenix (continued)

"M. S. G. A. Nominations For Second Semester at Regular Meeting." (1929/01/08) 3. Michener spoke against the publication of unsigned letters in the student newspaper at the mens student government meeting.

"Losing Streak Ends As Basketball Team Downs Ursinus Five." (1929/02/19) 5.

"Cast of Senior-Junior Play `Twelfth Night' Chosen After Tryout." (1929/03/05) 1.

"Delta Upsilon and Phi Psi in Final Round of Basketball Tourney." (1929/03/05) 3.

"Swarthmore Defeated By Main Line Quintet in Mediocre Struggle." (1929/03/05) 1+.

"James Michener Chosen to Deliver Ivy Oration Baccalaureate Sunday." (1929/03/19) 1.

"Students Launch Campaign to Aid Endowment Drive." (1929/04/23) 1-2. Michener supported 100% student participation in the alumni endowment drive.

"Student Body Unanimously Backs Endowment Drive." (1929/04/30) 6.

"Five Original Plays To Be Given By Curtain Theater." (1929/05/7) 3. Mentions Michener's one act play "Gold."

"Beatrice Beach Wins First Award in 1929 One-Act Play Contest." (1929/05/14) 1-2. Michener's play "Gold" won second.

"Phi Beta Kappa." (1929/06/03) 1. Michener is inducted and graduated with Highest Honors, the Swarthmore equivalent of Summa Cum Laude.

"Swarthmore Confers One Hundred Twelve Degrees on Students." (1929/06/03) 5.

"Men's Fall Handicap Tennis Matches Draw Big Crowd of Entries." (1929/09/29) 1+.

Tampa Tribune

"Emperor of the Epic." Feeney, Kathy. (1991/03/03) NewsBank, Names in the News, 1991, fiche 80, grid B9. Eckerd College Students pay for $10 seats for "A Conversation with James A. Michener," and to pay him homage.

Times Chronicle

"'You never know what sets a mind on fire.'" Gittings, Elizabeth A. (1985/05/30) ? Michener admires Bobby Fischer and Tennessee Williams, disappointed to lose congressional race, enjoyed working on Pennsylvania Constitution.

Torch (Doylestown High School)

"Basketball Team, 1922-23." (1923/06) Commencement Number of The Class of Nineteen Hundred and Twenty-three - Doylestown High School. Michener and team photo.

"Athletics." Van Pelt, J. 8:2 (1923/12) 14-15.

"Athletics." Van Pelt, J. 8: 2 (1923/12) 18, 23.

"Athletics." Van Pelt, J. 8: 4 (1924/02-03) 24.

Appendix II - Newspaper Articles About JAMES A. MICHENER

Torch (Doylestown High School) (continued)
"Athletics." Van Pelt, J. 8:4 (1924/02-03) 18-20.

"Athletics." Van Pelt, J. 8:5 (1924/05-06) 20-21.

"[Basketball Team, 1923-24]." (1924/June) Commencement Number of The
Class of 1924 - Doylestown High School. Michener and team photo.

"James Michener." (1925/06) Commencement Issue. A photograph and capsule
biography of Michener indicating his desire to become a mathematics teacher.
The stated date of birth is February 3, 1908? Michener served as Class President and Editor
of the Torch, the Doylestown High School newspaper. He played both baseball and basketball
and reputedly had the biggest feet in the class of '25. The Commencement Issue recaps the
four years activities of the class in a two page article titled "The Grand Army
of the Class of 1925."

USA Today
(1984/03/16). ABC's option on "Texas" for a ten-episode mini-series.

Variety
"Michener 'Source' May be NBC Mini; Durgan's Newsies." 268:13 (1972/11/08) 35.

Washington Post Children's Book World
(1967/11/05).

Wall Street Journal
"Bucks County Gets Michener Museum." MacLeod, Pamela J. (1989/04/10) A12.
James A. Michener Arts Center of Bucks County, Pennsylvania. Leisure and
Arts Section.

Washington Post
"James A. Michener's Imagination." Warga, Wayne. (1974/07/08) H18-20.

"South Pacific: How it Came About." Tuck, Lon. (1977/08/21) F1, 3-4.

"James Michener." Arana-Ward, Marie. 23:40 (1993/10/03). Biographical background.
Michener has just completed a new novel, "Recessional," about Florida retirement home
characters.

Washington Post Book World
"Paperbacks - Bizarre Bazaar." Petersen, Clarence. 3:45 (1969/11/09) 21.
Announces paperback publication of "Presidential Lottery."

"How the West Was Lost." Stafford, Jean. (1974/09/01) 1-2.

"James A. Michener: Life and Literature American Style." Eron, Carol.(1976/09/19) 1, 3.

"James Michener Bridges the Bay." Gibbons, Boyd. (1978/07/09) E1-4.

Washington Times
"Michener: 'Working at top energy.'" Hagman, Harvey. (1986/08/06)
NewsBank, Names in the News, 1986, fiche 13, grid B1. Interview of Michener following his
heart operation and at the time he was finalizing the writing of "Alaska."

Appendix II - Newspaper Articles About JAMES A. MICHENER

Washington Times (continued)

"'Working even more intensely.'" Hagman, Harvey. (1987/09/14) NewsBank, Names in the news, 1987, fiche 333, grid F5. Biographical information following the publication of "Legacy."

"Michener dives into Caribbean for novel." Hagman, Harvey. (1989/03/28) NewsBank, Names in the News, 1989, fiche 104, grid E11. Interview with Michener regarding his research for "Caribbean."

"Michener's writing takes a side trip to Cuba." Hagman, Harvey. (1989/09/28) NewsBank, Names in the News, 1989, fiche 290, grid G11. Michener and John Kings visit Cuba for background material for "Caribbean," and write "Six Days in Havana."

Appendix III - Critics' Reviews of Books by JAMES A. MICHENER

Alaska

"Alaska." *Magill Book Reviews.*

"Story of Alaska takes a big book." Hutshing, Ed. *San Diego Union*, (1988/06/19)
NewsBank, Literature, 1988, fiche 88, grid G14. A fairly clear picture of a state that
few know about. Michener fans will rejoice while others yawn.

"Michener's 'Alaska.' " Patty, Stanton H. *Seattle Times*, (1988/06/19)
NewsBank, Literature, 1988, fiche 89, grid A7. The author concludes
"The Great Alaskan Novel still has not been written."

"Michener's Cautionary Tale of the 49th State." Lehmann-Haupt, Christopher.
New York Times, 137:47,545 (1988/06/23) III, 21.

"A Nice Place For Mastodons." Jennings, Gary.
New York Times Book Review, 93:26. (1988/06/26) VII, 7.

"Book Review. (Fiction)." Hinkemeyer, Joan. *Library Journal*, 113:12 (1988/07) 93.

"Michener's 'Alaska' draws mixed reviews." Olson, Wallace M.
Juneau Empire, (1988/07/01) NewsBank, Literature, 1988, fiche 88, grid G13.
Reviewer finds "Alaska" superficial and contrived and misstating some
parts of Southeast native culture.

"Like life itself, 'Alaska' is sometimes a lot of work." Hunt, Bill. *Anchorage Daily News*,
(1988/07/03) NewsBank, Literature, 1988, fiche 88, grid G3. Critical of characterization,
plot, humor, contrived themes. Acknowledges Michener has a "decent message."

"A Magnum of Michener." McDaniel, Maude A. *Chicago Tribune*, (1988/07/03)
NewsBank, Literature, 1988, fiche 39, grid A2. Vowing not to be charmed again,
the reviewer admits "Michener has done it again."

"Michener's 'Alaska.'" Hunt, Bill. *Fairbanks Daily News-Miner*, (1988/07/03)
NewsBank, Literature, 1988, fiche 38, grid G10. Critical of characterization, plot, humor,
contrived themes. Reviewer acknowledges that Michener has a "decent message."

"Texas Was Too Small." Bodett, Tom. *Los Angeles Times Book Review*, (1988/07/03) 1, 7.

"James Michener's Alaska: Gold, Glaciers, and Grandeur." Brown, Chip.
Washington Post Book World, (1988/07/03) 1-2.

Time, 132:1 (1988/07/04) 70.

" 'Alaska' another hefty Michener melodrama." Finn, Robert. *Plain Dealer*, (1988/07/10)
NewsBank, Literature, 1988, fiche 89, grid A5. Melodrama, history, didacticism and
coincidence, leaving the reader feeling he knows the place.

"Michener Misses." Hamilton, Edith. *St. Petersburg Times*, (1988/07/10)
NewsBank, Literature, 1988, fiche 89, grid A1. Reviewer concludes "The brutal history
and the equally brutal beauty of Alaska deserve better than this."

Appendix III - Critics' Reviews of Books by JAMES A. MICHENER

Alaska (continued)

"Novel serves Natives but lacks in research." Olson, Wallace. *The Tundra Times*, (1988/07/11) NewsBank, Literature, 1988, fiche 88, grid G9. The positive impact of the book is to reveal the prejudice and unfair treatment suffered by natives.

"Michener's Alaska: Fine characters abound." Hauser. Jerald, *Milwaukee Journal*, (1988/07/12) NewsBank, Literature, 1988, fiche 76, grid C2. Reviewer discerns that Michener's animals have almost Disneylike identities. Believes praise is warranted.

"Michener's Alaskan installment." Nussbaum, Paul. *Philadelphia Inquirer*, (1988/07/12) NewsBank, Literature, 1988, fiche 76, grid B14. Siberians cross Bering land bridge, become Aleuts who are subjugated by Russians who sell to Americans.

"Few surprises on the long, long road to 'Alaska.'" Lehmann-Haupt, *Christopher Times Picayune*, (1988/07/17) NewsBank, Literature, 1988. fiche 89, grid A3.

"Alaska Comes to life in Michener's latest." Russo-Morin, Donna. *Journal*, (1988/07/19) NewsBank, Literature, 1988, fiche 76, grid C1. Reviewer believes that the novelistic portions are rewarding and overcome the textbook portions.

"Grit, stubbornness keys to survival in 'Alaska.'" Simon, Bruce R. *Richmond Times-Dispatch*, (1988/07/24) NewsBank, Literature, 1988, fiche 89, grid A6. It shall awaken reader's motivation to explore this kaleidoscopic state nicknamed "The Last Frontier."

"Michener On The Northern Frontier." Vines, Tom. *Wall Street Journal*, (1988/08/05) 15.

"Michener's 'Alaska' staggers in size, but shrinks in grandeur."Chandonnet, Ann. *Anchorage Times*, (1988/08/07) NewsBank, Literature, 1988, fiche 102, grid C12. Local citizens will find many shortcomings but the book may inspire strangers to explore.

America vs. America

"America vs. America." *Best Sellers*, (1969/06/15) 127.

"Just the Facts Please." Peterson, Clarence. *Chicago Tribune Book World*, (1969/01/08) 13.

The Bridge at Andau

Kirkus, 25 (1957/02/01) 123.

"Can You Spank a Child Who has Been Blowing Up Tanks?" Pisco, Ernest S. *Christian Science Monitor*, 49:79 (1957/02/28) 9.

Hogan, William. *San Francisco Chronicle*, (1957/02/28) 23.

"Books of the Times." Prescott, Orville. *New York Times*, 106:36,196 (1957/03/01) 21. Michener's dedication to good causes hurts his fiction but creates memorable reporting.

"Exodus to Freedom." Lengyel, Emil. *Saturday Review*, 40:9 (1957/03/02) 13.

Simmons, Walter. *Chicago Sunday Tribune*, (1957/03/03) 1.

Shuster, G.N. *New York Herald Tribune Book Review*, (1957/03/03) 3.

Appendix III - Critics' Reviews of Books by JAMES A. MICHENER

The Bridge at Andau (continued)
"Twelve Days that Shook the World." MacCormac, John.
New York Times Book Review, 52:9 (1957/03/03) VII, 1.
"Hungary's revolution is fought again in Mr. Michener's telling of the story."

Time, 69:9 (1957/03/04) 104.

"Books: Briefly Noted. (General)." *New Yorker*, 33:4 (1957/03/16) 149.

"Reader's Choice." Rolo, Charles J. *Atlantic*, 199:4 (1957/04) 86.

Bookmark, 16 (1957/04) 157.

"On Our List." Barrett, Mary Ellen, and Marvin Barrett.
Good Housekeeping, 144: 4 (1957/04) 275-78. Mentions Michener's TV essay
"Assignment Southeast Asia," to be a 90 minute NBC Program.

Booklist, 53 (1957/04/01) 401.

"Uneven Report." Wilhelmsen, Frederick D. *Commonweal*, 66:2 (1957/04/12) 45-46.

"New Books Appraised." Grimm, Ben E. *Library Journal*, 82:8 (1957/04/15) 1057.

Ignotus, Paul. *New Statesman & Nation,* 53 (1957/04/20) 521.

Cleveland Open Shelf, (1957/05) 14.

Wisconsin Library Bulletin, 53 (1957/05) 397.

"The Fight for Hungary." *Times[London] Literary Supplement*, 2881 (1957/05/17) 299.

Scoggin, M.C. *Horn Book*, 33 (1957/08) 318.

Catholic World, 186 (1957/10) V.

The Bridges at Toko-ri
"New Books Appraised." Walbridge, Earle F. *Library Journal*, 78:13 (1953/07) 1232.

Kirkus, 21 (1953/07/01) 395.

"Books of the Times." Poore, Charles. *New York Times*, 102:34,858 (1953/07/02) 21.
Published first in the current issue of *Life* magazine (5 million copies).

"The Few and the Many." Sawyer, Roland.
Christian Science Monitor, 45:189 (1953/07/09) 11.

"Books of the Times." Poore, Charles. *New York Times*, 102:34,865 (1953/07/09) 23.
Michener's book is contrasted with "The Deep Six," by Martin Dibner.

"The War Nobody Loves." Kelly, James. *Saturday Review*, 36:28 (1953/07/11) 22-23.

Havighurst, Walter. *Chicago Sunday Tribune*, (1953/07/12) 3.

Appendix III - Critics' Reviews of Books by JAMES A. MICHENER

The Bridges at Toko-ri (continued)
Reynolds, Quentin. *New York Herald Tribune Book Review*, (1953/07/12) 1.

"Once He Had Been Part of those Jets." Payne, Robert.
New York Times Book Review, 48:28 (1953/07/12) VII, 5.

Jackson, J. H. *San Francisco Chronicle*, (1953/07/12) 16.

"Books - Corn from Korea." *Newsweek*, 42:2 (1953/07/13) 89-90.

"Sacrifices of the Few." *Time*, 62:2 (1953/07/13) 102.

Kennebeck, Edwin. *Commonweal*, 58:17 (1953/07/31) 426-27.

"Books: Briefly Noted." *New Yorker*, 29:24 (1953/08/01) 55.

Webster, H. C. *New Republic*, 129 (1953/08/17) 20.

"Reader's Choice." Rolo, Charles J. *Atlantic*, 192:3 (1953/09) 78-79.

Booklist, 50 (1953/09/01) 13.

Bookmark, 13 (1953/10) 10.

Hughes, Riley. *Catholic World*, 178 (1953/10) 71.

Wisconsin Library Bulletin, 49 (1953/10) 211.

Horn Book, 29 (1953/12) 469.

Caravans
"Review of Caravans." Gilbert, Highet. *Book-of-the-Month Club*, (1963).
Book-of-the-Month Club Bulletin.

"Lost in the Mazes of Afghanistan." Prescott, Orville.
New York Times, 112: 38,548 (1963/08/09) 21.

"Bull Market." *Time*, 82:6 (1963/08/09) 76-79.

"Books: Briefly Noted." *New Yorker*, 39:25 (1963/08/10) 89.

Kluger, Richard. *New York Herald Tribune Book Review*, (1963/08/11) 5.

"Harem Girl From Bryn Mawr." Payne, Robert.
New York Times Book Review, 58:19 (1963/08/11) VII, 4-5.

"Geography Lesson." *Newsweek*, 62:7 (1963/08/12) 82.

Cargas, Harry J. *America,* 109:9 (1963/08/31) 217-18.

"The Atlantic Bookshelf." Weeks, Edward. *Atlantic*, 212:3 (1963/09) 118.

Grady, R. F. *Best Sellers*, 23:11 (1963/09/01) 181.

Appendix III - Critics' Reviews of Books by JAMES A. MICHENER

Caravans (continued)

"Calcified Country." Kalp, Bernard. *Saturday Review*, 46:36 (1963/09/07) 35.

"New Books Appraised." Sandoe, James. *Library Journal*, 88:16 (1963/09/15) 3225.

"Michener's New Novel." P.M.[?]. *Christian Science Monitor*, 55:256 (1963/09/26) 13.

Grumbach, Doris. *Critic*, 22 (1963/10) 83.

"Notes on Current Books." *Virginia Quarterly Review*, 40:1 (1964/Winter) ix.

Caribbean

"Caribbean." *Magill Book Reviews*, ISSN 0890-7722.

"Caribbean." Diehl, Digby. *Modern Maturity*, 32:5 (1989/10-11) 82.

"Caribbean." Bernikow, Louise. *Cosmopolitan*, 207:5 (1989/11) 50.

"The Caribbean As Lead Character In A Michener Novel." Mitgang,
Herbert. *New York Times*, 139:48,042 (1989/11/02) III, 23.

"'Caribbean' barely scratches islands surface." Lorber, Helene.
Detroit Free Press, (1989/11/05) NewsBank, Literature, 1989, fiche 127, grid C10.

"Encyclopedic Tone Of 'Caribbean' Is Also Entertaining." O'Briant, Don.
Journal (Atlanta), (1989/11/05) NewsBank, Literature, 1989, fiche 127, grid C9.

"Slimmer Epic: Michener novel has a narrower scope but still is powerful." Hauser, Jerald.
Milwaukee Journal, (1989/11/05) NewsBank, Literature, 1989, fiche 127, grid D2.

"Paradise Tales." Houston, Robert.
New York Times Book Review, 94:45 (1989/11/05) VII, 22.

"Michener navigates the Caribbean." Corbett, Christopher.
Philadelphia Inquirer, (1989/11/05) NewsBank, Literature, 1989, fiche 127, grid C11.

"Michener portrays 'Caribbean' islands as land of violence." Hutshing, Ed.
San Diego Union, (1989/11/05) NewsBank, Literature, 1989, fiche 127, grid C7.

"Choppy Waters for Michener's 'Caribbean.'" Jensen, Lisa.
San Francisco Examiner, (1989/11/05) NewsBank, Literature, 1989, fiche 127, grid C8.
Lacks the "soaring, concentrated power of a great novel."
Offers interesting minutiae of the islands.

"'CARIBBEAN': Michener weaves masterful tale from historical vantage point."
Acquaviva, Michael A. *Pittsburgh Press*, (1989/11/12) NewsBank, Literature, 1989,
fiche 127, grid C13. Meticulous research combined with masterful storytelling.

"The Middle C of The Americas." Hearne, John.
Washington Post Book World, (1989/11/12) 4.

"Michener sails formula 'Tales' into Caribbean." Mitgang, Herbert.
Tribune (Oakland), (1989/11/15) NewsBank, Literature, 1989, fiche 127, grid C6.

Appendix III - Critics' Reviews of Books by JAMES A. MICHENER

Caribbean (continued)

"Human drama saves 'Caribbean' from facts." O'Briant, Don.
Denver Post, (1989/11/19) D10.

"People - And the Ship Sailed On." Mitchell, E. *Time*, 134:21 (1989/11/20) 96.
Reports on Michener's new book that it is to be his last epic.

"Michener's Caribbean lacks color." Holwill, Richard N. *Washington Times* (D.C.),
(1989/11/27) NewsBank, Literature, 1989, fiche 127, grid C14.

"James A. Michener runs aground in Caribbean." Martin, Virginia.
Birmingham News, (1989/12/03) NewsBank, Literature, 1989, fiche 7, grid A11.

"Michener Leaves fans adrift in 'Caribbean.'" Hellmuth, Ann.
Orlando Sentinal, (1989/12/03) NewsBank, Literature, 1989, fiche 7, grid A12.

"Michener hits bull's-eye." Perry, Roy E. *Nashville Banner*, (1989/12/16)
NewsBank, Literature, 1989, fiche 7, grid A14. The reviewer considers this
Michener's best novel since "The Source." A master storyteller.

"'Caribbean' has its good, bad points." Alexander, James E.
Pittsburgh Post Gazette, (1989/12/16) NewsBank, Literature, 1989, fiche 7, grid A13.

"Caribbean - The Big Christmas Book." *Rave Reviews*, 22 (1989/12-1) 8.

"'Caribbean' visit is a welcome return." Cregan, Lori.
Wichita Eagle, (1990/01/14) NewsBank, Literature, 1990, fiche 18, grid A1.

Centennial

"Centennial." Hutchens, John K. *Book-of-the-Month Club News*, (1974/09) 1-3.

"LJ: Book Review." Eyth, Mary Jo. *Library Journal*, 99:15 (1974/09/01) 2091.

"Once Upon a Time 136,000,000 Years Ago." Frakes, James R.
New York Times Book Review, 79:36 (1974/09/08) VII, 6.

Javers, Ron. *Philadelphia Inquirer*, (1974/09/08) B10.

"Oehippus Opera." Cooper, Arthur. *Newsweek*, 84:12 (1974/09/16) 82-86.

"Stately American Novel." Stuart, James. *New Republic*, 171 (1974/09/21) 21-22.

Barnes, Julian. *Times Literary Supplement*, (1974/09/22) 1308.

"Happy Birthday, America." Morrow, Lance. *Time*, 104:13 (1974/09/23) 96-97.

Wilkinson, Burke. *Christian Science Monitor*, (1974/09/25) 11.

"From Heroic Acts to Hiccups." Lehmann-Haupt, Christopher.
New York Times, 124:42,615 (1974/09/27) 39.

Appendix III - Critics' Reviews of Books by JAMES A. MICHENER

Centennial (continued)
"Books and Authors: Two authors at top form." Newquist, Roy.
Palm Springs Life, 17:2 (1974/10) 118. "It is impossible to name a better
novel written by an American." Noted in "Authors in the News."

Grady, R. F. *Best Sellers*, 34:14 (1974/10/15) 323.

"The Peripatetic Reviewer." Weeks, Edward. *Atlantic*, 234:5 (1974/11) 118-19.

Hill, W. B. *America*, 131 (1974/11/16) 301.

"Michener's Deluge." Bryant, Rene Kuhn. *National Review*, 26:47 (1974/11/22) 1365.

"Passing pterodactyl." Barnes, Julian.
Times[London] Literary Supplement, 3794 (1974/11/22) 1308.

"Friendly Elephant." Straub, Peter. *New Statesman*, (1974/11/29) 794-95.

Chesapeake
"Book Review." Michaud, Charles. *Library Journal*, 103:13 (1978/07) 1436.

"Summer Reading." *Time,* 112:2 (1978/07/10) 80.

"An American Vision." Yardley, Jonathan.
New York Times Book Review, 83:30 (1978/07/23) VII, 11.

"My Best Advice." Beatty, Jack. *Newsweek*, 92 (1978/07/24) 82.

"Books of the Times." Lehmann-Haupt, Christopher.
New York Times, 127:44,019 (1978/08/01) III, 7.

"Books: Briefly Noted." *New Yorker*, 54:26 (1978/08/14) 98.

"Typhoon on the Bay." Wills, Gary. *New York Review of Books*, 25 (1978/08/17) 31-32.

O'Brien, Dominic V. *Best Sellers*, 38:6 (1978/09) 171.

"Poop Poop." Mano, D. Keith. *National Review*, 30 (1978/09/15) 1153-54.

"Maryland's Eastern Shore Gets Michener Touch." Phillips, Barbara.
Christian Science Monitor, 70:206 (1978/09/18) B3.

LaSalle, Peter. *America*, 139:8 (1978/09/23) 182.

Schene, Carol. *School Library Journal*, 25:4 (1978/12) 72.

The Covenant
"Book Review." Michaud, Charles.
Library Journal, 105:18 (1980/10/15) 2233.

"Skimming Over South Africa." Brink, Andre.
Washington Post Book World, (1980/11/02) 3.

Appendix III - Critics' Reviews of Books by JAMES A. MICHENER

The Covenant (continued)
"Michener's Sweeping South African Saga." Winder, David.
Christian Science Monitor, 72:344 (1980/11/10) B1, 11.

"Books of the Times." Leonard, John. *New York Times*, 130:44,767 (1980/11/14) III, 29.

"Michener: The Novelist As Teacher." Burns, John F.
New York Times Book Review, 85:47 (1980/11/23) VII, 3, 27.

"Lost in the Veldt." Anello, Ray. *Newsweek*, 96:21 (1980/11/24) 113-14.

"The Covenant." Gannon, Thomas M. *America*, 144 (1981/01/24) 66-67.

"Black and White." McWhirter, William. *Time,* 117:6 (1981/02/09) 94.

"James Michener's Docudramas." Bell, Pearl K. *Commentary*, 71:4 (1981/04) 71-73.
Concludes "What we have here is a new genre of the information age."

Cosgrave, M. S. *Horn Book*, 57 (1981/06) 335.

Washington Post Book World, (1981/12/06) 29.

Creatures of the Kingdom
"Creatures of the Kingdom: Stories of Animals and Nature." Hooper, Brad.
Booklist, 89 (1993/07) 1918.

"Creatures of the Kingdom: Stories About Animals and Nature."
Publishers Weekly, 240 (1993/08/23) 57.

"Creatures of the Kingdom: Stories of Animals and Nature." Stapler, Elizabeth.
Christian Science Monitor, 85 (1993/11/23) 11.

"Creatures of the Kingdom." *BookNews*, (1993) 24.
A Book-of-the-Month Club publication.

The Drifters
McCullough, David W. *Saturday Review*, 54:18 (1971/05/01) 39-40.

"The Peripatetic Reviewer." Weeks, Edward. *Atlantic*, 227:6 (1971/06) 100-1.

"Jim the Middle-Aged Youth-Watcher." Maddocks, Melvin. *Life*,
70:21 (1971/06/04) 12.

"Live It Up While You Can." Lask, Thomas. *New York Times*,
120:41,410 (1971/06/10) 41.

Phillipson, John S. *Best Sellers*, 31:6 (1971/06/15) 135.

"The Drifters." Sourian, Peter.
New York Times Book Review, 76:26 (1971/06/27) VII, 6, 31.

"Novels - Ah, Wilderness." Frakes, J. R.
Washington Post Book World, 5:29 (1971/07/18) 2.

Appendix III - Critics' Reviews of Books by JAMES A. MICHENER

The Drifters (continued)
"The Pick of The Paperbacks." Peterson, Clarence.
Washington Post Book World, (1972/06/08) 21. Crest $1.25.

"Adrift in Spain, Portugal, and Africa in the 1970's." Mosely, Bob.
La Busca, 29 (1993/11-12) 22-27.

The Eagle and The Raven
"The Eagle and the Raven." Steinberg, Sybil. *Publishers Weekly*,
237:29 (1990/07/20) 49.

"The Eagle and the Raven." Salzberg, Charles.
New York Times Book Review, 95:39 (1990/09/30) VII, 28.

"Michener's cuts find new life." Finn, Robert. *Plain Dealer*, (1990/10/14)
NewsBank, Literature, 1990, fiche 113, grid F12. A "wildly interesting story" told with
"practiced professionalism."

"Michener Draws on Research Of Texas." Bass, Calvin G. *Tulsa World*,
(1991/02/04) NewsBank, Literature, 1991, fiche 28, grid B4.
Strongly recommended by a longtime fan of James Michener.

The Fires of Spring
Kirkus, 16 (1948/12/01) 630.

"New Books Appraised." McDonald, Gerald D. *Library Journal*, 74:1 (1949/01/01) 60.

Jackson. J. H. *San Francisco Chronicle*, (1949/02/04) 16.

"Young Man Comes of Age, Grimly." DuBois, William. *New York Times
Book Review*, 44:6 (1949/02/06) VII, 7.

Prescott, Orville. *New York Times*, 98:33,252 (1949/02/07) 17.
Also in "In My Opinion." New York: Bobbs-Merrill, 1952, pp. 146-64.

Motley, Willard. *Chicago Sun*, (1949/02/09).

Trilling, Diana. *Nation*, 168:8 (1949/02/12) 192.

Burns, John Horne. *Saturday Review of Literature*, 32:7 (1949/02/12) 16-17.

Ross, J. D. *New York Herald Tribune Book Review*, (1949/02/13) 3.

Time, 53:7 (1949/02/14) 103.

"A Stream of American Life." Reynolds, Horace.
Christian ScienceMonitor, 41:68 (1949/02/15) 16.

"Briefly Noted - Fiction." *New Yorker*, 24:51 (1949/02/19) 90.

Rolo, Charles J. *Atlantic*, 183:3 (1949/03) 84-85.

Catholic World, 169 (1949/05) 158.

Appendix III - Critics' Reviews of Books by JAMES A. MICHENER

The Fires of Spring (continued)
"Outstanding Novels." Prescott, Orville. *The Yale Review*, 37:3 (1949/Spring) 573-76.

Firstfruits, A Harvest of Twenty-five Years of Israeli Writing.
"Firstfruits." Cohen, Arthur A.
New York Times Book Review, 78:39 (1973/09/30) VII, 46-47.

The Floating World
Kirkus, 22 (1954/11/15) 772.

"Books of the Times." Prescott, Orville. *New York Times*, 104:35,380 (1954/12/06) 25.
A history of the life and death of an art in the period from 1660 to 1860.

Priest, Alan. *New York Herald Tribune Book Review*, (1954/12/12) 4.

"The Japanese Print Makers." Paine, Robert T., Jr.
New York Times Book Review, 49:50 (1954/12/12) VII, 3.

Walls, Jim. *San Francisco Chronicle*, (1954/12/19) 16.

"Interpreting Japanese Prints." Davis, Saville R.
Christian Science Monitor, 47:24 (1954/12/23) 7.

Gentles, Margaret. *Chicago Sunday Tribune*, (1954/12/26) 3.

McCall, J. E. *Artibus Asiae*, 18:3-4 (1955) 324-26.

Booklist, 51 (1955/01/01) 195.

"Japanese Pattern." Stern, Harold Phillip. *Saturday Review*, 38:1 (1955/01/01) 59, 67.

"New Books Appraised." Plaut, Alice S. *Library Journal*, 80:3 (1955/02/01) 373.

"Books: Briefly Noted." *New Yorker*, 31:4 (1955/03/12) 139.

Print, 9 (1955/05) 24.

Arts Digest, 29 (1955/08) 23.

U.S. Quarterly Book Review, 11 (1955/09) 339.

Spectator, (1955/09/15) 372.

Apollo, 62 (1955/11) 158.

Gray, B. *Burl*, 97 (1955/11) 9.

Connoiseur (Am ed), 137 (1956/05) 205.

"Michener's World of the Woodblock." Morse, Marcia. *Honolulu Star-Bulletin*,
(1984/01/20) B1-3. "The Floating World" drove up prices of prints. The rudeness of a N.Y.
policeman and the courtesy of a Hawaiian policeman lead Michener to donate his print
collection to the Honolulu Academy of Arts.

Appendix III - Critics' Reviews of Books by JAMES A. MICHENER

Hawaii

Kirkus, 27 (1959/09/15) 707.

Bookmark, 19 (1959/11) 39.

"Some Enchanted Islands." Sutton, Horace. *Saturday Review*, 42:47 (1959/11/21) 40.

Butcher, Fanny. *Chicago Sunday Tribune*, (1959/11/22) 1.

Ross, Mary. *New York Herald Tribune Book Review*, (1959/11/22) 3.

"God, Missionaries and the Golden Men." Geismar, Maxwell. *New York Times Book Review*, 54:47 (1959/11/22) VII, 4-5.

Time, 74:21 (1959/11/23) 107-10.

Hogan, William. *San Francisco Chronicle*, (1959/11/24) 39.

Hogan, William. *San Francisco Chronicle*, (1959/11/25) 31.

"Books: Briefly Noted." *New Yorker*, 35:43 (1959/12/12) 235.

"New Books Appraised." Hopkinson, Shirley L. *Library Journal*, 84:22 (1959/12/15) 3870.

Wisconsin Library Bulletin, 65 (1960/01) 650.

Booklist, 56 (1960/01/01) 267.

Christian Century, 77 (1960/02/03) 140.

Hughes, Riley. *Catholic World*, 191 (1960/06) 185.

Shrapnel, Norman. *Manchester Guardian*, (1960/06/17) 7.

Bryden. Ronald. *Spectator*, (1960/06/17) 889.

Times [London] Literary Supplement, 54,800 (1960/06/17) 390.

West, Paul. *New Statesman*, 59 (1960/06/25) 953.

"Hawaii." Poppy, John. *Look*, 30:18 (1966/09/06) 48-55. Review of the book and film, with photographic interpretation by Dennis Stock.

The Hokusai Sketchbooks; Selections from the Manga

"In Common Things, a Nation's Charm." Paine, Robert T., Jr. *New York Times*, 107:36,716 (1958/08/03) 7. Hokusai was a Japanese print designer (1760-1849).

Priest, Alan. *New York Herald Tribune Book Review*, (1958/08/10) 4.

Saturday Review, 41:33 (1958/08/16) 15.

Hogan, William. *San Francisco Chronicle*, (1958/08/17) 27.

Appendix III - Critics' Reviews of Books by JAMES A. MICHENER

The Hokusai Sketchbooks; Selections from the Manga (continued)
Kirkus, 26 (1958/09/01) 705.

"The Sketches of Hokusai." Adlow, Dorothy.
Christian Science Monitor, 50:243 (1958/09/11) 13.

"The Atlantic Bookshelf." Weeks, Edward. *Atlantic*, 202:4 (1958/10) 84-86.

Booklist, 55 (1958/10/01) 67.

"New Books Appraised. " von Khrum, Paul. *Library Journal*, 83:17 (1958/10/01) 2770.

Woodcock, G. *Arts*, 33 (1958/12) 18.

Kirstein, Lincoln. *Nation,* 188:5 (1959/01/31) 106.

Connoiseur (Am ed), 145 (1960/04) 118.

Stern, H. P. *Artibus Asiae*, 25:2-3 (1962) 219-20.

Iberia
"The Book Review." Harlan, Robert D. *Library Journal*, 93:7 (1968/04/01) 1482.

"Reader's Choice." Handlin, Oscar. *Atlantic*, 221:5 (1968/05) 112-13.

"James A. Michener's Spanish Odyssey." Poore, Charles.
New York Times, 117:40,275 (1968/05/01) 45.

Welles, Benjamin. *Saturday Review*, 51 (1968/05/04) 28.

"To Spain with love and puzzlement." Pryce-Jones, Alan.
Washington Post Book World, 2:18 (1968/05/05) 1-3.

"Michener's Spain." Sokolov, Raymond A. *Newsweek*, 71:19 (1968/05/06) 112.

"Michener's Spain." Goodsell, James Nelson.
Christian Science Monitor, 60:140 (1968/05/09) 9.

"One Man's Spain." Payne, Robert.
New York Times Book Review, 73:18 (1968/05/12) VII, 8.

"The Infatuated Traveler." *Time,* 91:20 (1968/05/17) 106.

"Books: Briefly Noted." *New Yorker*, 44:14 (1968/05/25) 160.

Conlin, Richard. *Best Sellers*, 28:7 (1968/07/01) 152.

"The Book Review." Jacob, Helen. *Library Journal*, 93:18 (1968/10/15) 3997.

Besas, Peter. *Guidepost*, (1968/10/25) 35.

"Spanish Speculations." *Times[London] Literary Supplement*, 3480 (1968/11/07) 1259.

Appendix III - Critics' Reviews of Books by JAMES A. MICHENER

Iberia (continued)
Carr, Raymond. *New York Review of Books*, 11 (1968/12/19) 29.

Japanese Prints: From the Early Masters to the Modern
Kirkus, 27 (1959/10/01) 787.

"New Books Appraised." von Khrum, Paul.
Library Journal, 84:19 (1959/11/01) 3463.

"A Chance to Inspect the Choice of the Collector." Paine, Robert T., Jr.
New York Times Book Review, 54:45 (1959/11/08) VIII, 8.

Werner, Alfred. *Saturday Review*, 42:49 (1959/12/05) 22.

"Arts and Monuments." Kirstein, Lincoln. *Nation,* 189:20 (1959/12/12) 446.

Priest, Alan. *New York Herald Tribune Book Review*, (1959/12/20) 4.

Booklist, 56 (1960/01/01) 262.

Times [London] Literary Supplement, 54,699 (1960/02/19) 108.

Woodcock, G. *Arts*, 34 (1960/03) 14.

Connoiseur (Am ed), 145 (1960/06) 262-63.

Winzinger, F. *Kunstwerk,* 15 (1961/11) 80. Review of the German edition.

Gray, B. *Oriental Art*, 7:2 (1961/Summer) 88.

Journey
"Northern Follies: James Michener's tale of the gold rush." Bemrose, John.
Maclean's, 101:48 (1988/11/21) 61. "Possesses the timeless appeal
of a tale documenting the ancient struggle of mankind with nature."

Sherbaniuk, Richard. *Quill Quire*, 55 (1989/01) 30.

"Book Review." Scarinci, Florence. *Library Journal*, 114:7 (1989/04/15) 100.

"Journey." Steinberg, Sybil. *Publishers Weekly*, 235:19 (1989/05/12) 280.

"Michener book should appeal to many." Wisneski, Ken.
Minneapolis Star and Tribune, (1989/06/04) NewsBank, Literature, 1989, fiche 70, grid F6.
"An excellent yarn about a disastrous expedition to the Klondike during the Canadian
gold rush."

"A Stagey, Readable Leftover From Michener's 'Alaska.'" Newman, Peter C.
Chicago Tribune Books, (1989/07/02) 4.

"Michener offers rewarding 'Journey.'" Hauser, Jerald.
Milwaukee Journal, (1989/07/02) NewsBank, Literature, 1989, fiche 81, grid E1.
The reviewer believes that "Journey" is Michener's best novel.

Appendix III - Critics' Reviews of Books by JAMES A. MICHENER

Journey (continued)
"'Alaska' Or Bust." Fleming, Thomas.
New York Times Book Review, 94:28 (1989/07/09) VII, 15.

"Michener has his readers groping for solution." Finn, Robert. *Plain Dealer*, (1989/07/15)
NewsBank, Literature, 1989, fiche 81, grid D14.
The reviewer finds Michener didactic, parading results of research into time and period.

"A short but dull 'Journey' into the Klondike goldfields." Hunt, Bill.
Anchorage Daily News, (1989/07/23) NewsBank, Literature, 1989, fiche 81, grid D12.
Considers "Journey" a "dull piece of work," weak in characters and lacking in tensions
generated.

"Michener Trip No 'Journey' Of a Lifetime." O'Briant, Don. *Journal* (Atlanta),
(1989/07/23) NewsBank, Literature, 1989, fiche 91, grid D5. Reviewer believes
that Michener's novels are really only history and science made semi-entertaining.

"Prospecting for Fool's Gold." Kamine, Mark. *Newsday* (Long Island), (1989/07/23)
NewsBank, Literature, 1989, fiche 81, grid D13. The reviewer is critical of Michener's
improbabilities of character and coincidences of plot.

"Michener fills 'Journey' with power, feeling." Acquaviva, Michael A.
Pittsburgh Press, (1989/08/20) NewsBank, Literature, 1989, fiche 91, grid D6.
Spellbinding story of five Englishmen who journey across Canada in search of gold.

"'Journey' gold nugget from 'Alaska' vein." Perry, Roy E. *Nashville Banner*, (1989/09/02)
NewsBank, Literature, 1989, fiche 100, grid B3. "A golden nugget that will delight the
literary prospector." Though "skimpy," it has its charm.

"'Journey' takes reader on a search for gold in Canada." Brown, Ron.
Bangor Daily News, (1989/10/10) NewsBank, Literature, 1989, fiche 114, grid G9.
"Michener may be America's greatest storyteller." He explores with relish and enthusiasm.

"Michener Takes A Thread and Weaves It Into Another Fine Novel." McKenzie, J. Norman.
New York Tribune, (1989/10/12) NewsBank, Literature, 1989, fiche 114, grid G10.
The reviewer believes that Michener knows a good story when he sees it and knows
how to tell it.

"Journey." Dutton, Joy. *World Magazine*, (1989/11) 89.

"Michener's 'Journey' is a literary trip worth taking." Mackey, Neil.
St. Paul Pioneer Press-Dispatch, (1989/11/26) NewsBank, Literature, 1989, fiche 7, grid B1.

"Journey." Penny, Susan. *School Library Journal*, 35:16 (1989/12) 128-29.

"Journey." Diment, Barbara. *Wilson Library Bulletin*, 65:3 (1990/11) BT10.

Kent State: What Happened and Why
Playboy, (1971/03).

Time, 97:18 (1971/05/03) 90-93.

"Books." Muggeridge, Malcolm. *Esquire*, 75:6 (1971/06) 84.

Appendix III - Critics' Reviews of Books by JAMES A. MICHENER

Kent State: What Happened and Why (continued)
"Kent State." Wicker, Tom. *New York Times Book Review*, 76:23 (1971/06/06) VII, 31-32.

"Four Dead in Ohio." Brudnoy, David. *National Review*, 23:25 (1971/06/29) 707-8.

"The fourth of May, 1970 - Kent, Ohio." Alba, Victor.
Washington Post Book World, 5:27 (1971/07/04) 6.

"The Kent State Massacre." Walters, Robert. *Nation,* 213:2 (1971/07/19) 54-56.

"New Books." Calam, John. *Saturday Review*, 54:38 (1971/09/18) 80.

"In Cold Blood." Howard, Anthony. *New Statesman*, 82:2119 (1971/10/29) 592-93.
Published weekly at Great Turnstile, London.

Bazarov, Konstantin. *Books and Bookmen*, (1971/12) 73.

Legacy
"Legacy." *Magill Book Reviews.*

Hitchens, Christopher. *Times Literary Supplement*, (1987/08/21) 898.

Spitzer, Jane Stewart. *Christian Science Monitor*, (1987/09/04) B4.

"From Constitutionland To Iranorrama." Martin, Judith.
New York Times Book Review, 92:36 (1987/09/06) VII, 6.

"Patriots Don't Take The Fifth." Erlichman, John.
Los Angeles Times Book Review, (1987/09/13) 1, 21.

"Book Review." Hinkemeyer, Joan. *Library Journal*, 112:15 (1987/09/15) 95.

Literary Reflections
"Literary Reflections: Michener on Michener, Hemingway, Capote and Others."
Publishers Weekly, (1993/10/18) 54. "Interesting and witty."

"Literary Reflections." Braun, Janice. *Library Journal*, 118 (1993/11/15) 79.
"Imbued with warmth and even passion."

"Literary Reflections: Michener on Michener, Hemingway, Capote and Others."
Walton, David. *New York Times Book Review*, (1993/11/28) 26.
"Agreeable and unpretentious."

"Literary Reflections: Michener on Hemingway, Capote, and Others."
Joyce, Alice. *Booklist*, 90 (1993/12/01) 671.

Mexico
"Mexico." *Publishers Weekly*, 239 (1992/09/21) 74.

"Mexico." Seaman, Donna. *Booklist*, 117 (1992/10/01) 195.

"Mexico." Michaud, Charles. *Library Journal*, 117 (1992/11/01) 118.

Appendix III - Critics' Reviews of Books by JAMES A. MICHENER

Mexico (continued)
"Michener plods through 1,500 years of Mexican history." Schleier, Curt.
San Jose Mercury News, (1992/11/15) NewsBank, Literature, 1992, fiche 103, grid G1

"Michener manages 'Mexico.'" Pintarich, Paul. *The Oregonian*, (1992/11/15)
NewsBank, Literature, 1992, fiche 103, grid G2.

"Michener mining Mexico for minutiae." Miron, Susan.
Philadelphia Inquirer, (1992/11/29) NewsBank, Literature, 1992, fiche 103, grid G3.

"Mexico." Irving, Clifford. *New York Times Book Review*, (1992/12/20) 8.

"Mexico." Scott, David Clark. *Christian Science Monitor*, 85 (1993/02/04) 14.

"Mexico." Conover, Don. *La Busca*, 29 (1993/11-12) 28-33.

A Michener Miscellany: 1950-1970
"'Michener Miscellany' - Both Fascinating and Informative." Cromie, Robert.
Chicago Tribune Book World, 126:112 (1973/04/22) Sect. 7, 5.

"Michener, James Albert. A Michener Miscellany: 1950-1970." *Choice*, (1973/11) 1375.
"A 'mariner's platter' representing the Michener scope of interest and ability."

Modern Japanese Prints. An Appreciation
Priest, Alan. *New York Herald Tribune*.

"An Ancient Art in Modern Dress." Preston, Stuart.
New York Times Book Review, 58:28 (1963/07/14) VII, 7.

Swann, P.C. *Oriental Art*, 9:4 (1963/Winter) 259.

My Lost Mexico
"James Michener's Lost Mexico." Carpenter, Richard P.
Boston Sunday Globe, (1992/11/01) B22.

"My Lost Mexico." *Publishers Weekly*, 239 (1992/11/09) 69.

"My Lost Mexico." Irving, Clifford. *New York Times Book Review*, (1992/12/20) 8.
"A rewarding experience...... a treat...... the tough old bird is no has-been."

"My Lost Mexico." Scott, David Clark. *Christian Science Monitor*, 85 (1993/02/04) 14.

"My Lost Mexico." Conover, Don. *La Busca*, 29 (1993/11-12) 42-43.

Los Angeles Times Book Review, (1993/01/25) E8. "Marvelous, really."

The Novel
"'The Novel,' Michener's Novel About a Novel." Lehmann-Haupt, Christopher.
New York Times, 140:48,553 (1991/03/28) II, 2. Living Arts Pages.

"The Novel." Isaacs, Susan. *New York Times Book Review*, 96:13 (1991/03/31) VII, 12.

Appendix III - Critics' Reviews of Books by JAMES A. MICHENER

The Novel (continued)
"With Michener, inside a writer's life." Rohland, Pamela.
Philadelphia Inquirer, (1991/03/31) NewsBank, Literature, 1991, fiche 36, grid D6.
Strongly autobiographical, Michener reveals an unknown side, and a glimpse of the publishing world.

"Michener challenges - and loses." Gagliani, William D. *Milwaukee Journal*, (1991/04/07) NewsBank, Literature, 1991, fiche 36, grid D7.

"'Novel': shaping of a book." Seago, Kate. *Daily News* (Los Angeles), (1991/04/14) NewsBank, Literature, 1991, fiche 36, grid C14. Not great, but satisfying on many levels. An interesting "self-analysis" of a writer.

"Michener's 34th Work Is Different." Hartman, Diane. *Denver Post*, (1991/04/14) NewsBank, Literature, 1991, fiche 36, grid D2. The reviewer recommends that you "Keep your memories of good Michener books; pass this one up."

"Michener's latest explores the world of publishing." Lorber, Helene.
Detroit News and Free Press, (1991/04/14) NewsBank, Literature, 1991, fiche 36, grid D3.

"Michener's 'The Novel' smaller, but rewarding." West Larry.
Seattle Times, (1991/04/14) NewsBank, Literature, 1991, fiche 60, grid G12.

"Michener's 'Novel' Wooden Wisdom." Pate, Nancy. *Orlando Sentinel*, (1991/04/21) F8.

"Michener falls short in a story about self." Pintarich, Paul.
The Oregonian, (1991/04/28) NewsBank, Literature, 1991, fiche 36, grid D4.

"The Novel." Rubin, Merle. *Christian Science Monitor*, (1991/05/13) 13.

"The Novel." Scott, Jay. *Chatelaine*, 64 (1991/06) 10.

Pilgrimage: A Memoir of Poland and Rome
"Book Review." Cridland, Nancy C. *Library Journal*, 115:16 (1990/10/01) 98.

"Pilgrimage." Forbes, Malcolm S., Jr. *Forbes*, 147:10 (1991/05/13) 24.

Poland
"Poland." *Publishers Weekly*, 224 (1983/07/15) 41.

"Book Notes." Lochte, Dick. *Los Angeles Times Book Review*, (1983/07/31) II, 10.

"Book Review." McCully, William C. *Library Journal*, 108:15 (1983/09/01) 1721.

"'Poland': Bound by The Past." Osnos, Peter. *Washington Post*, (1983/09/02) C1, 8.

"Polish Romanticism." Darnton, John. *New York Times*, 132:45,790 (1983/09/03) 12.

"From Michener, a monumental retelling of Poland's tragic history." Kurtle, Bill.
Chicago Tribune, 137:247 (1983/09/04) Sect. 12, 2.

"Cycles of devastation, endurance, renewal." Hegi, Ursula.
Los Angeles Times Book Review, (1983/09/04) pp. 1,8.

Appendix III - Critics' Reviews of Books by JAMES A. MICHENER

Poland (continued)
"The Nation That Disappeared in 123 Years." Schott, Webster.
New York Times Book Review, 88:36 (1983/09/04) VII, 5, 10.

Schaufele, William E. *Christian Science Monitor*, (1983/09/14) 11.

"A rattling good read: The ever-observant Michener offers a timely portrait of Poland."
Schwarzbaum, Lisa. *Detroit News*, (1983/09/18) 2-E.

"Michener probes the solidarity, diversity of Poland's past." Cross, Robert.
Chicago Tribune, 137:272 (1983/09/29) Sect. 5, 3.

"Low Altitude." Blake, Patricia. *Time,* 122:14 (1983/10/03) 81-82.

"James Michener's "Poland" Significant, but Novel Skimps on Polish Jewry."
Madison, Charles. *Detroit Jewish News*, 84 (1983/10/28) 76.

"Dead End." Pleszczynski, Wladyslaw. *National Review*, 35 (1983/11/11) 1418, 1420.

"On James Michener's Poland." Nordon, Haskell.
New York Times Book Review, 88:47 (1983/11/20) VII, 43.

Roodkowsky, Nikita D. *America*, 149 (1983/12/03) 359.

"Poland: Michener's Harsh Reading." Guttenplan, D. D., Douglas
Stranglin, and Tessa Namuth. *Newsweek*, 103:3 (1984/01/16) 45.

Presidential Lottery
"Presidential Lottery." Sorensen, Theodore C. *Saturday Review*, 52:15 (1969/04/12) 33-36.

"The Book Review." Summers, F. William. *Library Journal*, 94:10 (1969/05/15) 1997.

"In Brief." Mee, Charles L., Jr. *New York Times Book Review*, 74:21 (1969/05/25) VII, 26.

"Playboy After Hours - Books." *Playboy*, 16:1 (1969/06) 39.

"White House roulette." Koenig, Louis W.
Washington Post Book World, 3:22 (1969/06/01) 8.

Evans, M. S. *National Review*, 21 (1969/09/09) 919.

"The Book Review." Faria, Judy. *Library Journal*, 94:16 (1969/09/15) 3235.

The Quality of Life
"Reservations: Arts and Letters." *Antioch Review*, 30:3-4 (1970-71/Fall) 461.

"The Book Review." Welsch, Erwin K. *Library Journal*, 95:17 (1970/10/01) 3297.

Nordberg, Robert B. *Best Sellers*, 30:18 (1970/12/15) 398.

"We may overcome." *Times[London] Literary Supplement*, 3621 (1971/07/23) 852.

Appendix III - Critics' Reviews of Books by JAMES A. MICHENER

Rascals in Paradise
    Kirkus, 25 (1957/04/01) 293.

    Teilhet, Darwin. *Saturday Review*, 40:23 (1957/06/08) 33-34.

    Hogan, William. *San Francisco Chronicle*, (1957/06/11) 21.

    Booklist, 53 (1957/06/15) 524.

    "New Books Appraised." Dillon, Richard H. *Library Journal*, 82:12 (1957/06/15) 1672.

    Searles, P. J. *New York Herald Tribune Book Review*, (1957/06/16) 1.

    "Evil Spirits in a Magic Setting." Whipple, A. B. C.
    New York Times, 106:36,303 (1957/06/16) 6.

    McCutcheon, J. T. *Chicago Sunday Tribune*, (1957/06/23) 3.

    "Books: Briefly Noted." *New Yorker*, 33:19 (1957/06/29) 86.

    Bookmark, 16 (1957/07) 236.

    Times [London] Literary Supplement, 53,951 (1957/09/20) 564.

Recessional
    "James Michener's September Song." Lindbergh, Reeven.
    Washington Post Book World, 24:42 (1994/10/16) 1.

Report of the County Chairman
    Kirkus, 29 (1961/03/15) 288.

    Hogan, William. *San Francisco Chronicle*, (1961/05/03) 35.

    Mitchell, S. A. *Chicago Sunday Tribune*, (1961/05/07) 2.

    Parton, Margaret. *New York Herald Tribune*, (1961/05/28) 25. Lively Arts Section.

    Johnson, G. W. *New Republic*, 144 (1961/05/29) 18.

    Booklist, 57 (1961/06/01) 603.

    "New Books Appraised." Woodward, Robert C. *Library Journal*, 86:11 (1961/06/01) 2112.

    "White House Pathfinder." Hyman, Sidney. *Saturday Review*, 44:23 (1961/06/10) 42.

    "On the Road for J.F.K." Lubell, Samuel.
    New York Times Book Review, 56:25 (1961/06/18) VII, 12.

    Christian Century, 78 (1961/06/28) 797.

    Manchester Guardian, (1961/11/10) 7.

    Brogan, D. W. *Spectator*, (1961/11/10) 673.

Appendix III - Critics' Reviews of Books by JAMES A. MICHENER

Report of the County Chairman (continued)
>   *Times [London] Literary Supplement,* 55,241 (1961/11/17) 828.

Return to Paradise
>   "Review of Return to Paradise." Marquand, John P.
>   *Book-of-the-Month Club,* (1951) 1. Book-of-the-Month Club Bulletin.

>   *Kirkus,* 19 (1951/03/01) 131.

>   *Booklist,* 47 (1951/04/15) 285.

>   Espey, J. J. *New York Herald Tribune Book Review,* (1951/04/22) 7.

>   "For Michener, It's Still the South Pacific." Karig, Walter.
>   *New York Times Book Review,* 46:16 (1951/04/22) VII, 7.

>   *Time,* 57:17 (1951/04/23) 114-16.
>   The book was based on eight articles written for *Holiday* magazine.

>   Farrell, Paul V. *Commonweal,* 54:3 (1951/04/27) 67.

>   "South Pacific Revisited." Payne, Robert.
>   *Saturday Review of Literature,* 34:17 (1951/04/28) 10-11.
>   Also biographical information in column titled "Author" on page 10.

>   *Booklist,* 47 (1951/05/01) 308.

>   "Back to the Pacific." Chapin, Ruth. *Christian Science Monitor,* 43:132 (1951/05/01) 9.

>   "Books: Briefly Noted." *New Yorker,* 27:12 (1951/05/05) 114.

>   Guilfoil, Kelsey. *Chicago Sunday Tribune,* (1951/05/06) 3.

>   Jackson, J. H. *San Francisco Chronicle,* (1951/05/06) 22.

>   Swados, Harvey. *Nation,* 172:19 (1951/05/12) 446-47.

>   Grattan, C. H. *New Republic,* 124 (1951/05/14) 18.

>   Weeks, Edward. *Bookmark,* 10 (1951/06) 208.

>   "The Atlantic Bookshelf." Weeks, Edward. *Atlantic,* 188:3 (1951/07) 82.

>   *Cleveland Open Shelf,* (1951/07) 16.

>   *Wisconsin Library Bulletin,* 47 (1951/07) 190.

>   Hughes, Riley. *Catholic World,* 173 (1951/08) 390.

>   *U.S. Quarterly Book Review,* 7 (1951/09) 242.

>   *Times [London] Literary Supplement,* 52,142 (1951/10/26) 680.

Appendix III - Critics' Reviews of Books by JAMES A. MICHENER

Return to Paradise (continued)
"Paperbacks of the Month." *New York Times Book Review*, 79:6 (1974/02/10) VII, 22.

Sayonara
Kirkus, 21 (1953/12/01) 766.

"Review of Sayonara." Buck, Pearl. *Book-of-the-Month Club*, (1954). Book-of-the-Month Club Bulletin.

"New Books Appraised." Forbes, Harriett R. *Library Journal*, 79:2 (1954/01/15) 142.

"Books: Briefly Noted." *New Yorker*, 24:49 (1954/01/23) 100-1.

Smith, Bradford. *New York Herald Tribune Book Review*, (1954/01/24) 4.

"My Love Goodby." Sneider, Verne. *New York Times Book Review*, 49:4 (1954/01/24) VII, 4.

"James Michener: Again the Warm Voice of Asia." *Newsweek*, 43:4 (1954/01/25) 92-95. Condensed as "Michener of the South Pacific" in *Reader's Digest*, 64:384 (1954/04) 20.

"Books of the Times." Prescott, Orville. *New York Times*, 103:35,067 (1954/01/27) 25.

Jackson, J. H. *San Francisco Chronicle*, (1954/01/29) 15.

Butcher, Fanny. *Chicago Sunday Tribune*, (1954/01/31) 3.

Booklist, 50 (1954/02/01) 222.

"Case of Military Miscegenation." Gibney, Frank. *Saturday Review*, 36:6 (1954/02/06) 11.

Pfaff, William. *Commonweal*, 59:19 (1954/02/12) 480.

Wisconsin Library Bulletin, 50 (1954/03) 73.

Conover, Robert. *Christian Century*, 71 (1954/04/07) 431.

Hughes, Riley. *Catholic World*, 179 (1954/05) 155.

Cleveland Open Shelf, (1954/05) 161.

Metcalf, John. *Spectator*, (1954/06/25) 792.

Times [London] Literary Supplement, 52,979 (1954/07/09) 437.

Six Days in Havana
"Briefly Noted." *Library Journal*, 114:13 (1989/08) 154.

"Six Days in Havana." Hoelterhoff, Manuela. *Wall Street Journal*, (1989/12/05) A20. Leisure and Arts Section. Written by Michener with John Kings.

Appendix III - Critics' Reviews of Books by JAMES A. MICHENER

Six Days in Havana (continued)
"Havana: once over too lightly." Seib, Philip. *Dallas Morning News*,
(1989/12/24) NewsBank, Literature, 1989, fiche 16, grid F3. The strength of the
book is in the photography, otherwise an "inconsequential book."

The Source
"New Books Appraised." Lazenby, Francis D. *Library Journal*, 90:9 (1965/05/01) 2160.

"Israel Down the Ages." Payne, Robert.
New York Times Book Review, 70:21 (1965/05/23) VII, 45.

"Old Testament Man." *Newsweek*, 65:21 (1965/05/24) 118.

Time, 85:22 (1965/05/28) 110-12.

"The Hidden Spring that Succored Man." Comay, Joan.
Saturday Review, 48:22 (1965/05/29) 27.

Schary, Dore. *Book Week*, (1965/05/30) 6.

"Michener's Dig." Harrison, Joseph G. *Christian Science Monitor*, 57: 159 (1965/06/03) 4.

Hart, Mary. *Best Sellers*, 25:6 (1965/06/15) 129.

"Books: Briefly Noted." *New Yorker*, 41:19 (1965/06/26) 106.

Klausler, A. P. *Christian Century*, 82 (1965/07/28) 041.

Critic, 24 (1965/08) 87.

Times [London] Literary Supplement, 56,452 (1965/10/14) 912.

Morgan, Edwin. *New Statesman*, 70 (1965/10/29) 658.

Hill, W. B. *America*, 113 (1965/11/07) 688.

South Pacific. as told by James A. Michener
"South Pacific." *Publishers Weekly*, 239 (1992/06/29) 61.
With illustrations by Michael Hague.

"South Pacific." Cooper, Illene. *Booklist*, 89 (1992/09/01) 60.

"South Pacific." Margolis, Sally T. *School Library Journal*, 38 (1992/11) 112.

Space
"Book Review." Donahugh, Robert H. *Library Journal*, 107:15 (1982/09/01) 1677.

"James Michener Blasts Off." Bova, Ben. *Washington Post Book World*, (1982/09/12) 1, 4.

"A Novel of Very High Adventure." Wilford, John Noble.
New York Times Book Review, 87:38 (1982/09/19) VII, 3, 26.

"Books of the Times." Broyard, Anatole. *New York Times*, 132:45,451 (1982/09/29) III, 24.

Appendix III - Critics' Reviews of Books by JAMES A. MICHENER

Space (continued)

"Faulty Craft Plagues Michener's Space Mission." Rhodes, Richard. *Chicago Tribune*, 136:276 (1982/10/03) Sect. 7, 1.

"Launching a winner: Michener's space epic probes man's imagination." Eatherly, Ken. *Detroit News*, (1982/10/03) 2-E.

"The great American ennobler: Michener at a new altitude." Keller, Karl. *Los Angeles Times Book Review*, (1982/10/03) V2.

"Fact-laden Novel On Space Program." Harrell, Don. *Christian Science Monitor*, 74:219 (1982/10/06) 14.

Bell, Pearl K. *Times Literary Supplement*, (1983/02/25) 200.

"No. 1 on the Best-seller List." Smith, Michael L. *Nation,* 236:9 (1983/03/05) 279-81.

"Space." Kirwan, Jack. *National Review*, 35 (1983/05/27) 640.

Sports in America

"Book Review. (Sports and Recreation - A Sober View of Sports)." DeLapo, Josephine A. *Library Journal*, 101:11 (1976/06/01) 1304.

"Michener Leaves Fiction for Astute Look at Athletics." Anderson, Terry R. *Sunday Denver Post*, 84:325 (1976/06/20) 23.

"Two in the End Zone." Plimpton, George. *Saturday Review*, 3:19 (1976/06/26) 38-39.

"Sports in America." Lipsyte, Robert. *New York Times Book Review*, 81:26 (1976/06/27) VII, 2-3.

"Jock Lit 101." Maddocks, Melvin. *Time,* 107:27 (1976/06/28) 63-64.

"Bring on the Second Team." Broyard, Anatole. *New York Times*, 125:43,258 (1976/07/01) 27.

"Michener comes to grips with American sports mania." Plimpton, George. *Los Angeles Times*, (1976/07/25) 3-7.

"Books Considered - Sports in America." Weintraub, Stanley. *National Review*, 175:6-7 (1976/08/07-14) 37-38.

"Sports in America by James Michener." Weintraub, Stanley. *New Republic*, 175:6-7 (1976/08/07-14) 37-38.

Forman, Jack. *School Library Journal*, 23:2 (1976/10) 125.

Stopa, Peter J. *Best Sellers*, 36:8 (1976/11) 269.

Choice, 13 (1976/11) 1171.

Appendix III - Critics' Reviews of Books by JAMES A. MICHENER

Sports in Amercia (continued)
"Don't just sit there, play something." Hoffman, Matthew.
Times[London] Literary Supplement, 3932 (1977/07/22) 888.
British title - "Michener On Sport."

Tales of the South Pacific
Kirkus, 14 (1946/12/01) 605.

"New Books Appraised." Boyle, Frances Alter. *Library Journal*, 72:2 (1947/01/15) 159.

Textor, Clinton. *Chicago Sun Book Week*, (1947/02/02) 2.

Searles, P. J. *New York Herald Tribune Book Review*, (1947/02/02) 6.

"Atolls of the Sun." Dempsey, David.
New York Times Book Review, 42:5 (1947/02/02) VII, 5, 30.

"Books of the Times." Prescott, Orville. *New York Times*, 96:32,517 (1947/02/03) 17.
Also in "In My Opinion." New York: Bobbs-Merrill, 1952, pp. 146-64.

Booklist, 43 (1947/03/01) 205.

U.S. Quarterly Book Review, 3 (1947/06) 138.

"Outstanding Novels." Prescott, Orville. *The Yale Review*, 36:3 (1947/Spring) 573-76.

Texas
"Texas." *Magill Book Reviews*.

"Book Review." Whealler, Cynthia Johnson.
Library Journal, 110:17 (1984/10/15) 102.

"Texas overwhelms Michener, and vice versa." Leary, Mike. *Denver Post*, (1985/06/09) D22.
Michener explores Texas and Texans in preparation for the novel "Texas."

"Eyes of Michener are Upon Texas." Leary, Mike.
Chicago Tribune, 139: 178 (1985/06/27) Sect. 5, 1, 5.

"James Michener's Ten-Gallon Epic." Lemann, Nicholas.
Washington Post Book World, (1985/09/29) 1, 13.

"Books of the Times." Kakutani, Michiko. *New York Times*, 135:46,557 (1985/10/09) III, 20.

"'Texas': Wooden and as long as Lone Star Brag." King, Larry L.
Chicago Tribune, 139:286 (1985/10/13) Sect. 14, 41, 46. Book World Section.

"Four Centuries of Tex Arcana." Rudd, Hughes.
New York Times Book Review, 90:41 (1985/10/13) VII, 9.

"Michener burrows deep into the heart of the Lone Star State."
Becker, Alida. *Detroit News*, (1985/10/27) 2-F.

"James Michener Casts a Publishing Shadow as Big as 'Texas.'" Casey, Constance.

Appendix III - Critics' Reviews of Books by JAMES A. MICHENER

Texas (continued)
>
> *Chicago Tribune*, 139:290 (1985/10/17) Sect. 5, 2.
>
> "Bookends." *Time,* 126:17 (1985/10/28) 96.
>
> "Wait For The Miniseries." Applebome, Peter. *Wall Street Journal*, (1985/11/12) 26.
>
> "Michener Gets the Draw on Texas." LaSalle, Peter. *Los Angeles Times*, (1985/11/21) V30.
>
> Bueter, Robert J. *America*, 154 (1986/01/18) 36.

The Voice of Asia
>
> *Booklist*, 48 (1951/09/01) 2.
>
> *Kirkus*, 19 (1951/09/01) 506.
>
> Duffield, Marcus. *New York Herald Tribune Book Review*, (1951/10/28) 5.
>
> "The Word from the Rice Paddies." Trumbull, Robert.
> *New York Times Book Review*, 46:43 (1951/10/28) VII, 6.
>
> "Books of the Times." Prescott, Orville. *New York Times*, 101:34,247 (1951/10/30) 27.
> Also in "In My Opinion." New York: Bobbs-Merrill, 1952, pp. 146-64.
>
> Jackson, J. H. *San Francisco Chronicle*, (1951/10/31) 18.
>
> *Cleveland Open Shelf*, (1951/11) 25.
>
> Peel, Robert. *Christian Science Monitor*, (1951/11/01) 11.
>
> "Books: Briefly Noted." *New Yorker*, 27:39 (1951/11/10) 162.
>
> *Booklist*, 48 (1951/11/15) 99.
>
> "New Books Appraised." Linton, Howard P.
> *Library Journal*, 76:20 (1951/11/15) 1932.
>
> Fischer, Max. *Commonweal*, 55 (1951/11/16) 154.
>
> Bader, A. L. *Chicago Sunday Tribune*, (1951/11/25) 4.
>
> *Bookmark*, 11 (1951/12) 58.
>
> Brown, W. N. *Nation,* 173 (1951/12/15) 529.

The Watermen
>
> "On the Deck of A Chesapeake Skipjack." Simon, Anne W.
> *Washington Post Book World*, (1979/09/30) 6.

The World is My Home
>
> "The World is My Home." *Publishers Weekly*, 238:50 (1991/11/15) 60.
>
> "Book Review." Saylor, V. Louise. *Library Journal*, 116:21 (1991/12) 158.

Appendix III - Critics' Reviews of Books by JAMES A. MICHENER

The World is My Home (continued)
Mitgang, Herbert. *New York Times*, 141 (1991/12/30) III, 16.

"Michener: All Business." Mehren, Elizabeth. *Orlando Sentinel*, (1992/01/01) E1.

"Michener spins a world of yarns, from his Pa. days and his travels." Williams, Edgar.
Philadelphia Inquirer, (1992/01/05) NewsBank, Literature, 1992, fiche 11, grid G12.

"Michener's memoir a page-turner but flawed." Winders, Glenda.
San Diego Union, (1992/01/05) NewsBank, Literature, 1992, fiche 11, grid G10.

"Michener's own story has breadth of his novels." Courtney, Steve.
Hartford Courant, (1992/01/19) NewsBank, Literature, 1992, fiche 11, grid G11.

Grumbach, Doris. *New York Times Book Review*, 97:3 (1992/01/19) VII, 11.

"Being humble not a Michener trait." Robbins, Jhan.
State (Columbia, S. C.), (1992/01/19) NewsBank, Literature, 1992, fiche 11, grid G14.

Germani, Clare. *Christian Science Monitor*, 84 (1992/02/04) 13.

"Michener still has that storytelling magic." Kernan, Michael.
Rocky Mountain News, (1992/02/23) NewsBank, Literature, 1992, fiche 20, grid B5.

"Rambling through the life of that traveling man - James Michener." Marvel, Bill.
Dallas Morning News, (1992/03/01) NewsBank, Literature, 1992, fiche 20, grid B6.

"Michener's life story as compelling as his popular books." Voboril, Mary.
Miami Herald, (1992/04/28) NewsBank, Literature, 1992, fiche 40, grid F5.

"James A. Michener." *BookNews*, (1992/05) 32. A Book-of-the-Month Club publication.

"The World is My Home: A Memoir." Kreyche, Gerald F.
USA Today, 121 (1992/09) 96.

Appendix IV - Michener Miscellany

ART AND POSTERS

IBERIA: THREE SIGNED PHOTOGRAPHS BY ROBERT VAVRA.
Random House, New York: n.d. Written with Robert Vavra, introduction by Michener.

JAPANESE WOODBLOCK PRINT MASTERPIECES.
Rutland: Charles E. Tuttle, [1959?]. 8 color reproductions of print masterpieces appearing in "Japanese Prints: From the Early Masters to the Modern." Each print is matted and ready for framing. 6 prints per portfolio. Portfolio #1: Kabuki Actors; Portfolio #2: Beautiful Women. Size of portfolio: 11" x 15." Size of prints: approximately 7" x 10 1/4". Original price per portfolio - $2.75

"JAMES A. MICHENER RETELLS SOUTH PACIFIC" [POSTER].
Harcourt Brace Jovanovich, 1992. Hague, Michael. ISBN 0-15-200618-4. Various illustrations from the book on an attractive colorful 19" x 22" poster.

"TEXAS" POSTER.
University of Texas, Austin: 1985. Shaw, Charles. 22"x 29". Rifleman on horseback, and notation that it commemorates the sesquicentennial publication of "Texas."

BOOK BAG

BOOK BAG with an illustration of James A. Michener. New York: Barnes & Noble, 1984.

BOOKS DEDICATED TO JAMES A. MICHENER

HAWAII: FIFTIETH STAR.
Day, A. Grove. New York: Duell, Sloan and Pearce, 1960.

JAPANESE INN. Statler, Oliver.
- a   New York: Random House, 1961.
- b   New York: Pyramid Books, 1962/02.
- c   New York: Arena Books, 1972/08.
- d   Honolulu: University of Hawaii Press, 1982.

MASTERS OF THE JAPANESE PRINT.
Lane, Richard Douglas, London: Thames and Hudson, 1962.

CALENDARS

LYRICAL VISIONS. Japanese Prints From the James A. Michener Collection, Honolulu Academy of Arts. A Universal Calendar.
New York: Universe Publishing, 1984.

JAMES A. MICHENER'S ALASKA: The Nineteen Eighty-Nine Alaska.
Greatland Graphics, 1988/08. ISBN 0-936425-04-0. Photographer's calendar. Sold for $8.95.

COFFEE CUPS

COFFEE CUP with an illustration of James A. Michener.
New York: Barnes & Noble, 1994.

CROSSWORD PUZZLES

SERIES 157 CROSSWORD PUZZLE BOOK. [No. 33]
Gersch, Charles E., New York: Simon & Schuster, 1990. A crossword puzzle titled "A Michener Treasury" created as a tribute to a popular American author. ISBN 0-671-72351-0.

SERIES 169 CROSSWORD PUZZLE BOOK. [No. 8]
Gersch, Charles E., New York: Simon & Schuster, 1992. A crossword puzzle titled "Tribute to JM." ISBN 0-671-79178-9.

NOTEPAD

THE MICHENER NOTE PAD: FOR THOSE DAY TO DAY IDEAS.
New York: Fawcett Crest (1979). A paperback sized book of blank pages, presumably published as a promotional gimmick. (See A.040.)

STUDY GUIDES

A VIEWER'S GUIDE TO CENTENNIAL.
NBC-TV, 1978. Brussat, Frederic A. Six modules are developed on the major themes of "Centennial." Gives discussion starters, project ideas and further readings.

JAMES A. MICHENER'S SPACE.
Cultural Information Service, New York: 1985. Viewer's guide to "Space," prepared by a nonprofit educational organization and publisher of resources for lifelong learners. This guide is an educational tool to be used in conjunction with the viewing of the TV series. Topics presented for discussion include the use of space by industry, multi-national cooperation in the use of space technology, military use of space, the feasibility of space colonies, and the question of life elsewhere in the universe. The guide provides a "Space" poster for discussion purposes. The guide was made possible by CBS.

T-SHIRT

T-SHIRT with an illustration of James A. Michener.
New York: Barnes & Noble, 1994.

Appendix V - A Biographical Chronology

1907	Birth	1953	**The Bridges at Toko-ri**
1921-25	Doylestown High School	1954	**Sayonara**
	"Torch" Assoc. Editor, 2 yrs		**The Floating World**
	Editor-in-Chief 1 yr		Doctor of Humane Letters,
	Basketball, Class President		Swarthmore College.
1925-29	Swarthmore College	1955	Divorced by Vange Nord
	Contributions to "Portfolio"		Married Mari Yoriko Sabusawa
	Grad. BA-English & History,	1956	Aids Hungarian refugees.
	Summa Cum Laude	1957	Appointed to Fed. Advisory
	Phi Beta Kappa		Arts Commission
1928	Traveled with Swarthmore		Honorary Doctorate of Laws,
	Chautauqua Group		Temple University
1929-31	Teacher -The Hill School		**The Bridge at Andau**
1931-33	Traveled and studied abroad		**Rascals in Paradise**
	Joshua Lippincott Fellowship.		**Selected Writings of**
	Studied at St. Andrews, Scotland.		**James A. Michener**
	Served in the British		Oct., plane crashed in Pacific
	Merchant Marine		off of Iwo Jima
1935	Married Patti Koon	1958	Overseas Press Club Award for
1933-36	Teacher-The George School		Reader's Digest article (Andau)
1936-39	Associate Professor at		Ed., **The Hokusai Sketchbooks**
	Colorado State College of Ed.	1959	Places collection of Japanese
	Completed M.A. in 1937.		Prints at Honolulu Academy of
1938-40	Co-founded Angells Club,		Arts.
	discussion group with faculty,		**Hawaii**
	community and farmers.		**Japanese Prints**
1939-40	Visiting lecturer at the	1960	Chairman of the Bucks
	Graduate School of Education,		County Citizens for Kennedy
	Harvard University.	1961	**Report of the County Chairman**
1939	**The Future of the Social Studies**		Appointed by JFK to manage U.S.
1940	**The Unit in the Social Studies.**		Food for Peace. Program failed.
1940-49	Social Studies editor,	1962	Dem. candidate for Congress
	MacMillan Publishing Co.		from 8th District, Pa. Lost.
1943-46	Activated from Naval Reserve in	1963	**Caravans**
	1943 and sent to the South	1965	**The Source**
	Pacific in the spring of 1944.		Heart attack
1944-46	South Pacific Naval Historian	1967	Helped establish Bucks County
1946	Leaves service as Lt. Comdr.		Arts Festival
1947	**Tales of the South Pacific.**		Joined Americans for Permanent
1948	Divorced by Patti Koon		Peace in the Middle East
	Married Vange Nord		Received Einstein Award
	Pulitzer Prize-Fiction		Einstein Medical College
1949	**The Fires of Spring**	1967-68	Pres., PA Electoral College
	South Pacific, the Musical Play		Sec. PA Constitutional Conv.
1950	Doctor of Humane Letters,	1968	**Adickes**
	Rider College	1968	**Iberia**
1951	**Return to Paradise**		Collection of contemporary
	The Voice of Asia		American painting placed at
1952-70	Roving Editor for *Readers Digest*		University of Texas, Austin.
1953	President of the Asia Institute	1969	**Presidential Lottery**

Appendix V - A Biographical Chronology

1969	**America vs. America**
1970	**Facing East**
	The Quality of Life
	Donates $100,000 to Swarthmore programs for black studies and race relations.
	American-Hungarian Studies Award (George Washington)
1970-74	Member of U.S. Advisory Commission on Information. Donates $100,000 to Kent State University for arts program.
1971	**Kent State**
	The Drifters
1972	Correspondent to China and Russia with President Nixon. Doctor of Humane Letters, Univ. of Northern Colorado, dedication of library to him
1973	**A Michener Miscellany:1950-1970** Ed., **Firstfruits**
1974	**Centennial**
	About Centennial Honorary degree, Yeshiva Univ.
1975	Represented President Ford at Okinawa World Exposition. Appointed to the Bi-Centennial Advisory Committee
1975	Appointed to Citizens Advisory Stamp Committee
1976	**Sports in America**
1977	Medal of Freedom by Pres. Ford Begins series of TV programs, "The World of JAM"
1978	**Chesapeake** Recipient Pa. Society Gold Medal
1979	**The Watermen**
1979	Serves on NASA Adv. Council
1980	**The Covenant**
	The Quality of Life The Franklin Award Spanish Institute Gold Medal $500,000 endowment to fund Univ. of Iowa Writer's Workshop
1982	**Space**
1983	**Collector, Forgers--and a Writer** **Poland** **Testimony**
1983	Board for Int. Broadcasting (Radio Free Europe)

1983	Recognized by White House Arts Program for fin. asst. to artists
1984	Donated $2 mil. to Swarthmore
1985	Dedication of James A. Michener Arts Center in Bucks County Exemplar Award from Central Bucks Chamber of Commerce
1985	**Texas**
1987	**Legacy**
1988	**Alaska** **Journey**
1989	**Caribbean** **Six Days in Havana**
1990	**The Eagle and the Raven** **Pilgrimage**
1991	**James A. Michener on the Social Studies** **The Novel** Donated $15 million to the U.T. Graduate Writing Program Funded the writing program at the University of Houston $5 million more to Swarthmore Appointed to Smithsonian Nat. Postal Museum Adv. Committee
1992	**The World is My Home** **James A. Michener's Writer's Handbook** **South Pacific as told by JAM** **Mexico** **My Lost Mexico** Donated $600,000 to University of Northern Colorado Library
1993	**Creatures of the Kingdom** **Literary Reflections**
1994	**Recessional** **William Penn** Mari Michener passes away Pledges to Art Museums in Doylestown and Texas $5,000,000 each
1995	**Miracle in Seville** **Ventures in Editing**
1996	Outstanding Philanthropist by the National Society of Fund Raising Executives

** Michener has received more than 30 honorary doctorates in Humane Letters, Law, Theology and Science.

Indexes

ADICKES
Critique by James A. Michener

Adickes. A.021.

Name Index

285

Name Index

Name Index

Name Index

Name Index

Name Index

Name Index

Name Index

Periodical Index

Periodical Index

Publisher Index

Publisher Index

Publisher Index

WILLIAM PENN

by
JAMES A. MICHENER

William Penn. A.067.

Title Index

Title Index

Title Index

301

Title Index

Title Index

Title Index

Title Index

Title Index

Title Index

Title Index

Title Index

Title Index

Title Index

312

Title Index

Topical Index of Michener Works

Topical Index of Michener Works

315

About the Author

DAVID GROSECLOSE, a graduate of Harvard University and the University of Arizona School of Law, is a lawyer in Phoenix, Arizona, and an avid Michener bibliophile who has spent thirteen years gathering information on Michener's work. His impressive collection of Michener material is one of the most comprehensive private collections in the country. He is married to Karen Anne Monrad and they have three children.